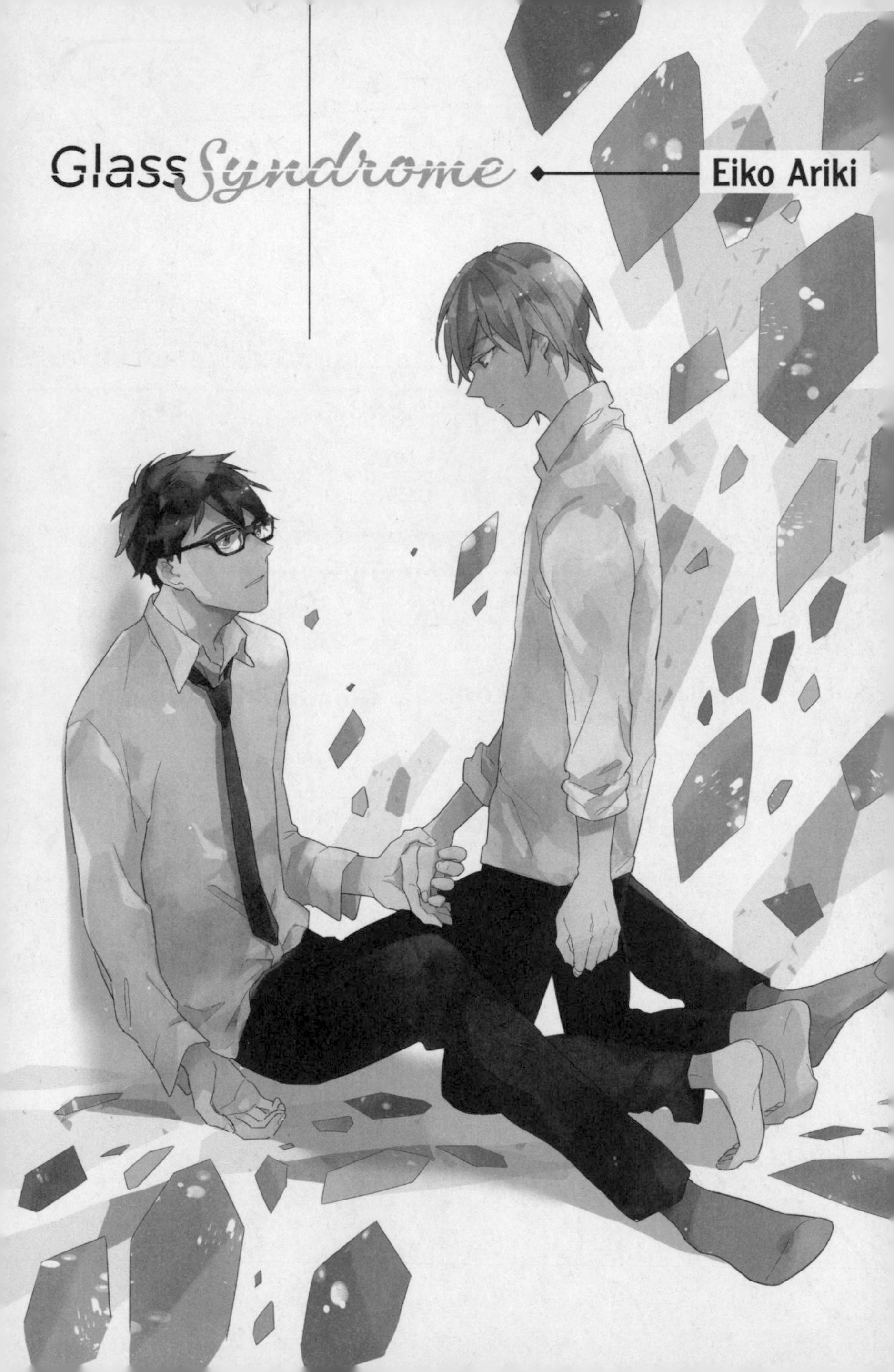
Glass Syndrome
Eiko Ariki

glass syndrome

CONTENTS

glass syndrome

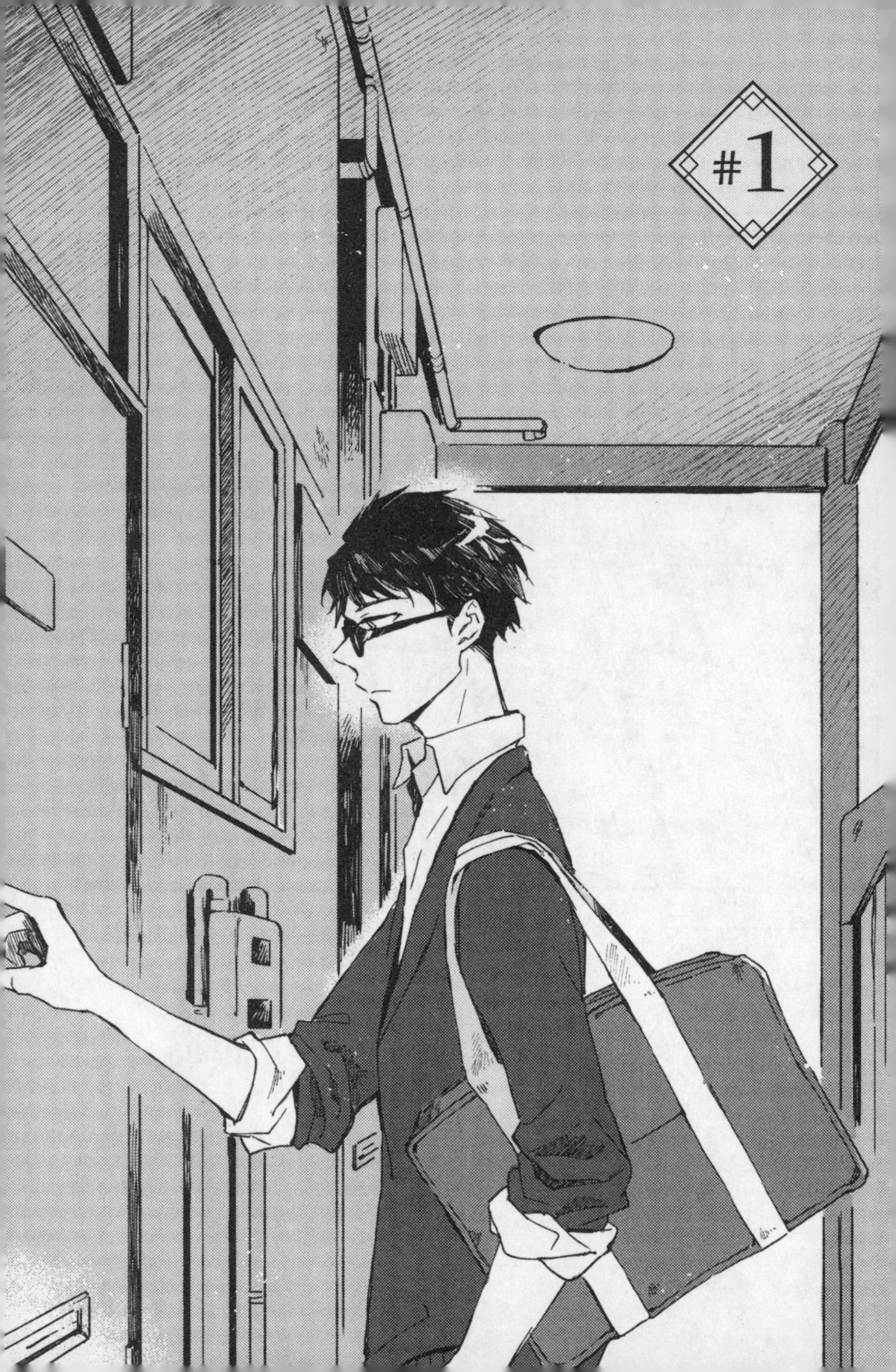
#1

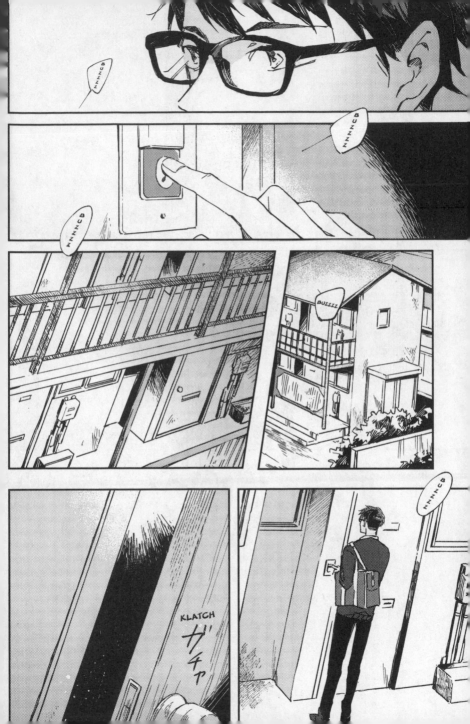

BUZZZZ

BUZZZ

BUZZZZ

BUZZZZ

BUZZZZ

KLATCH ガチャ

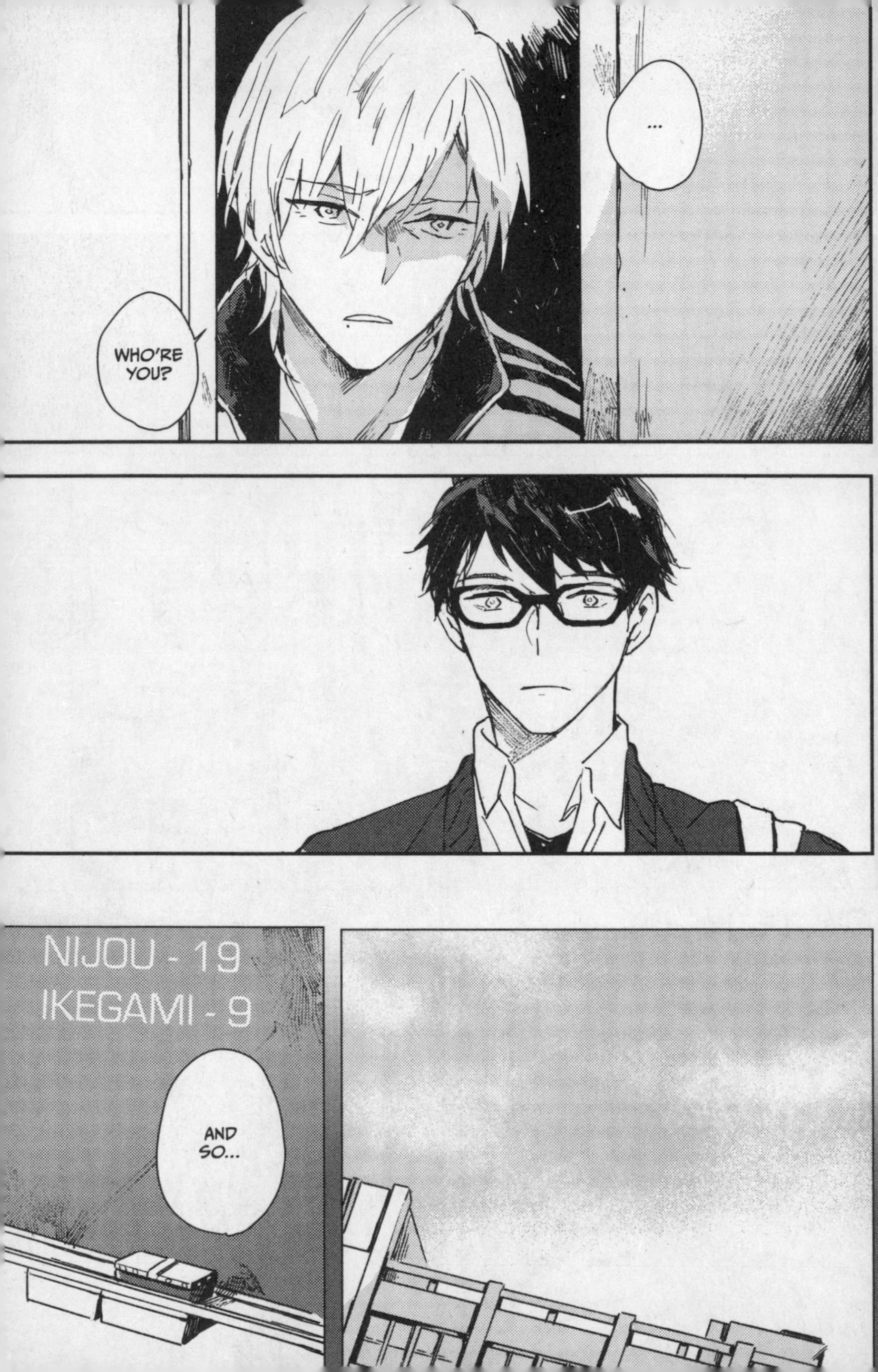
...
WHO'RE YOU?
NIJOU - 19
IKEGAMI - 9
AND SO...

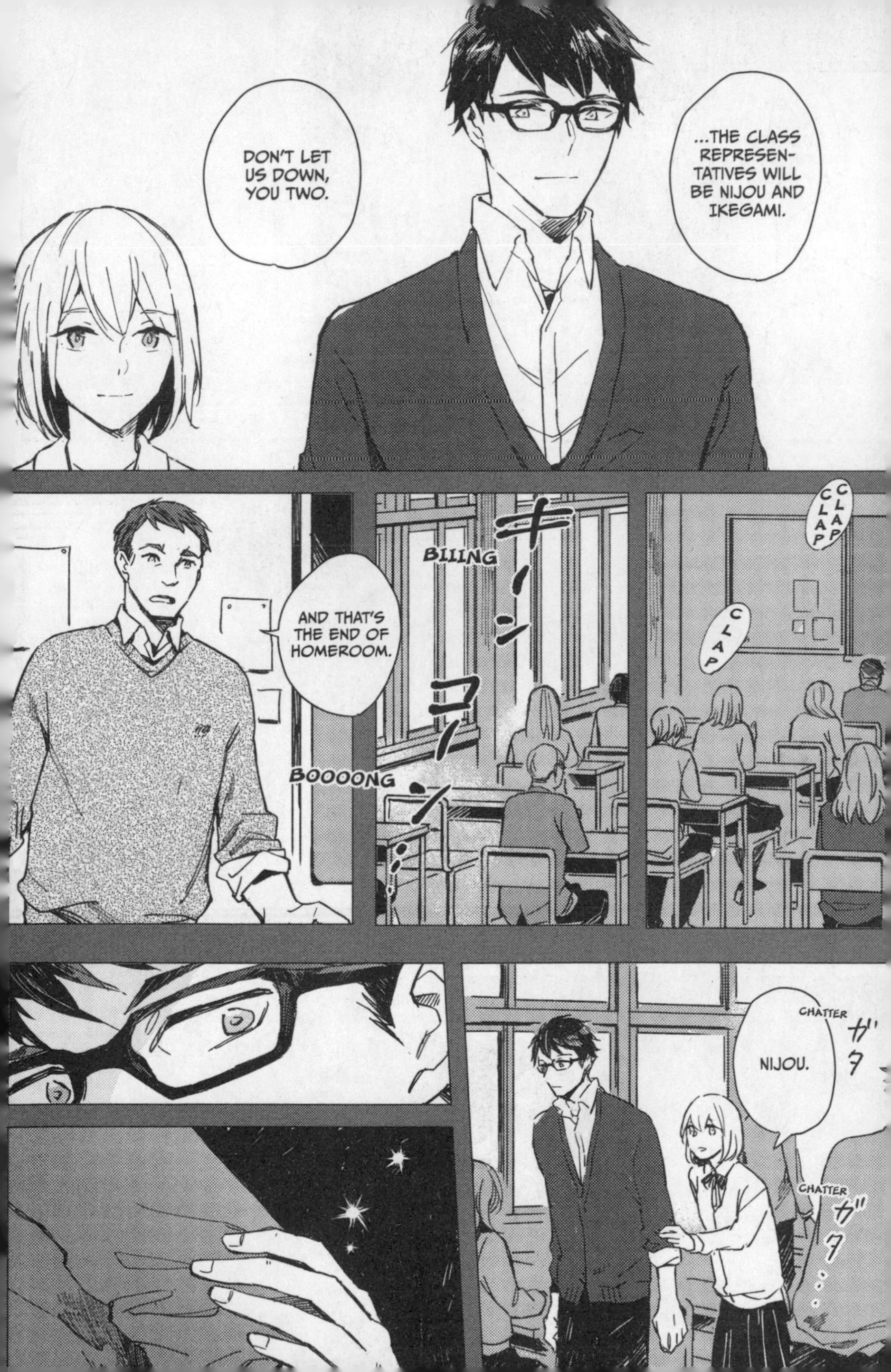

DON'T LET US DOWN, YOU TWO.

...THE CLASS REPRESENTATIVES WILL BE NIJOU AND IKEGAMI.

AND THAT'S THE END OF HOMEROOM.

BIIING

CLAP CLAP

CLAP

CLAP

BOOOONG

NIJOU.

CHATTER

CHATTER

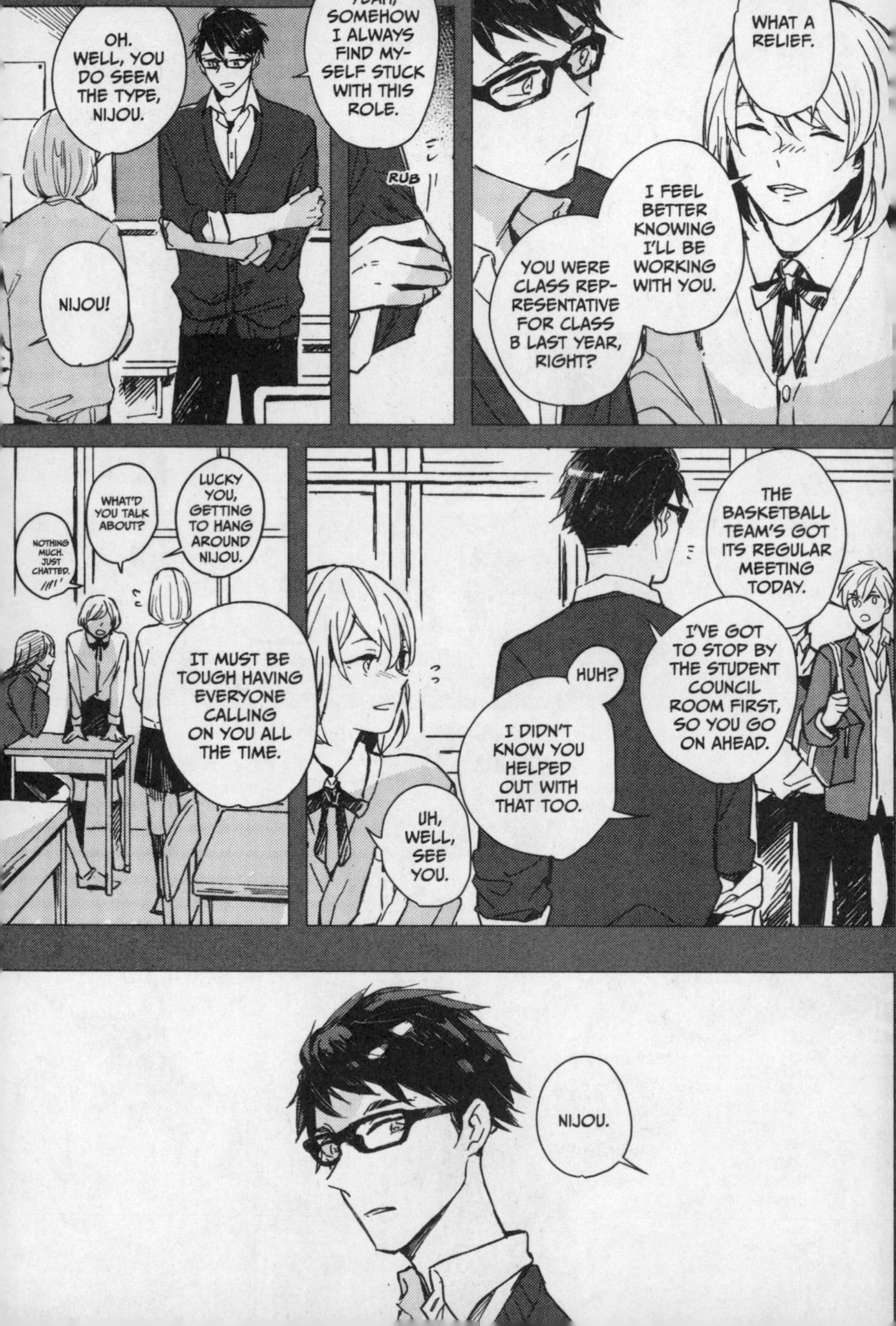
WHAT A RELIEF.
I FEEL BETTER KNOWING I'LL BE WORKING WITH YOU.
YOU WERE CLASS REPRESENTATIVE FOR CLASS B LAST YEAR, RIGHT?
YEAH, SOMEHOW I ALWAYS FIND MYSELF STUCK WITH THIS ROLE.
RUB
OH. WELL, YOU DO SEEM THE TYPE, NIJOU.
NIJOU!
THE BASKETBALL TEAM'S GOT ITS REGULAR MEETING TODAY.
I'VE GOT TO STOP BY THE STUDENT COUNCIL ROOM FIRST, SO YOU GO ON AHEAD.
HUH?
I DIDN'T KNOW YOU HELPED OUT WITH THAT TOO.
UH, WELL, SEE YOU.
LUCKY YOU, GETTING TO HANG AROUND NIJOU.
WHAT'D YOU TALK ABOUT?
NOTHING MUCH. JUST CHATTED.
IT MUST BE TOUGH HAVING EVERYONE CALLING ON YOU ALL THE TIME.
NIJOU.

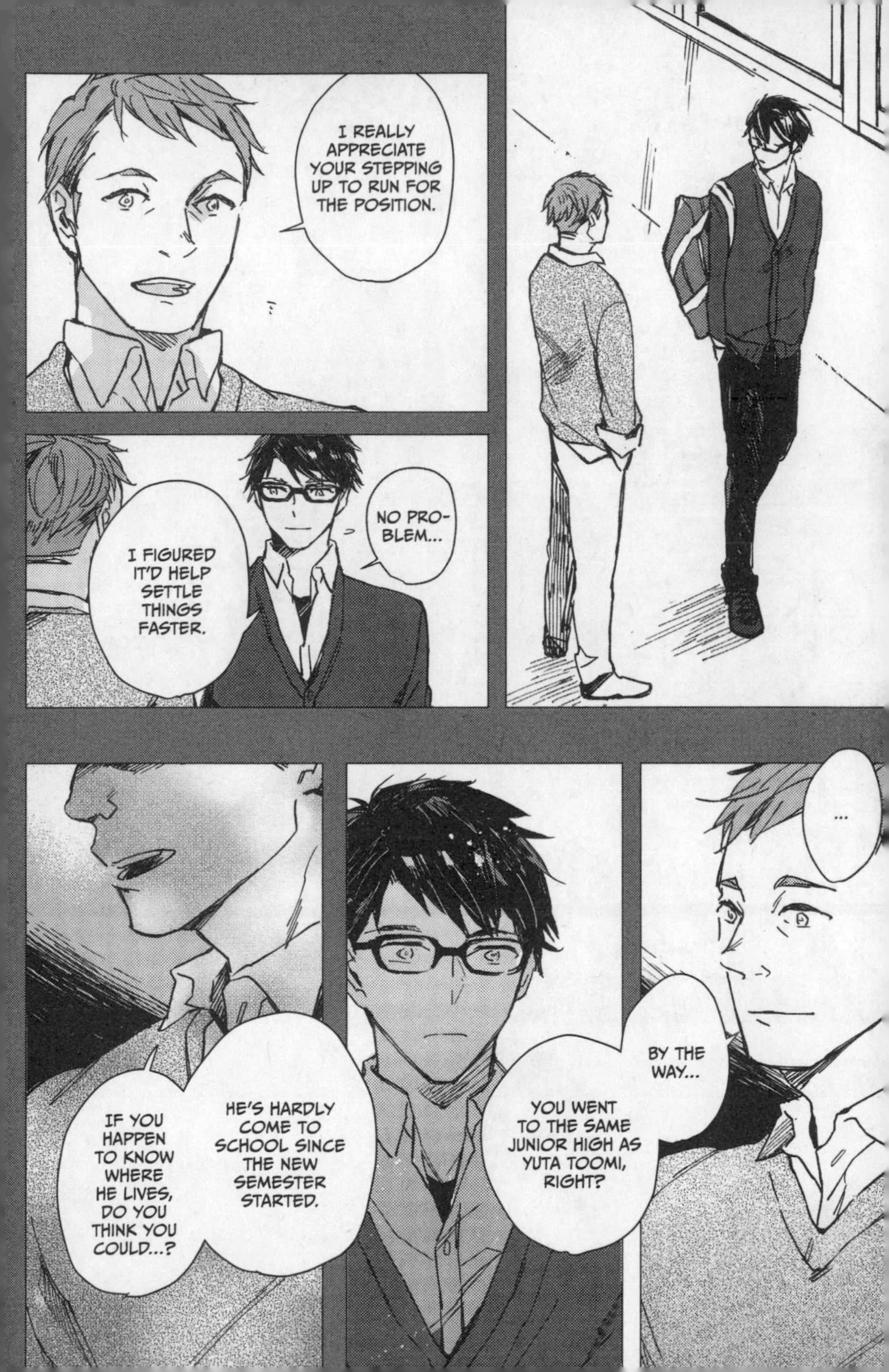
I REALLY APPRECIATE YOUR STEPPING UP TO RUN FOR THE POSITION.
NO PRO-BLEM...
I FIGURED IT'D HELP SETTLE THINGS FASTER.
...
BY THE WAY...
YOU WENT TO THE SAME JUNIOR HIGH AS YUTA TOOMI, RIGHT?
HE'S HARDLY COME TO SCHOOL SINCE THE NEW SEMESTER STARTED.
IF YOU HAPPEN TO KNOW WHERE HE LIVES, DO YOU THINK YOU COULD...?

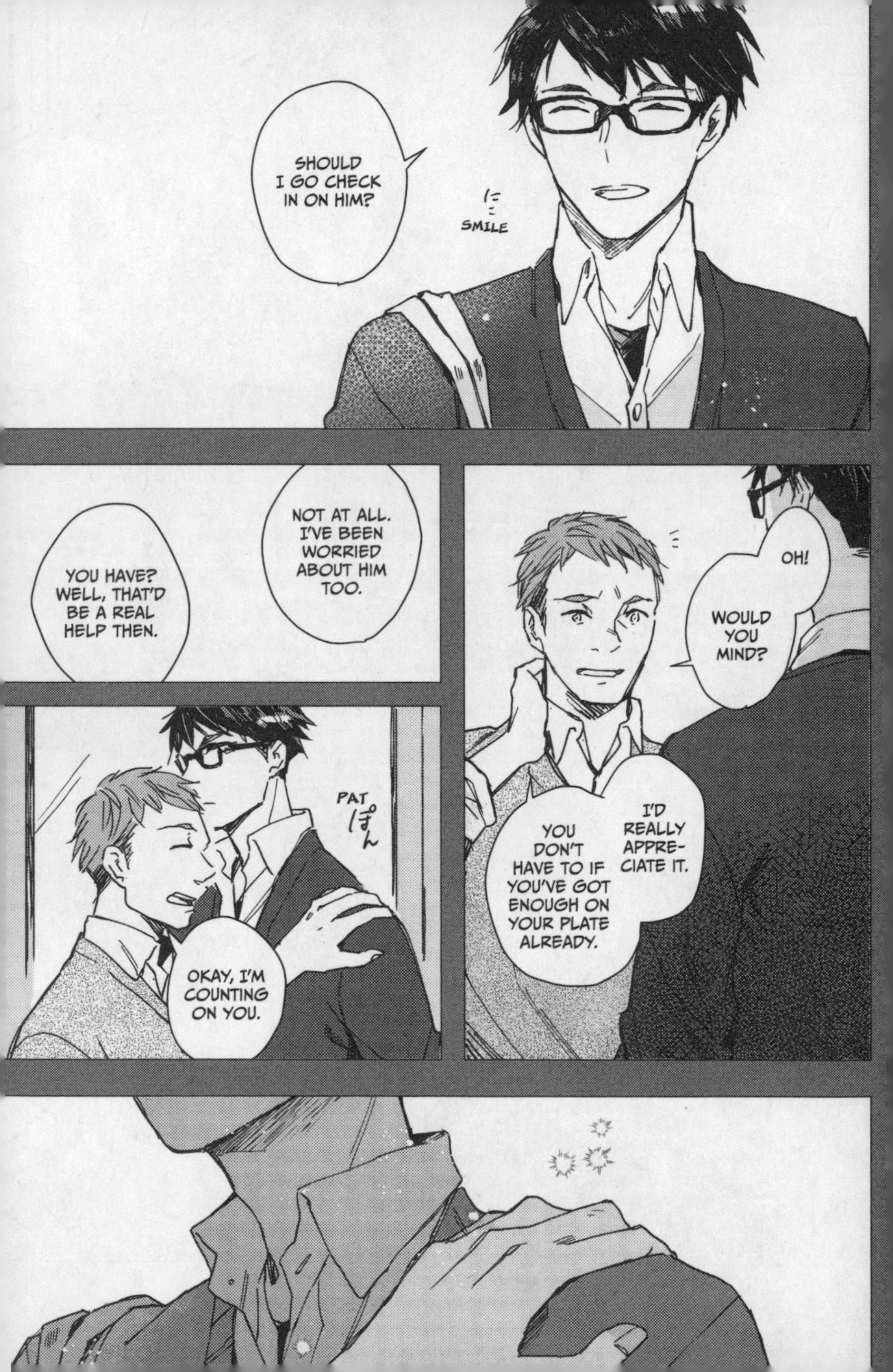
SHOULD I GO CHECK IN ON HIM?
SMILE
OH!
WOULD YOU MIND?
I'D REALLY APPRECIATE IT.
YOU DON'T HAVE TO IF YOU'VE GOT ENOUGH ON YOUR PLATE ALREADY.
NOT AT ALL. I'VE BEEN WORRIED ABOUT HIM TOO.
YOU HAVE? WELL, THAT'D BE A REAL HELP THEN.
PAT
ぽん
OKAY, I'M COUNTING ON YOU.

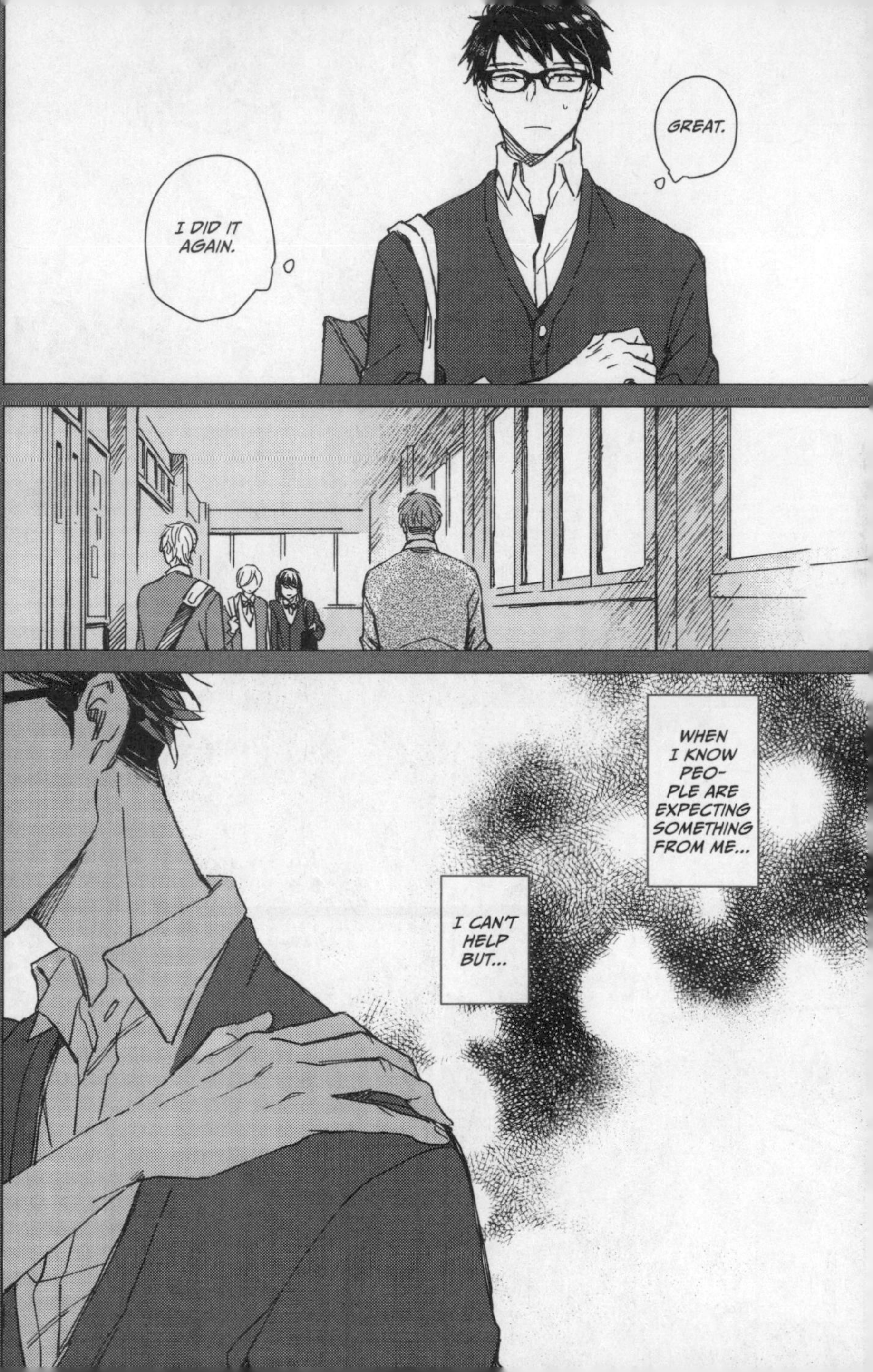
GREAT.
I DID IT AGAIN.
WHEN I KNOW PEO-PLE ARE EXPECTING SOMETHING FROM ME...
I CAN'T HELP BUT...

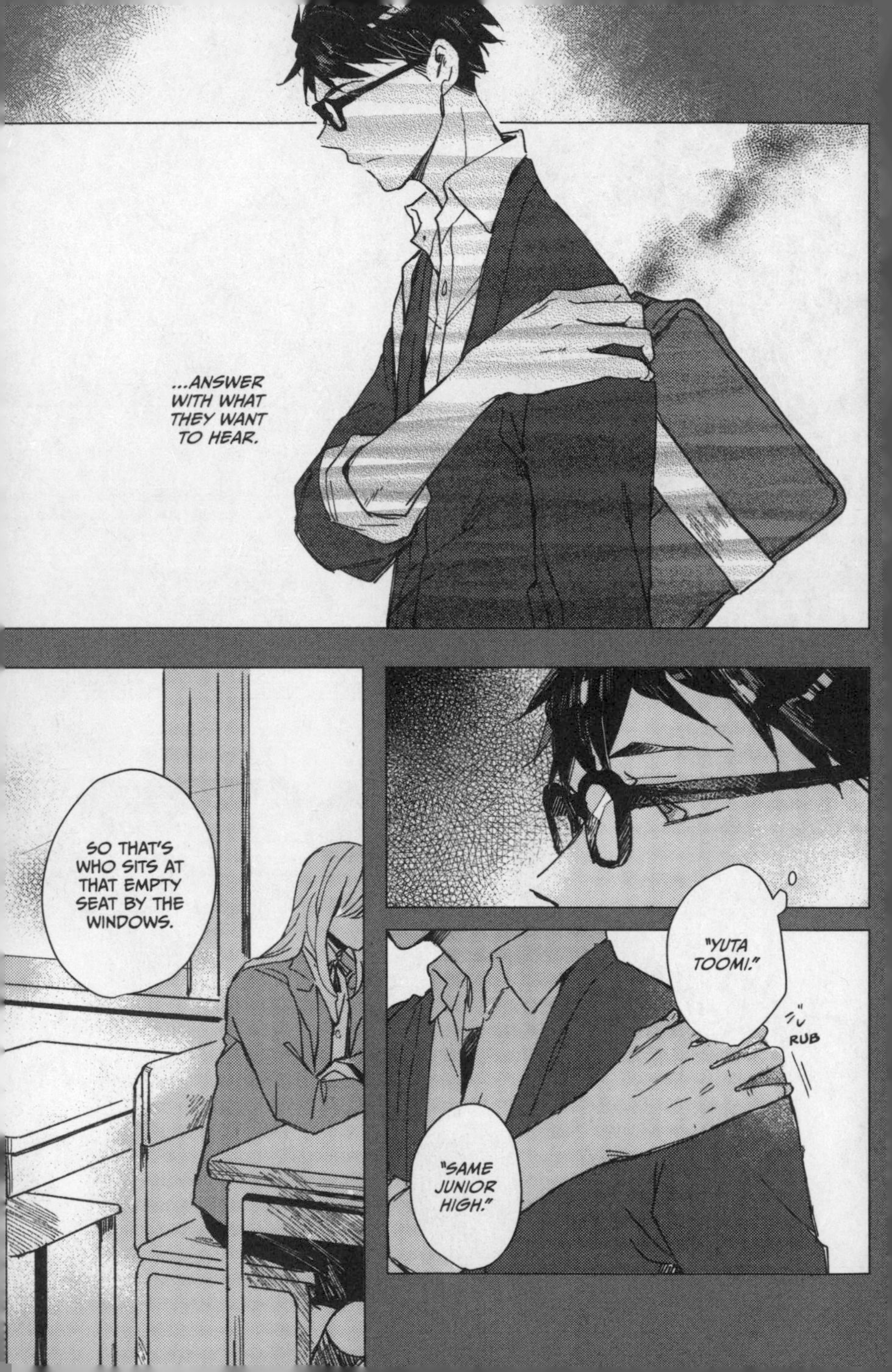
...ANSWER WITH WHAT THEY WANT TO HEAR.
"YUTA TOOMI."
RUB
"SAME JUNIOR HIGH."
SO THAT'S WHO SITS AT THAT EMPTY SEAT BY THE WINDOWS.

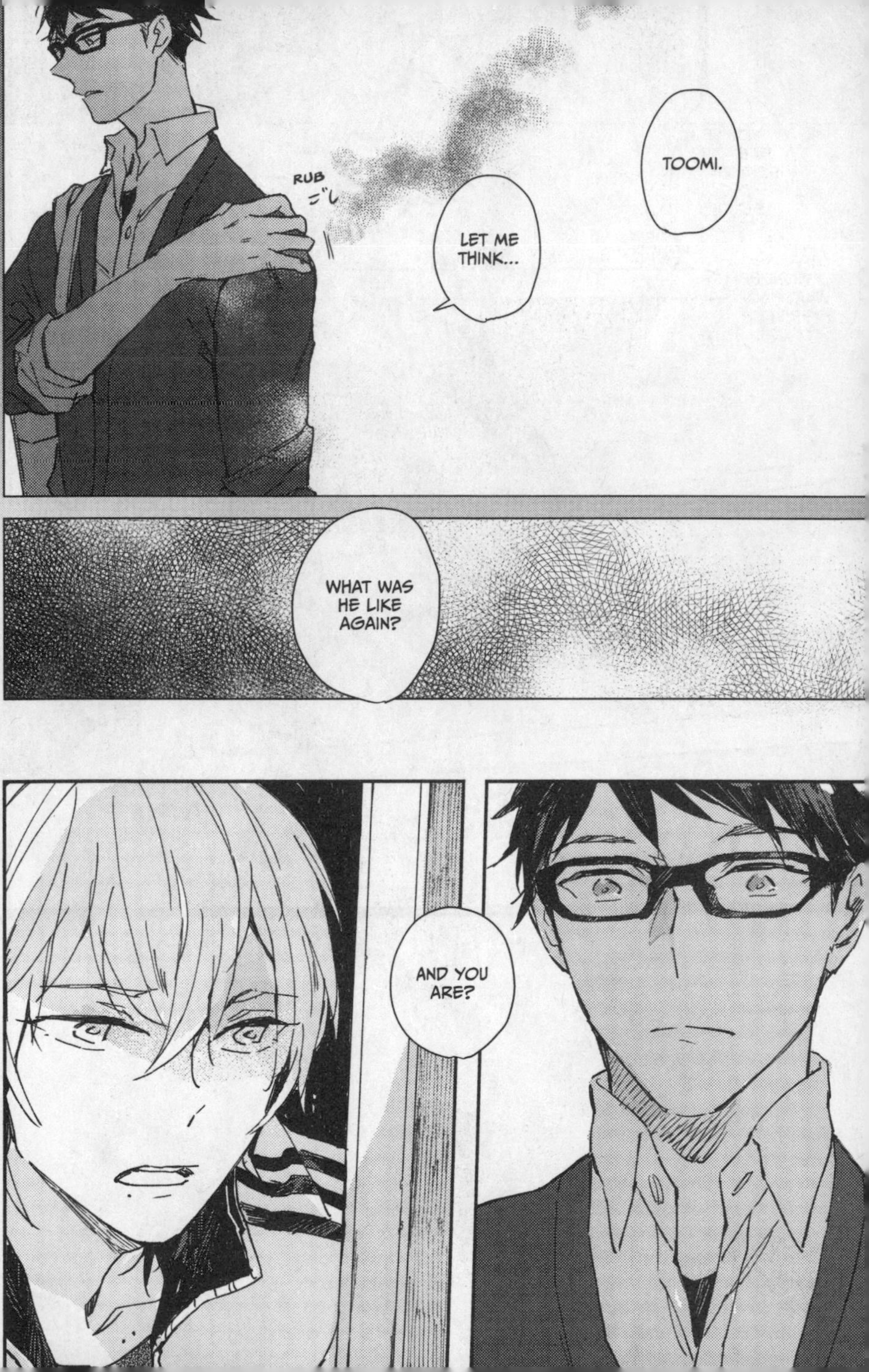
TOOMI.
LET ME THINK...
RUB
ごし
WHAT WAS HE LIKE AGAIN?
AND YOU ARE?

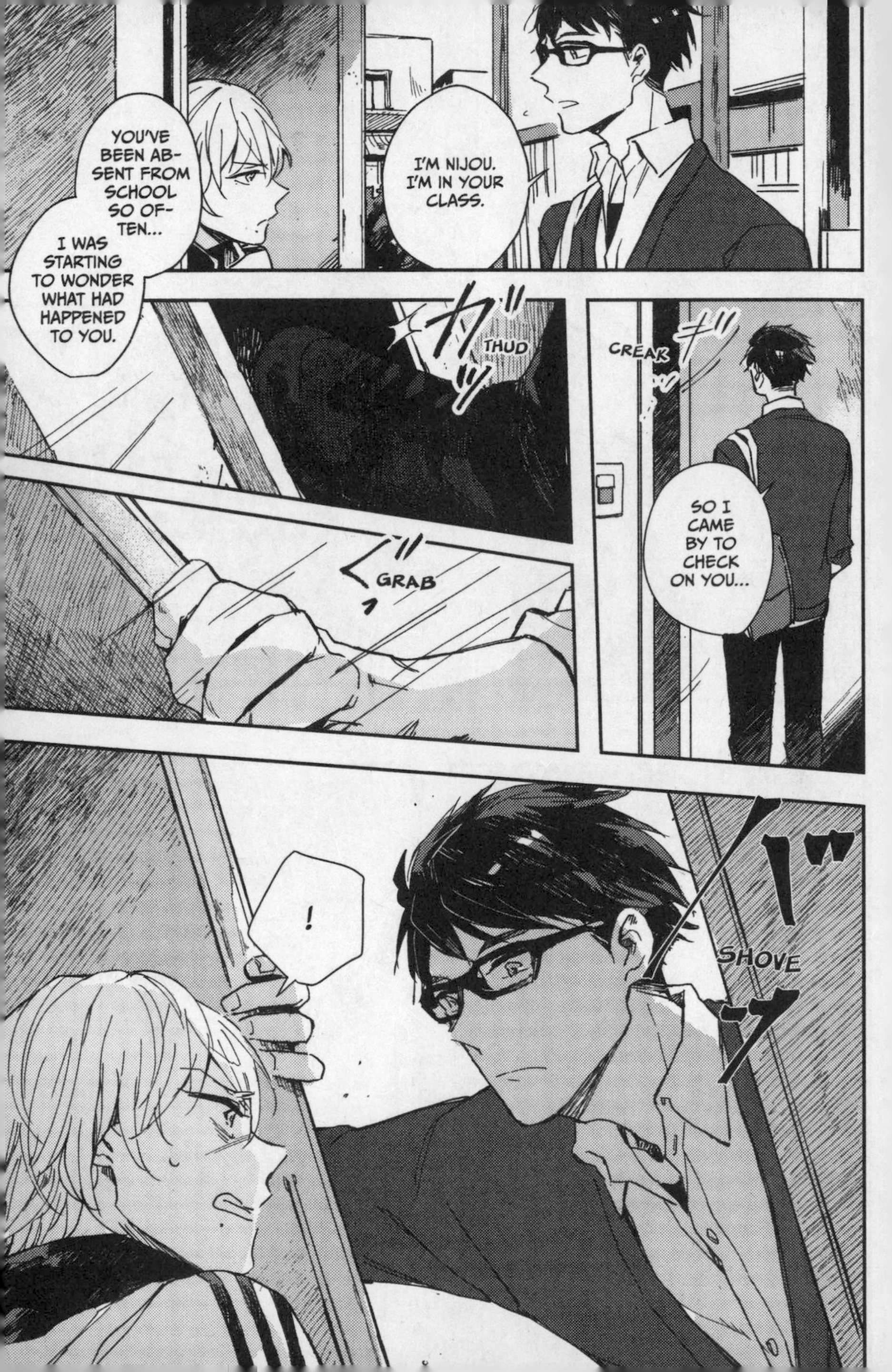
I'M NIJOU. I'M IN YOUR CLASS.
YOU'VE BEEN ABSENT FROM SCHOOL SO OFTEN...
I WAS STARTING TO WONDER WHAT HAD HAPPENED TO YOU.
CREAK
SO I CAME BY TO CHECK ON YOU...
THUD
GRAB
SHOVE
!

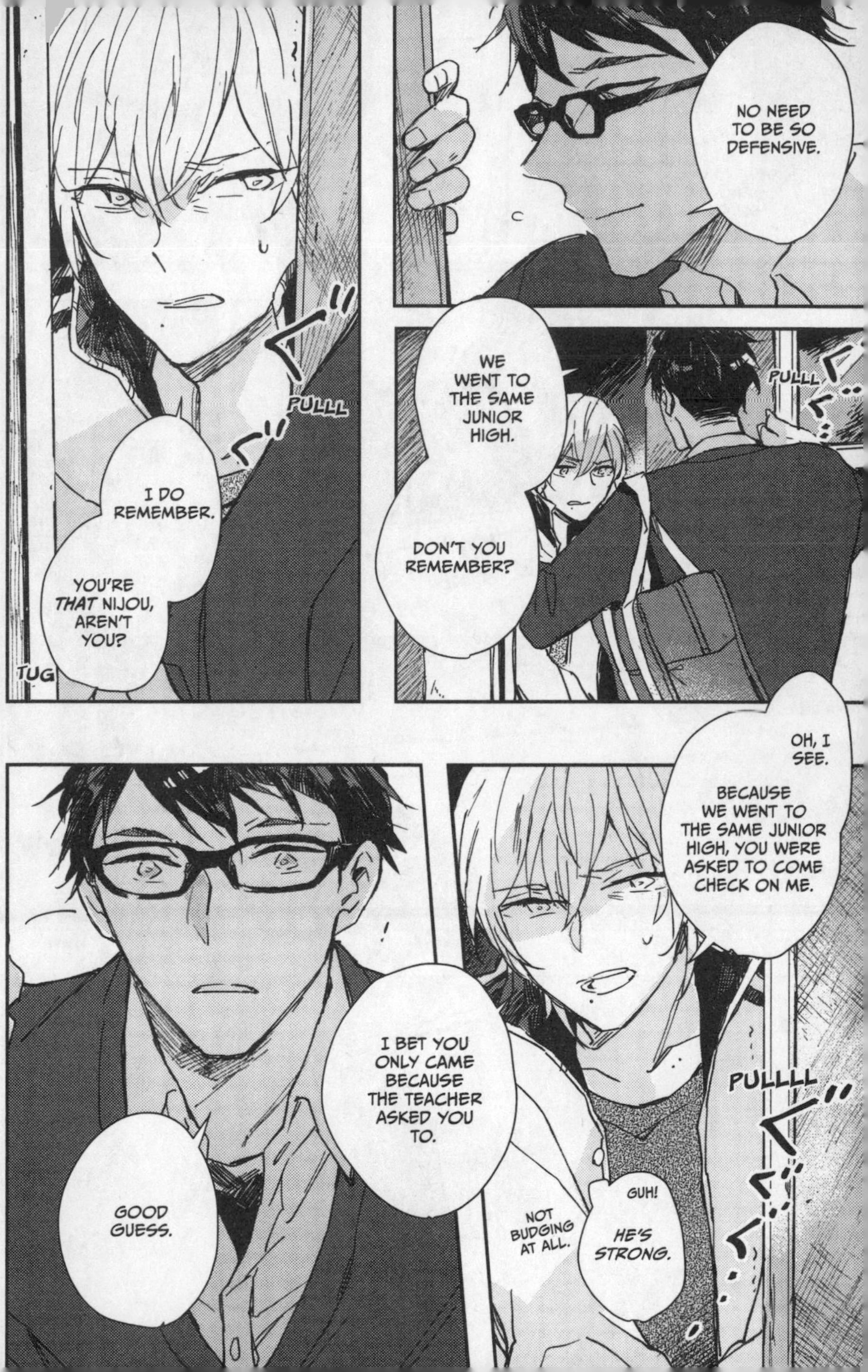
NO NEED TO BE SO DEFENSIVE.
WE WENT TO THE SAME JUNIOR HIGH.
DON'T YOU REMEMBER?
PULLL
PULLL
I DO REMEMBER.
YOU'RE *THAT* NIJOU, AREN'T YOU?
TUG
OH, I SEE.
BECAUSE WE WENT TO THE SAME JUNIOR HIGH, YOU WERE ASKED TO COME CHECK ON ME.
I BET YOU ONLY CAME BECAUSE THE TEACHER ASKED YOU TO.
PULLLL
GUH!
HE'S STRONG.
NOT BUDGING AT ALL.
GOOD GUESS.

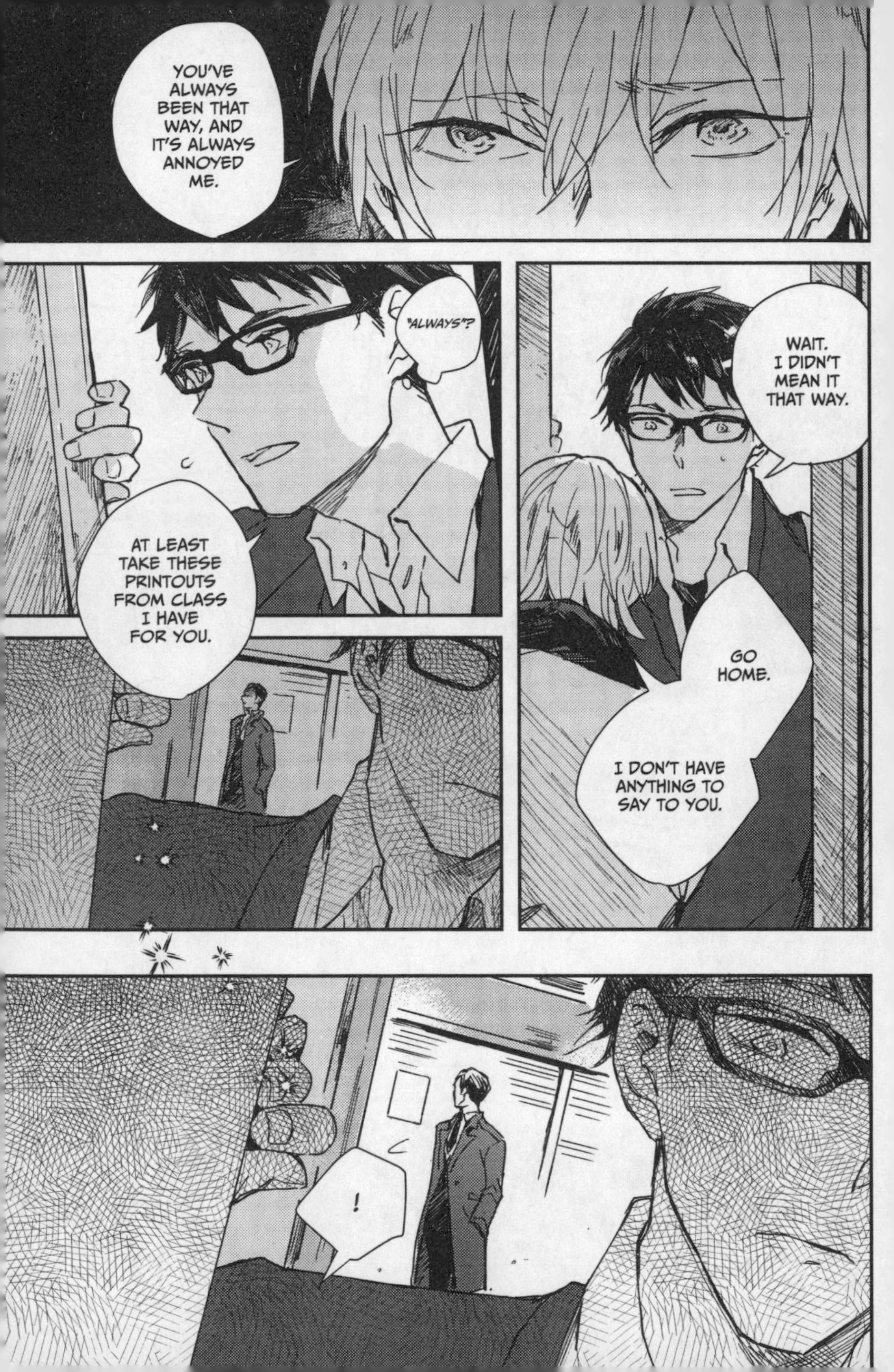
YOU'VE ALWAYS BEEN THAT WAY, AND IT'S ALWAYS ANNOYED ME.
WAIT. I DIDN'T MEAN IT THAT WAY.
GO HOME.
I DON'T HAVE ANYTHING TO SAY TO YOU.
"ALWAYS"?
AT LEAST TAKE THESE PRINTOUTS FROM CLASS I HAVE FOR YOU.
!

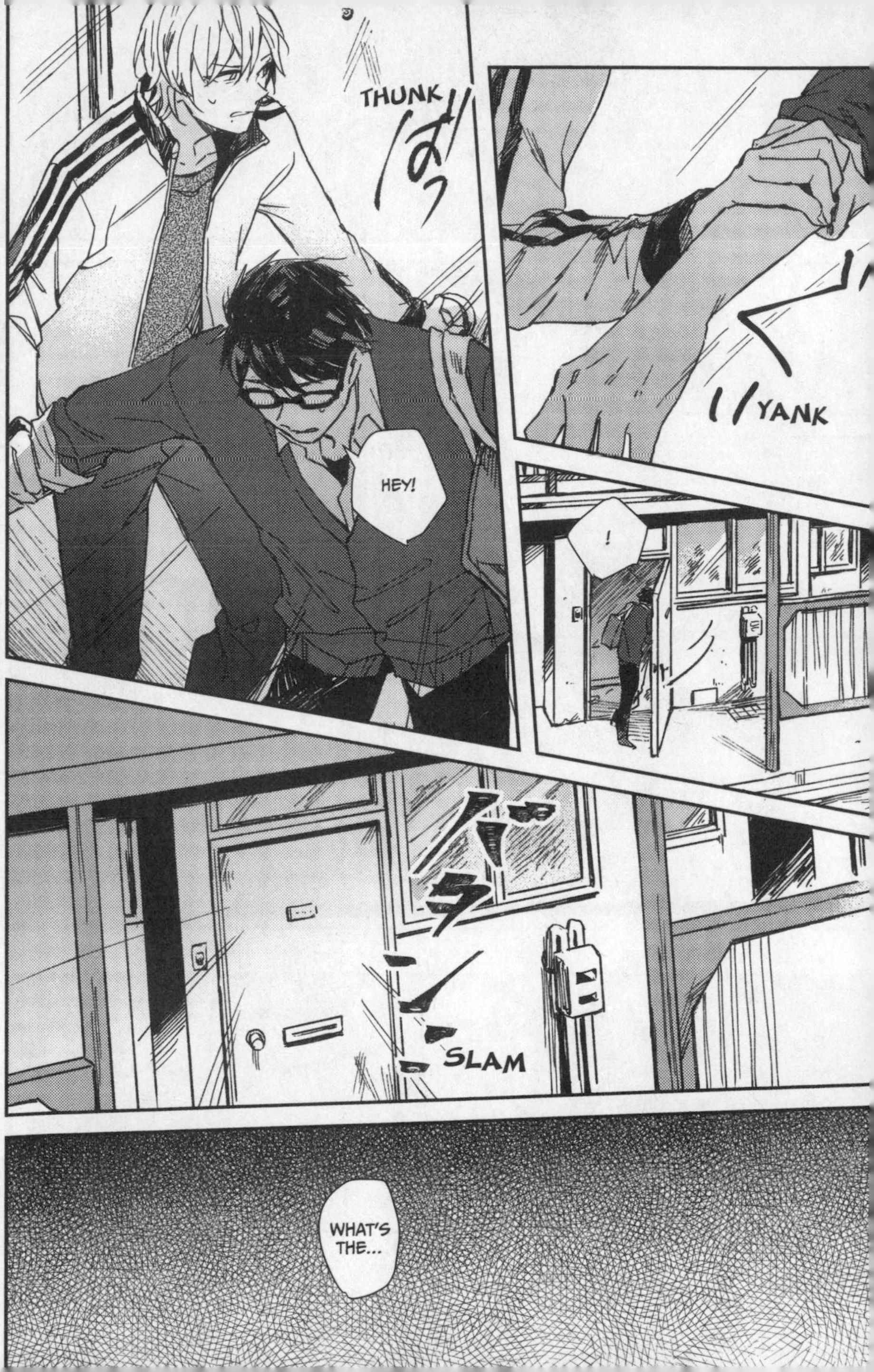
YANK
!
THUNK
HEY!
SLAM
WHAT'S THE...

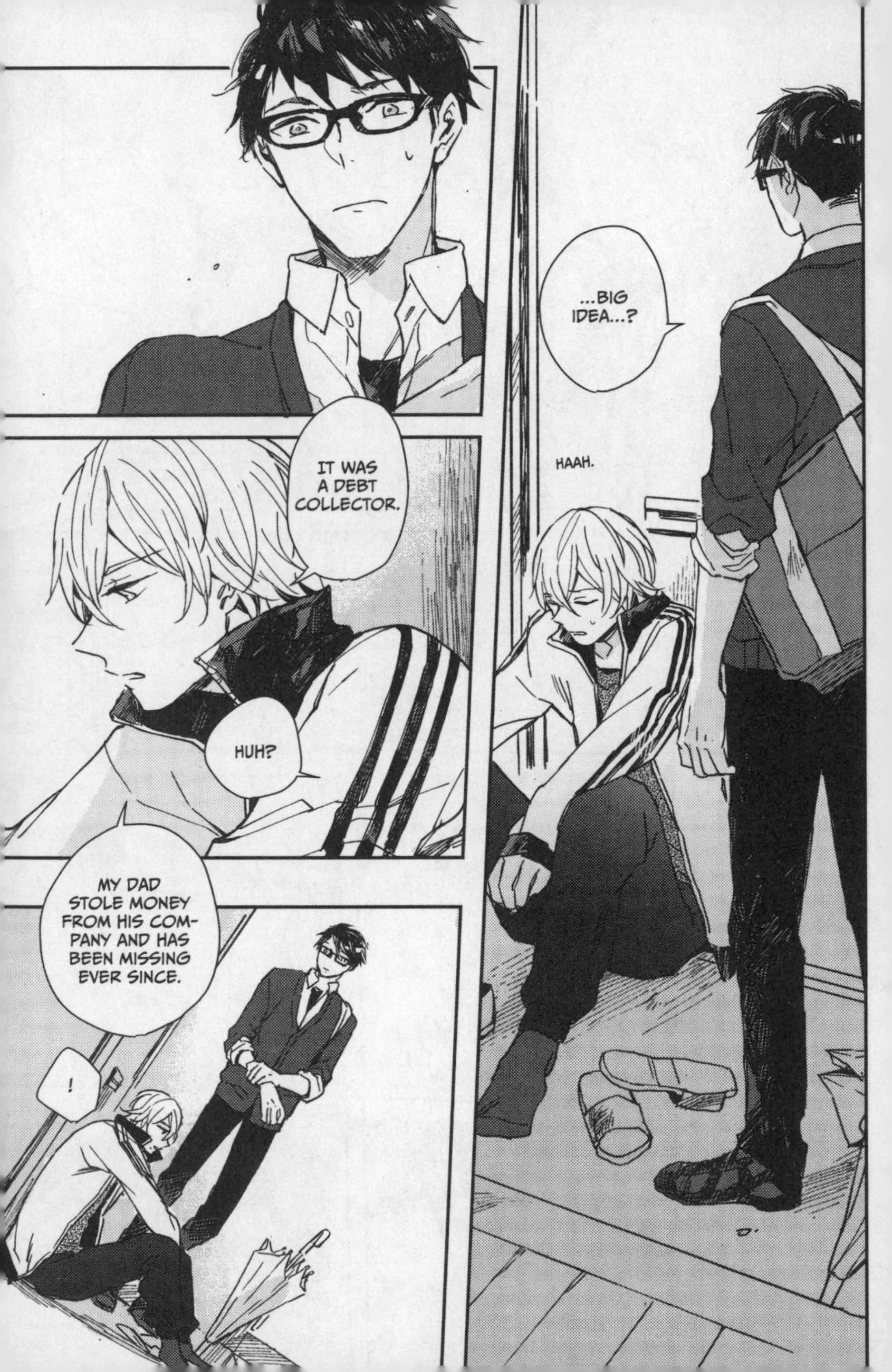
...BIG IDEA...?
HAAH.
IT WAS A DEBT COLLECTOR.
HUH?
MY DAD STOLE MONEY FROM HIS COM- PANY AND HAS BEEN MISSING EVER SINCE.
!

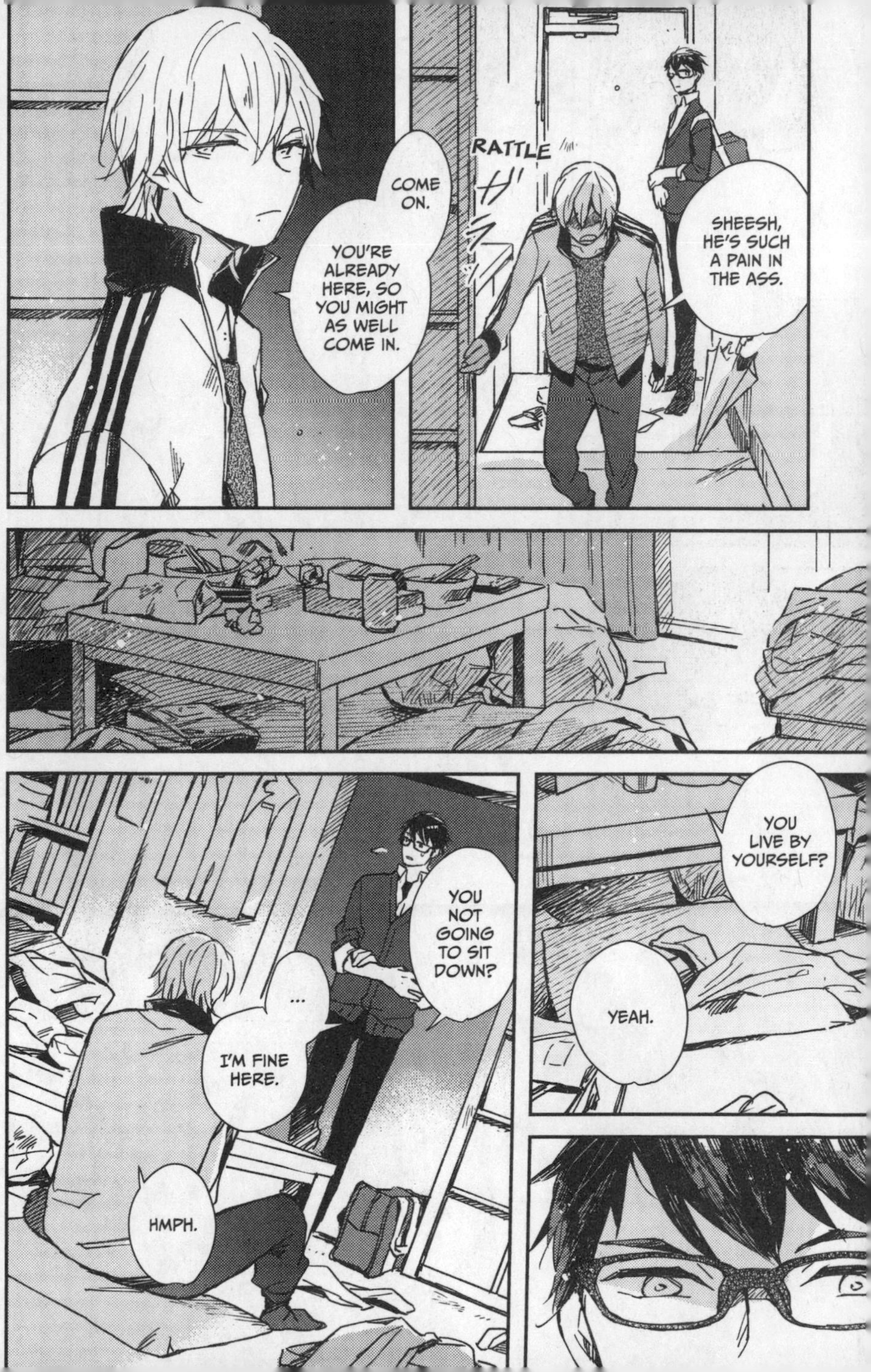
SHEESH, HE'S SUCH A PAIN IN THE ASS.
RATTLE
COME ON.
YOU'RE ALREADY HERE, SO YOU MIGHT AS WELL COME IN.
YOU LIVE BY YOURSELF?
YEAH.
YOU NOT GOING TO SIT DOWN?
...
I'M FINE HERE.
HMPH.

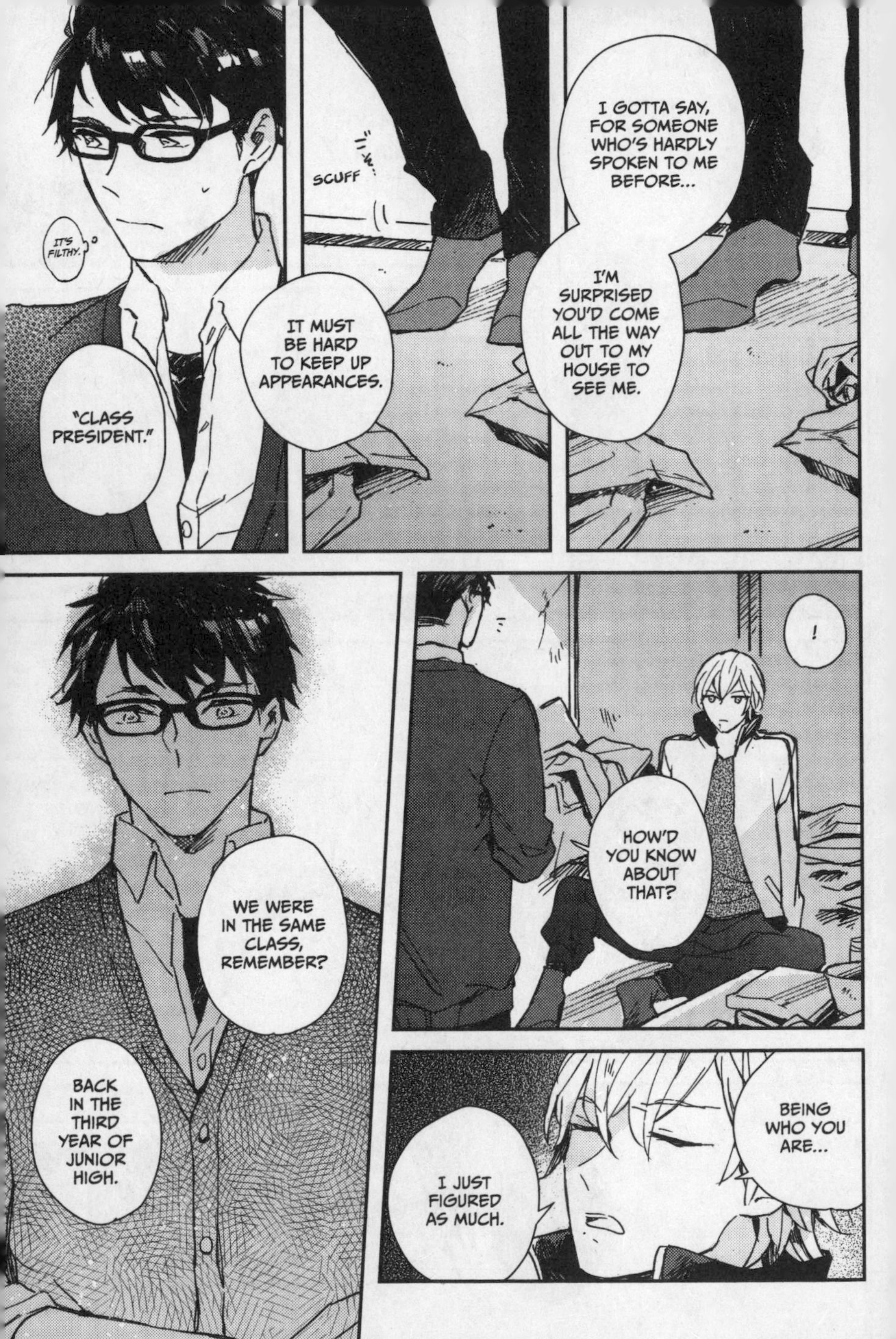
I GOTTA SAY, FOR SOMEONE WHO'S HARDLY SPOKEN TO ME BEFORE...
I'M SURPRISED YOU'D COME ALL THE WAY OUT TO MY HOUSE TO SEE ME.
SCUFF
IT MUST BE HARD TO KEEP UP APPEARANCES.
IT'S FILTHY.
"CLASS PRESIDENT."
!
HOW'D YOU KNOW ABOUT THAT?
BEING WHO YOU ARE...
I JUST FIGURED AS MUCH.
WE WERE IN THE SAME CLASS, REMEMBER?
BACK IN THE THIRD YEAR OF JUNIOR HIGH.

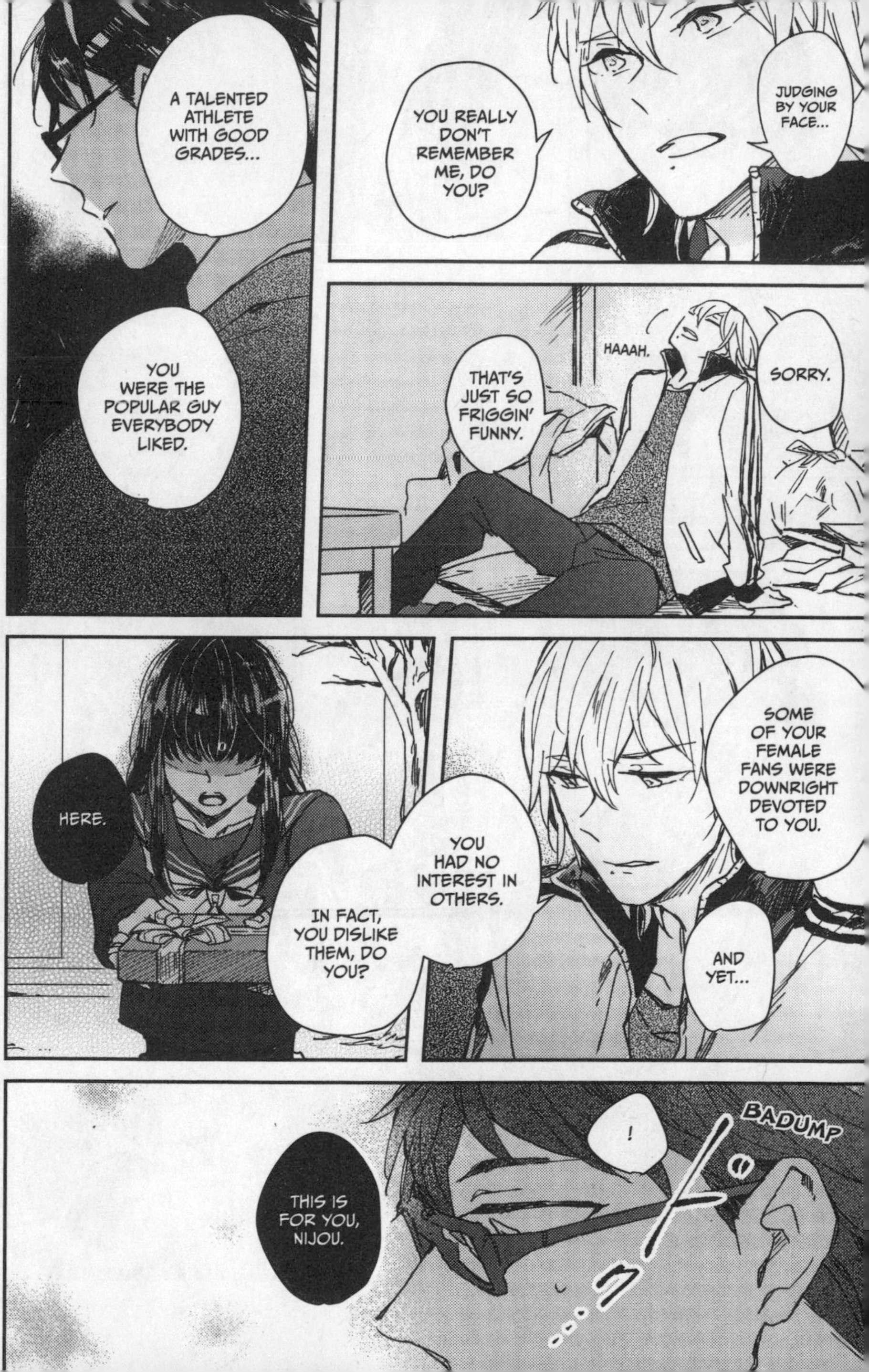
JUDGING BY YOUR FACE...
YOU REALLY DON'T REMEMBER ME, DO YOU?
SORRY.
HAAAH.
THAT'S JUST SO FRIGGIN' FUNNY.
A TALENTED ATHLETE WITH GOOD GRADES...
YOU WERE THE POPULAR GUY EVERYBODY LIKED.
SOME OF YOUR FEMALE FANS WERE DOWNRIGHT DEVOTED TO YOU.
AND YET...
YOU HAD NO INTEREST IN OTHERS.
IN FACT, YOU DISLIKE THEM, DO YOU?
HERE.
BADUMP
!
THIS IS FOR YOU, NIJOU.

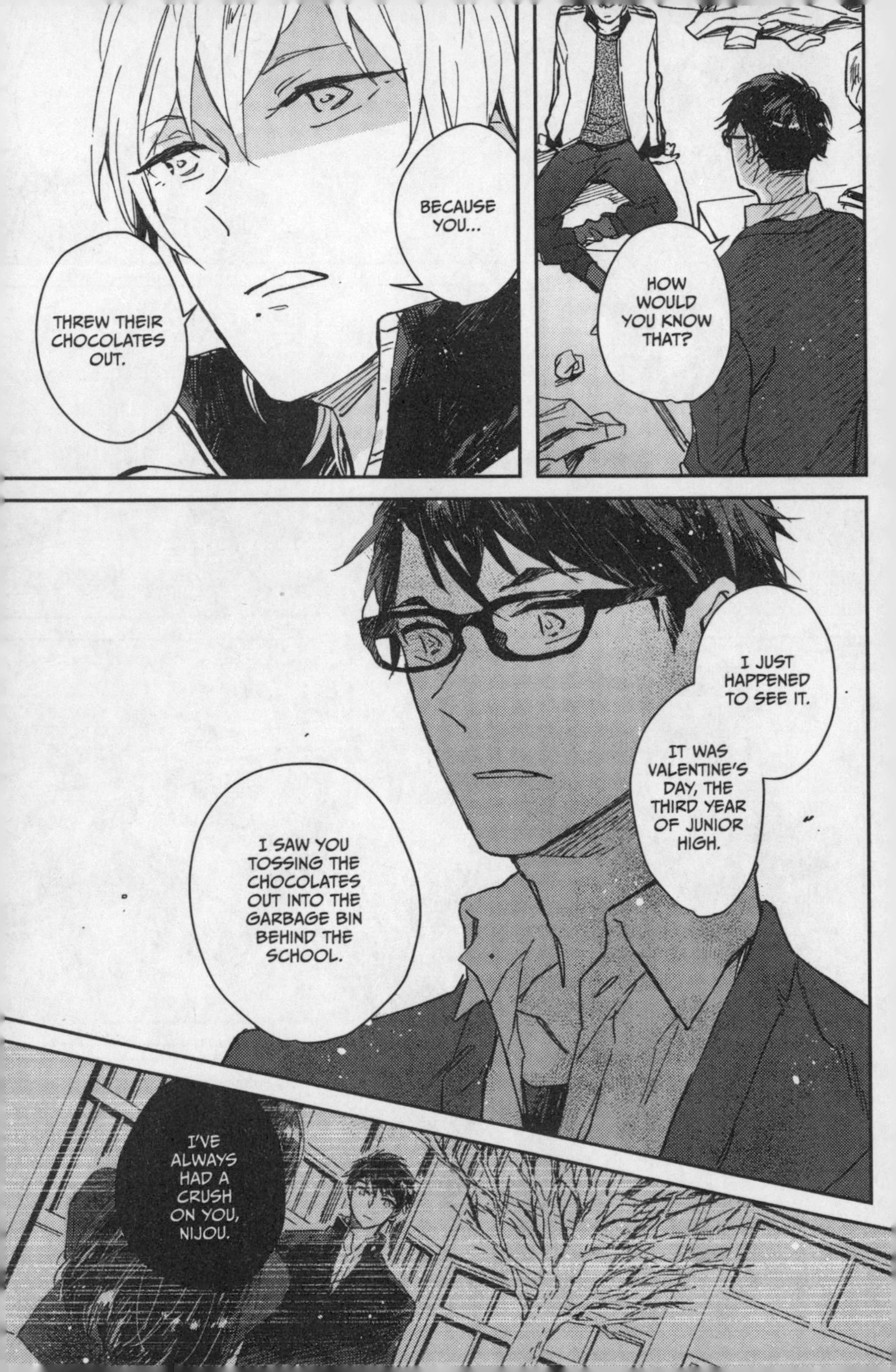
HOW WOULD YOU KNOW THAT?
BECAUSE YOU...
THREW THEIR CHOCOLATES OUT.
I JUST HAPPENED TO SEE IT.
IT WAS VALENTINE'S DAY, THE THIRD YEAR OF JUNIOR HIGH.
I SAW YOU TOSSING THE CHOCOLATES OUT INTO THE GARBAGE BIN BEHIND THE SCHOOL.
I'VE ALWAYS HAD A CRUSH ON YOU, NIJOU.

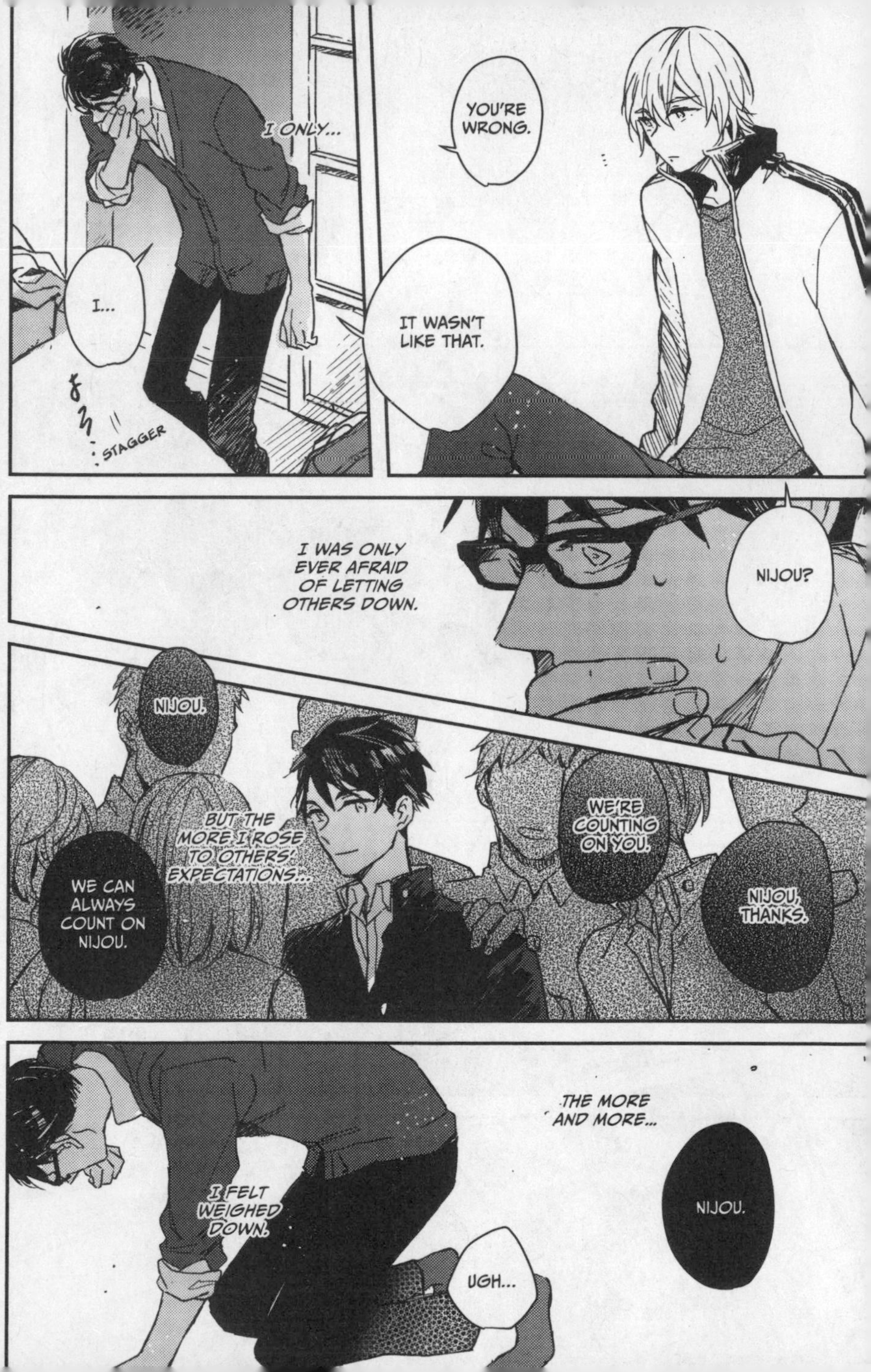
YOU'RE WRONG.
IT WASN'T LIKE THAT.
I ONLY...
I...
STAGGER
NIJOU?
I WAS ONLY EVER AFRAID OF LETTING OTHERS DOWN.
WE'RE COUNTING ON YOU.
NIJOU, THANKS.
NIJOU.
BUT THE MORE I ROSE TO OTHERS' EXPECTATIONS...
WE CAN ALWAYS COUNT ON NIJOU.
THE MORE AND MORE...
NIJOU.
UGH...
I FELT WEIGHED DOWN.

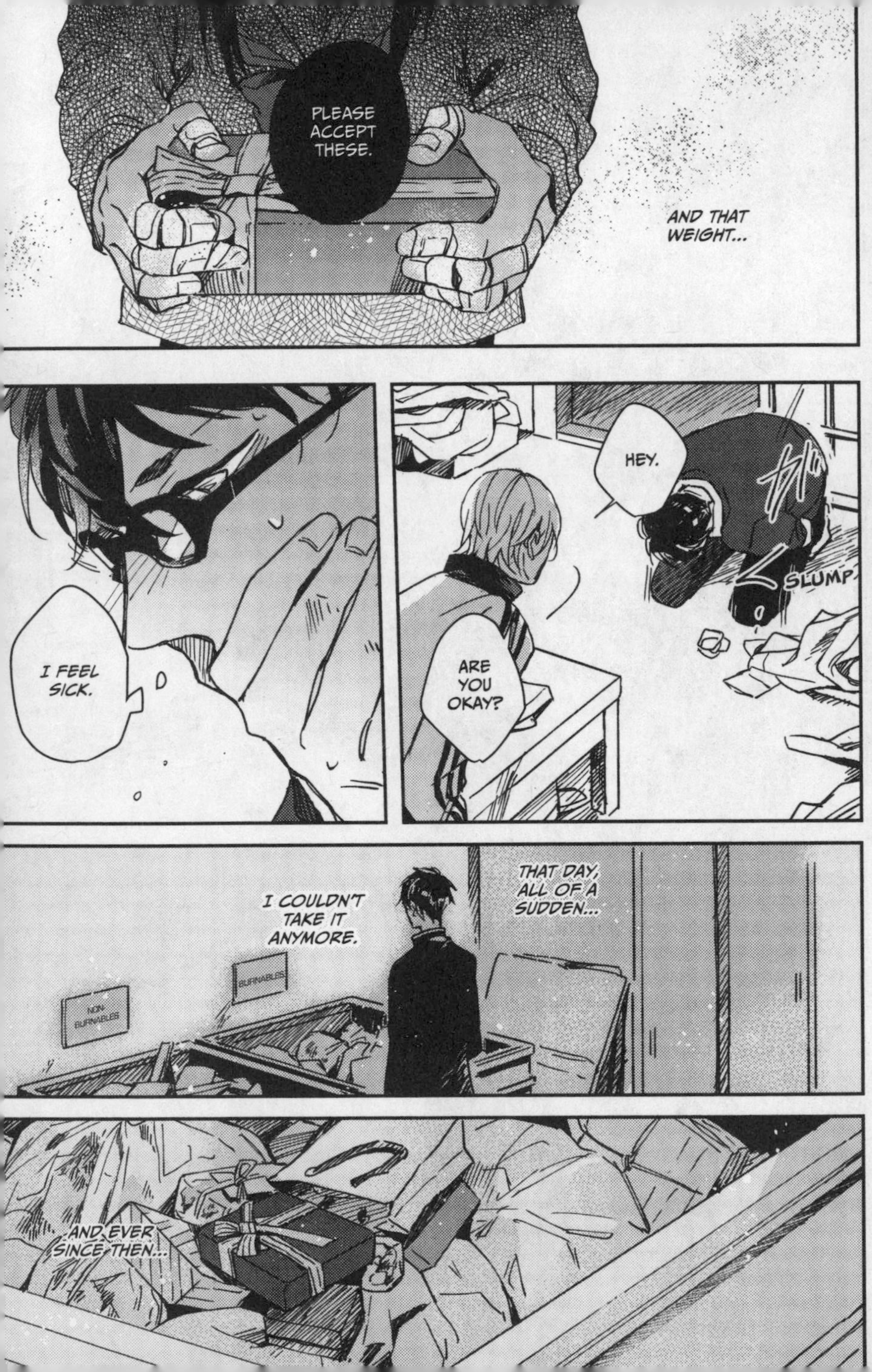
PLEASE ACCEPT THESE.
AND THAT WEIGHT...
HEY.
SLUMP
ARE YOU OKAY?
I FEEL SICK.
THAT DAY, ALL OF A SUDDEN...
I COULDN'T TAKE IT ANYMORE.
BURNABLES
NON-BURNABLES
AND EVER SINCE THEN...

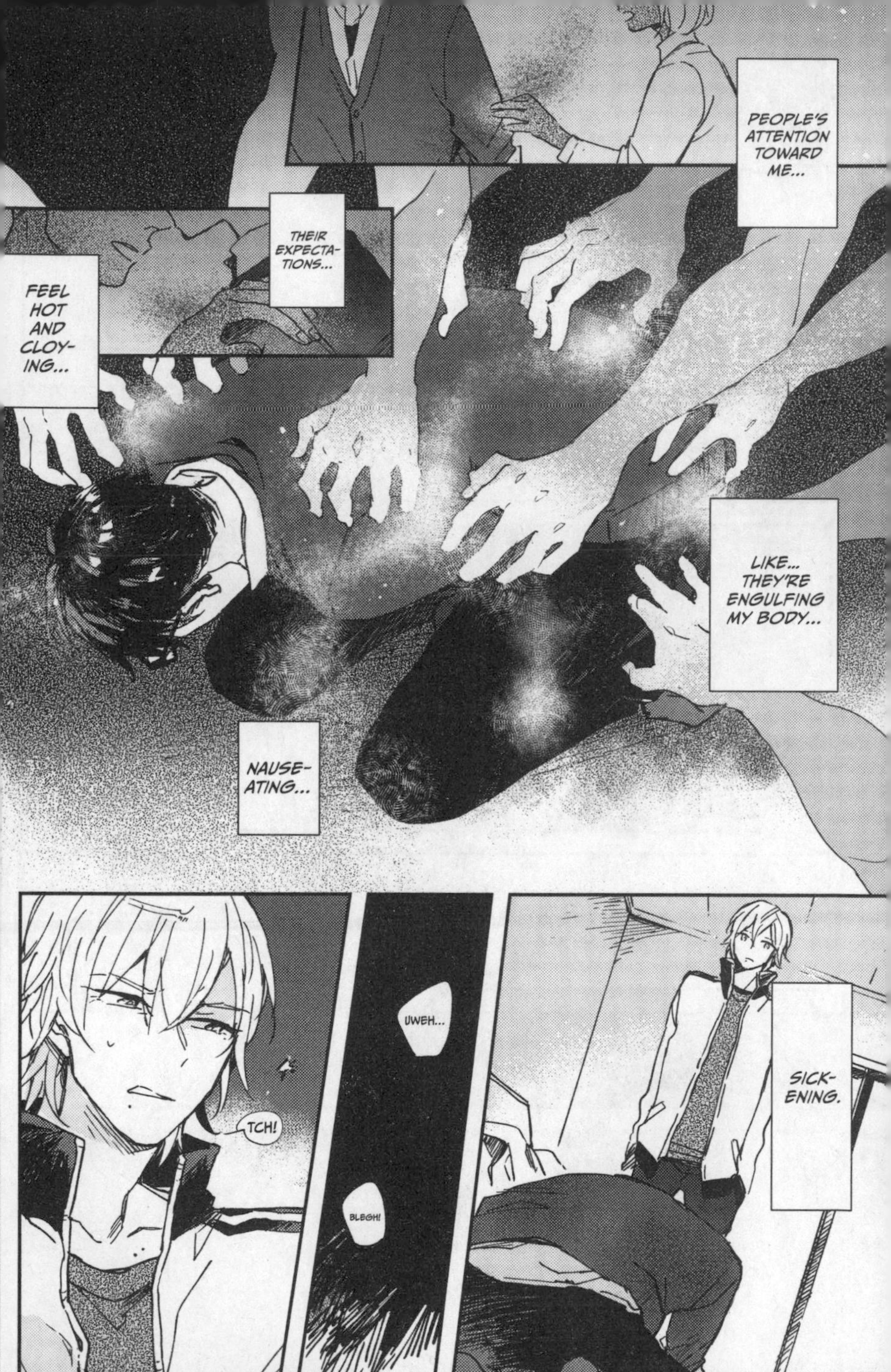
PEOPLE'S ATTENTION TOWARD ME...
THEIR EXPECTATIONS...
FEEL HOT AND CLOYING...
LIKE... THEY'RE ENGULFING MY BODY...
NAUSEATING...
SICKENING.
UWEH...
BLEGH!
TCH!

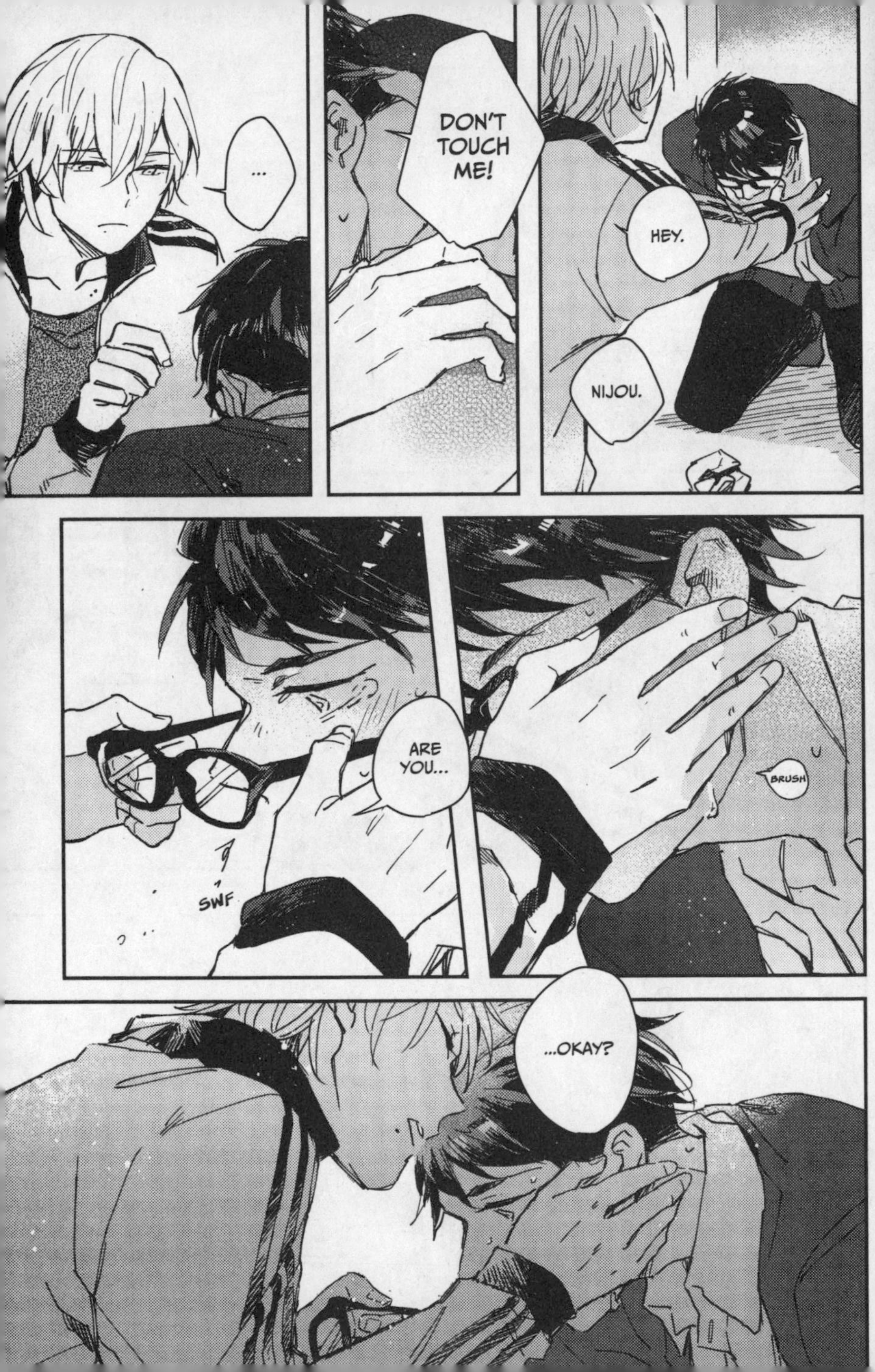
HEY.
NIJOU.
DON'T TOUCH ME!
...
BRUSH
ARE YOU...
SWF
...OKAY?

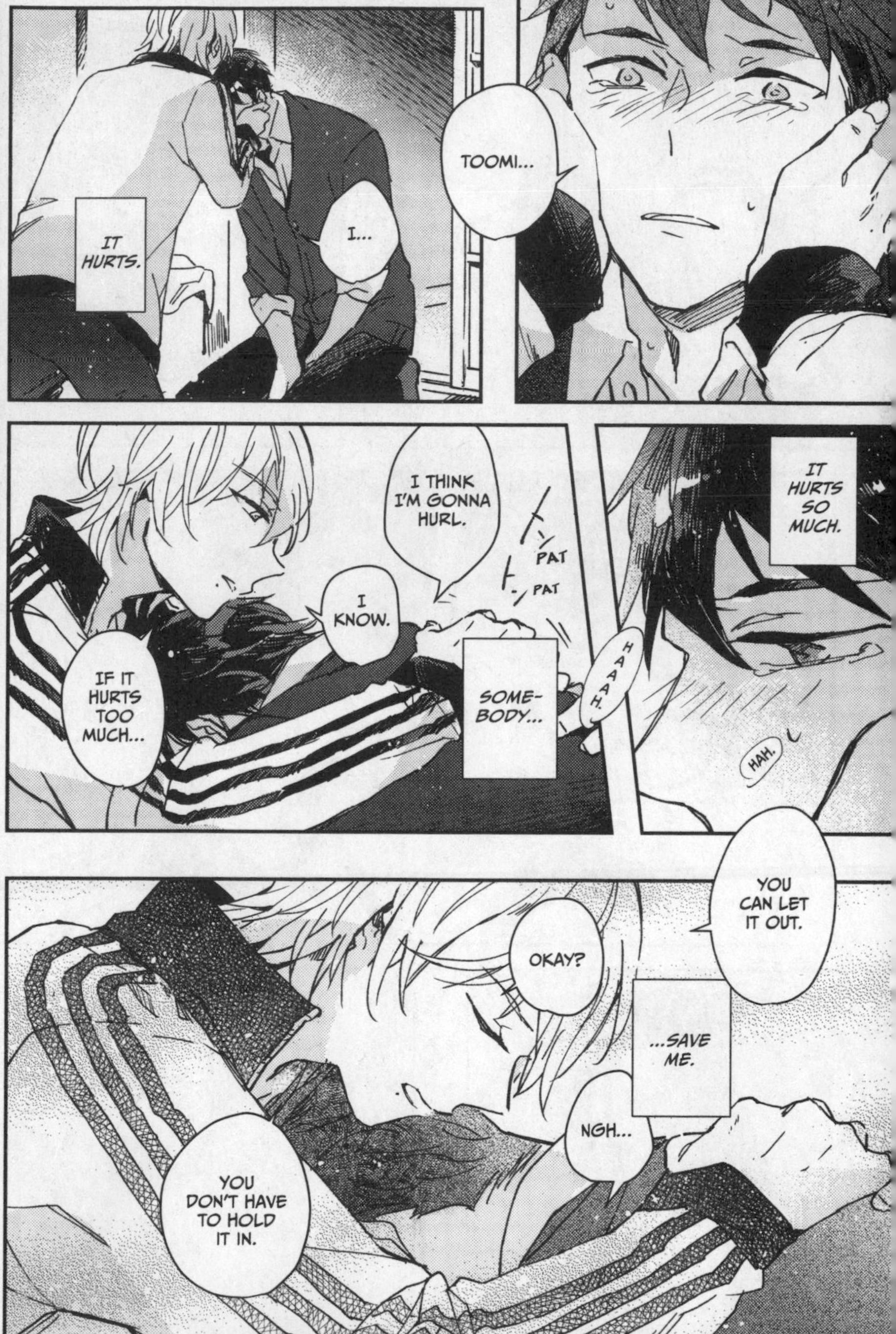
TOOMI...
I...
IT HURTS.
IT HURTS SO MUCH.
HAAAH.
HAH.
I THINK I'M GONNA HURL.
PAT
PAT
I KNOW.
SOME-BODY...
IF IT HURTS TOO MUCH...
YOU CAN LET IT OUT.
OKAY?
...SAVE ME.
NGH...
YOU DON'T HAVE TO HOLD IT IN.

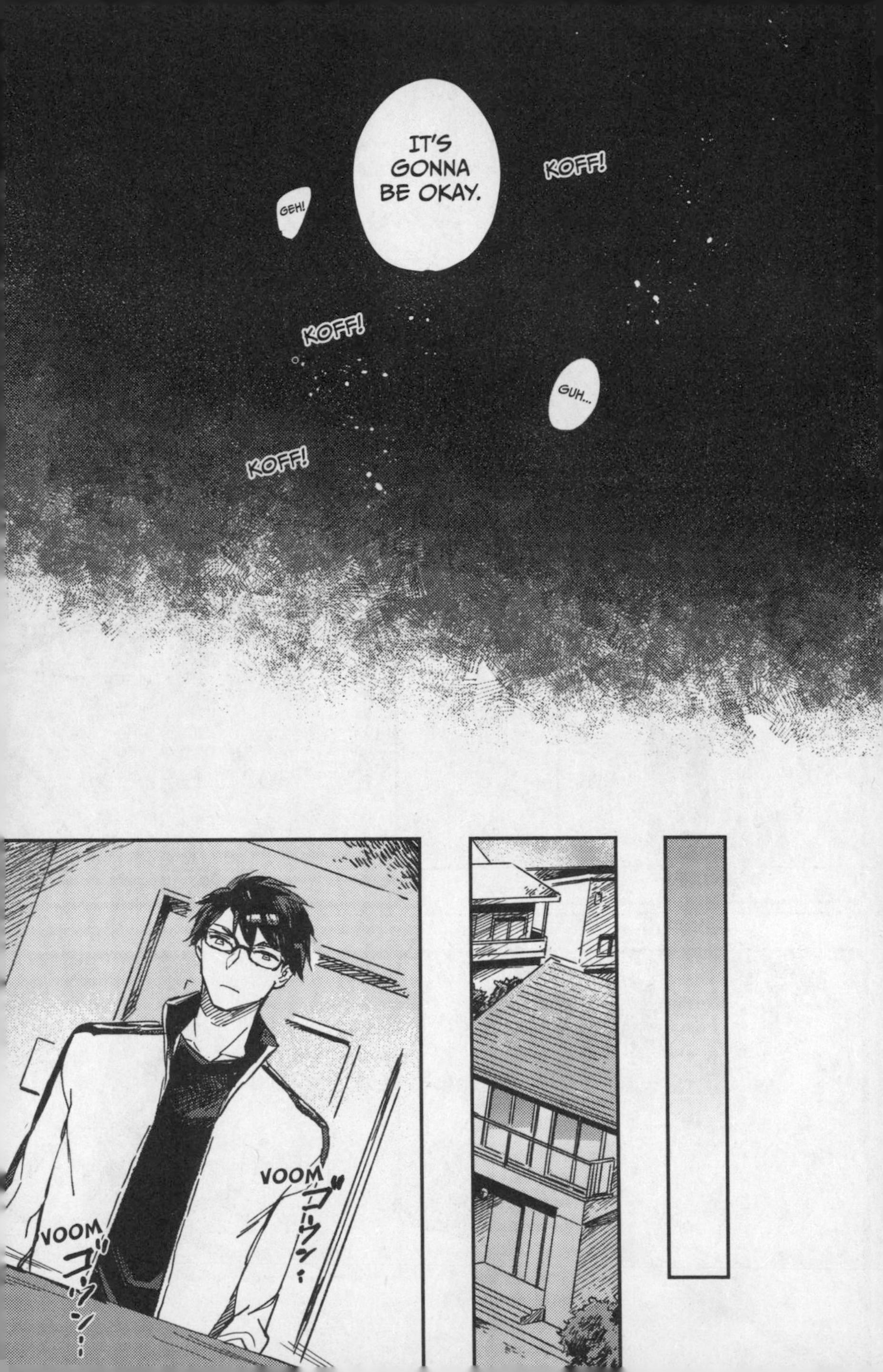
KOFF!
IT'S GONNA BE OKAY.
GEH!
KOFF!
GUH...
KOFF!
VOOM
ゴウン…
VOOM
ゴウン…

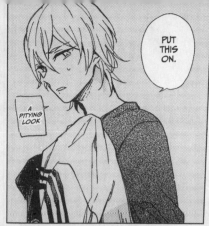

PUT THIS ON.

A PITYING LOOK

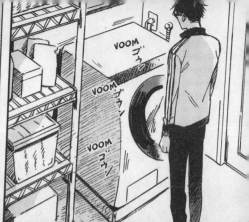

VOOM ブゥン

VOOM ブゥン

VOOM ブゥン

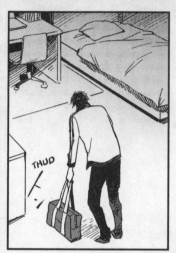

THUD トン

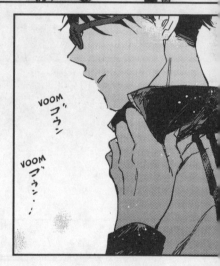

VOOM ブゥン

VOOM ブゥン...

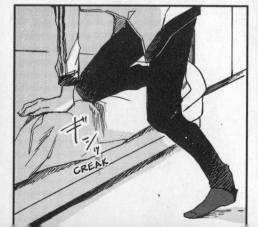

ギィ =/ ィ

CREAK

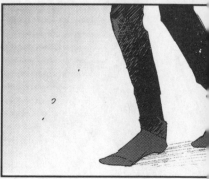

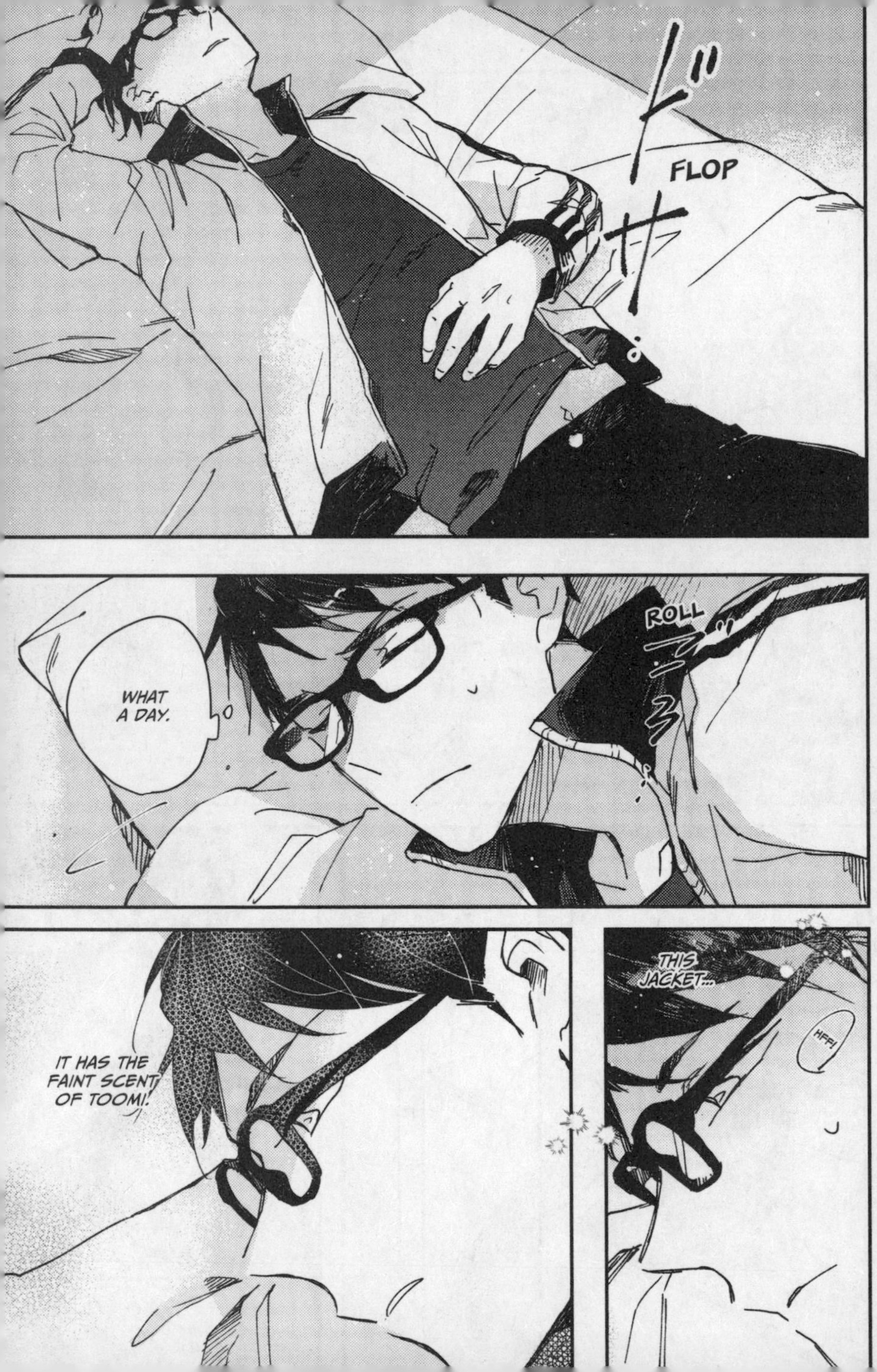
FLOP
ROLL
WHAT A DAY.
THIS JACKET...
HFF!
IT HAS THE FAINT SCENT OF TOOMI!

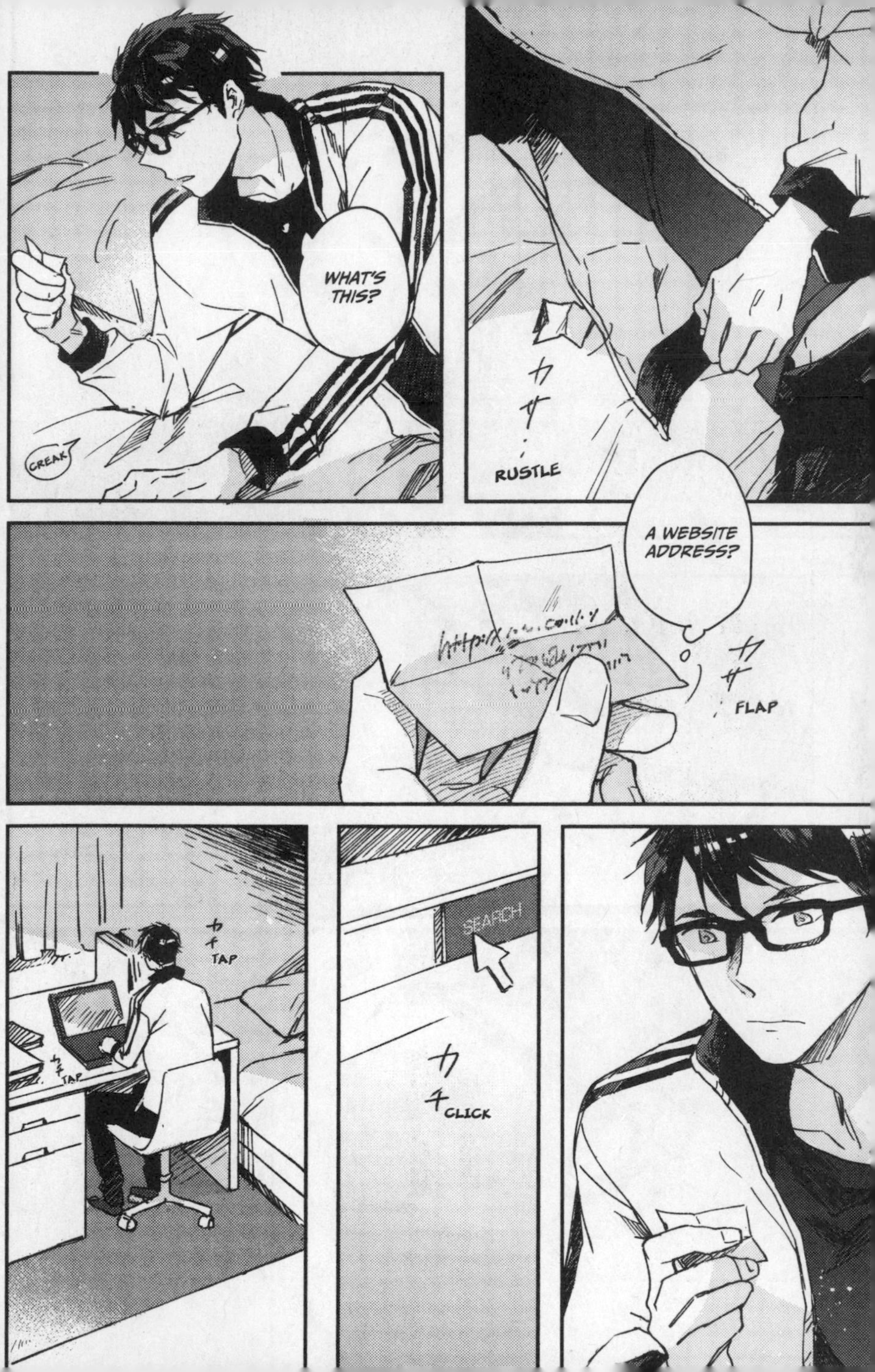
カサ…
RUSTLE
WHAT'S THIS?
CREAK
A WEBSITE ADDRESS?
カサ…
FLAP
SEARCH
カチ
CLICK
カチ
TAP
カチ
TAP

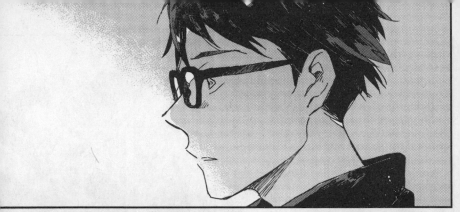

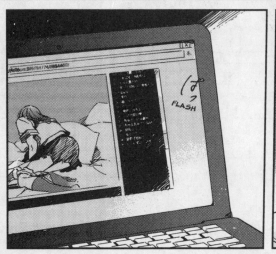

FLASH

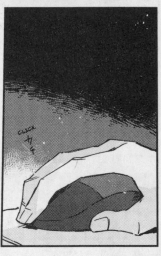

CLICK

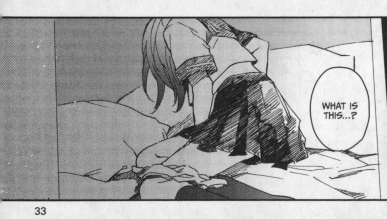

WHAT IS THIS...?

> SO HOT.
> WHAT A CUTIE
> HAWT.
> SHOW US ALR
> LET'S GET A R
> WE SHOULD
> TAKE IT OFF.
> NICE AND SL
> SHOW US M
> WHAT COLO
> MORE MORE
> SPREAD THO
> RIGHT NOW

33

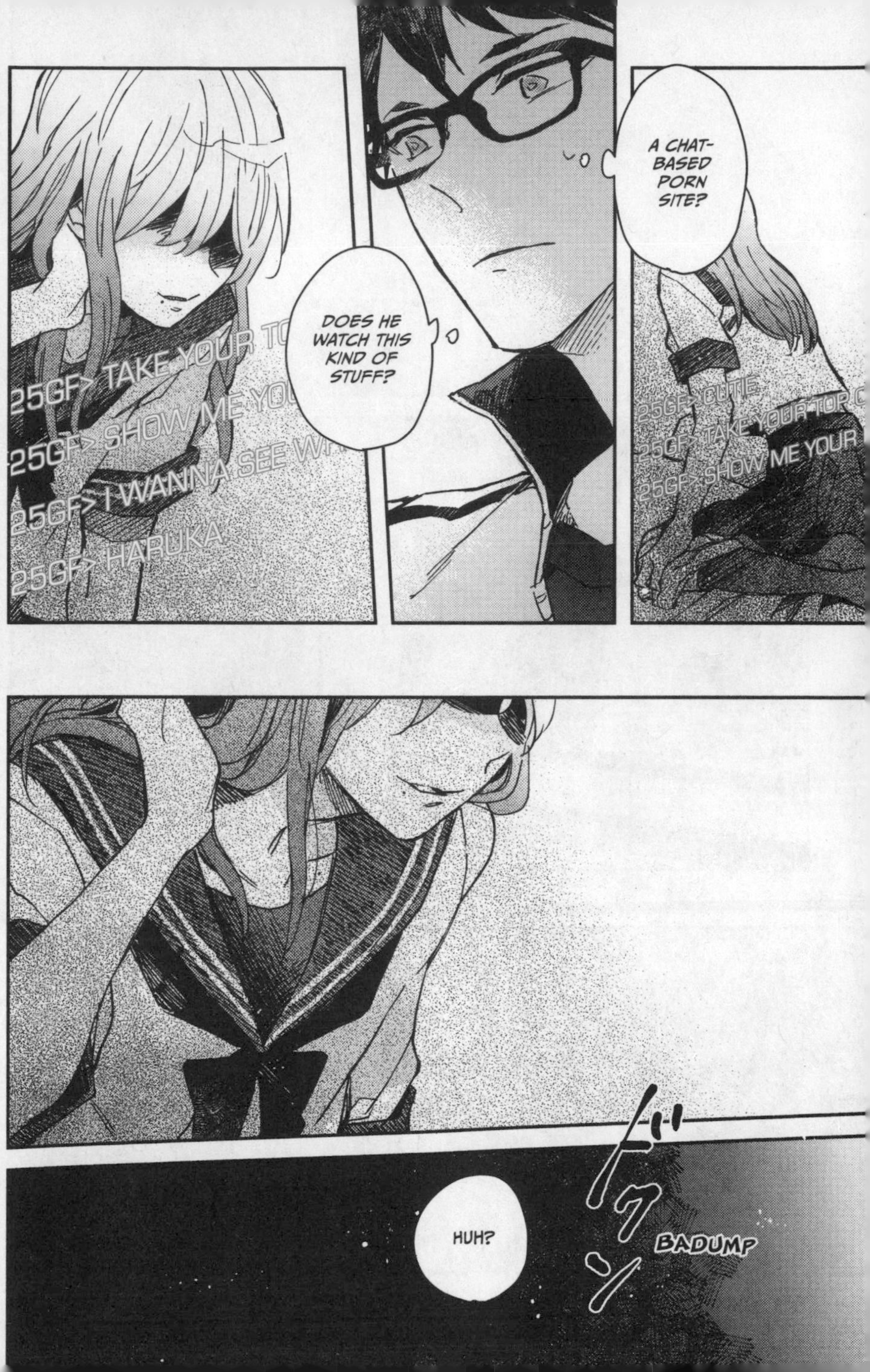
A CHAT-BASED PORN SITE?
25GF> CUTIE
25GF> TAKE YOUR TOP
25GF> SHOW ME YOUR
DOES HE WATCH THIS KIND OF STUFF?
25GF> TAKE YOUR
25GF> SHOW ME
25GF> I WANNA SEE
25GF> HARUKA
ドクン
BADUMP
HUH?

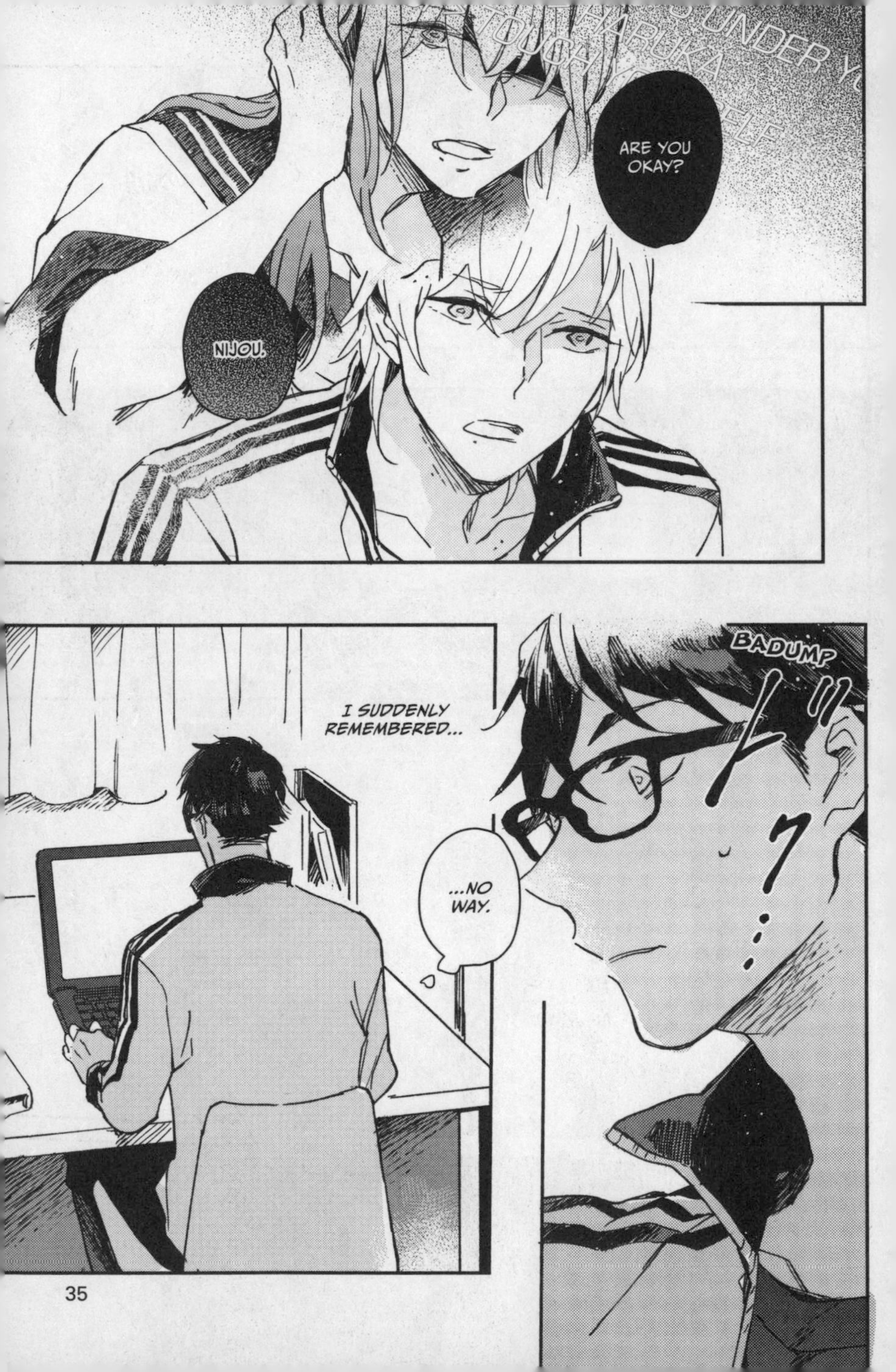
ARE YOU OKAY?
NIJOU.
BADUMP
I SUDDENLY REMEMBERED...
...NO WAY.

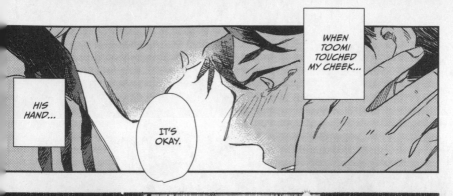

WHEN TOOMI TOUCHED MY CHEEK...

HIS HAND...

IT'S OKAY.

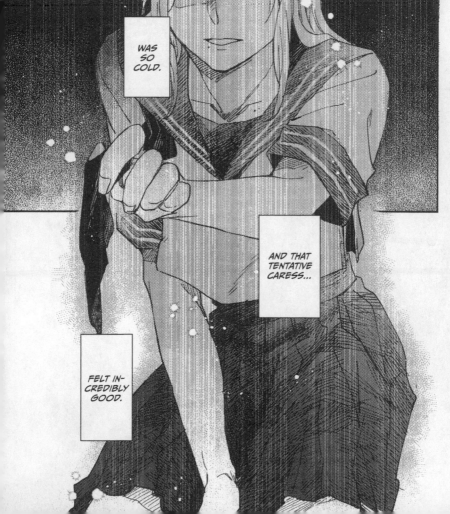

WAS SO COLD.

AND THAT TENTATIVE CARESS...

FELT IN-CREDIBLY GOOD.

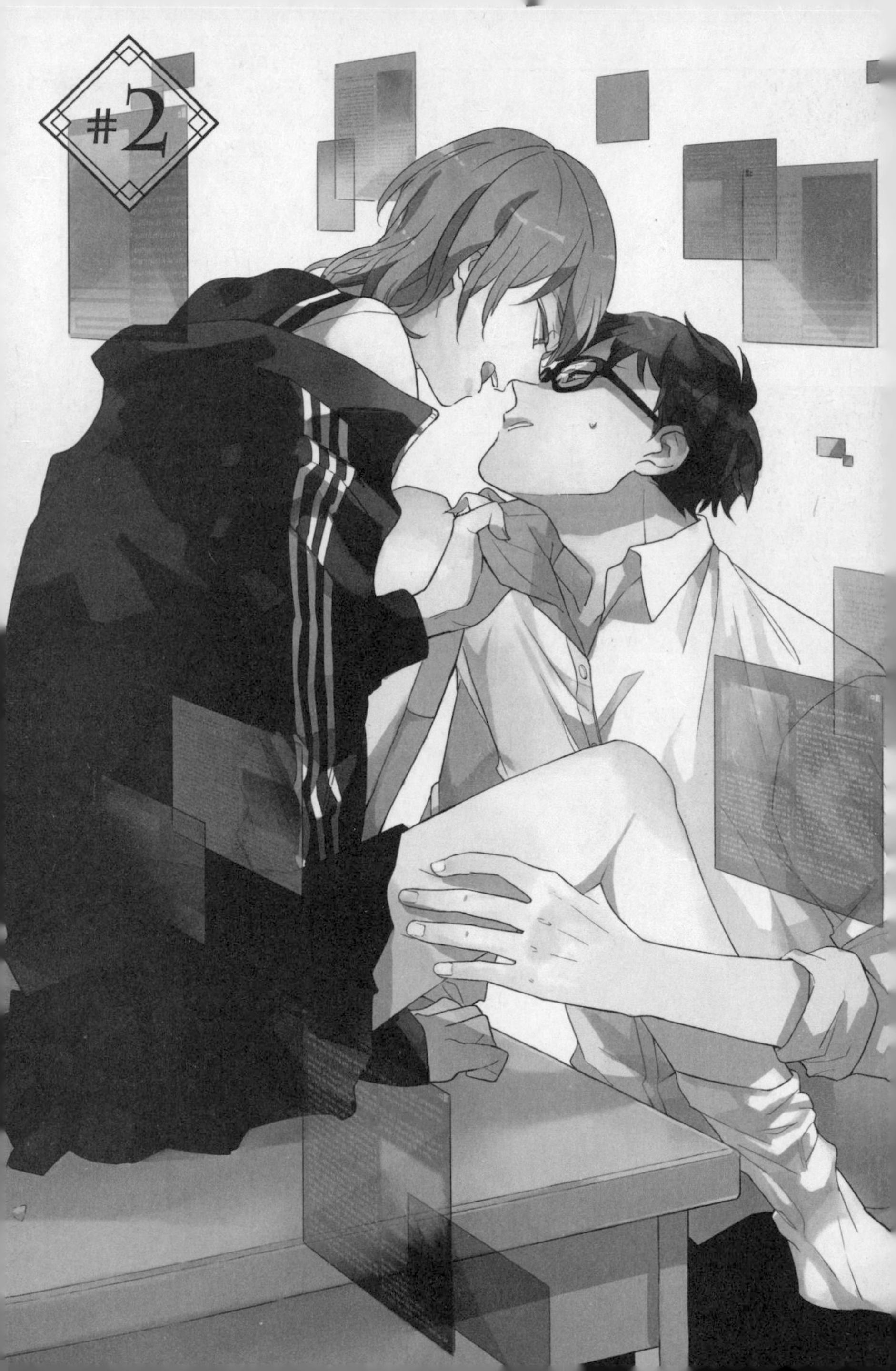
#2

glass syndrome

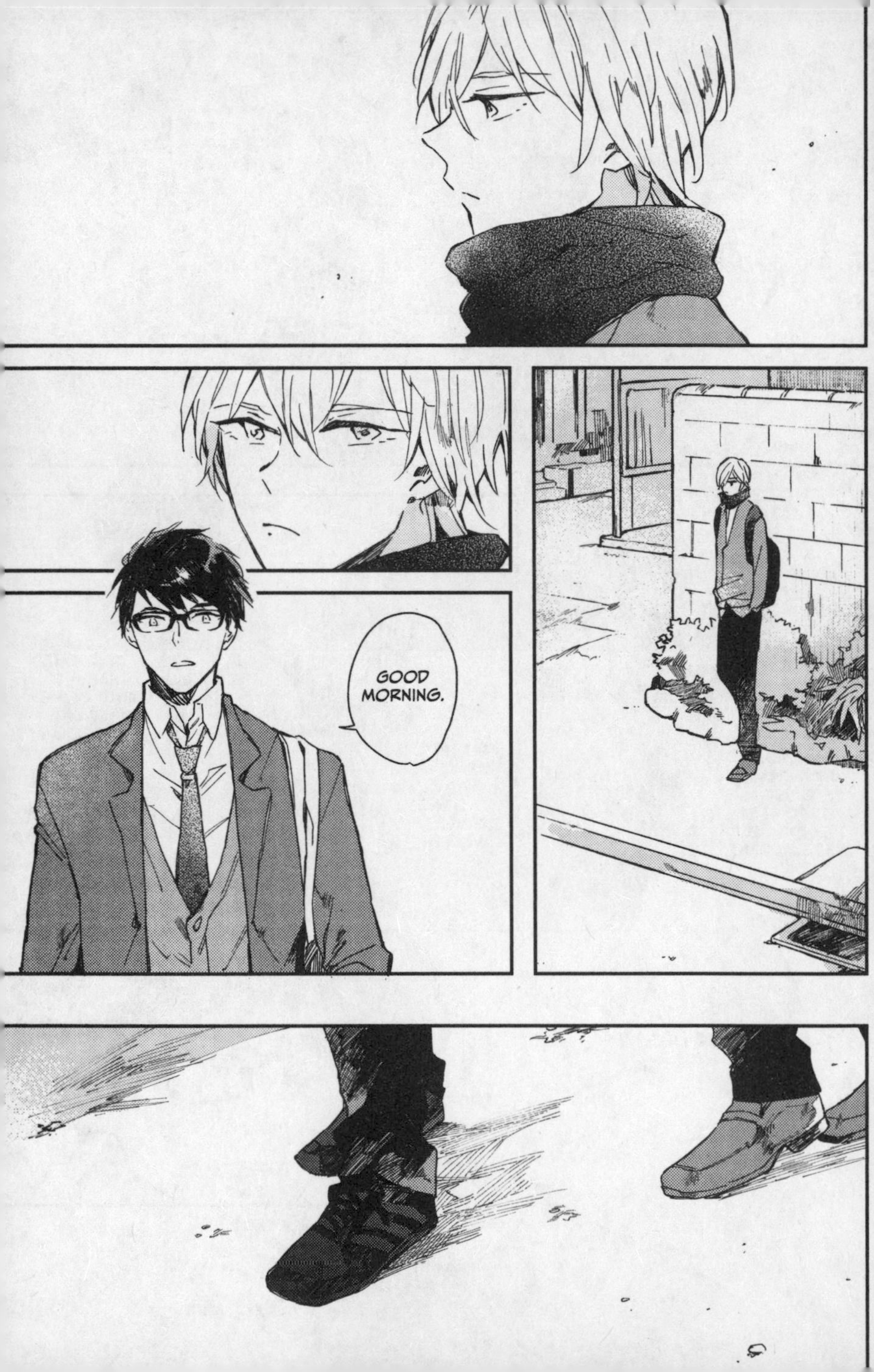
GOOD MORNING.

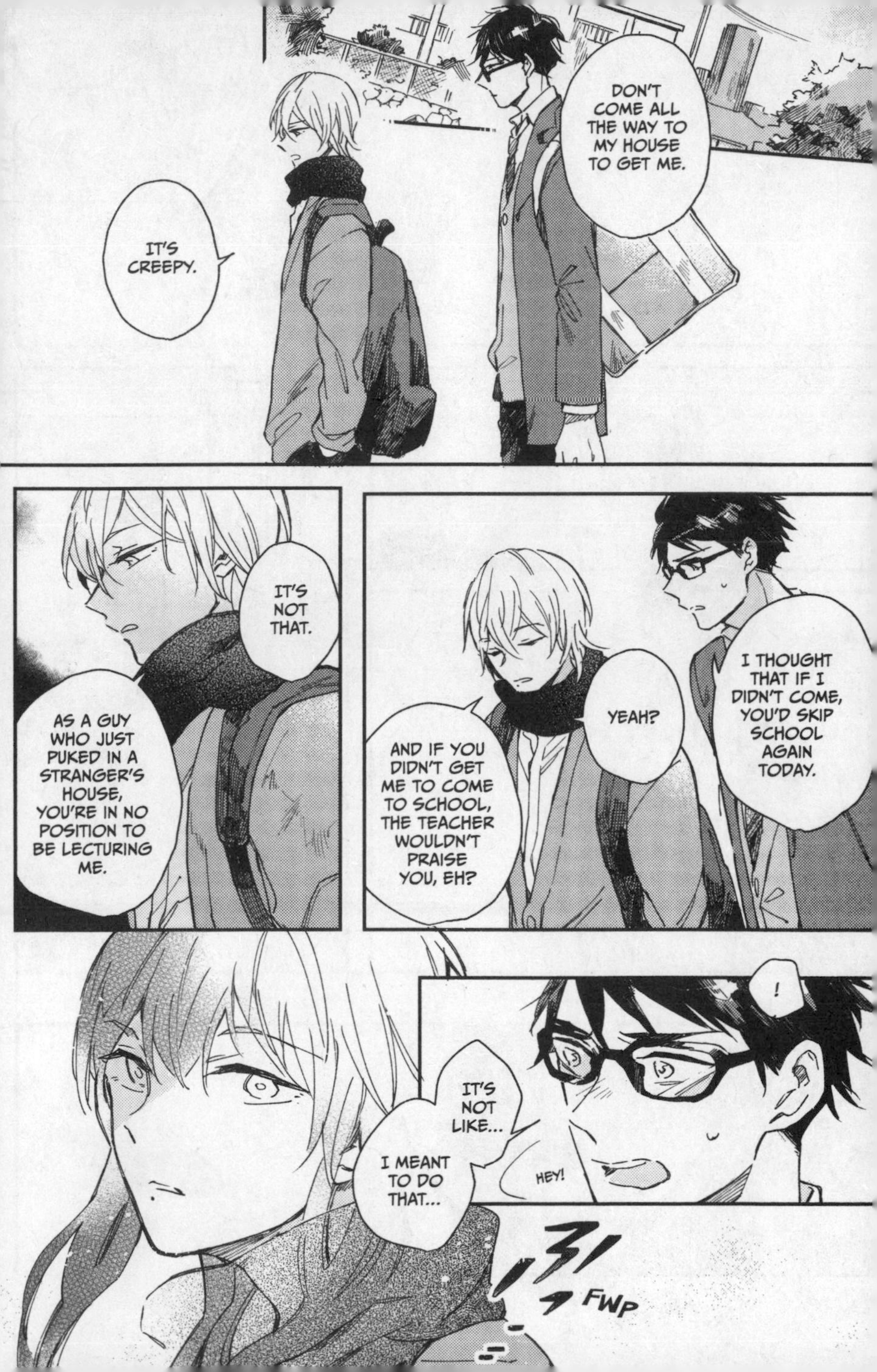
DON'T COME ALL THE WAY TO MY HOUSE TO GET ME.
IT'S CREEPY.
I THOUGHT THAT IF I DIDN'T COME, YOU'D SKIP SCHOOL AGAIN TODAY.
YEAH?
AND IF YOU DIDN'T GET ME TO COME TO SCHOOL, THE TEACHER WOULDN'T PRAISE YOU, EH?
IT'S NOT THAT.
AS A GUY WHO JUST PUKED IN A STRANGER'S HOUSE, YOU'RE IN NO POSITION TO BE LECTURING ME.
!
IT'S NOT LIKE...
I MEANT TO DO THAT...
HEY!
FWP

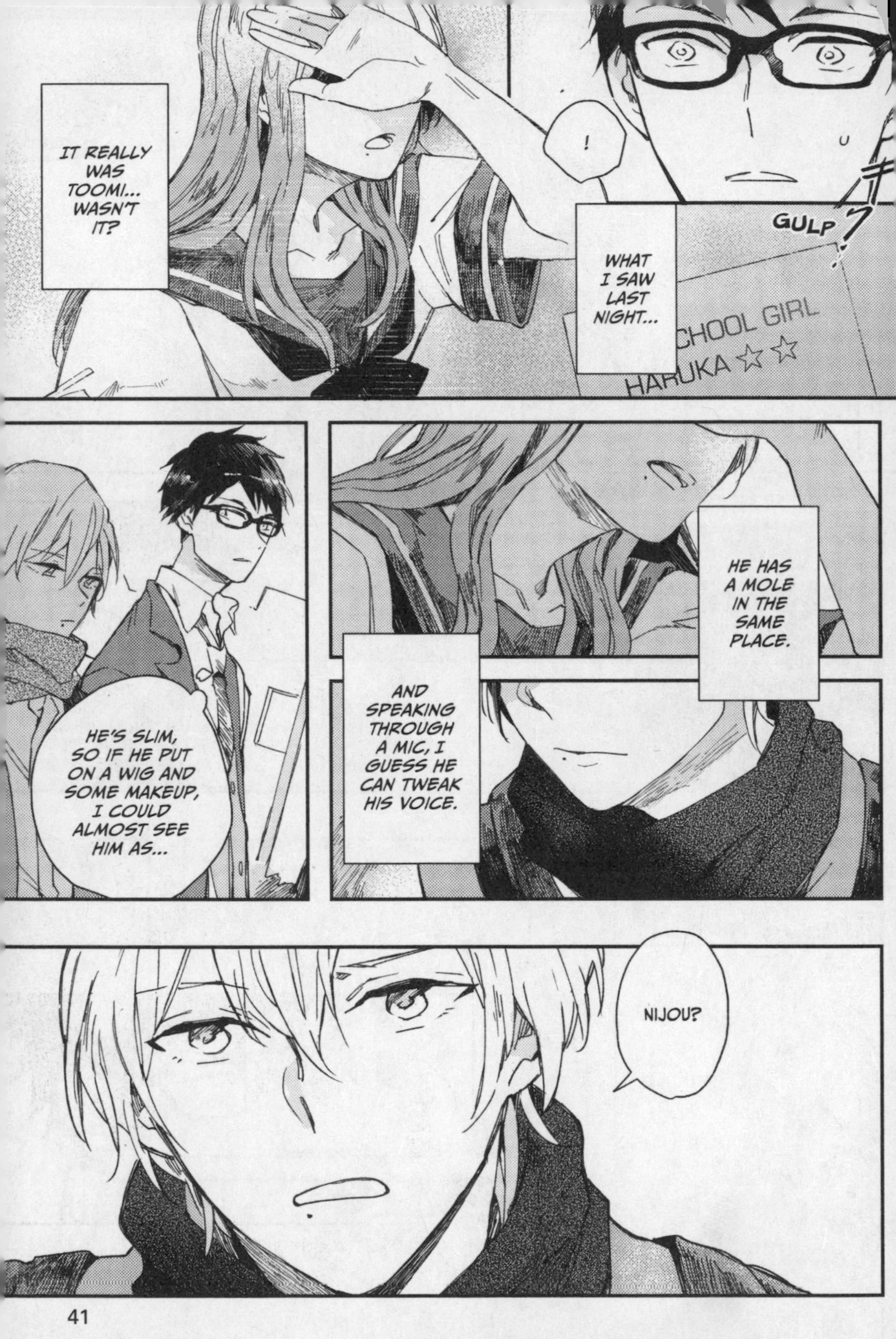
!
GULP
WHAT I SAW LAST NIGHT...
CHOOL GIRL
HARUKA ☆☆
IT REALLY WAS TOOMI... WASN'T IT?
HE HAS A MOLE IN THE SAME PLACE.
AND SPEAKING THROUGH A MIC, I GUESS HE CAN TWEAK HIS VOICE.
HE'S SLIM, SO IF HE PUT ON A WIG AND SOME MAKEUP, I COULD ALMOST SEE HIM AS...
NIJOU?

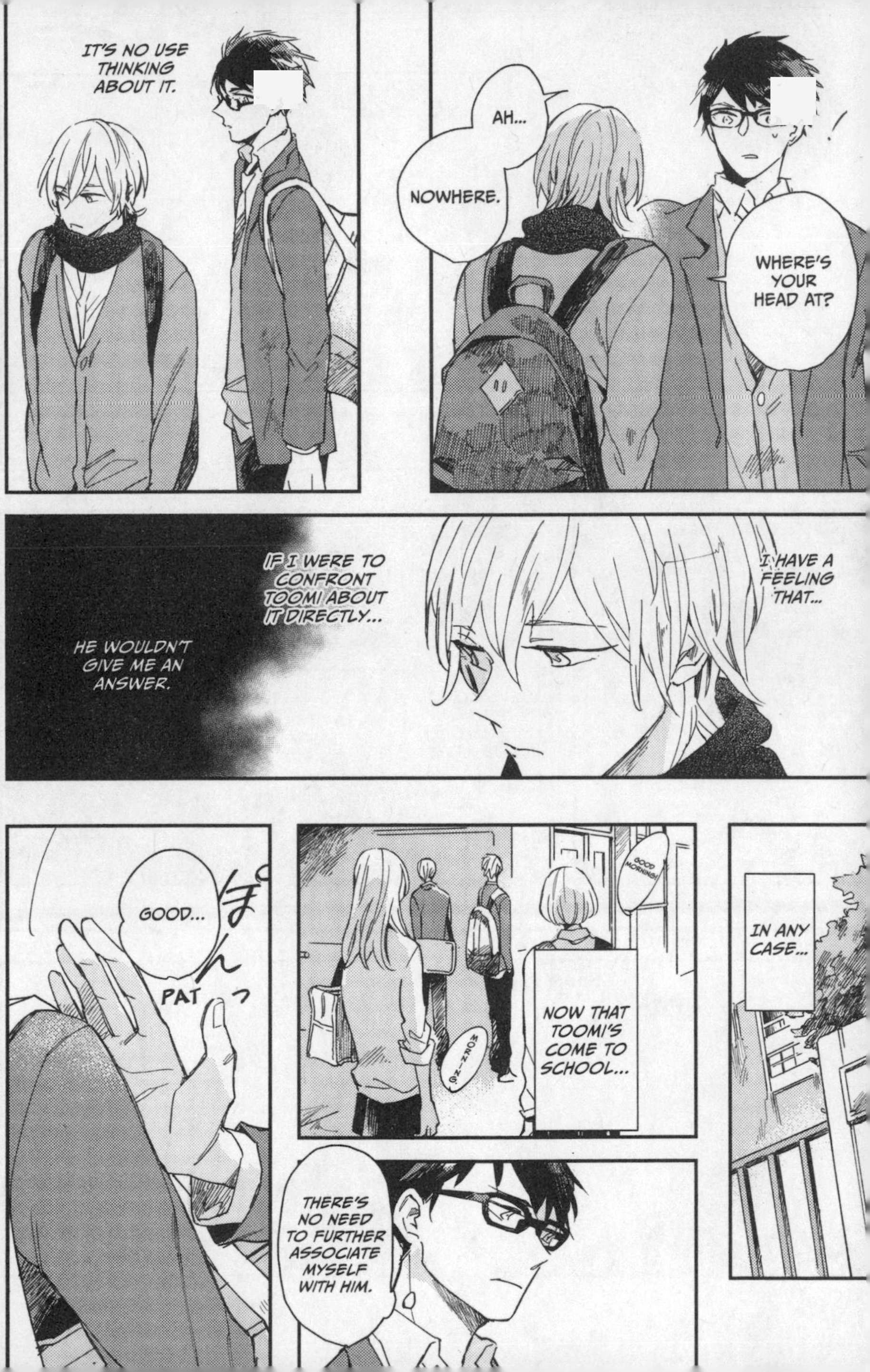
WHERE'S YOUR HEAD AT?
AH...
NOWHERE.
IT'S NO USE THINKING ABOUT IT.
I HAVE A FEELING THAT...
IF I WERE TO CONFRONT TOOMI ABOUT IT DIRECTLY...
HE WOULDN'T GIVE ME AN ANSWER.
IN ANY CASE...
GOOD MORNING!
NOW THAT TOOMI'S COME TO SCHOOL...
MORNING.
THERE'S NO NEED TO FURTHER ASSOCIATE MYSELF WITH HIM.
GOOD...
ぽんっ
PAT

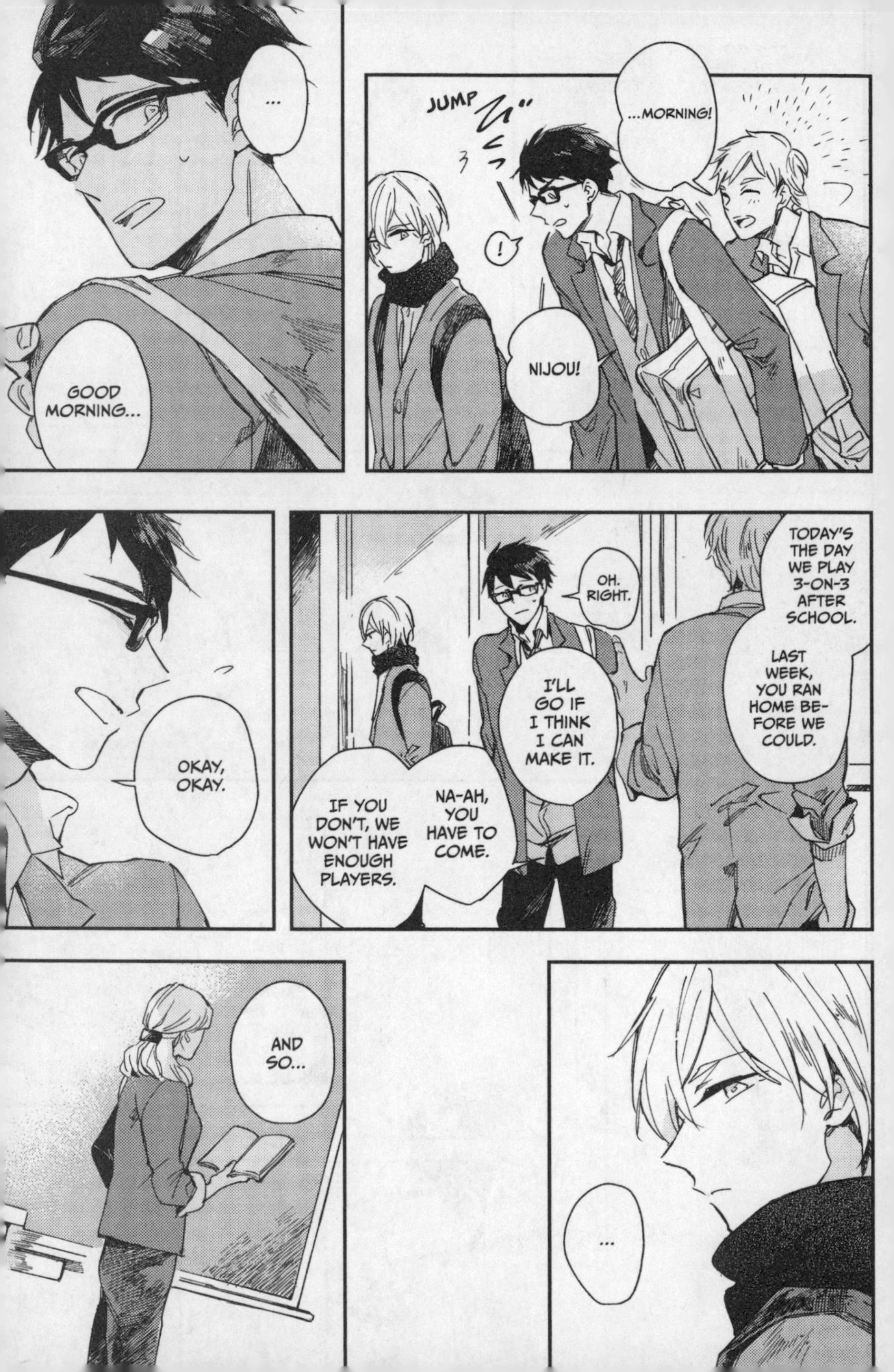
...MORNING!
JUMP
!
NIJOU!
...
GOOD MORNING...
TODAY'S THE DAY WE PLAY 3-ON-3 AFTER SCHOOL.
LAST WEEK, YOU RAN HOME BE-FORE WE COULD.
OH. RIGHT.
I'LL GO IF I THINK I CAN MAKE IT.
NA-AH, YOU HAVE TO COME.
IF YOU DON'T, WE WON'T HAVE ENOUGH PLAYERS.
OKAY, OKAY.
...
AND SO...

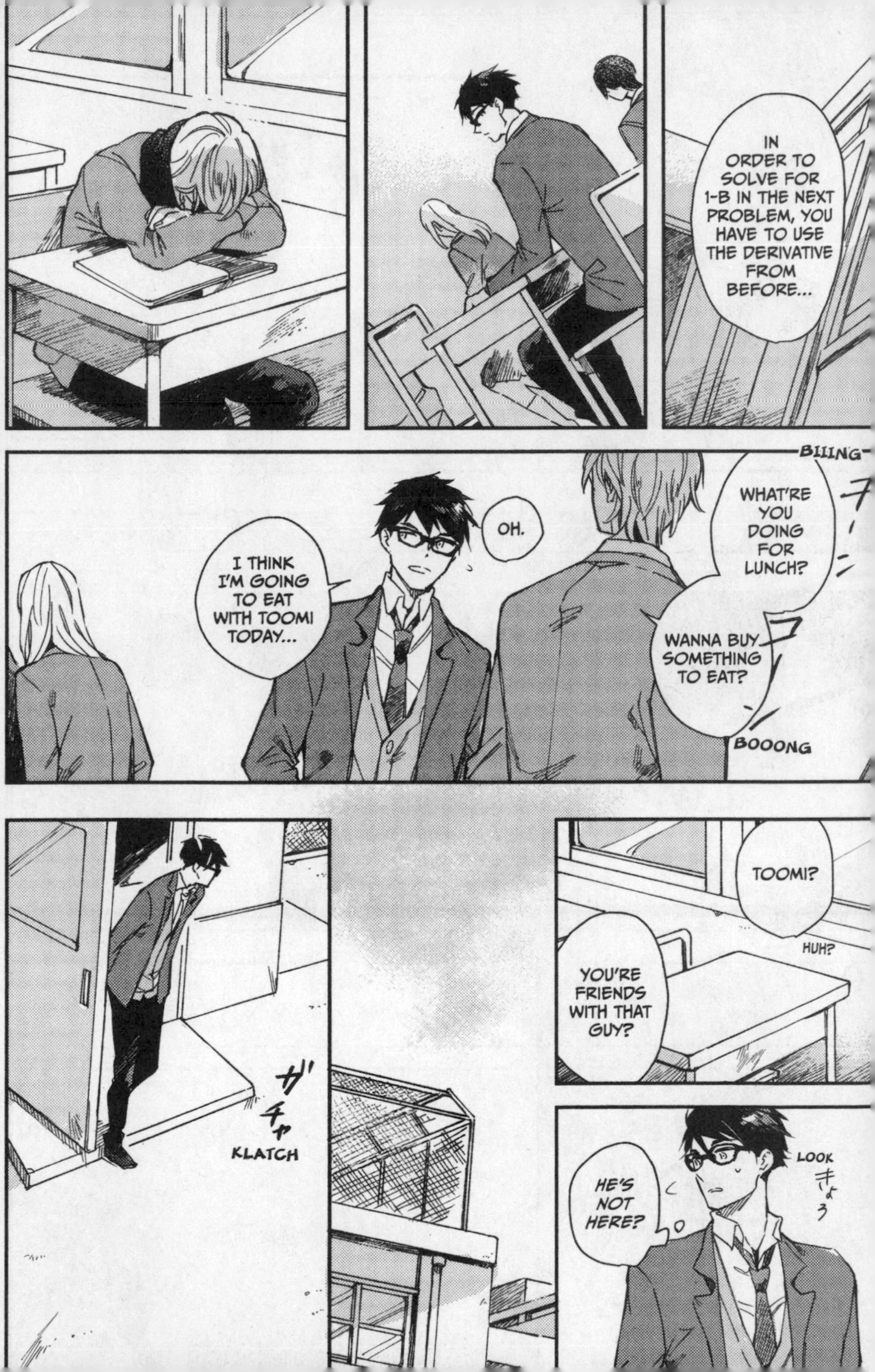
IN ORDER TO SOLVE FOR 1-B IN THE NEXT PROBLEM, YOU HAVE TO USE THE DERIVATIVE FROM BEFORE...
BIIING
WHAT'RE YOU DOING FOR LUNCH?
WANNA BUY SOMETHING TO EAT?
BOOONG
OH.
I THINK I'M GOING TO EAT WITH TOOMI TODAY...
TOOMI?
HUH?
YOU'RE FRIENDS WITH THAT GUY?
LOOK
きょろ
HE'S NOT HERE?
ガチャ
KLATCH

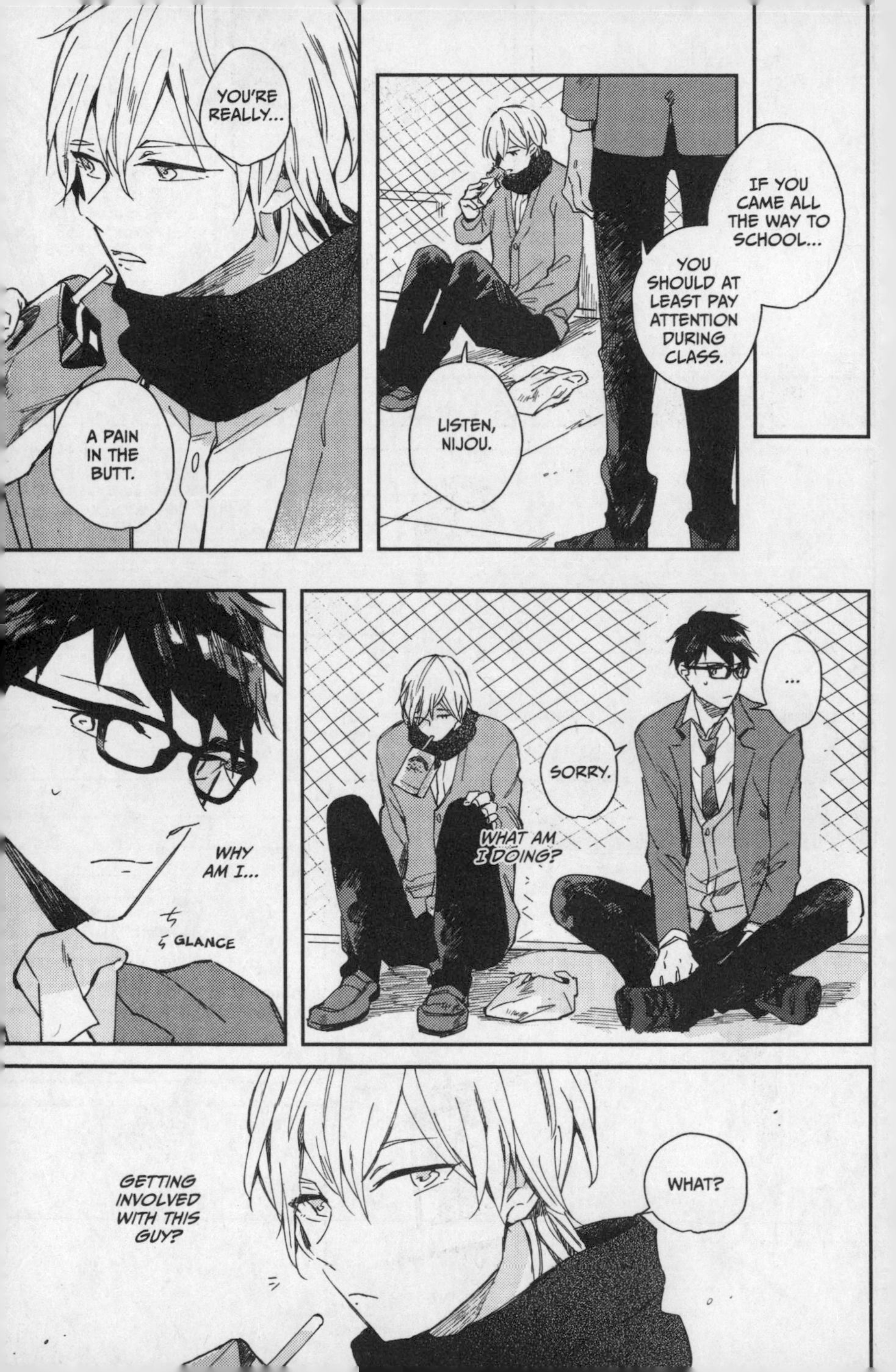
IF YOU CAME ALL THE WAY TO SCHOOL...
YOU SHOULD AT LEAST PAY ATTENTION DURING CLASS.
LISTEN, NIJOU.
YOU'RE REALLY...
A PAIN IN THE BUTT.
...
SORRY.
WHAT AM I DOING?
WHY AM I...
GLANCE
WHAT?
GETTING INVOLVED WITH THIS GUY?

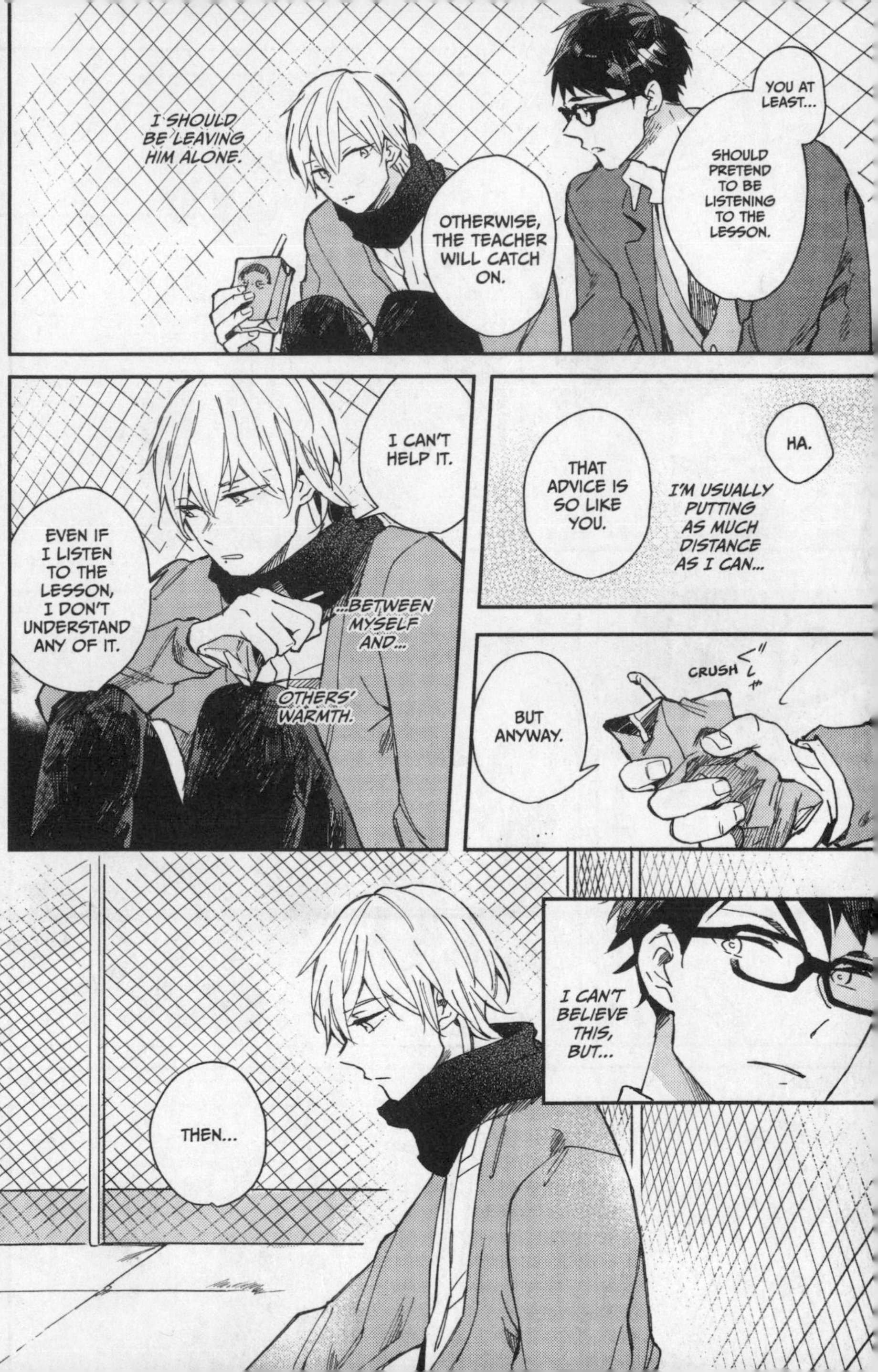
YOU AT LEAST...
SHOULD PRETEND TO BE LISTENING TO THE LESSON.
OTHERWISE, THE TEACHER WILL CATCH ON.
I SHOULD BE LEAVING HIM ALONE.
HA.
I'M USUALLY PUTTING AS MUCH DISTANCE AS I CAN...
THAT ADVICE IS SO LIKE YOU.
CRUSH
BUT ANYWAY.
...
I CAN'T HELP IT.
...BETWEEN MYSELF AND...
EVEN IF I LISTEN TO THE LESSON, I DON'T UNDERSTAND ANY OF IT.
OTHERS' WARMTH.
I CAN'T BELIEVE THIS, BUT...
THEN...

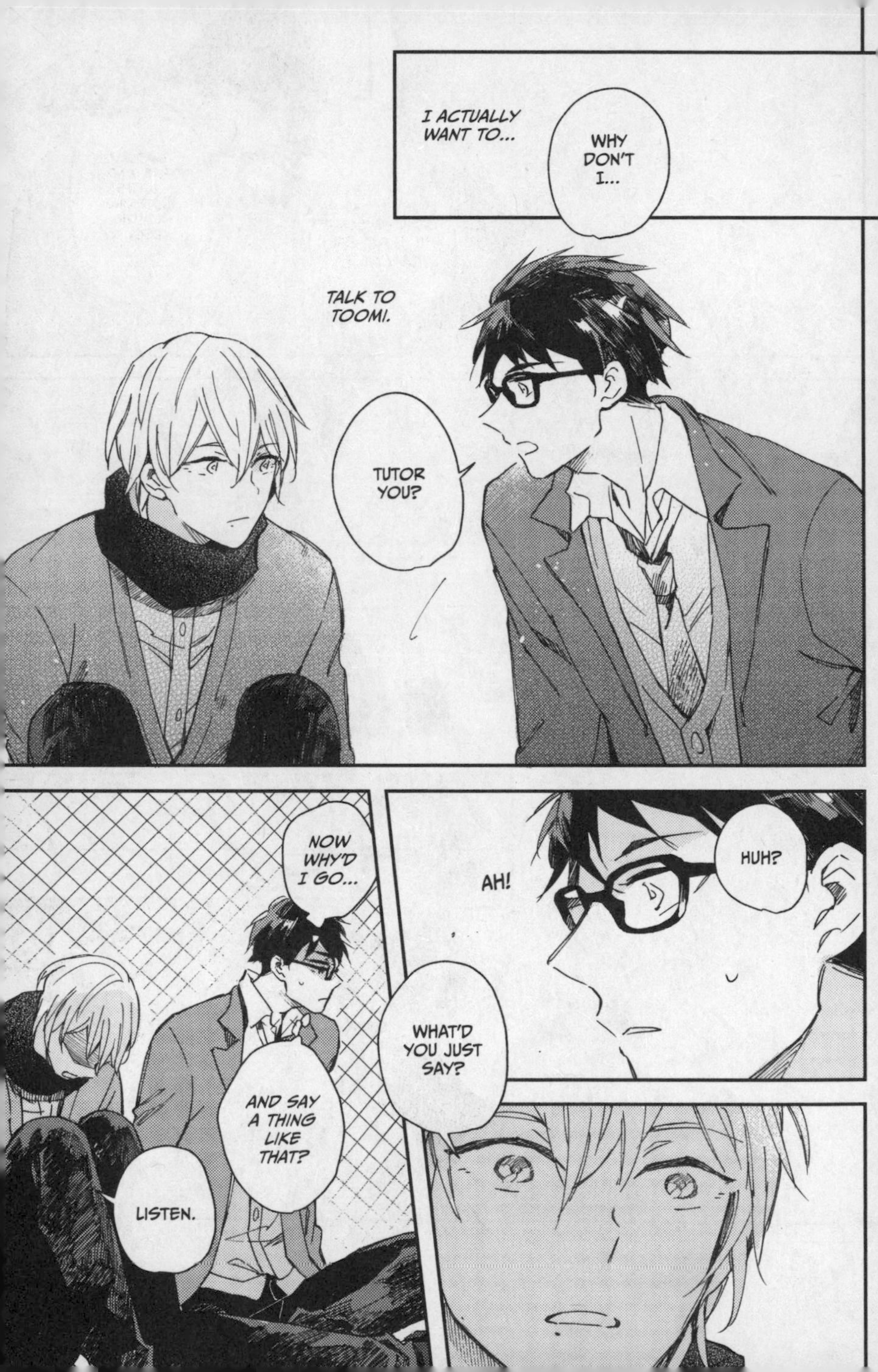
WHY DON'T I...
I ACTUALLY WANT TO...
TALK TO TOOMI.
TUTOR YOU?
HUH?
AH!
WHAT'D YOU JUST SAY?
NOW WHY'D I GO...
AND SAY A THING LIKE THAT?
LISTEN.

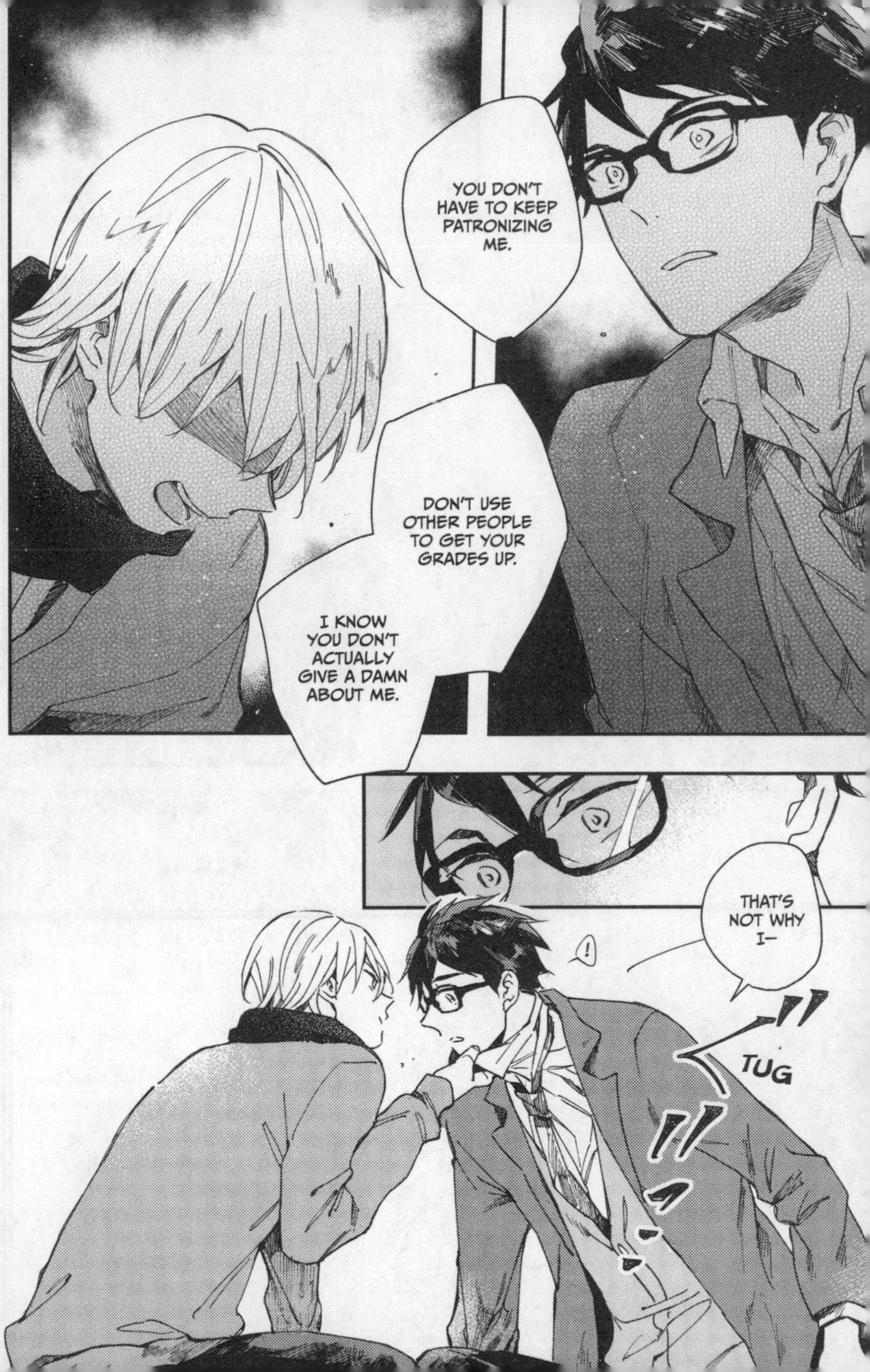
YOU DON'T HAVE TO KEEP PATRONIZING ME.
DON'T USE OTHER PEOPLE TO GET YOUR GRADES UP.
I KNOW YOU DON'T ACTUALLY GIVE A DAMN ABOUT ME.
THAT'S NOT WHY I—
!
TUG

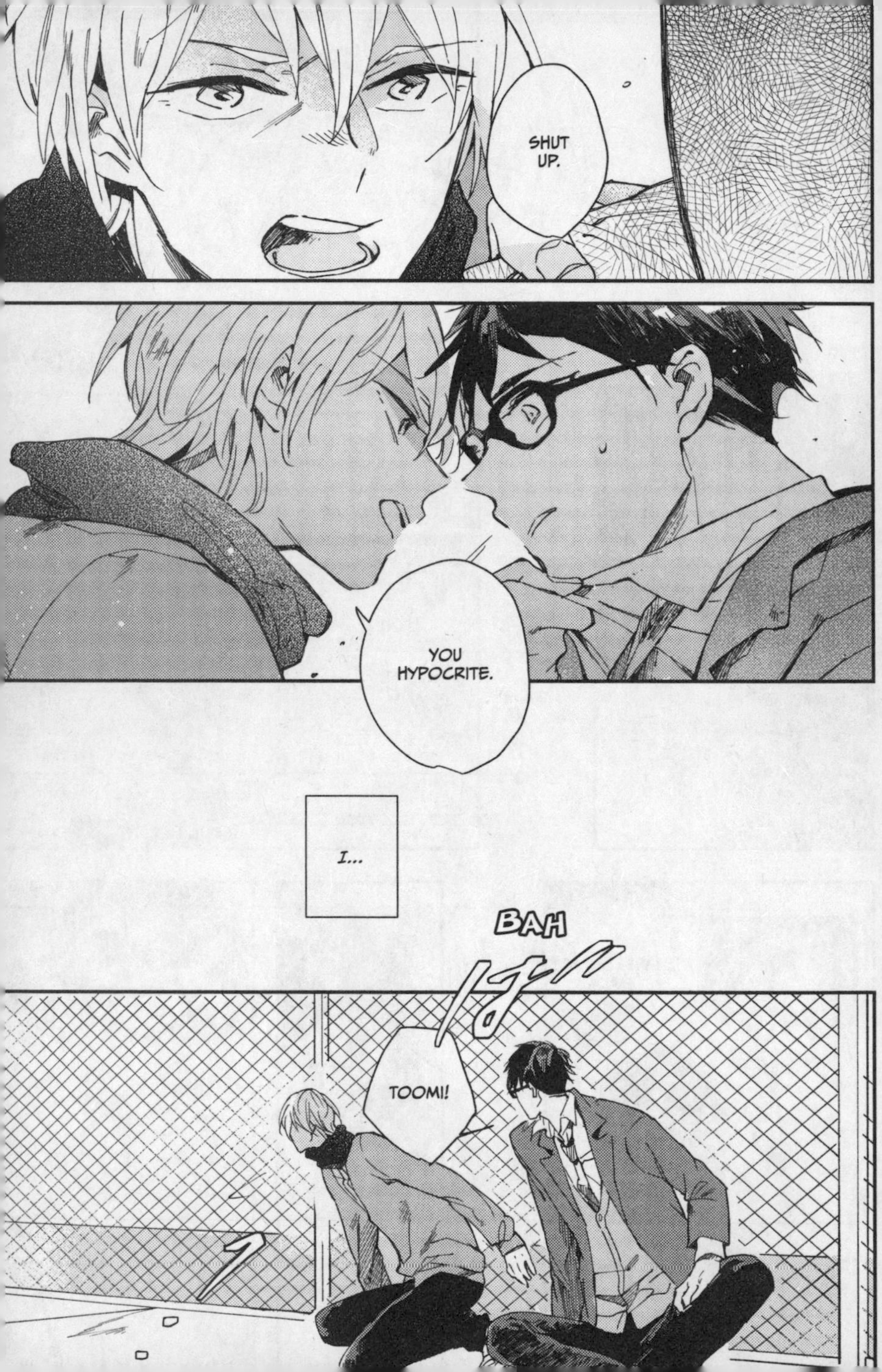
SHUT UP.
YOU HYPOCRITE.
I...
BAH
TOOMI!

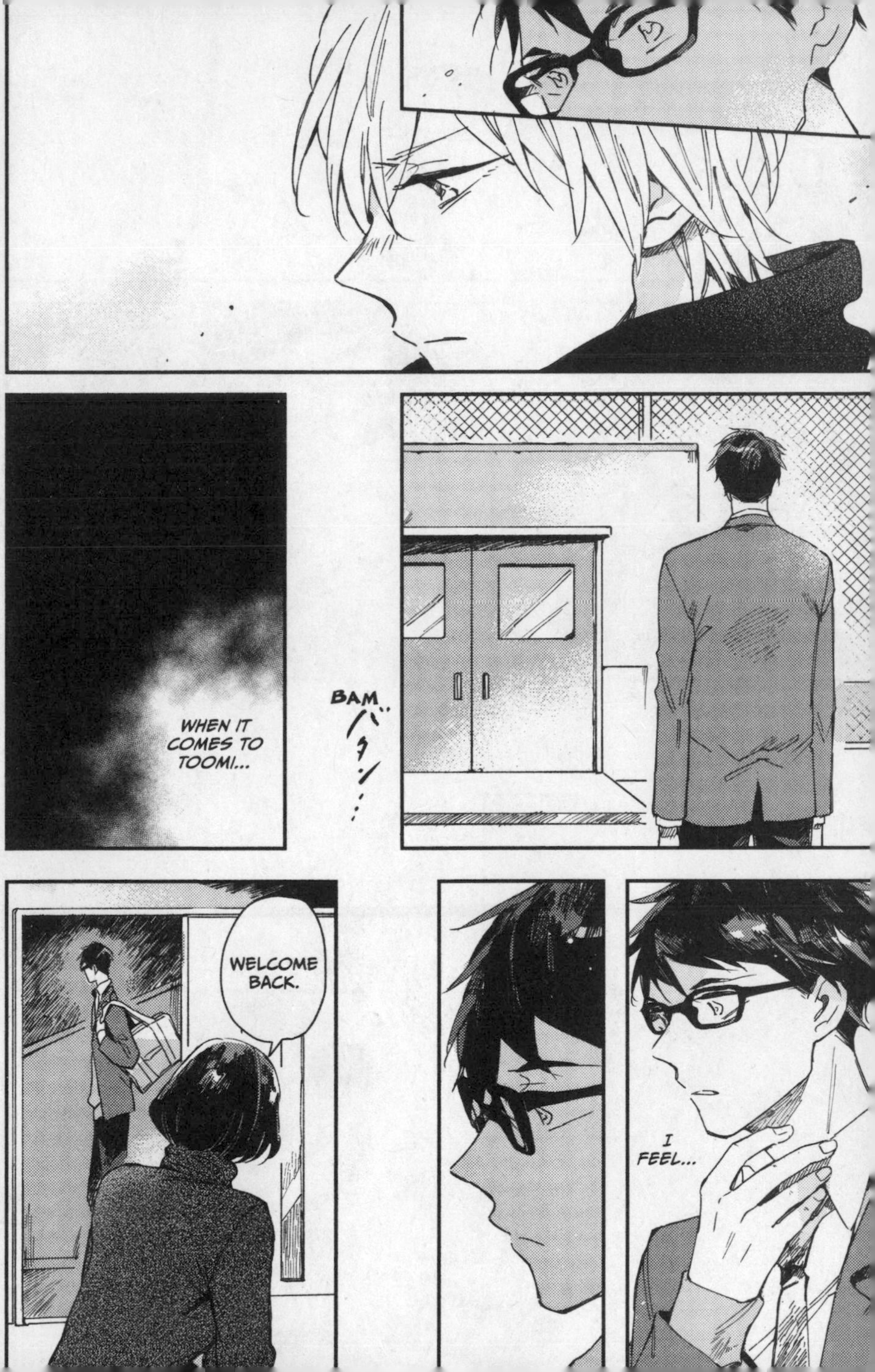
BAM
WHEN IT COMES TO TOOMI...
I FEEL...
WELCOME BACK.

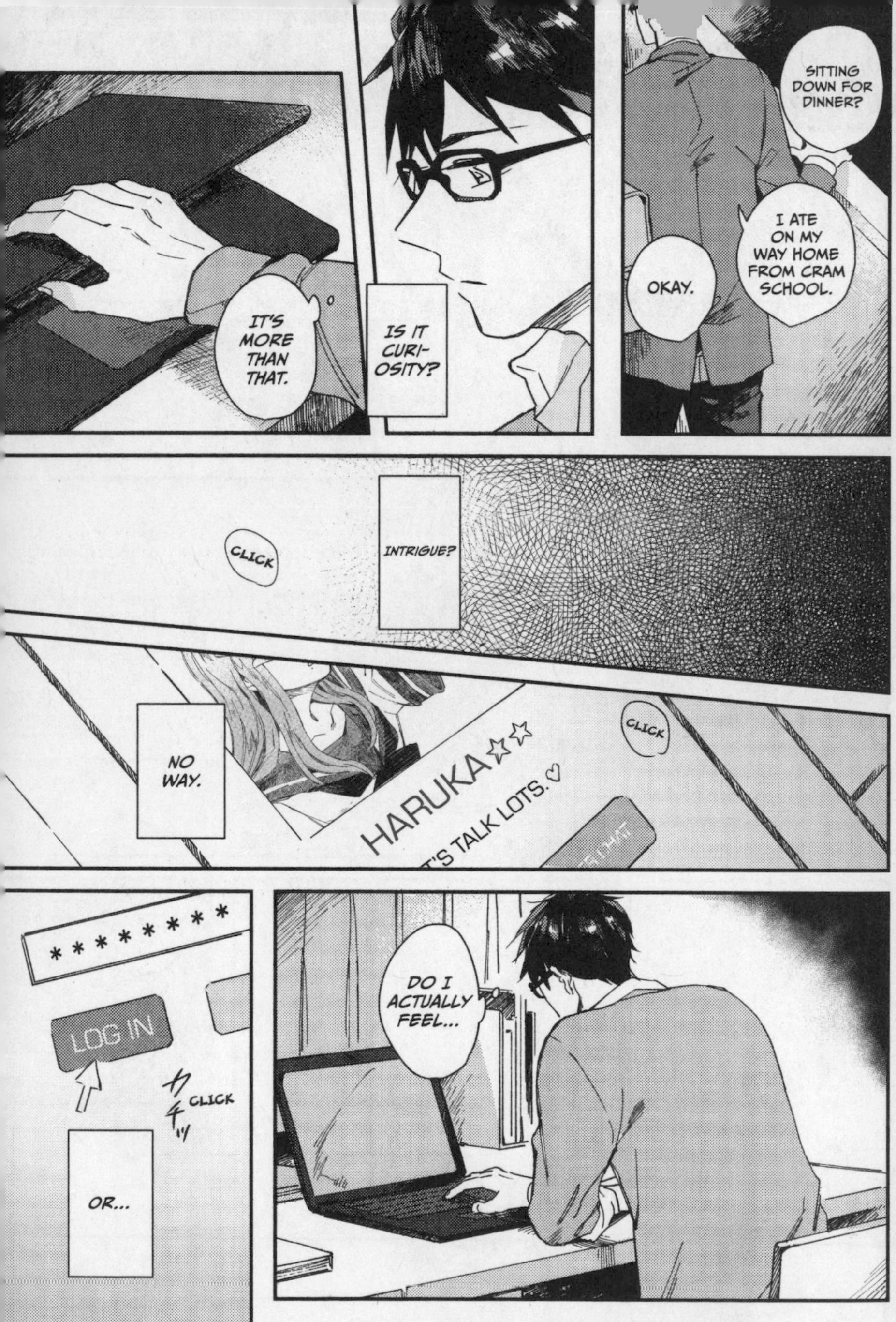
SITTING DOWN FOR DINNER?
I ATE ON MY WAY HOME FROM CRAM SCHOOL.
OKAY.
IS IT CURI-OSITY?
IT'S MORE THAN THAT.
INTRIGUE?
CLICK
CLICK
HARUKA☆☆
NO WAY.
DO I ACTUALLY FEEL...
****
LOG IN
CLICK
OR...

> ROOT HAS LOGGED IN.

PING

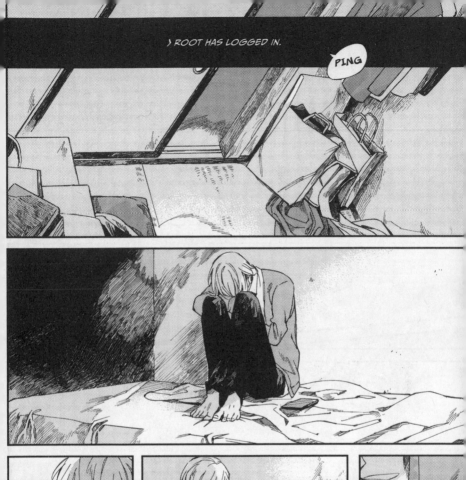

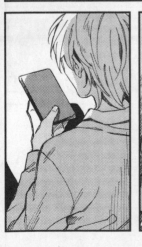

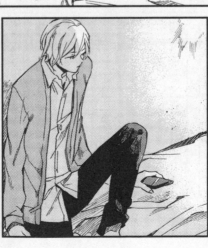

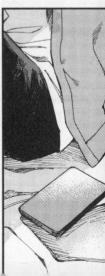

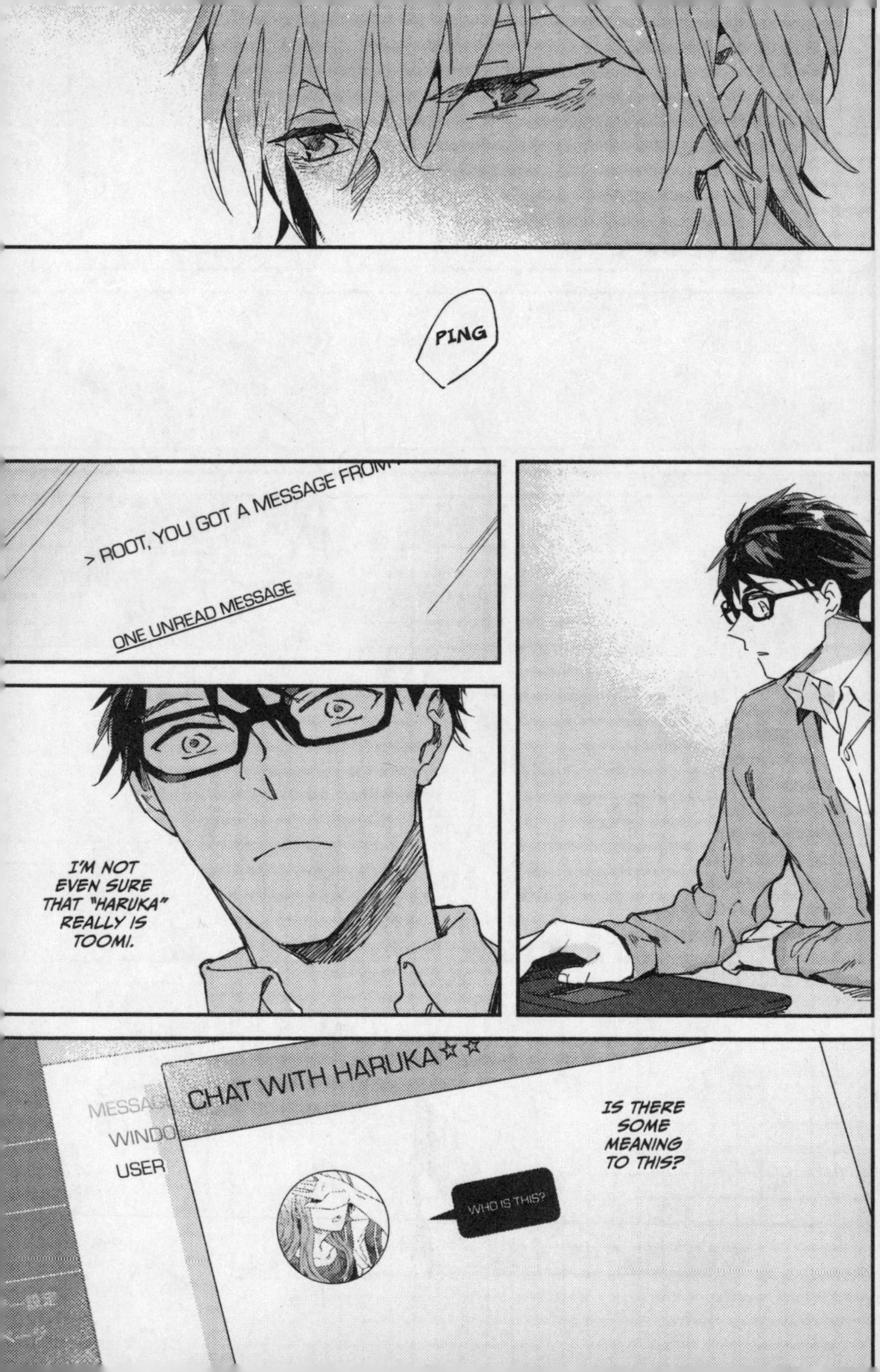
PING
> ROOT, YOU GOT A MESSAGE FROM
ONE UNREAD MESSAGE
I'M NOT EVEN SURE THAT "HARUKA" REALLY IS TOOMI.
IS THERE SOME MEANING TO THIS?
CHAT WITH HARUKA☆☆
MESSAG
WINDO
USER
WHO IS THIS?

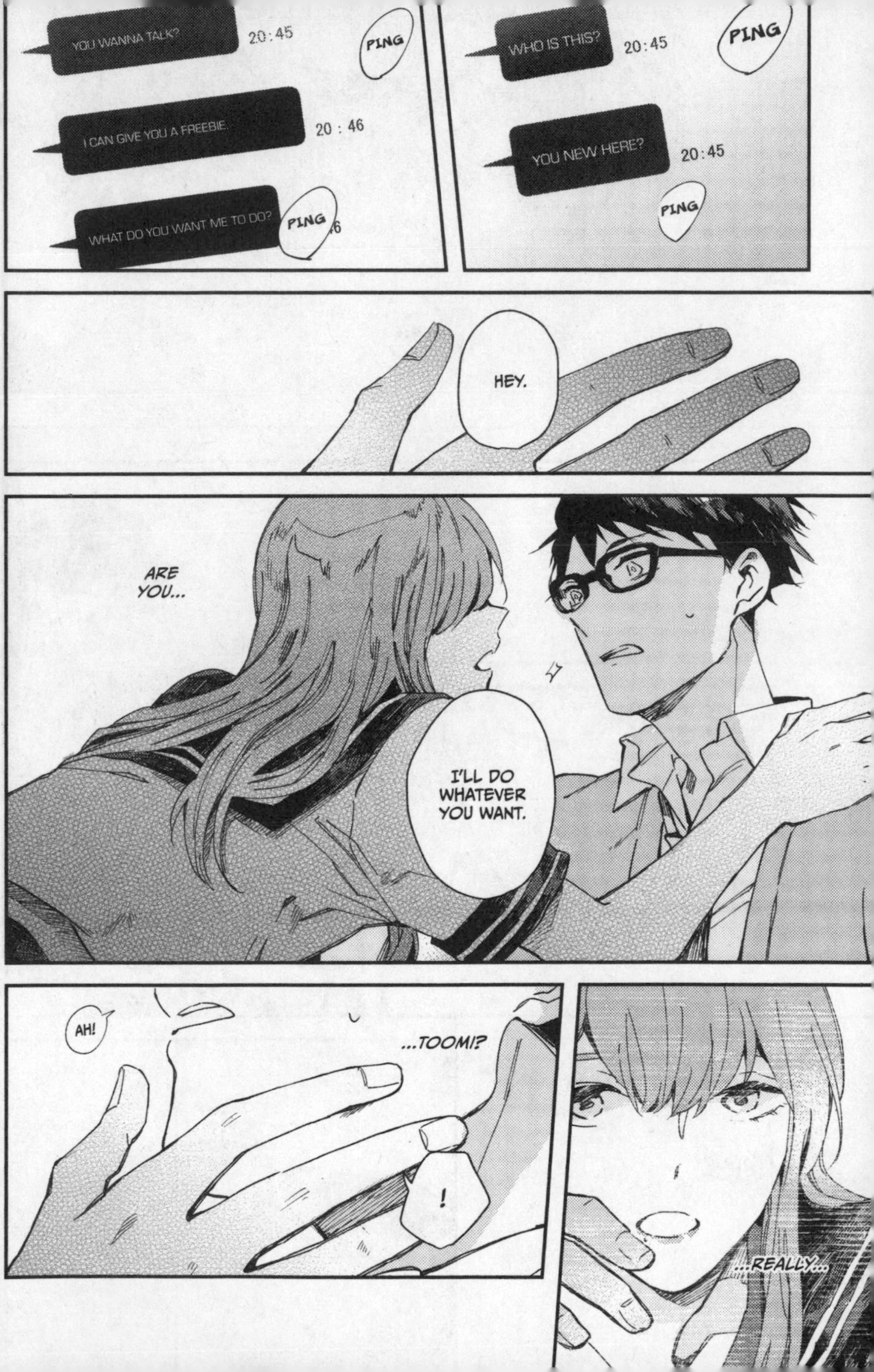
WHO IS THIS?
20:45
PING
YOU NEW HERE?
20:45
PING
YOU WANNA TALK?
20:45
PING
I CAN GIVE YOU A FREEBIE.
20 : 46
WHAT DO YOU WANT ME TO DO?
PING
HEY.
ARE YOU...
I'LL DO WHATEVER YOU WANT.
...REALLY...
...TOOMI?
AH!
!

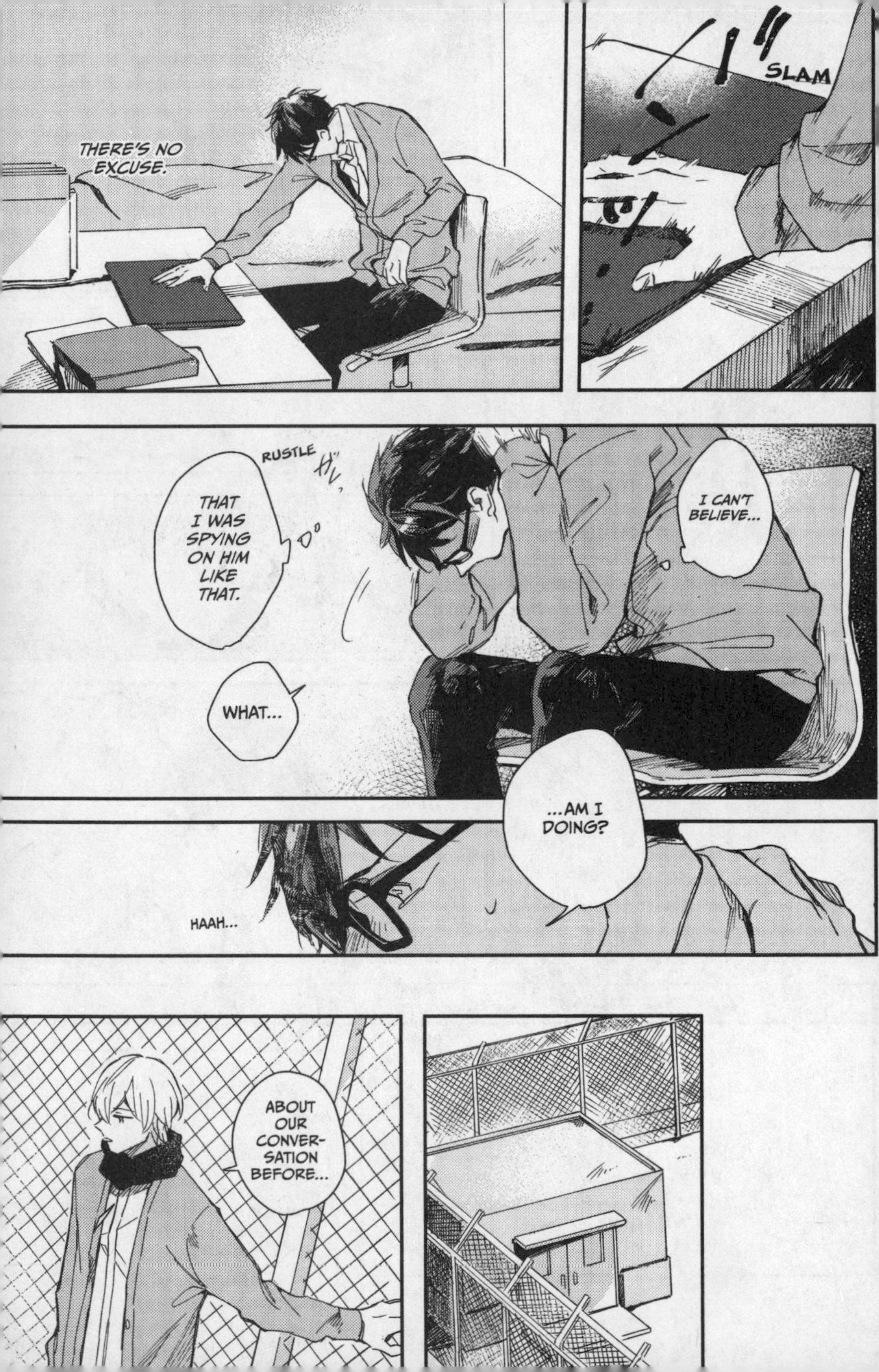
SLAM
THERE'S NO EXCUSE.
I CAN'T BELIEVE...
RUSTLE
THAT I WAS SPYING ON HIM LIKE THAT.
WHAT...
...AM I DOING?
HAAH...
ABOUT OUR CONVER-SATION BEFORE...

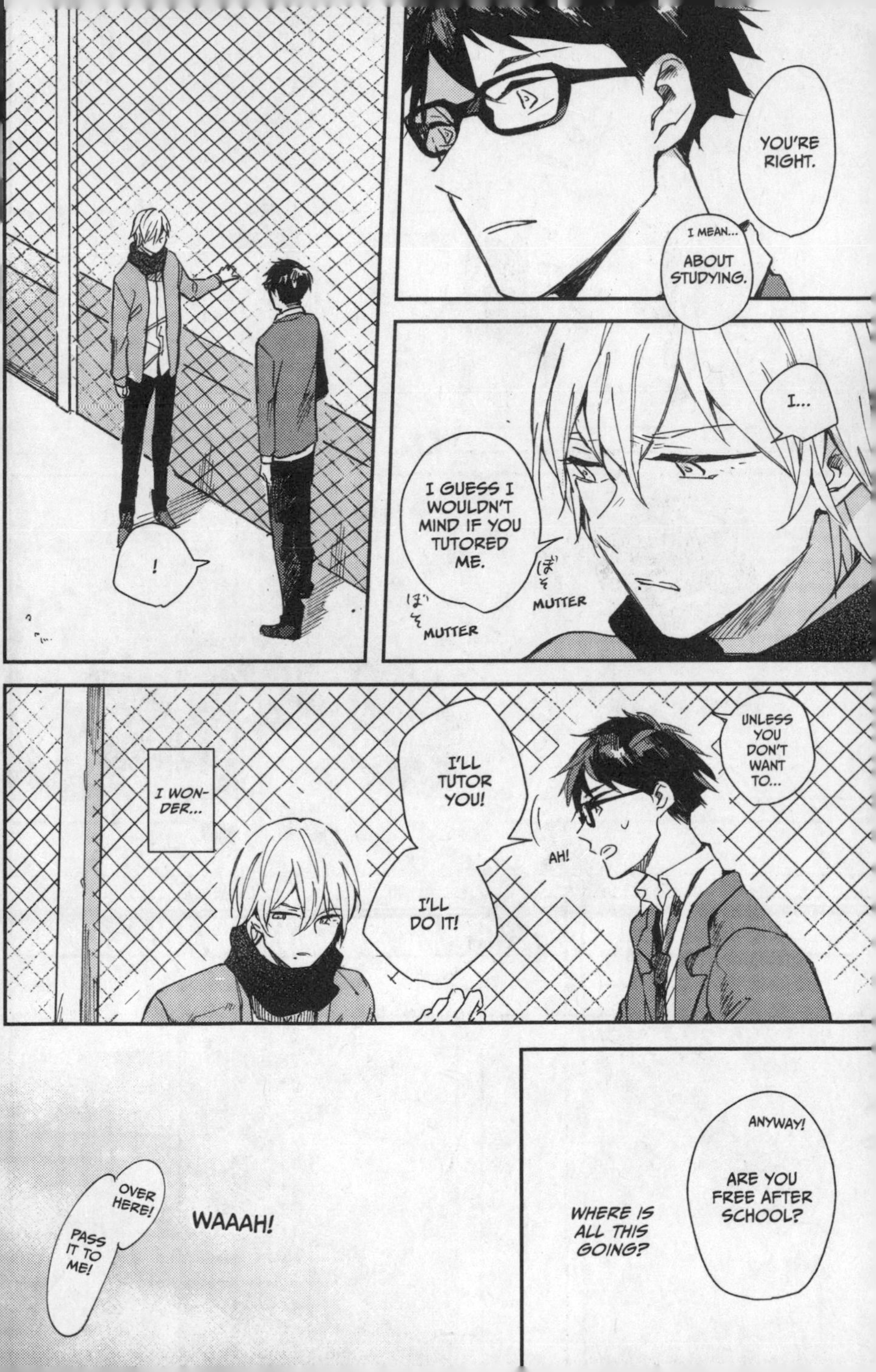
YOU'RE RIGHT.
I MEAN... ABOUT STUDYING.
I...
I GUESS I WOULDN'T MIND IF YOU TUTORED ME.
ぼそ
MUTTER
ぼそ
MUTTER
!
UNLESS YOU DON'T WANT TO...
AH!
I'LL TUTOR YOU!
I'LL DO IT!
I WONDER...
ANYWAY!
ARE YOU FREE AFTER SCHOOL?
WHERE IS ALL THIS GOING?
WAAAH!
OVER HERE!
PASS IT TO ME!

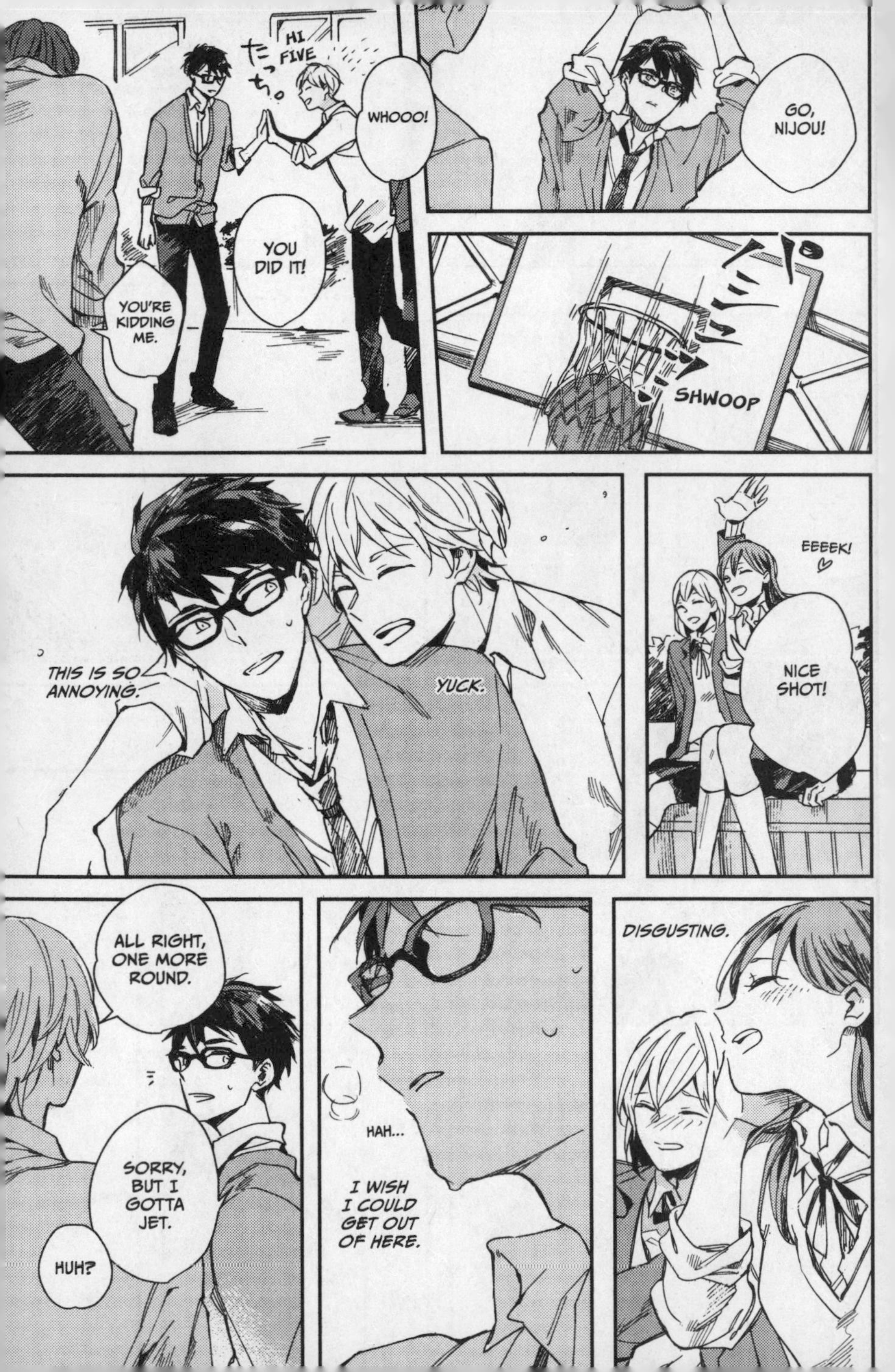

GO, NIJOU!
SHWOOP
WHOOO!
HI FIVE
YOU DID IT!
YOU'RE KIDDING ME.
EEEEK! ♡
NICE SHOT!
YUCK.
THIS IS SO ANNOYING.
DISGUSTING.
HAH...
I WISH I COULD GET OUT OF HERE.
ALL RIGHT, ONE MORE ROUND.
SORRY, BUT I GOTTA JET.
HUH?

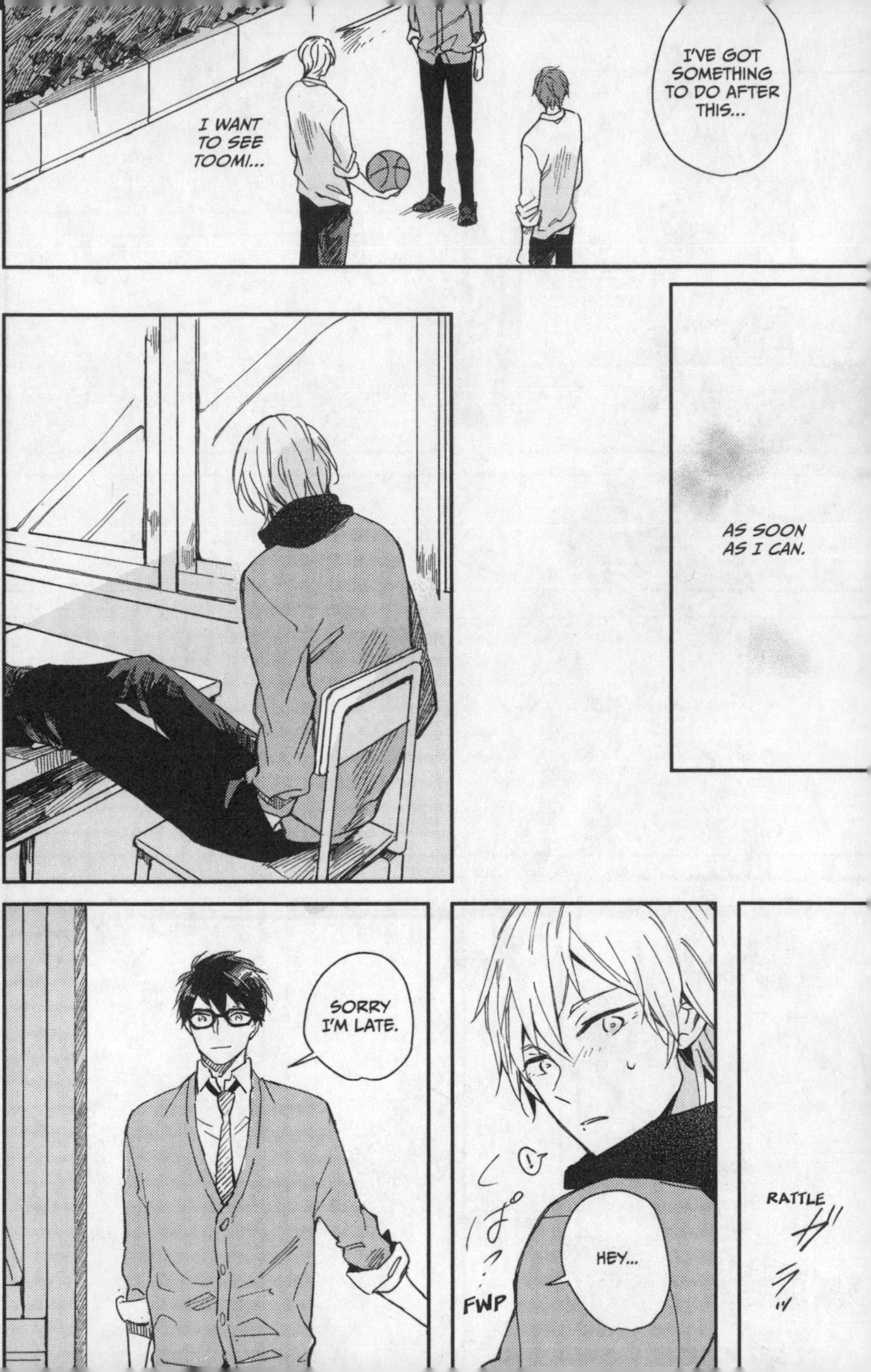
I'VE GOT SOMETHING TO DO AFTER THIS...
I WANT TO SEE TOOMI...
AS SOON AS I CAN.
RATTLE
!
FWP
HEY...
SORRY I'M LATE.

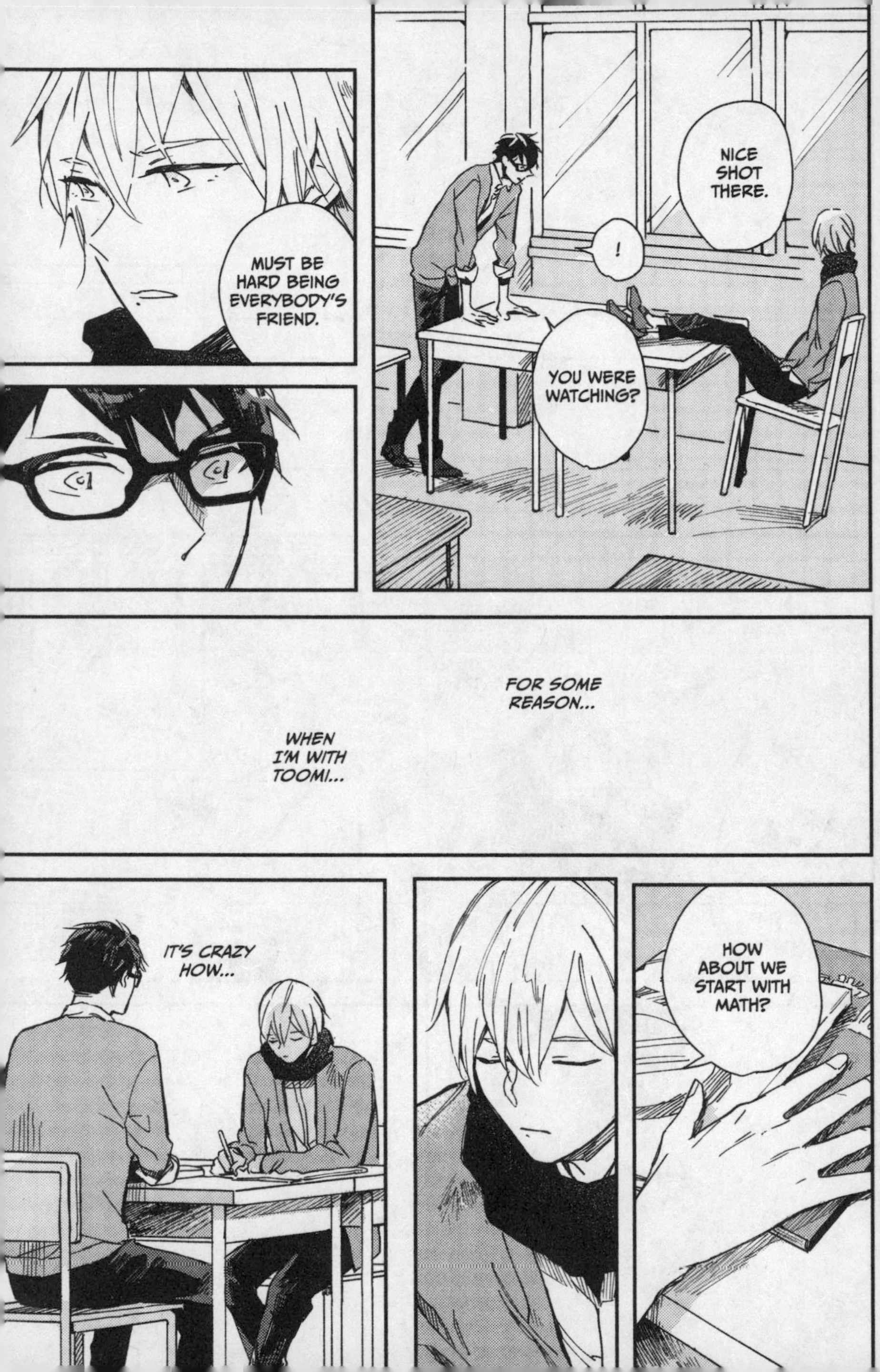
NICE SHOT THERE.
!
YOU WERE WATCHING?
MUST BE HARD BEING EVERYBODY'S FRIEND.
FOR SOME REASON...
WHEN I'M WITH TOOMI...
HOW ABOUT WE START WITH MATH?
IT'S CRAZY HOW...

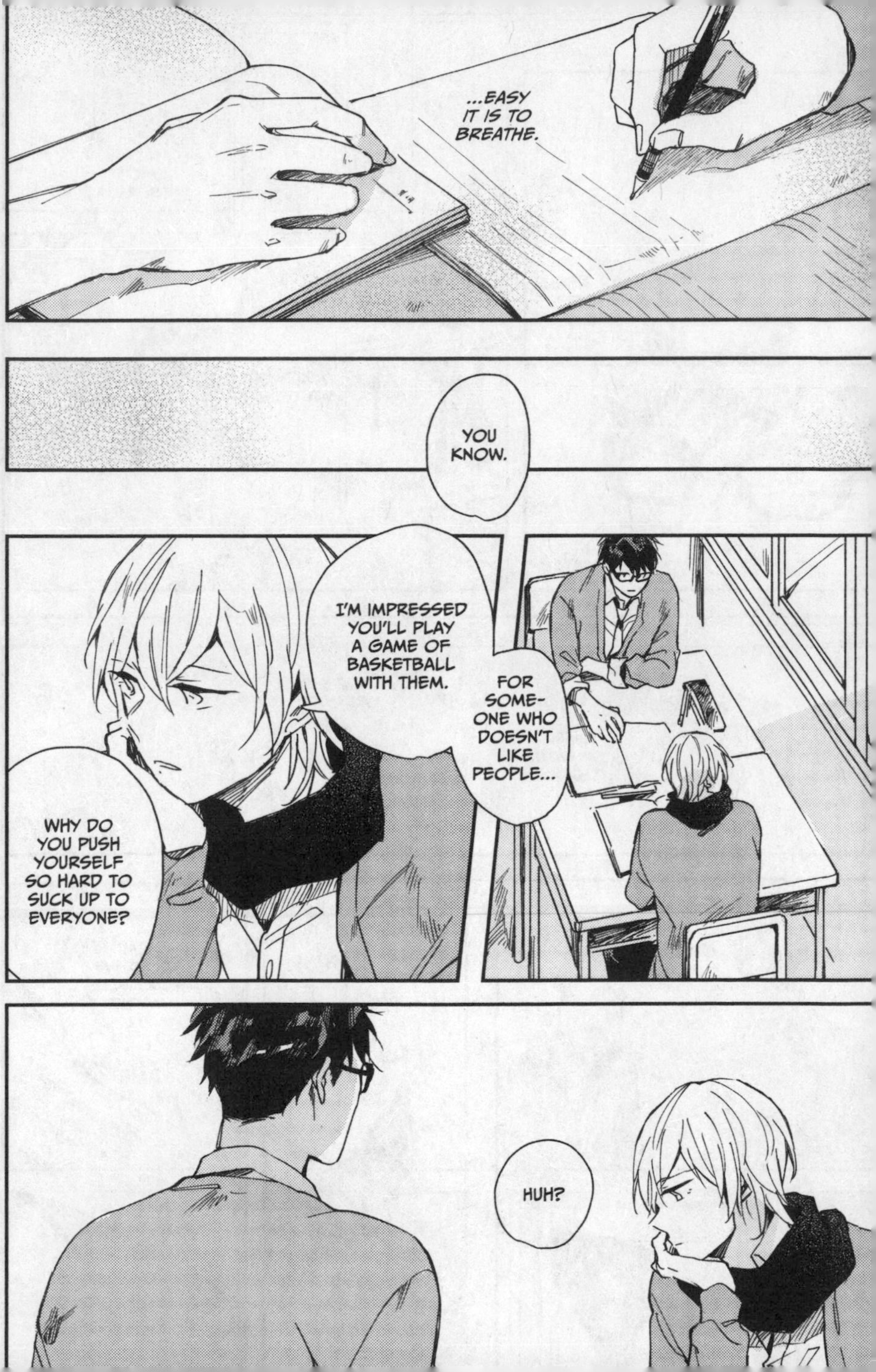
...EASY IT IS TO BREATHE.
YOU KNOW.
FOR SOME-ONE WHO DOESN'T LIKE PEOPLE...
I'M IMPRESSED YOU'LL PLAY A GAME OF BASKETBALL WITH THEM.
WHY DO YOU PUSH YOURSELF SO HARD TO SUCK UP TO EVERYONE?
HUH?

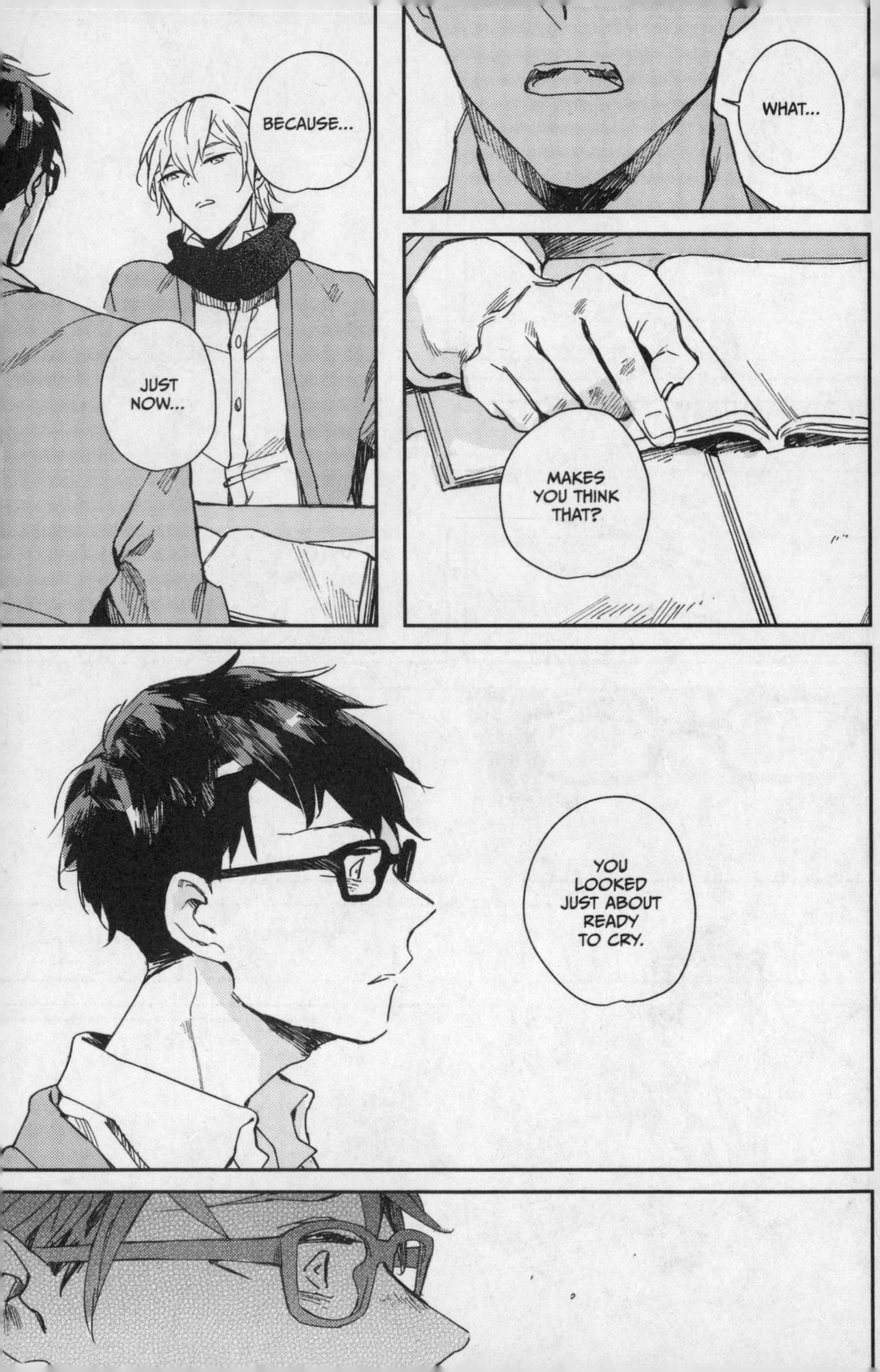
WHAT...
MAKES YOU THINK THAT?
BECAUSE...
JUST NOW...
YOU LOOKED JUST ABOUT READY TO CRY.

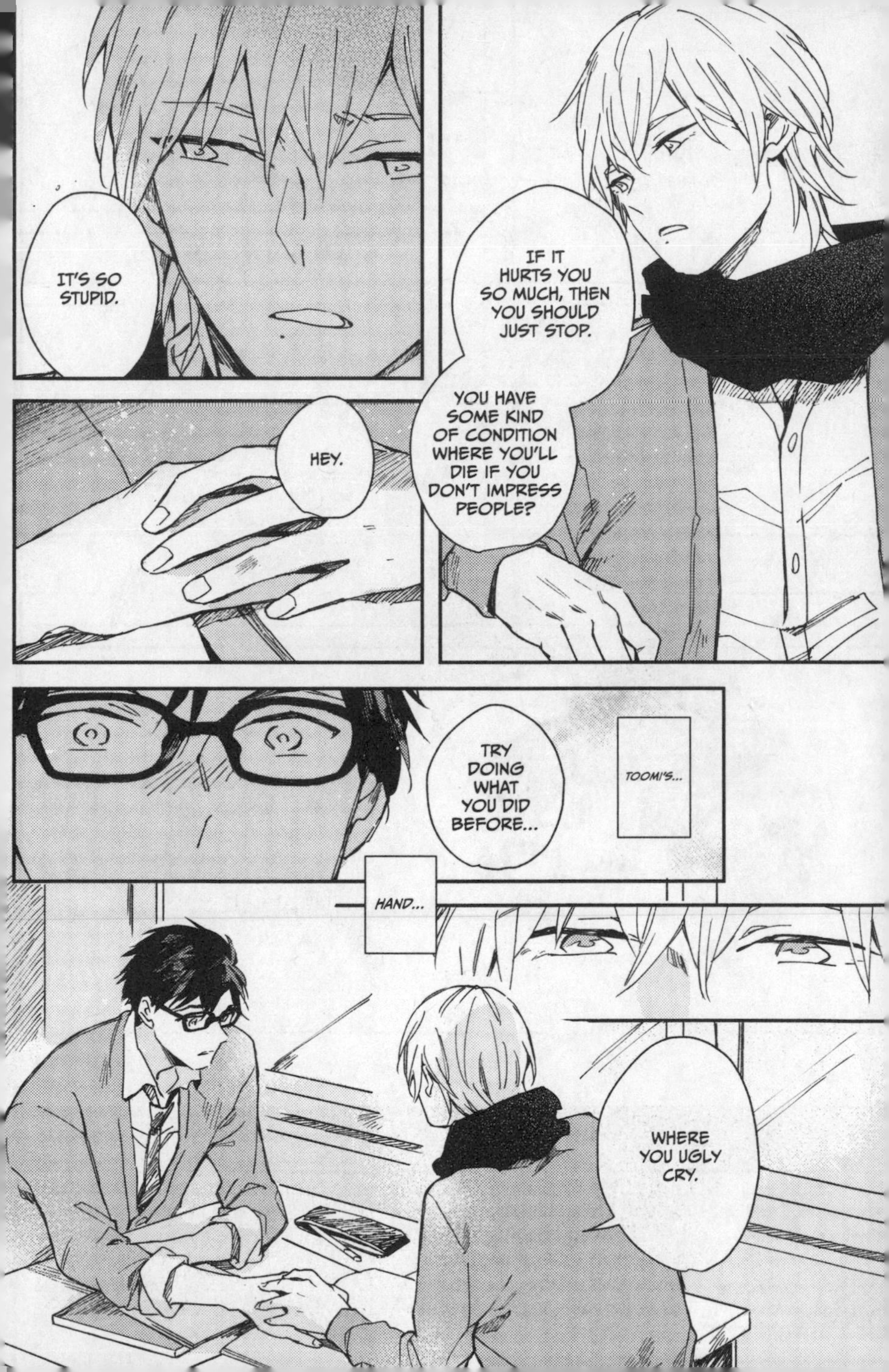
IF IT HURTS YOU SO MUCH, THEN YOU SHOULD JUST STOP.
YOU HAVE SOME KIND OF CONDITION WHERE YOU'LL DIE IF YOU DON'T IMPRESS PEOPLE?
IT'S SO STUPID.
HEY.
TOOMI'S...
TRY DOING WHAT YOU DID BEFORE...
HAND...
WHERE YOU UGLY CRY.

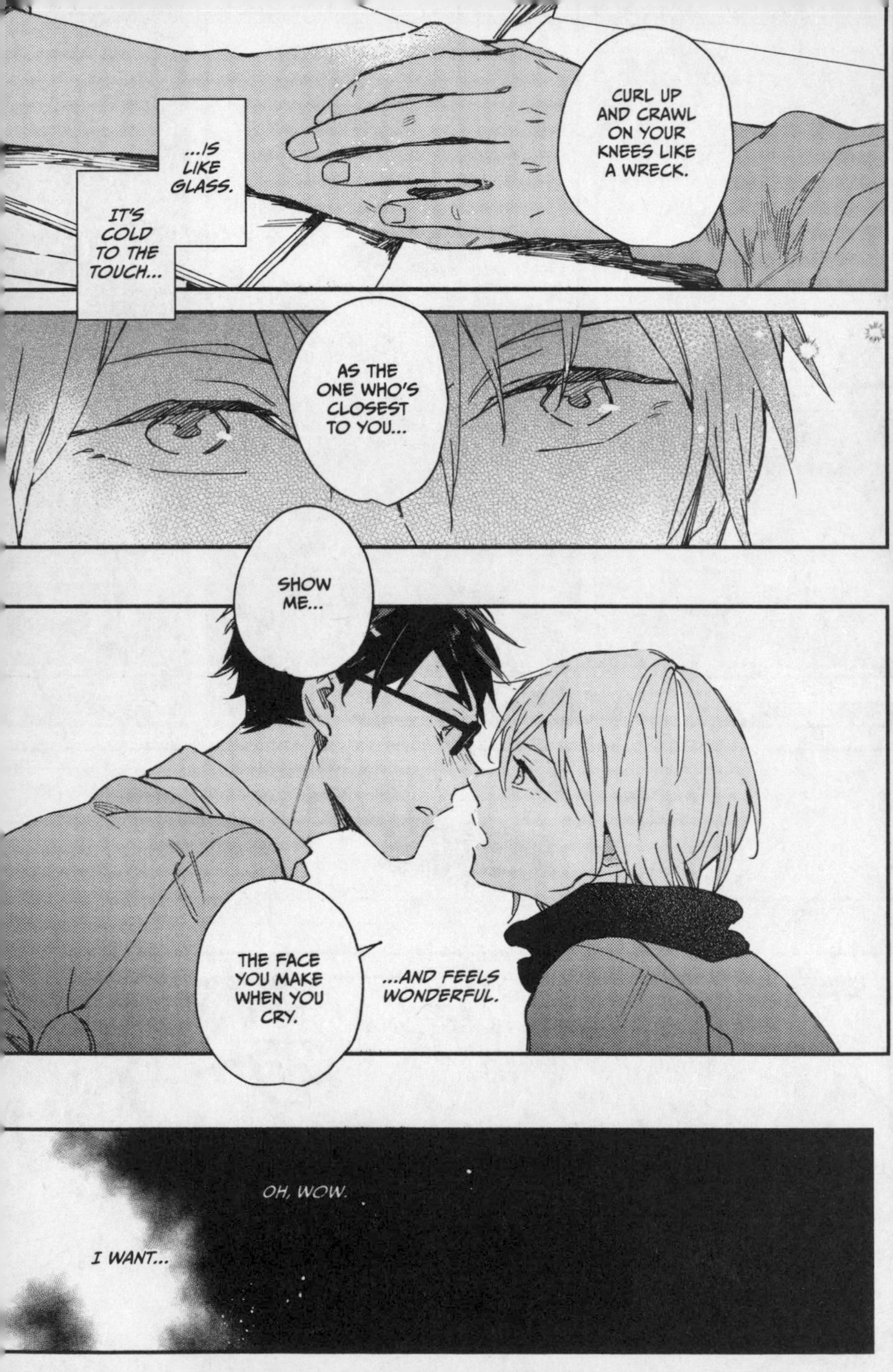
CURL UP AND CRAWL ON YOUR KNEES LIKE A WRECK.
...IS LIKE GLASS.
IT'S COLD TO THE TOUCH...
AS THE ONE WHO'S CLOSEST TO YOU...
SHOW ME...
THE FACE YOU MAKE WHEN YOU CRY.
...AND FEELS WONDERFUL.
OH, WOW.
I WANT...

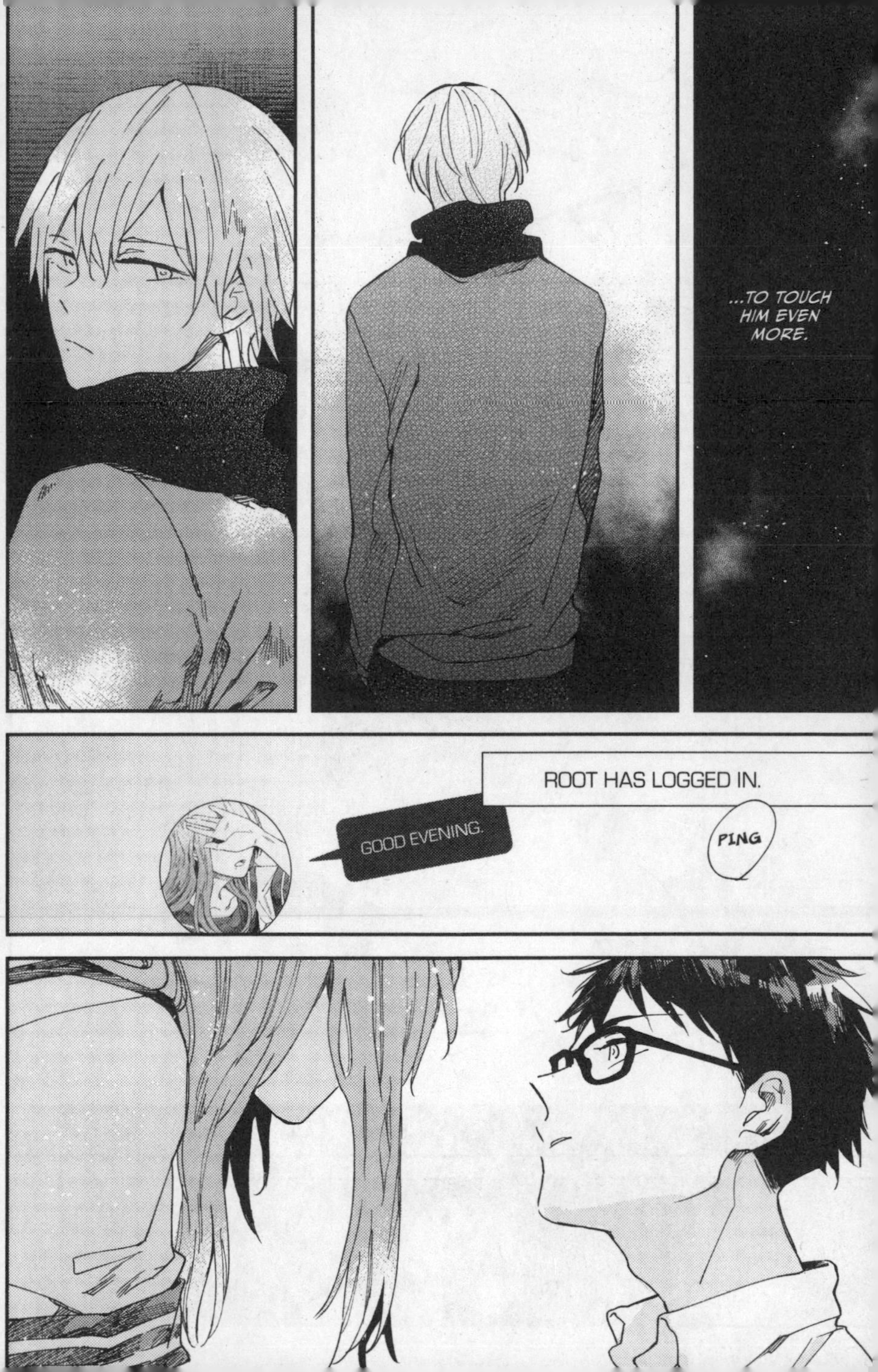
...TO TOUCH HIM EVEN MORE.
ROOT HAS LOGGED IN.
PING
GOOD EVENING.

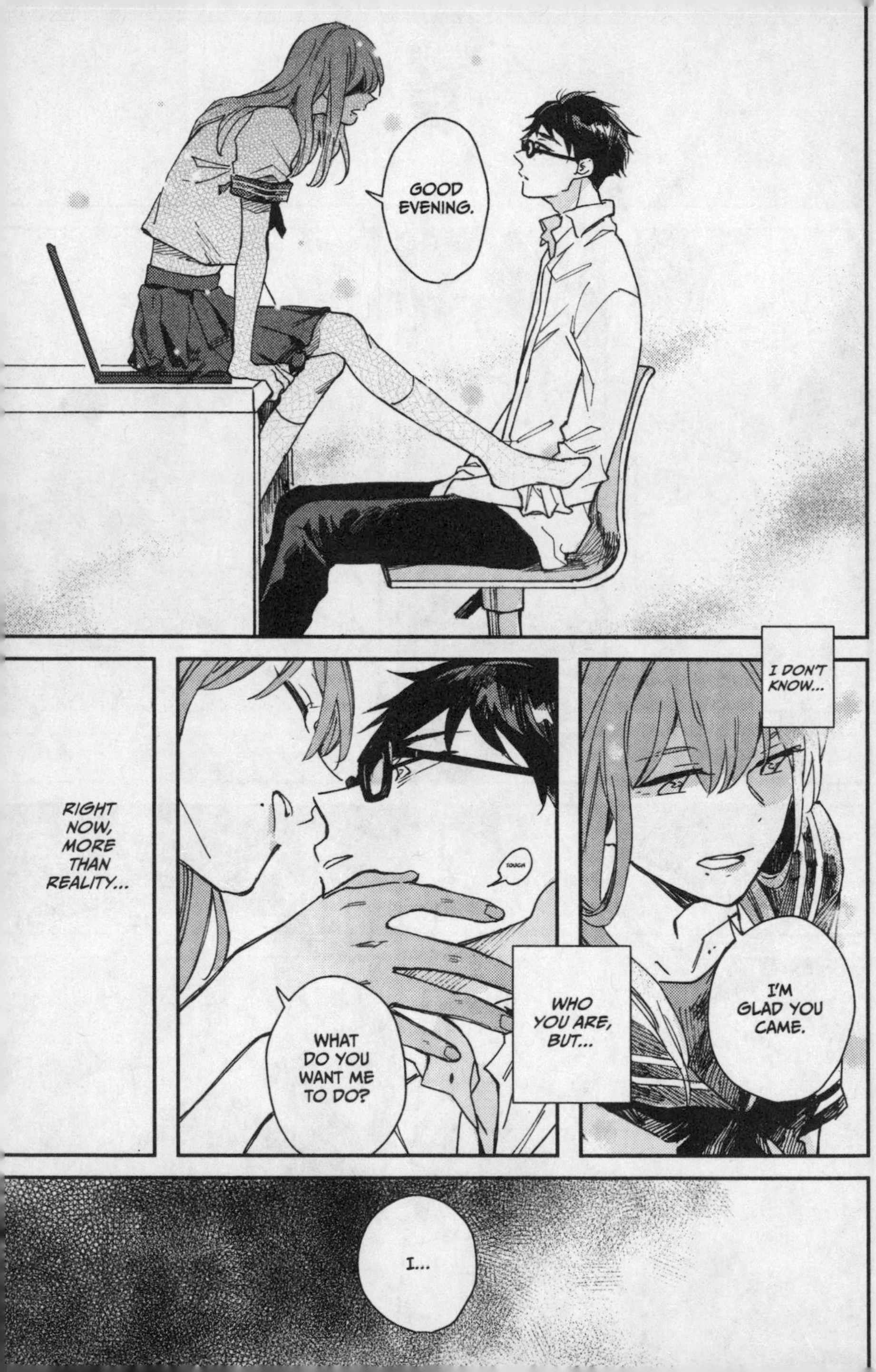
GOOD EVENING.
I DON'T KNOW...
I'M GLAD YOU CAME.
WHO YOU ARE, BUT...
TOUCH
WHAT DO YOU WANT ME TO DO?
RIGHT NOW, MORE THAN REALITY...
I...

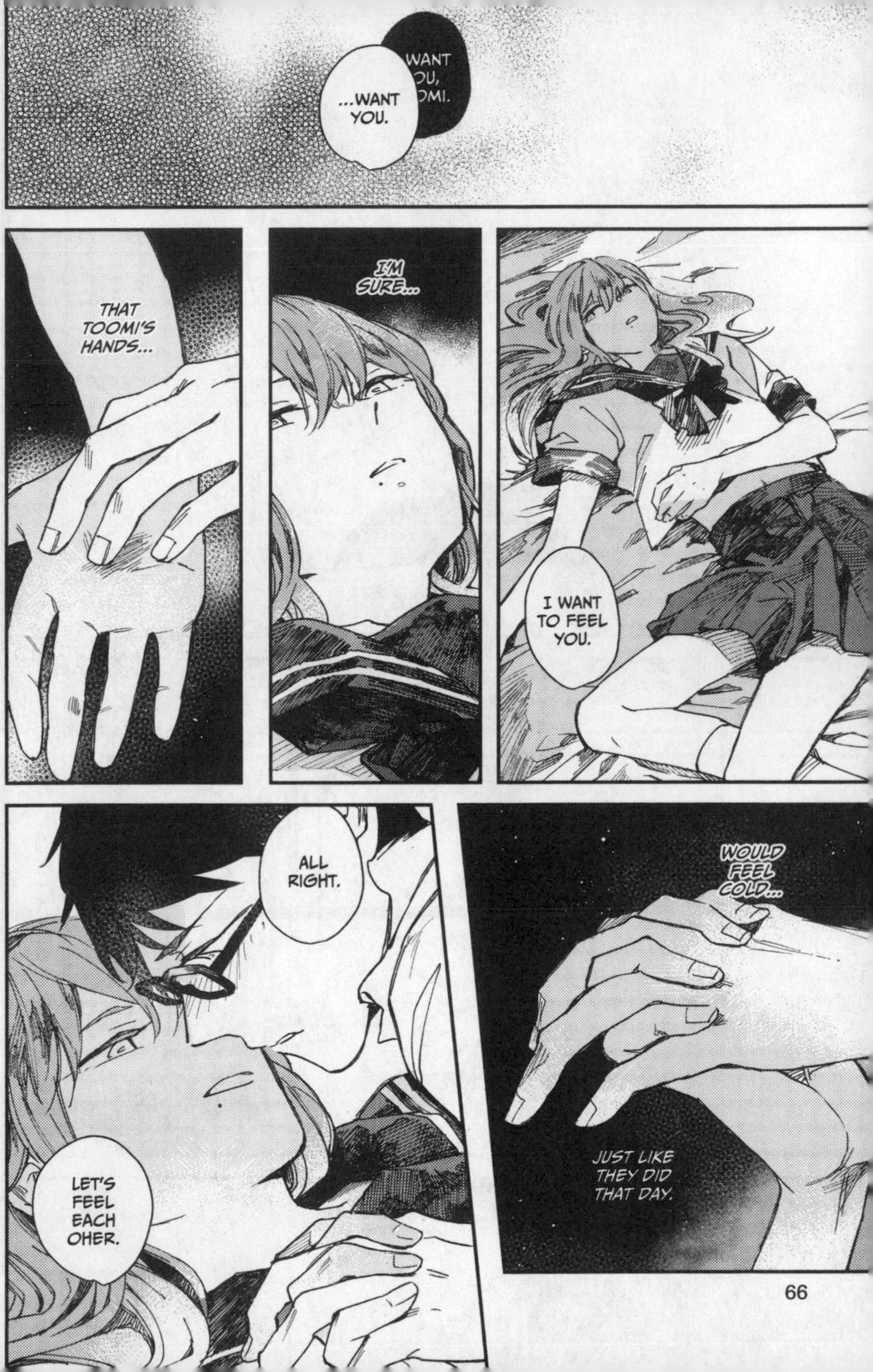
WANT
OU,
OMI.
...WANT YOU.
I WANT TO FEEL YOU.
I'M SURE...
THAT TOOMI'S HANDS...
WOULD FEEL COLD...
JUST LIKE THEY DID THAT DAY.
ALL RIGHT.
LET'S FEEL EACH OHER.

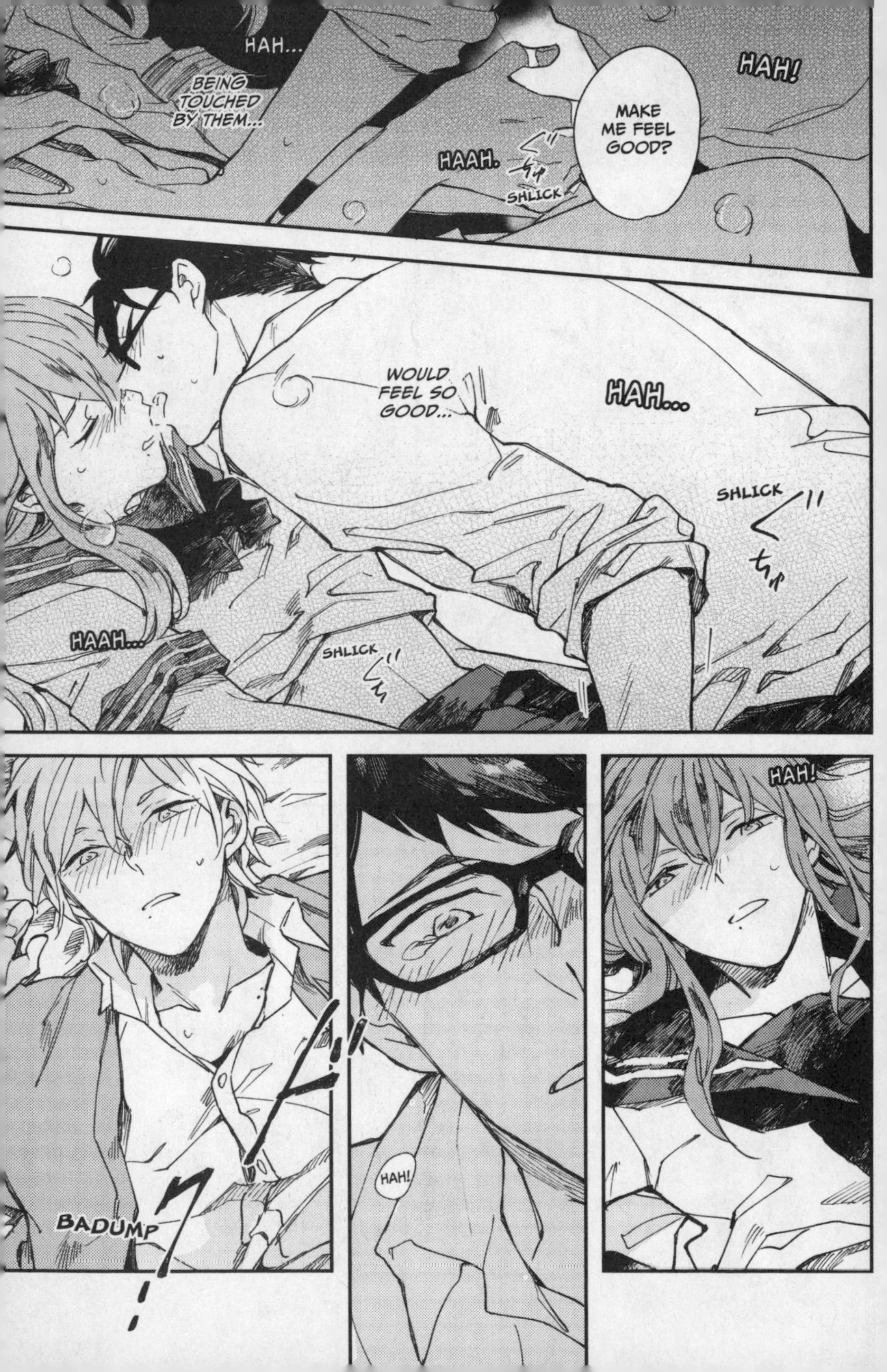
HAH!
MAKE ME FEEL GOOD?
SHLICK
HAAH.
HAH...
BEING TOUCHED BY THEM...
HAH...
WOULD FEEL SO GOOD...
SHLICK
SHLICK
HAAH...
HAH!
HAH!
BADUMP

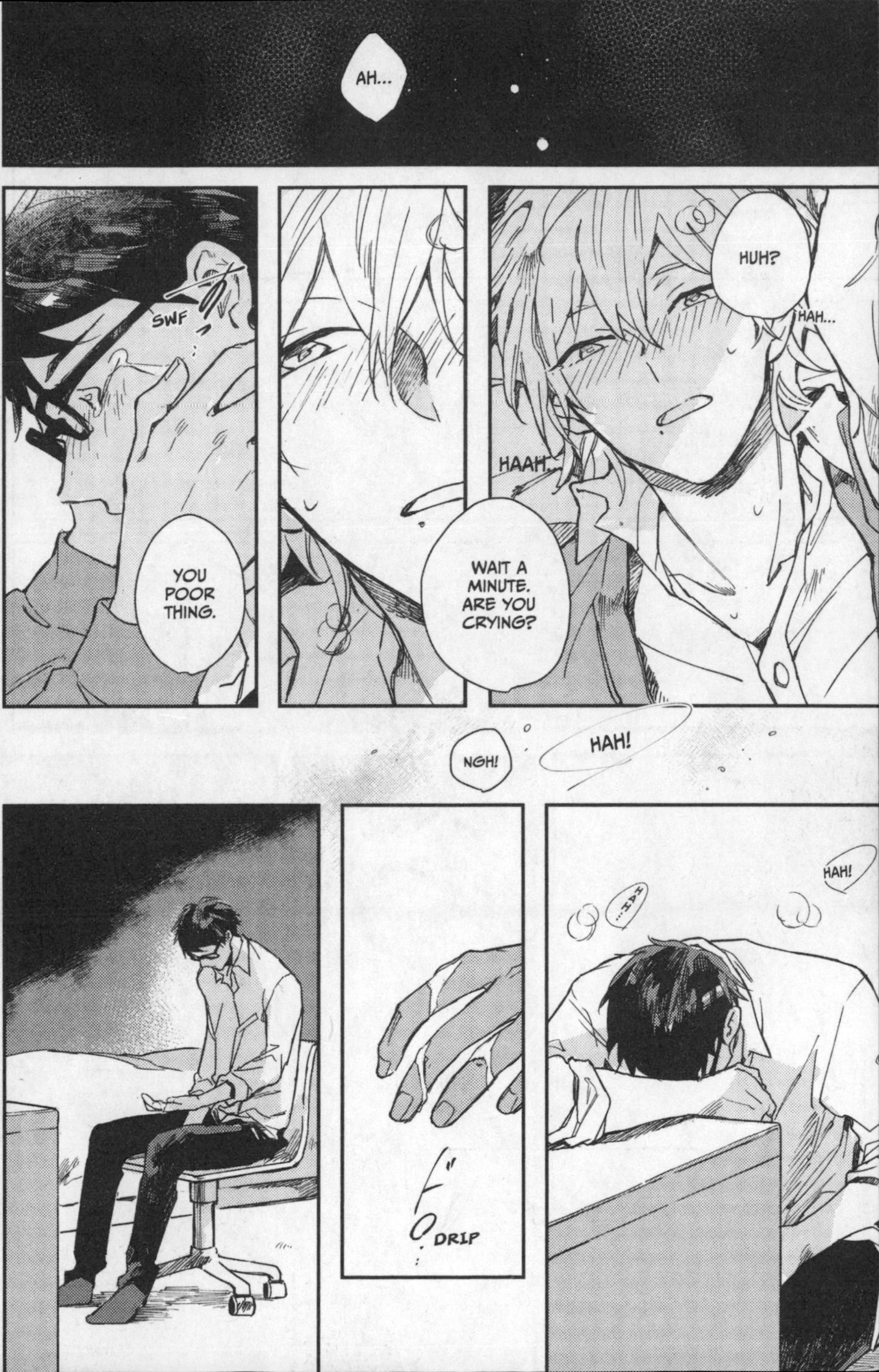
AH...
HUH?
HAH...
HAAH...
WAIT A MINUTE. ARE YOU CRYING?
SWF
YOU POOR THING.
HAH!
NGH!
HAH!
...HAH
DRIP

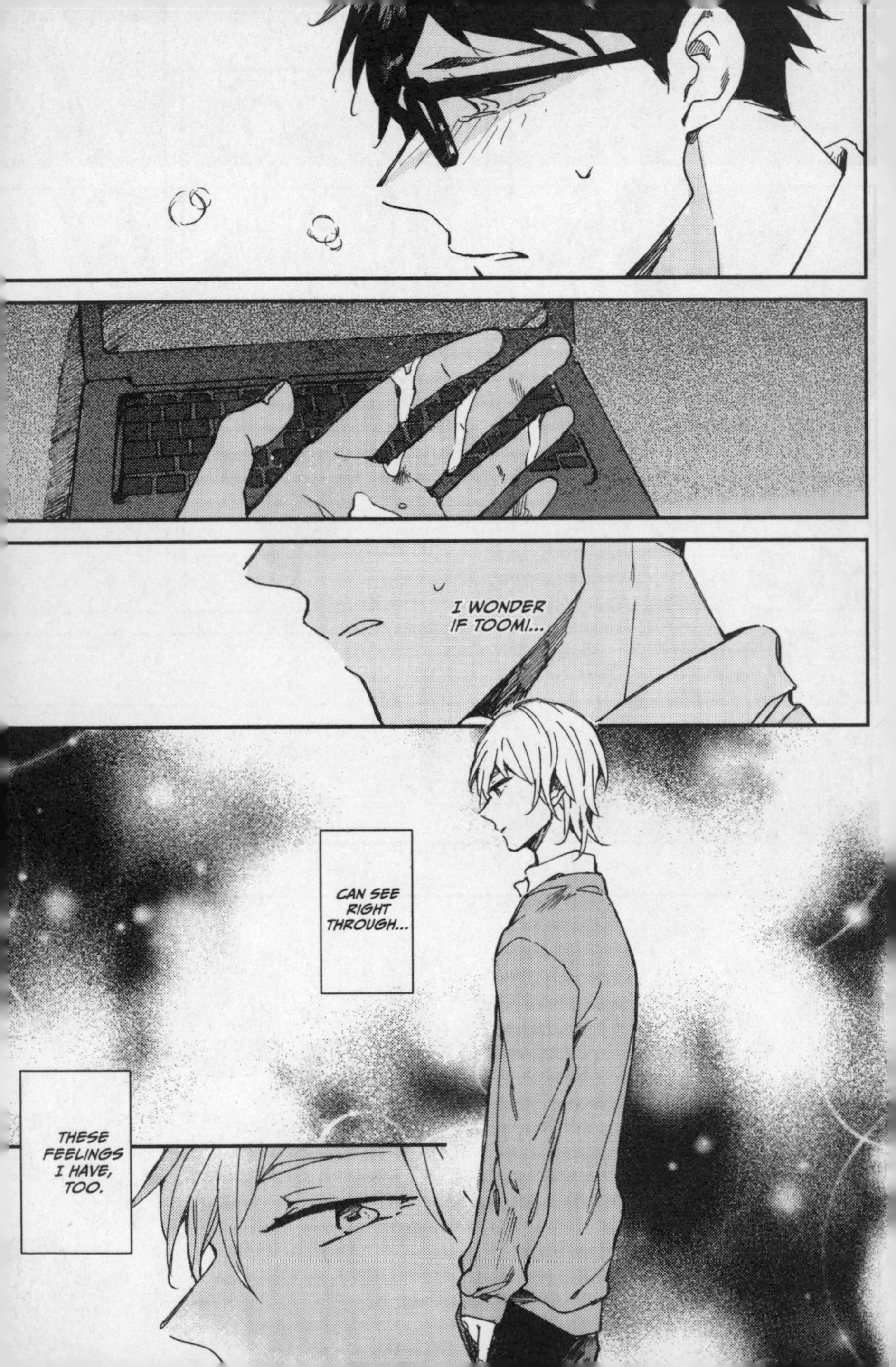
I WONDER IF TOOMI...
CAN SEE RIGHT THROUGH...
THESE FEELINGS I HAVE, TOO.

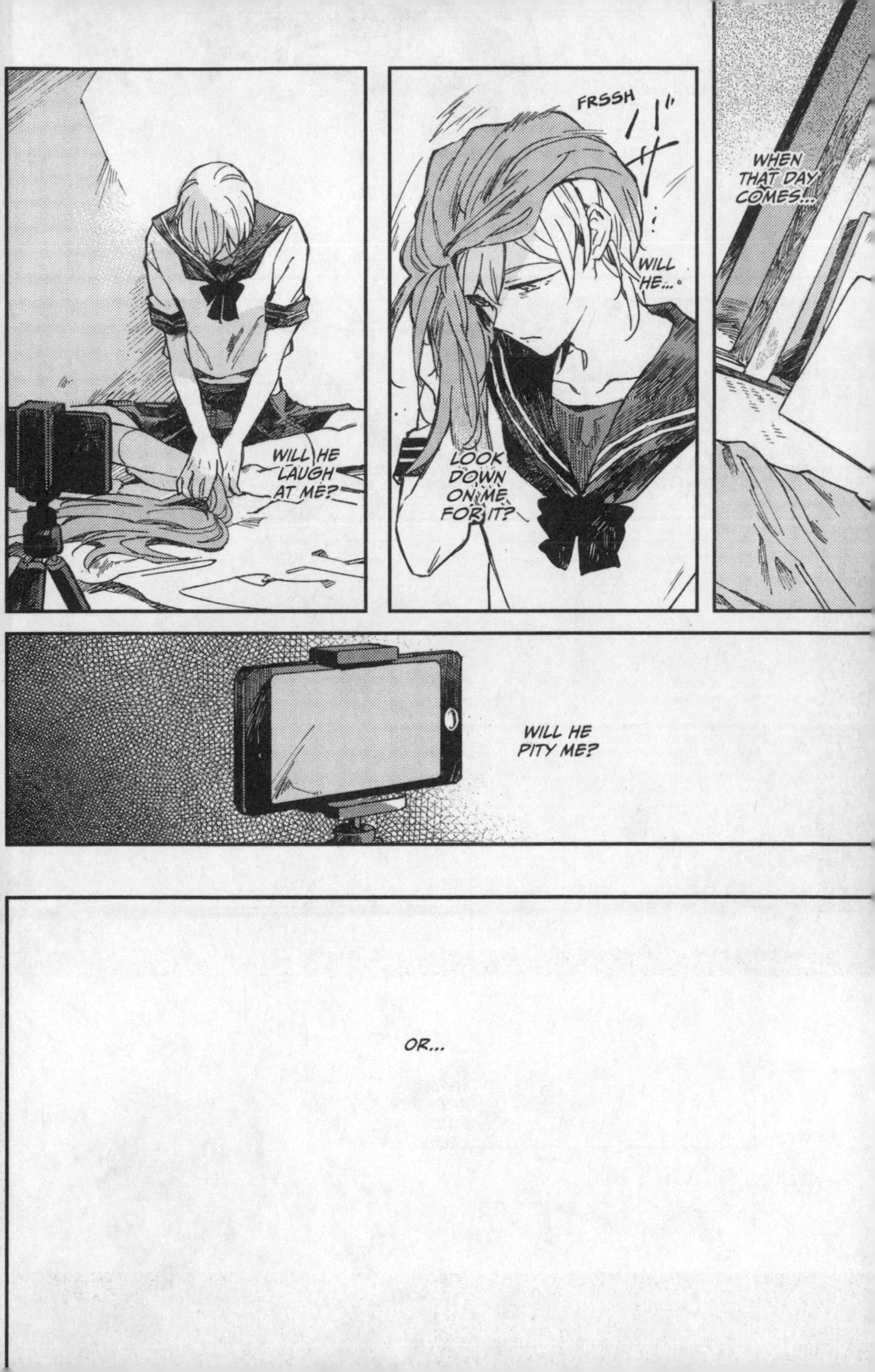
WHEN THAT DAY COMES...
FRSSH
WILL HE...
LOOK DOWN ON ME FOR IT?
WILL HE LAUGH AT ME?
WILL HE PITY ME?
OR...

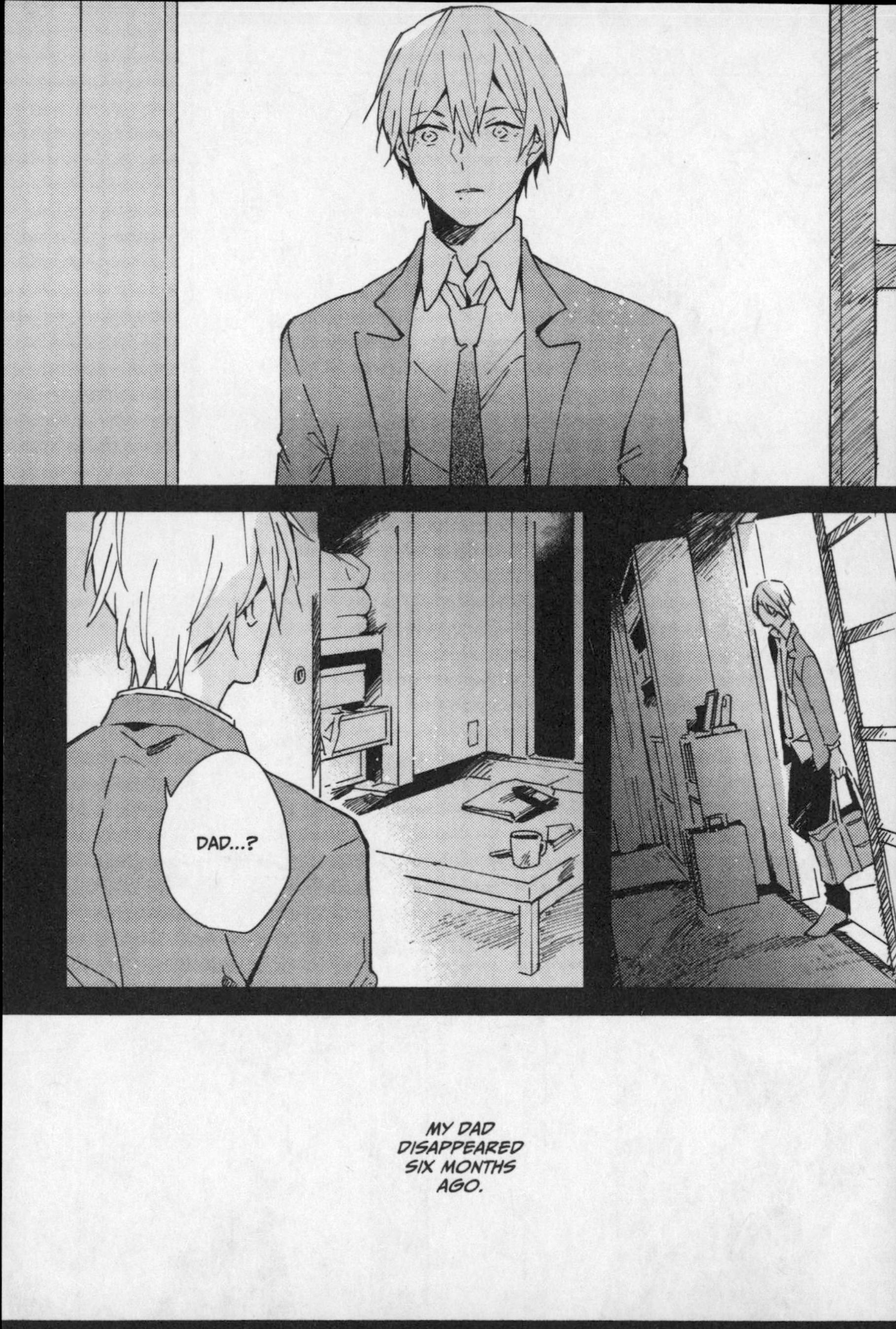
DAD...?
MY DAD DISAPPEARED SIX MONTHS AGO.

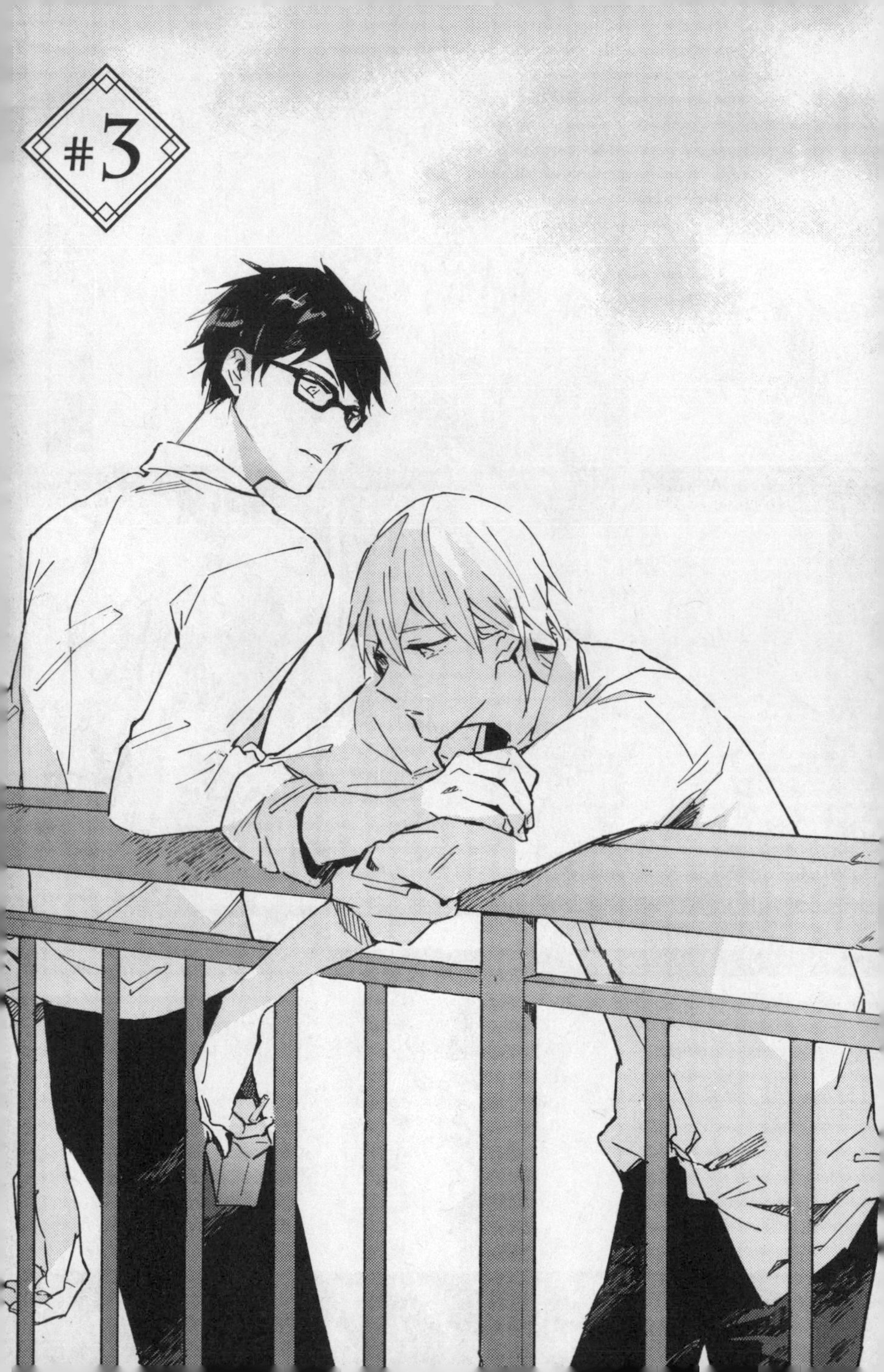
#3

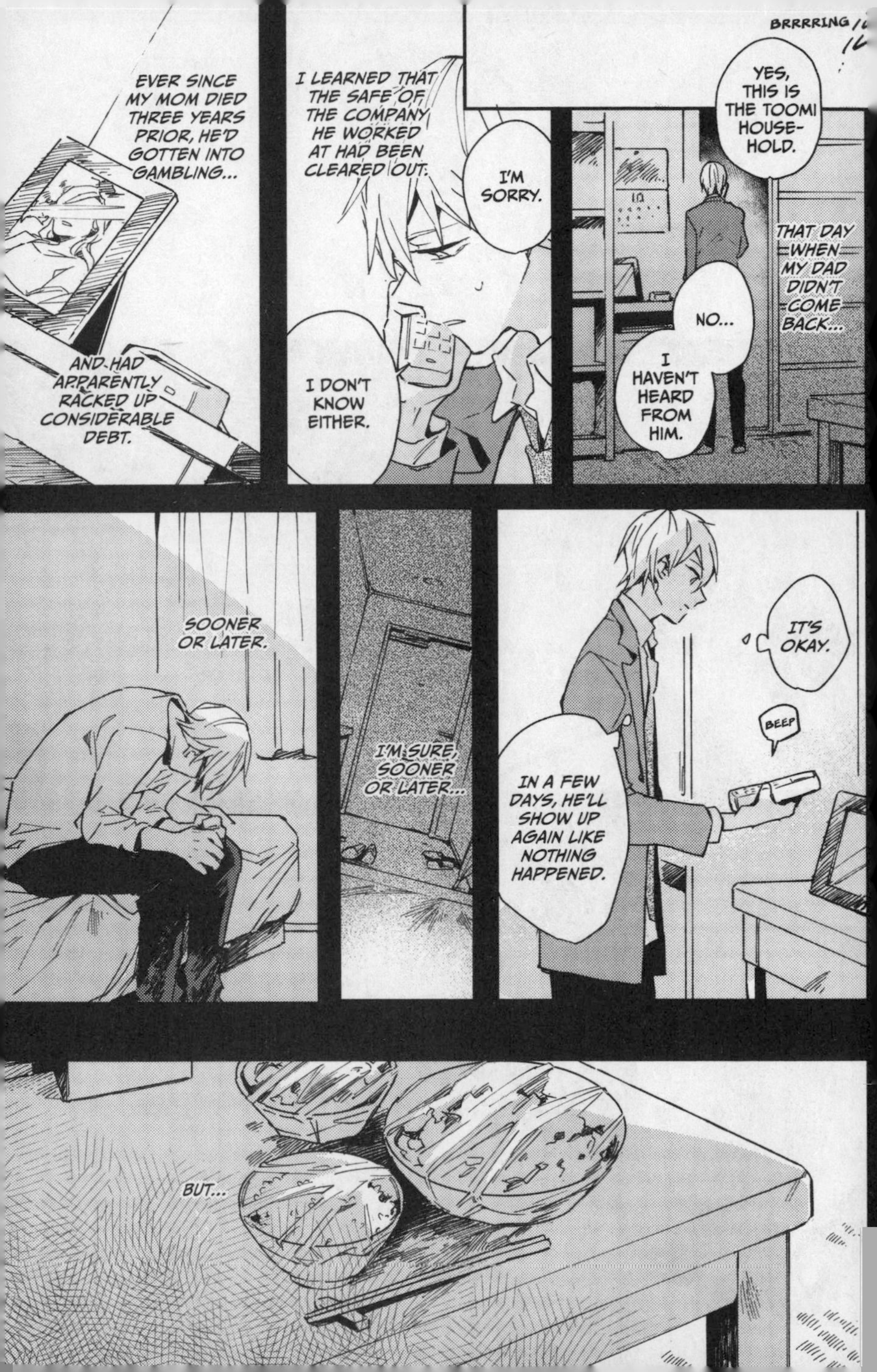
BRRRRING
YES, THIS IS THE TOOMI HOUSE-HOLD.
THAT DAY WHEN MY DAD DIDN'T COME BACK...
NO...
I HAVEN'T HEARD FROM HIM.
I LEARNED THAT THE SAFE OF THE COMPANY HE WORKED AT HAD BEEN CLEARED OUT.
I'M SORRY.
I DON'T KNOW EITHER.
EVER SINCE MY MOM DIED THREE YEARS PRIOR, HE'D GOTTEN INTO GAMBLING...
AND HAD APPARENTLY RACKED UP CONSIDERABLE DEBT.
IT'S OKAY.
BEEP
IN A FEW DAYS, HE'LL SHOW UP AGAIN LIKE NOTHING HAPPENED.
I'M SURE, SOONER OR LATER...
SOONER OR LATER.
BUT...

THAT DAY NEVER CAME.

THAT'S RIGHT.

AH.

SO, YEAH...

HA HA HA.

IF I'M NOT CAREFUL AND THIS GETS TURNED INTO A HUGE THING...

BUT...

I'M NOT ALLOWED TO HOLD A PART-TIME JOB WITHOUT GUARDIAN CONSENT.

WHAT AM I GOING TO DO...

ABOUT MONEY?

WHO SHOULD I TALK TO?

AND I'M NOT ABLE TO GO TO SCHOOL OR STAY IN MY APARTMENT...

AH HA HA.

MESSAGE
YOU HAVE 27 NEW MESSAGES IN YOUR CHAT ROOM.

BUZZ BUZZ

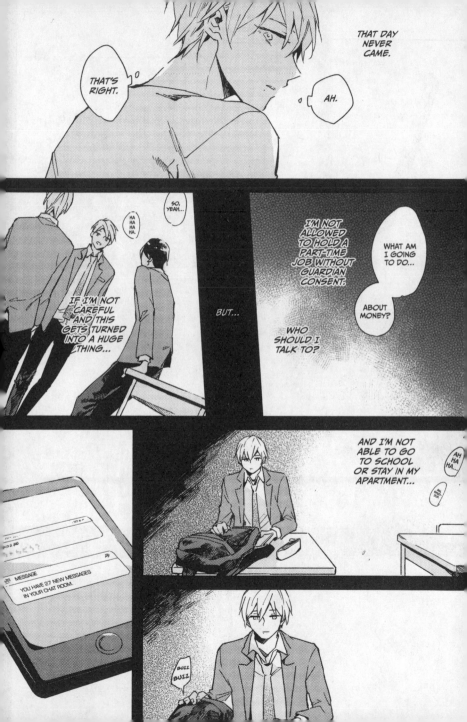

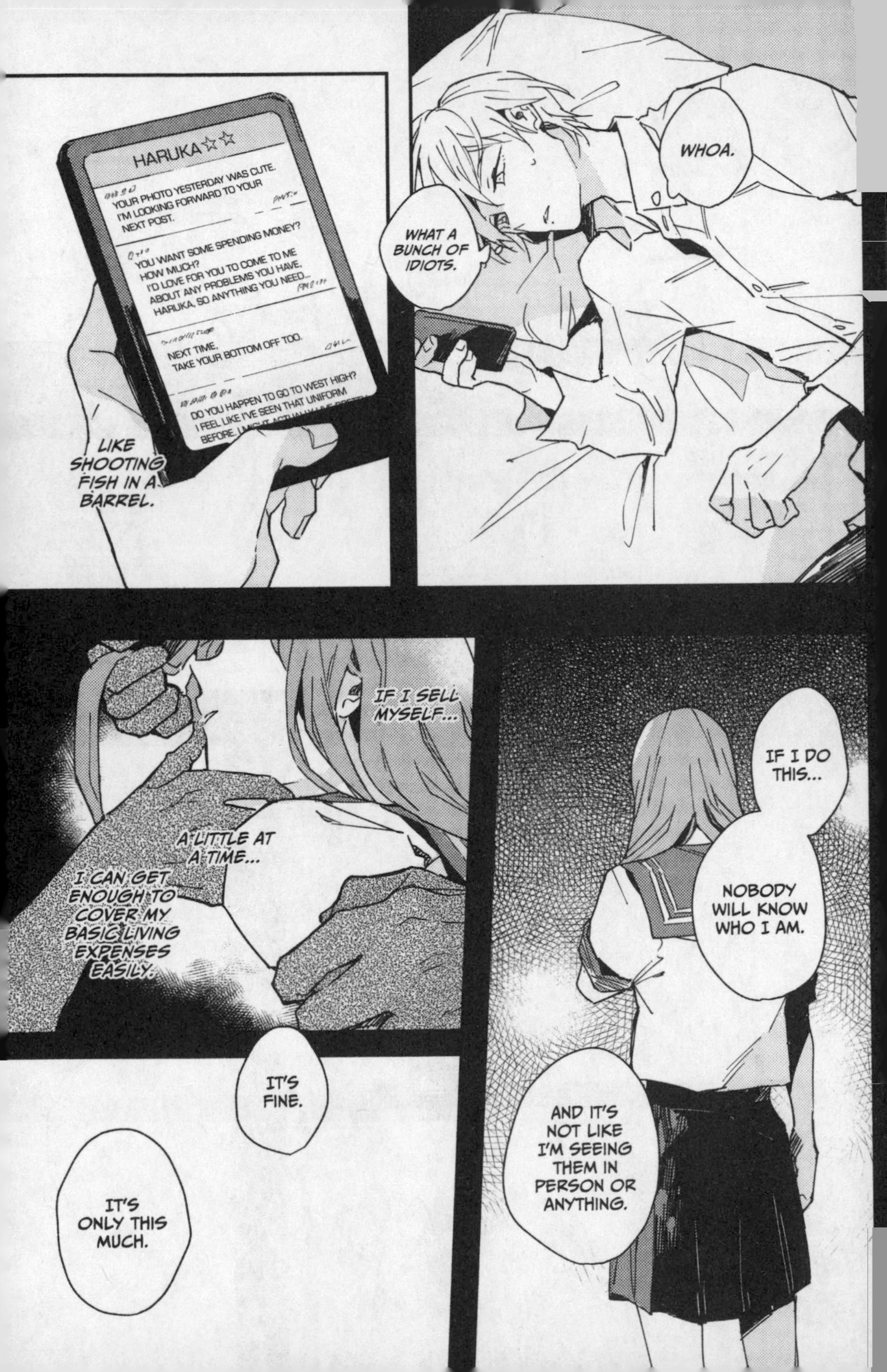
WHOA.
WHAT A BUNCH OF IDIOTS.
HARUKA☆☆
YOUR PHOTO YESTERDAY WAS CUTE. I'M LOOKING FORWARD TO YOUR NEXT POST.
YOU WANT SOME SPENDING MONEY? HOW MUCH? I'D LOVE FOR YOU TO COME TO ME ABOUT ANY PROBLEMS YOU HAVE, HARUKA, SO ANYTHING YOU NEED...
NEXT TIME, TAKE YOUR BOTTOM OFF TOO.
DO YOU HAPPEN TO GO TO WEST HIGH? I FEEL LIKE I'VE SEEN THAT UNIFORM BEFORE.
LIKE SHOOTING FISH IN A BARREL.
IF I DO THIS...
NOBODY WILL KNOW WHO I AM.
AND IT'S NOT LIKE I'M SEEING THEM IN PERSON OR ANYTHING.
IF I SELL MYSELF...
A LITTLE AT A TIME...
I CAN GET ENOUGH TO COVER MY BASIC LIVING EXPENSES EASILY.
IT'S FINE.
IT'S ONLY THIS MUCH.

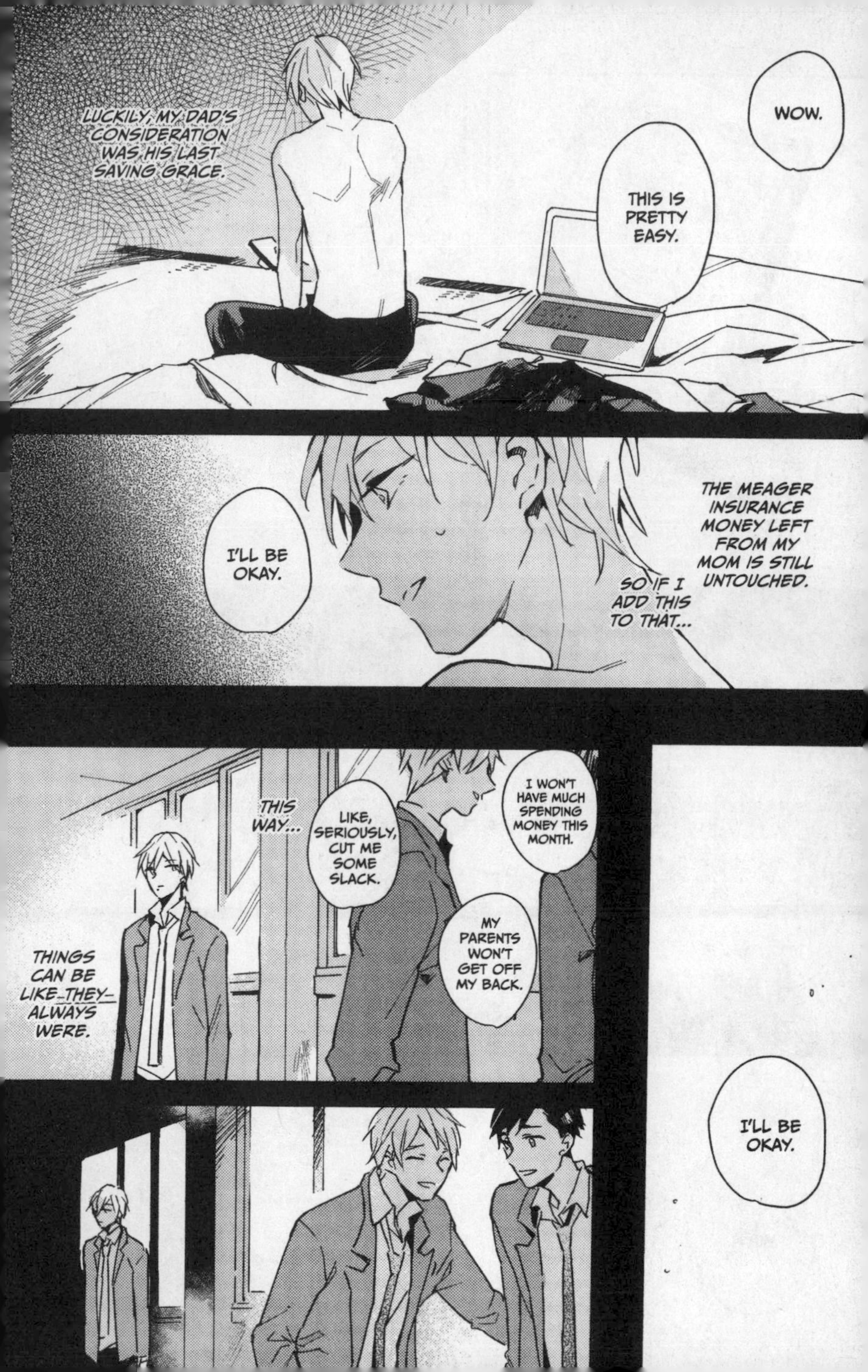
WOW.
THIS IS PRETTY EASY.
LUCKILY, MY DAD'S CONSIDERATION WAS HIS LAST SAVING GRACE.
THE MEAGER INSURANCE MONEY LEFT FROM MY MOM IS STILL UNTOUCHED.
SO IF I ADD THIS TO THAT...
I'LL BE OKAY.
I'LL BE OKAY.
I WON'T HAVE MUCH SPENDING MONEY THIS MONTH.
MY PARENTS WON'T GET OFF MY BACK.
LIKE, SERIOUSLY, CUT ME SOME SLACK.
THIS WAY...
THINGS CAN BE LIKE THEY ALWAYS WERE.

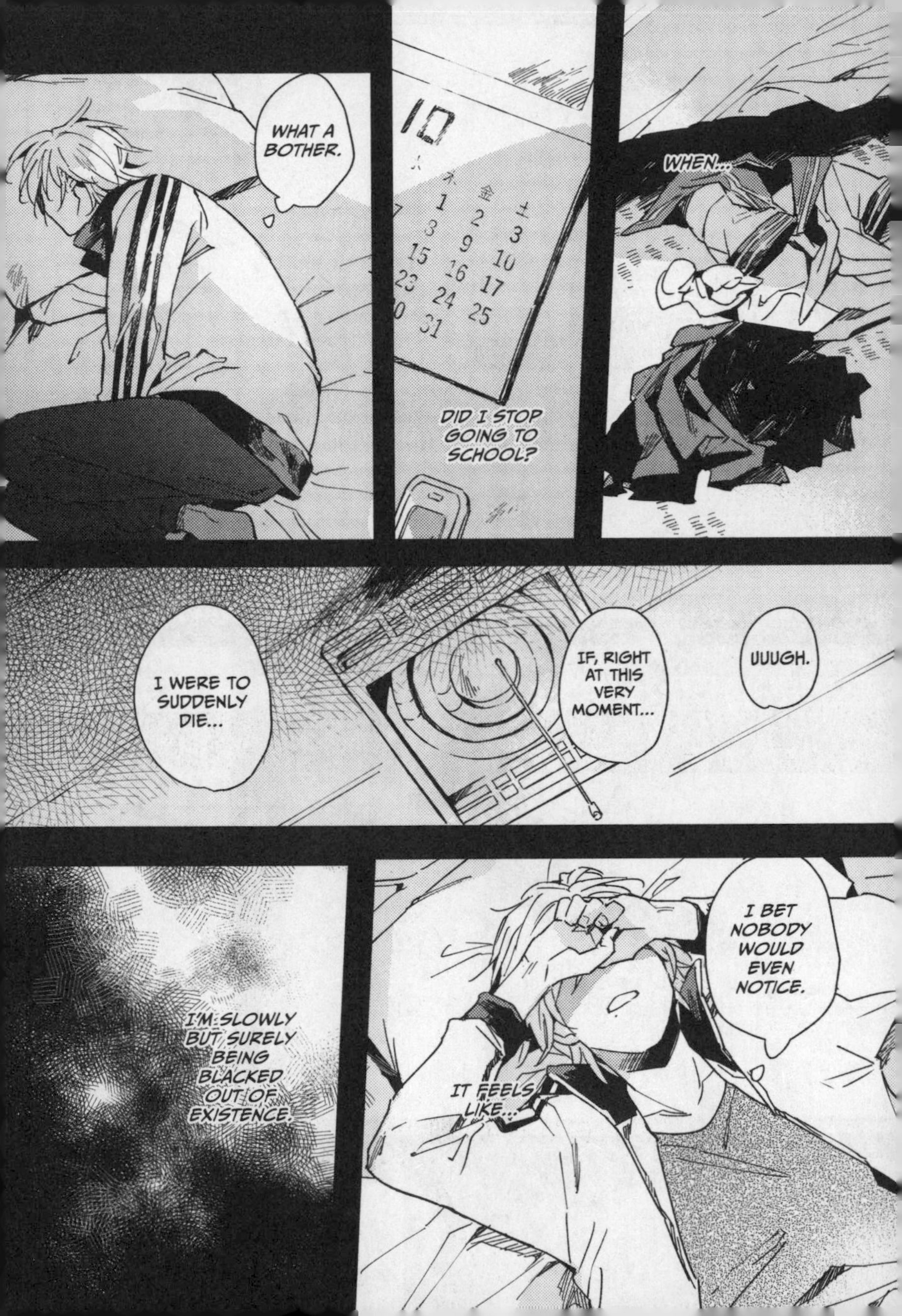
WHEN...
DID I STOP GOING TO SCHOOL?
WHAT A BOTHER.
UUUGH.
IF, RIGHT AT THIS VERY MOMENT...
I WERE TO SUDDENLY DIE...
I BET NOBODY WOULD EVEN NOTICE.
IT FEELS LIKE...
I'M SLOWLY BUT SURELY BEING BLACKED OUT OF EXISTENCE.

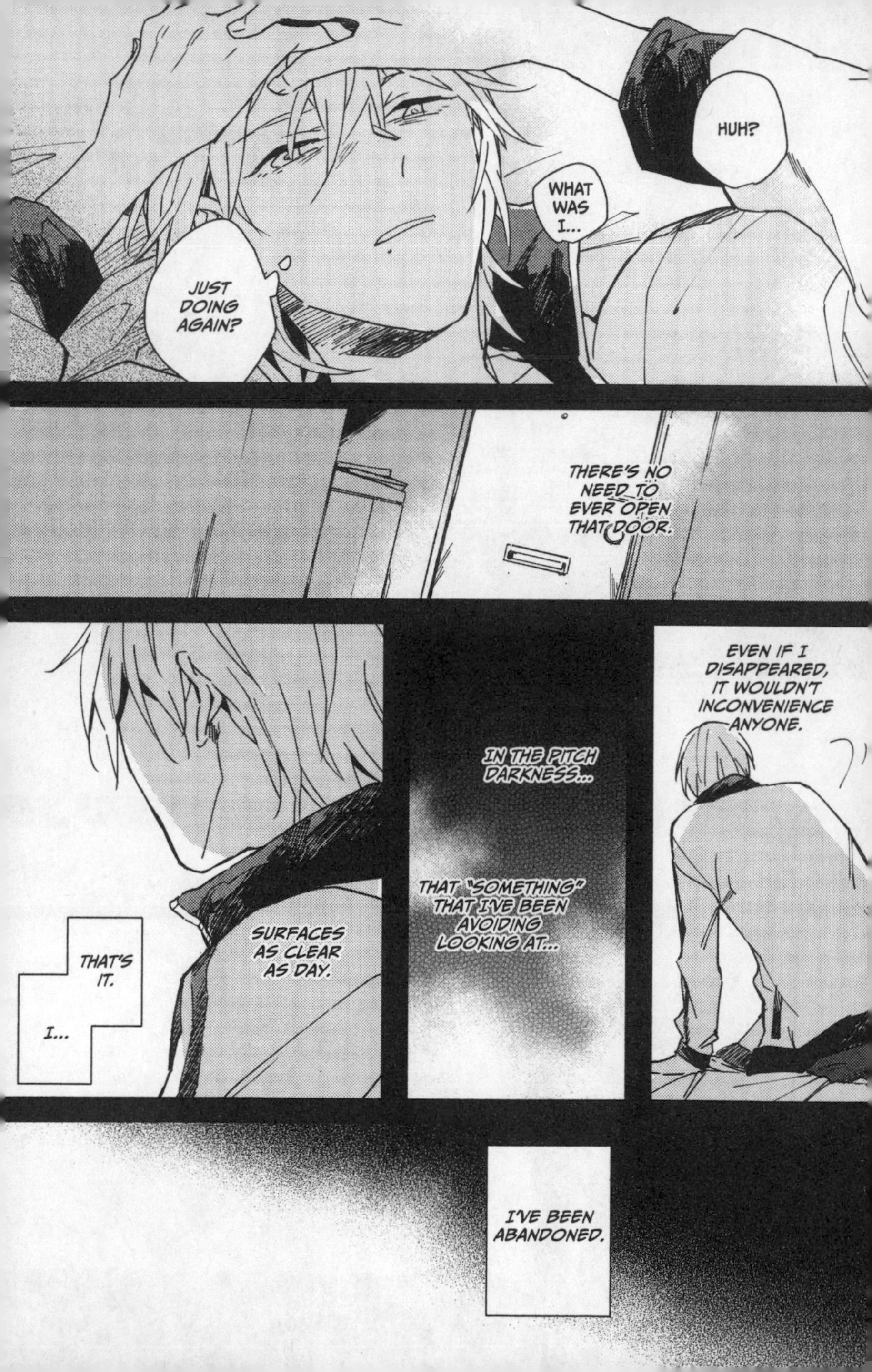
HUH?
WHAT WAS I...
JUST DOING AGAIN?
THERE'S NO NEED TO EVER OPEN THAT DOOR.
EVEN IF I DISAPPEARED, IT WOULDN'T INCONVENIENCE ANYONE.
IN THE PITCH DARKNESS...
THAT "SOMETHING" THAT I'VE BEEN AVOIDING LOOKING AT...
SURFACES AS CLEAR AS DAY.
THAT'S IT.
I...
I'VE BEEN ABANDONED.

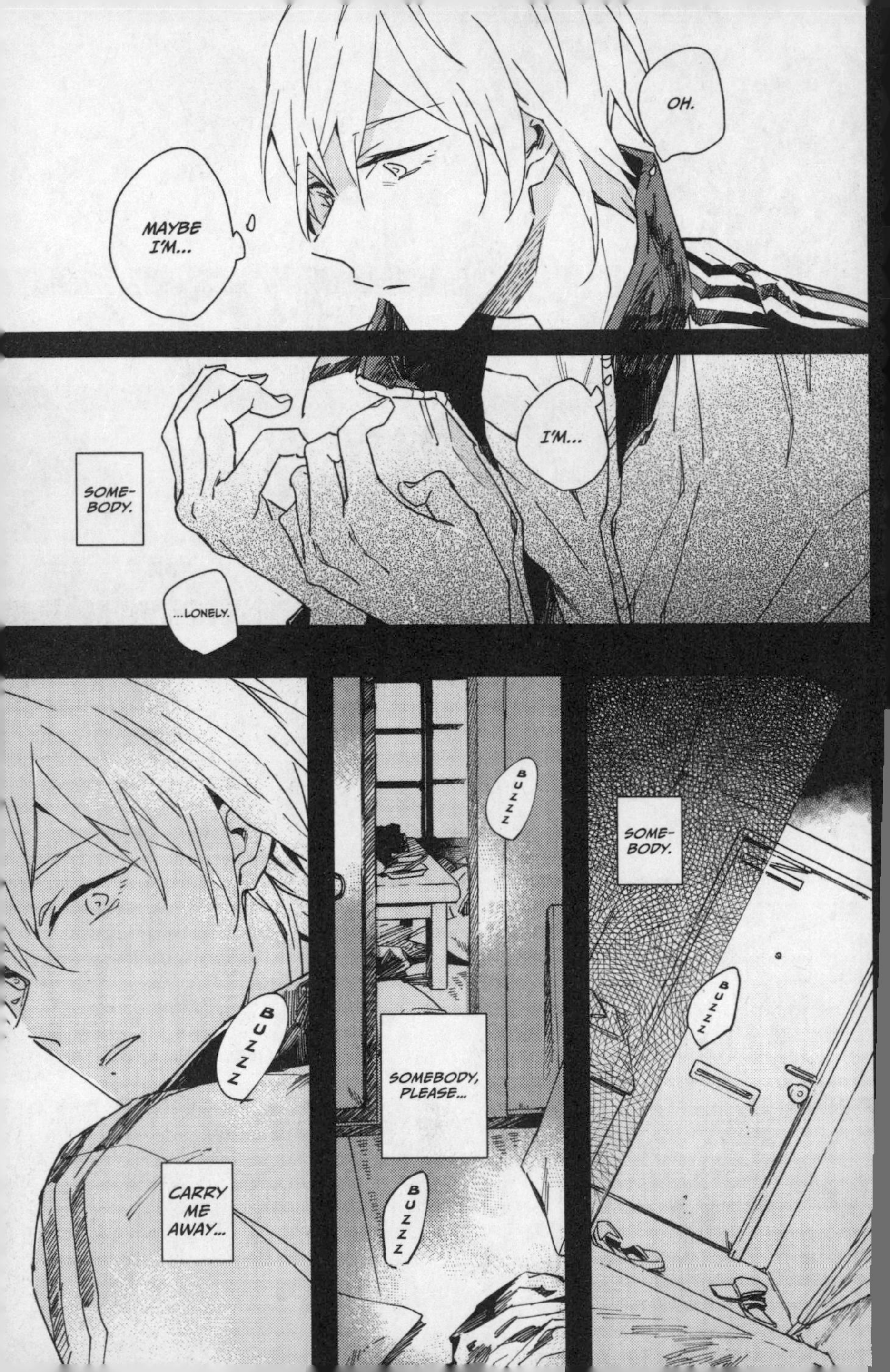
OH.
MAYBE I'M...
I'M...
SOME-BODY.
...LONELY.
SOME-BODY.
BUZZZ
BUZZZ
SOMEBODY, PLEASE...
BUZZZ
BUZZZ
CARRY ME AWAY...

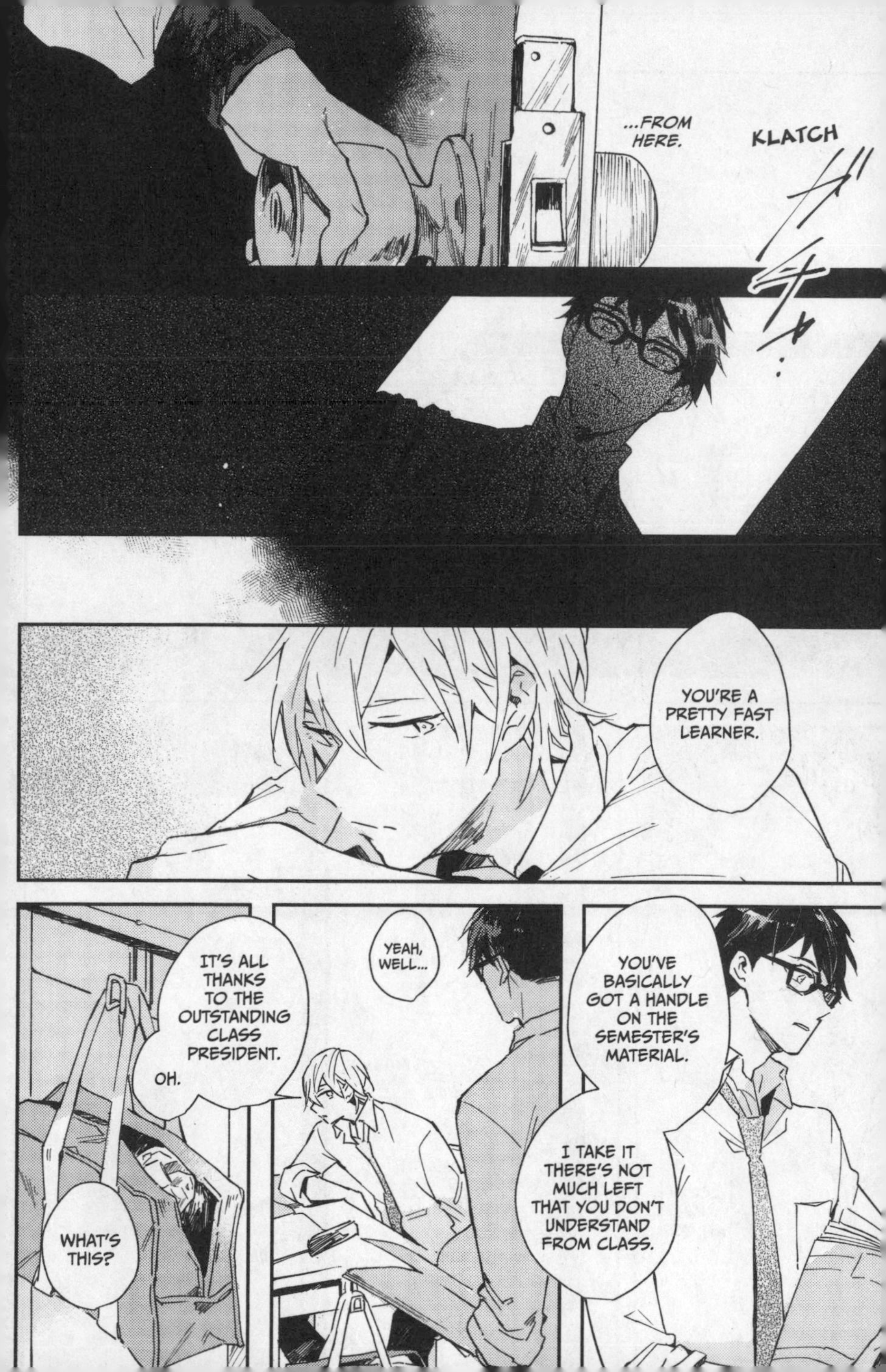
KLATCH
...FROM HERE.
YOU'RE A PRETTY FAST LEARNER.
YOU'VE BASICALLY GOT A HANDLE ON THE SEMESTER'S MATERIAL.
I TAKE IT THERE'S NOT MUCH LEFT THAT YOU DON'T UNDERSTAND FROM CLASS.
YEAH, WELL...
IT'S ALL THANKS TO THE OUTSTANDING CLASS PRESIDENT.
OH.
WHAT'S THIS?

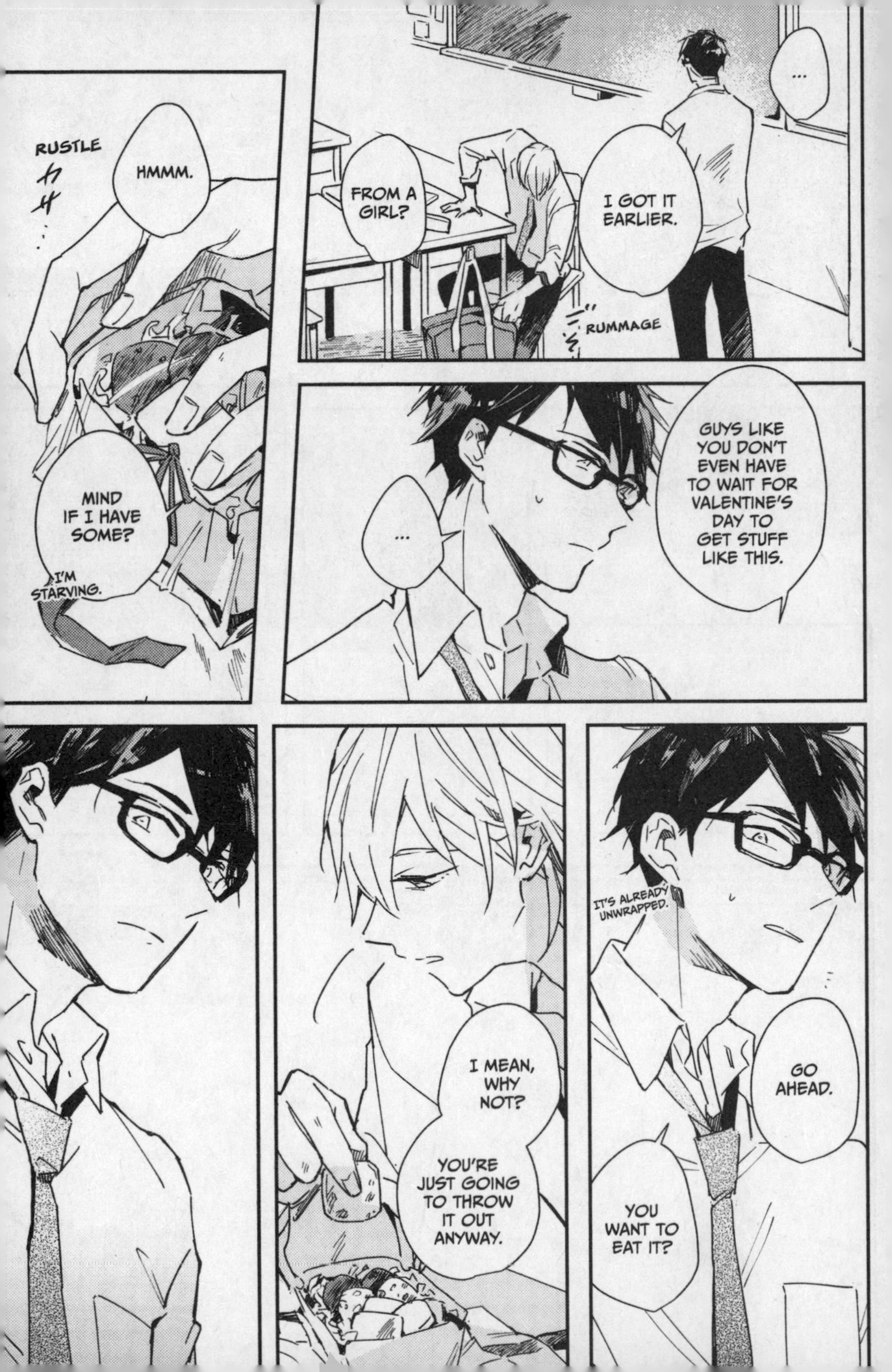
...
I GOT IT EARLIER.
FROM A GIRL?
RUMMAGE
GUYS LIKE YOU DON'T EVEN HAVE TO WAIT FOR VALENTINE'S DAY TO GET STUFF LIKE THIS.
...
RUSTLE
HMMM.
MIND IF I HAVE SOME?
I'M STARVING.
IT'S ALREADY UNWRAPPED.
GO AHEAD.
YOU WANT TO EAT IT?
I MEAN, WHY NOT?
YOU'RE JUST GOING TO THROW IT OUT ANYWAY.

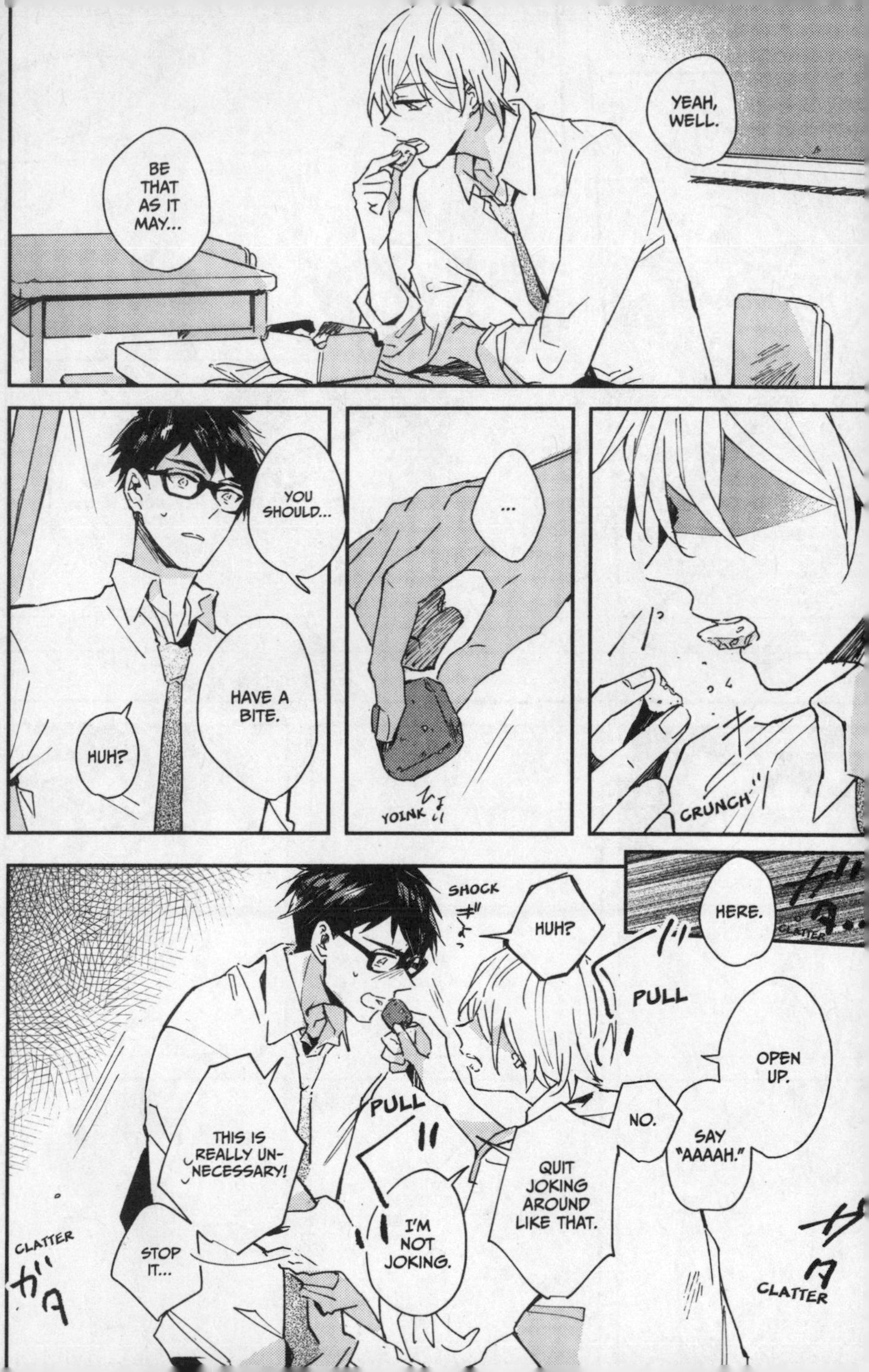
YEAH, WELL.
BE THAT AS IT MAY...
CRUNCH
...
YOINK
YOU SHOULD...
HAVE A BITE.
HUH?
HERE.
CLATTER
HUH?
SHOCK
PULL
OPEN UP.
SAY "AAAAH."
NO.
QUIT JOKING AROUND LIKE THAT.
PULL
I'M NOT JOKING.
THIS IS REALLY UN-NECESSARY!
STOP IT...
CLATTER
CLATTER

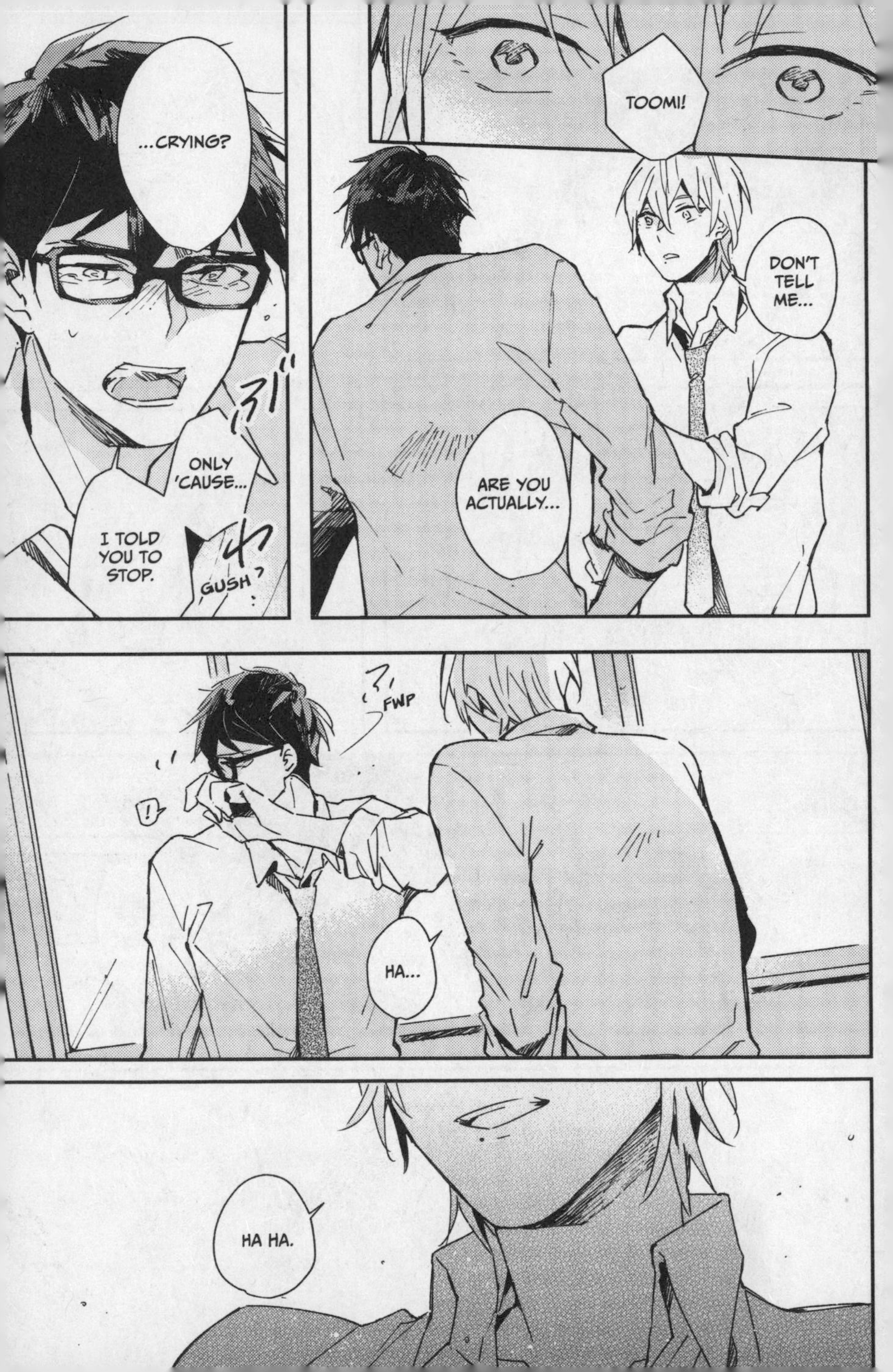
TOOMI!
DON'T TELL ME...
ARE YOU ACTUALLY...
...CRYING?
ONLY 'CAUSE...
I TOLD YOU TO STOP.
GUSH
FWP
!
HA...
HA HA.

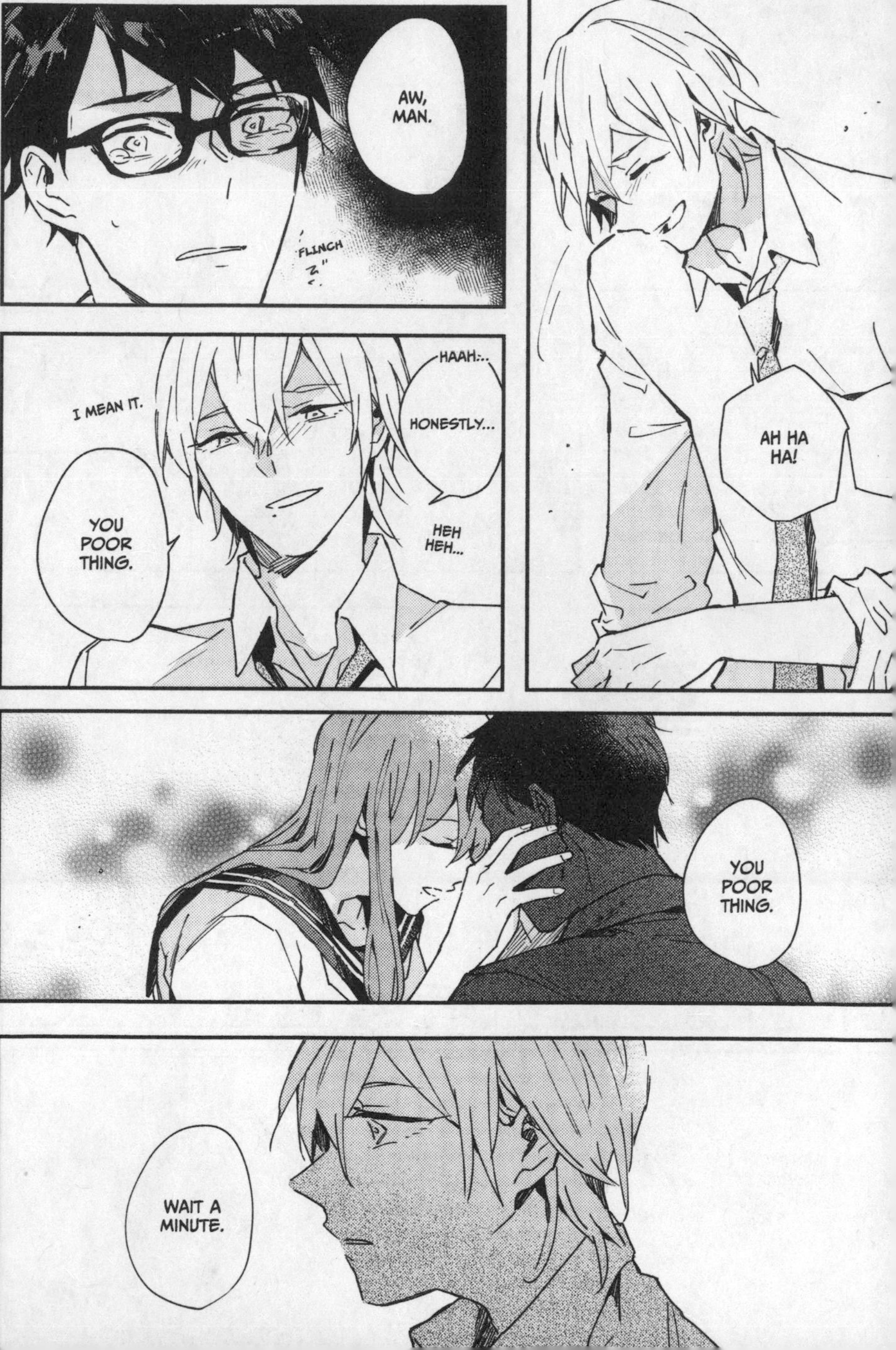
AH HA HA!
AW, MAN.
FLINCH
HAAH...
HONESTLY...
HEH HEH...
I MEAN IT.
YOU POOR THING.
YOU POOR THING.
WAIT A MINUTE.

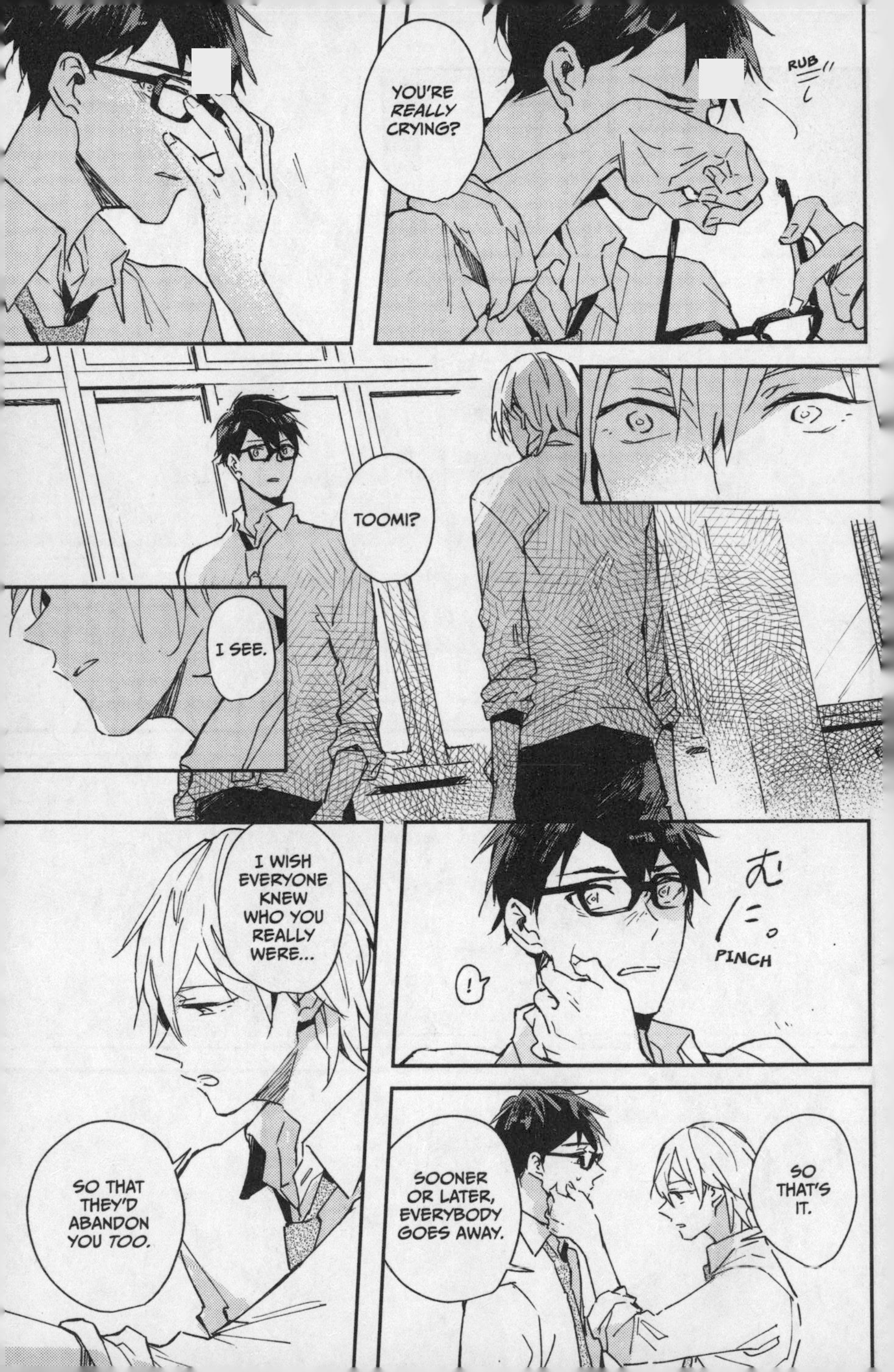

RUB
YOU'RE REALLY CRYING?
TOOMI?
I SEE.
むに。
PINCH
!
SO THAT'S IT.
SOONER OR LATER, EVERYBODY GOES AWAY.
I WISH EVERYONE KNEW WHO YOU REALLY WERE...
SO THAT THEY'D ABANDON YOU TOO.

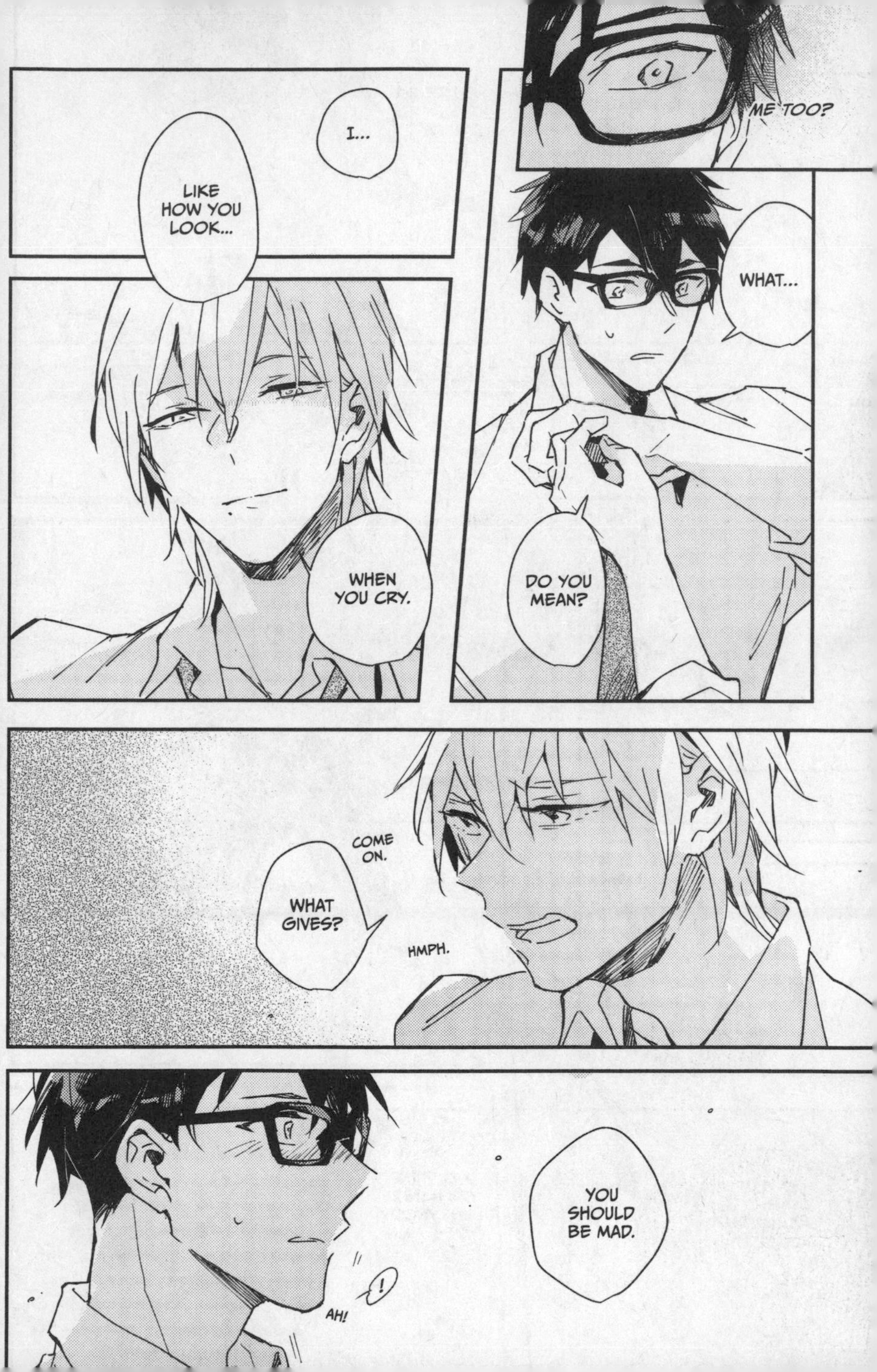
ME TOO?
WHAT...
DO YOU MEAN?
I...
LIKE HOW YOU LOOK...
WHEN YOU CRY.
COME ON.
WHAT GIVES?
HMPH.
YOU SHOULD BE MAD.
!
AH!

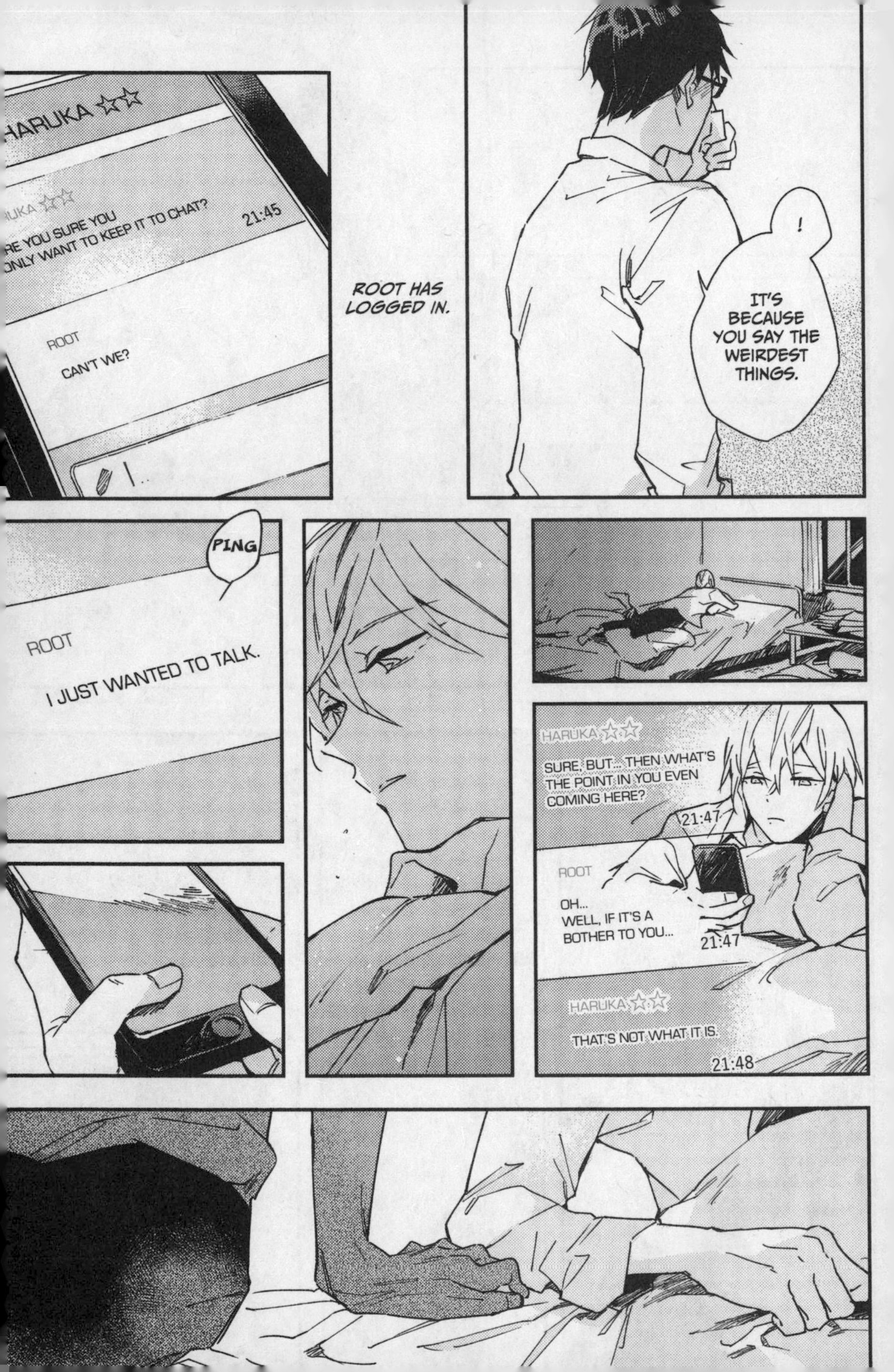
!
IT'S BECAUSE YOU SAY THE WEIRDEST THINGS.
ROOT HAS LOGGED IN.
ARUKA☆☆
RUKA☆☆
RE YOU SURE YOU ONLY WANT TO KEEP IT TO CHAT?
21:45
ROOT
CAN'T WE?
HARUKA☆☆
SURE, BUT... THEN WHAT'S THE POINT IN YOU EVEN COMING HERE?
21:47
ROOT
OH... WELL, IF IT'S A BOTHER TO YOU...
21:47
HARUKA☆☆
THAT'S NOT WHAT IT IS.
21:48
PING
ROOT
I JUST WANTED TO TALK.

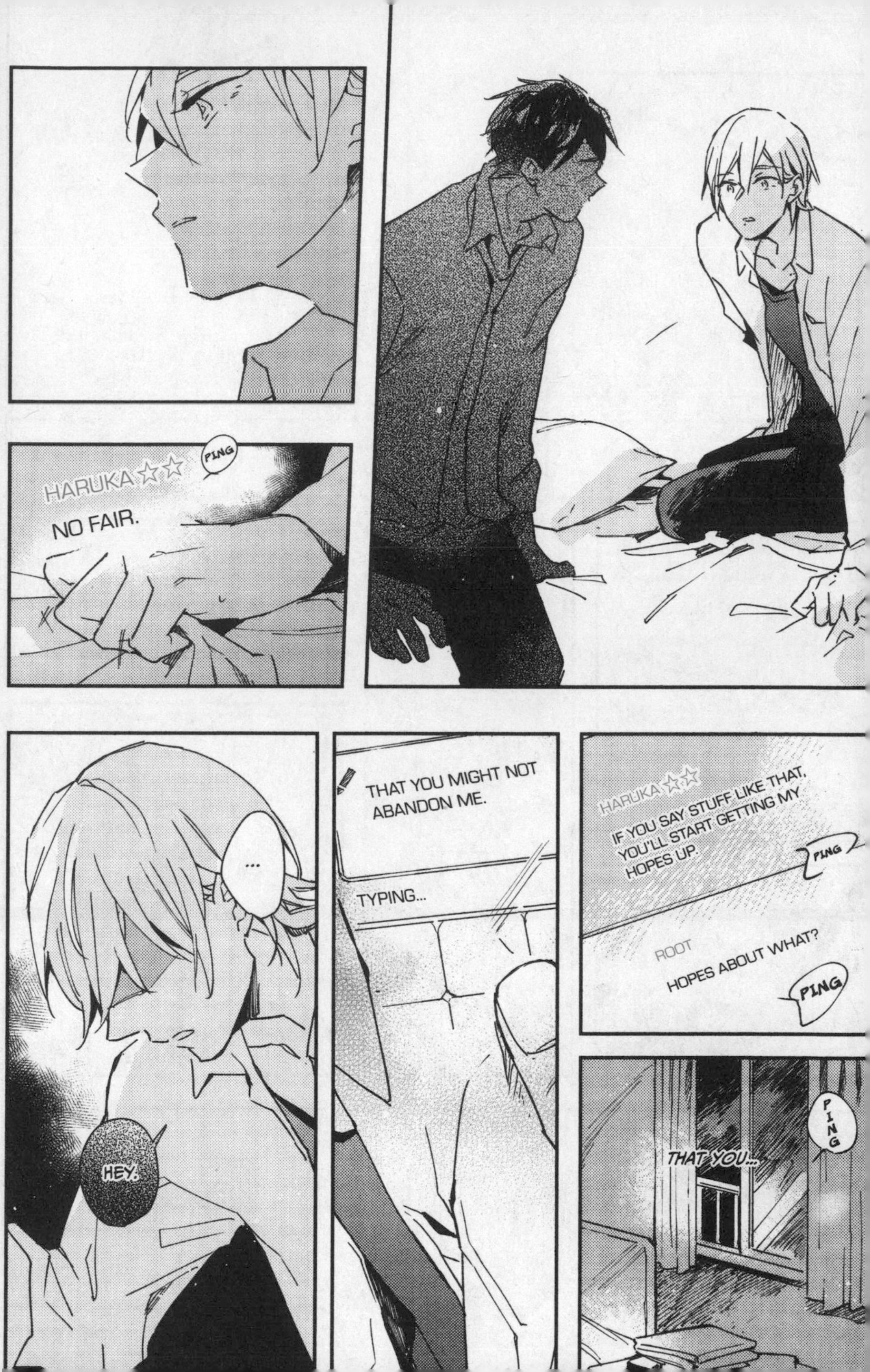
HARUKA☆☆
PING
NO FAIR.
HARUKA☆☆
IF YOU SAY STUFF LIKE THAT, YOU'LL START GETTING MY HOPES UP.
PING
ROOT
HOPES ABOUT WHAT?
PING
PING
THAT YOU...
THAT YOU MIGHT NOT ABANDON ME.
TYPING...
...
HEY.

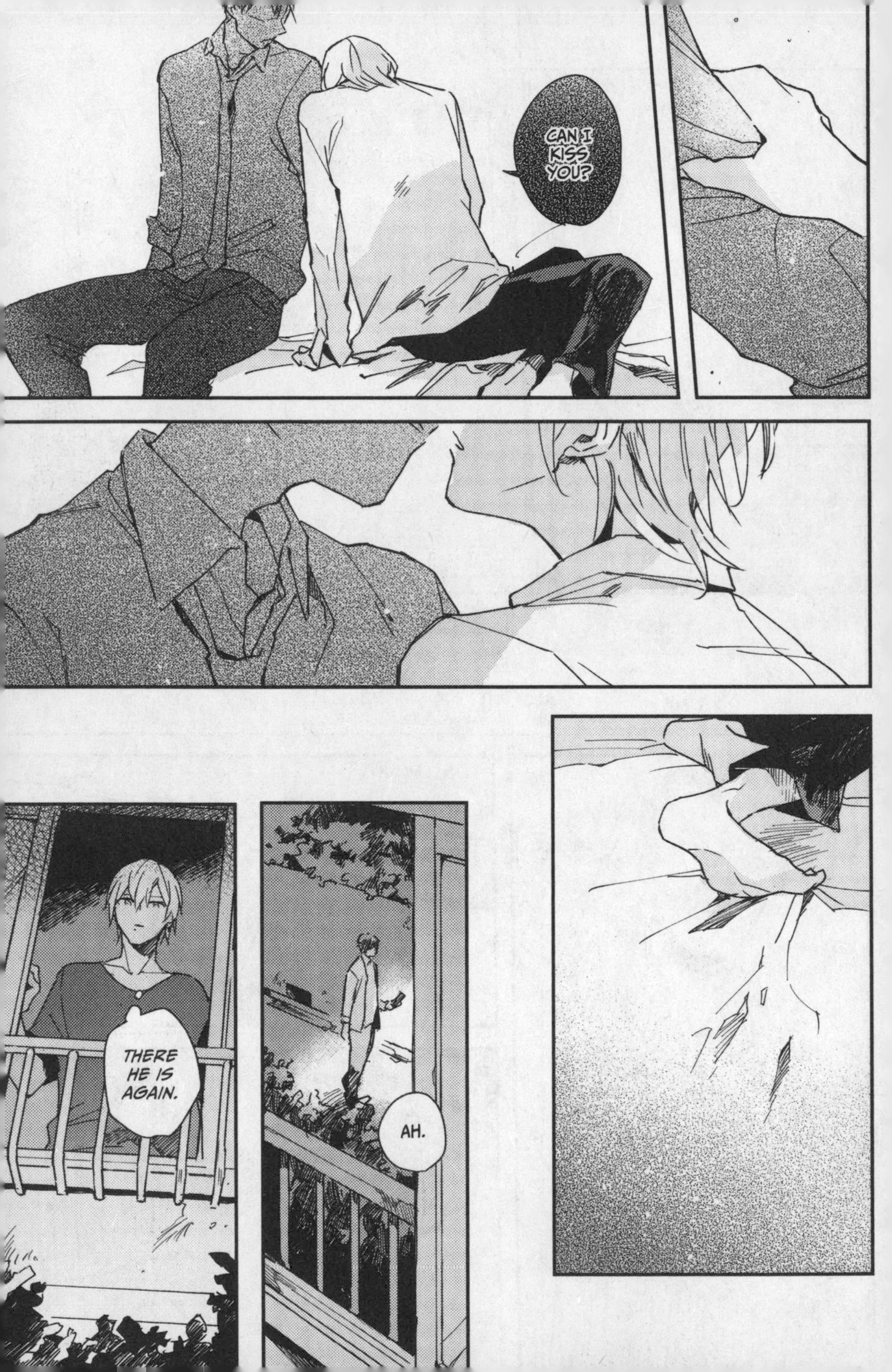
CAN I KISS YOU?
AH.
THERE HE IS AGAIN.

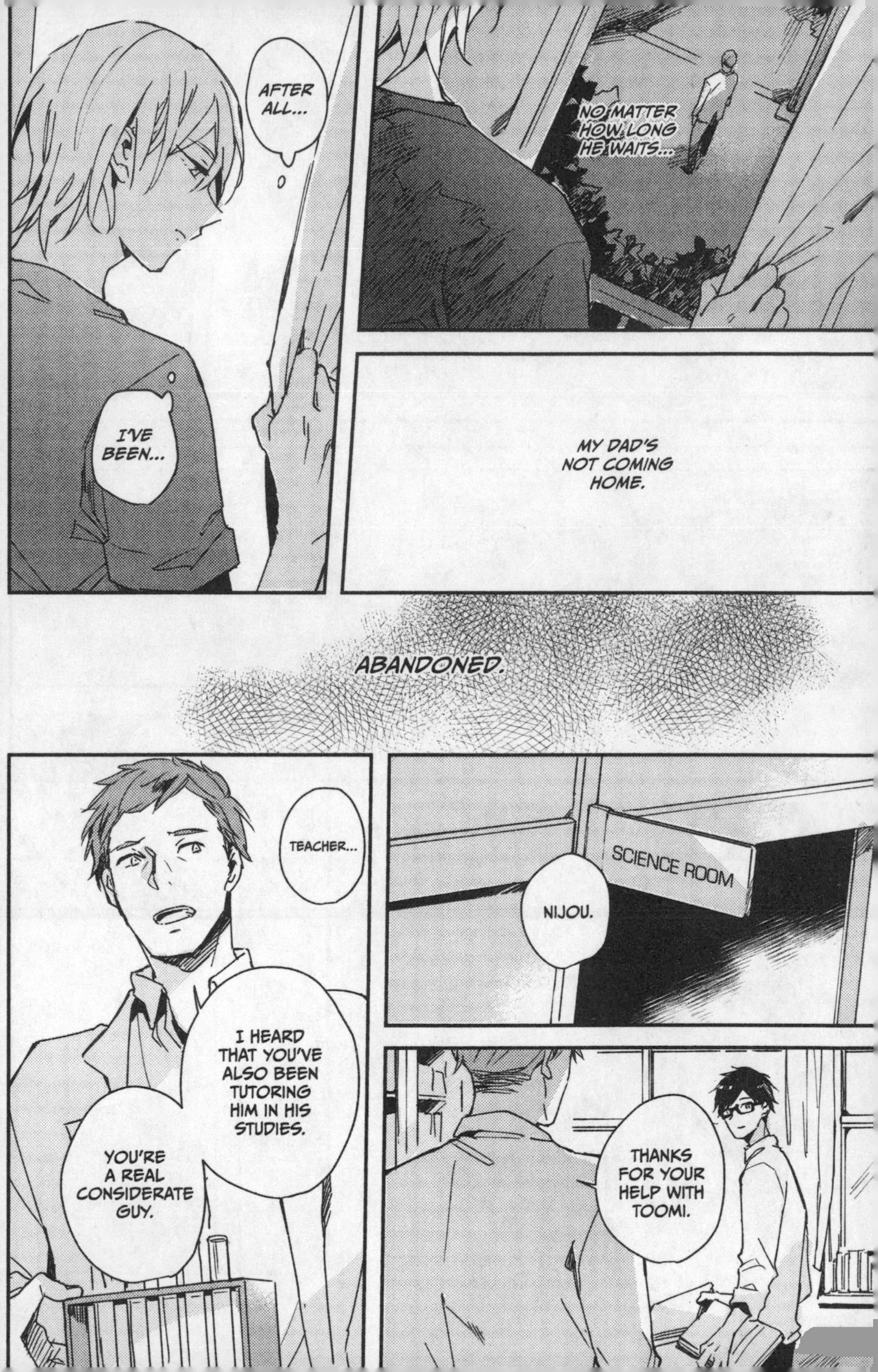
NO MATTER HOW LONG HE WAITS...
MY DAD'S NOT COMING HOME.
AFTER ALL...
I'VE BEEN...
ABANDONED.
SCIENCE ROOM
NIJOU.
THANKS FOR YOUR HELP WITH TOOMI.
TEACHER...
I HEARD THAT YOU'VE ALSO BEEN TUTORING HIM IN HIS STUDIES.
YOU'RE A REAL CONSIDERATE GUY.

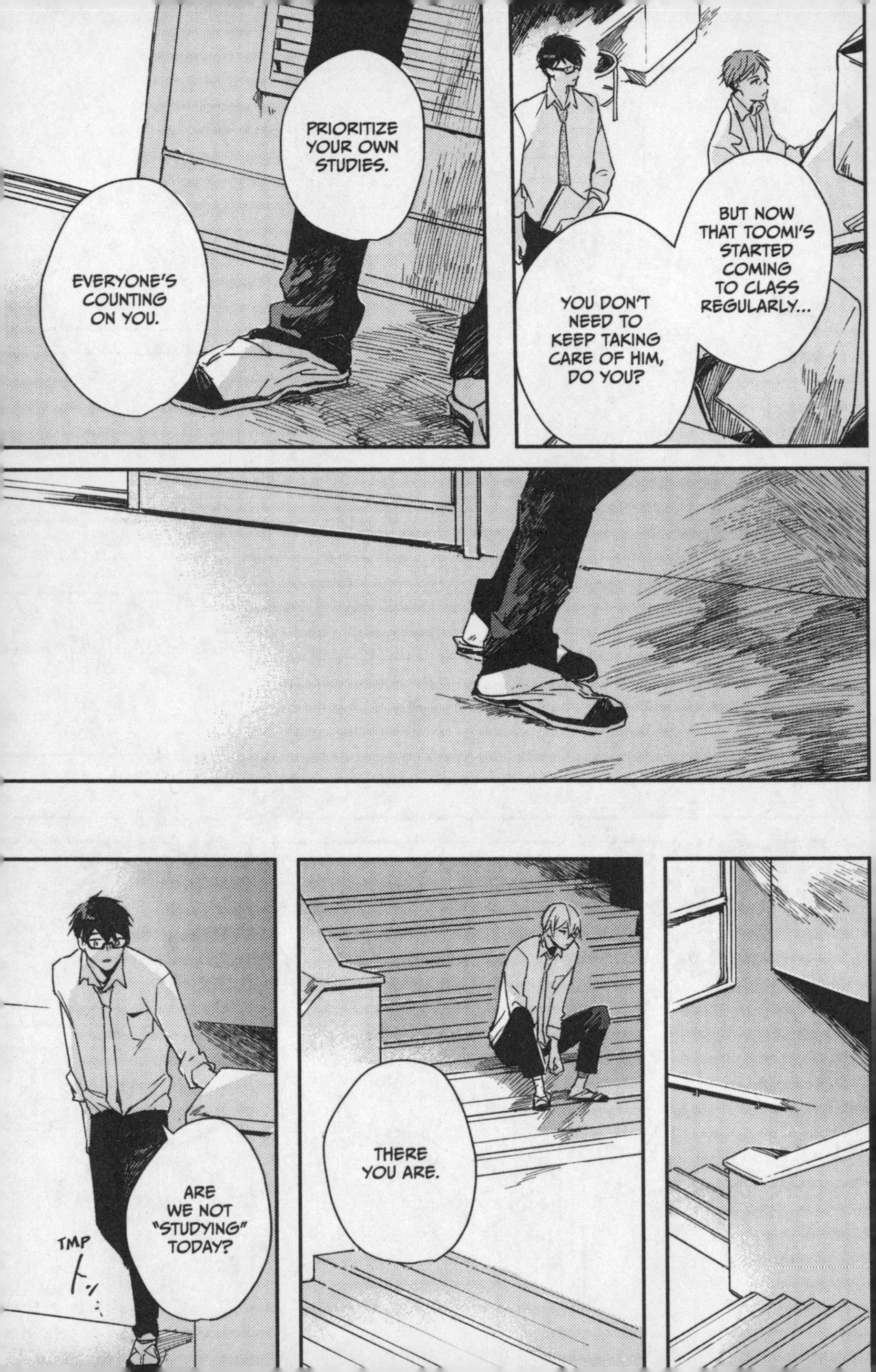
BUT NOW THAT TOOMI'S STARTED COMING TO CLASS REGULARLY...
YOU DON'T NEED TO KEEP TAKING CARE OF HIM, DO YOU?
PRIORITIZE YOUR OWN STUDIES.
EVERYONE'S COUNTING ON YOU.
THERE YOU ARE.
ARE WE NOT "STUDYING" TODAY?
TMP
ト

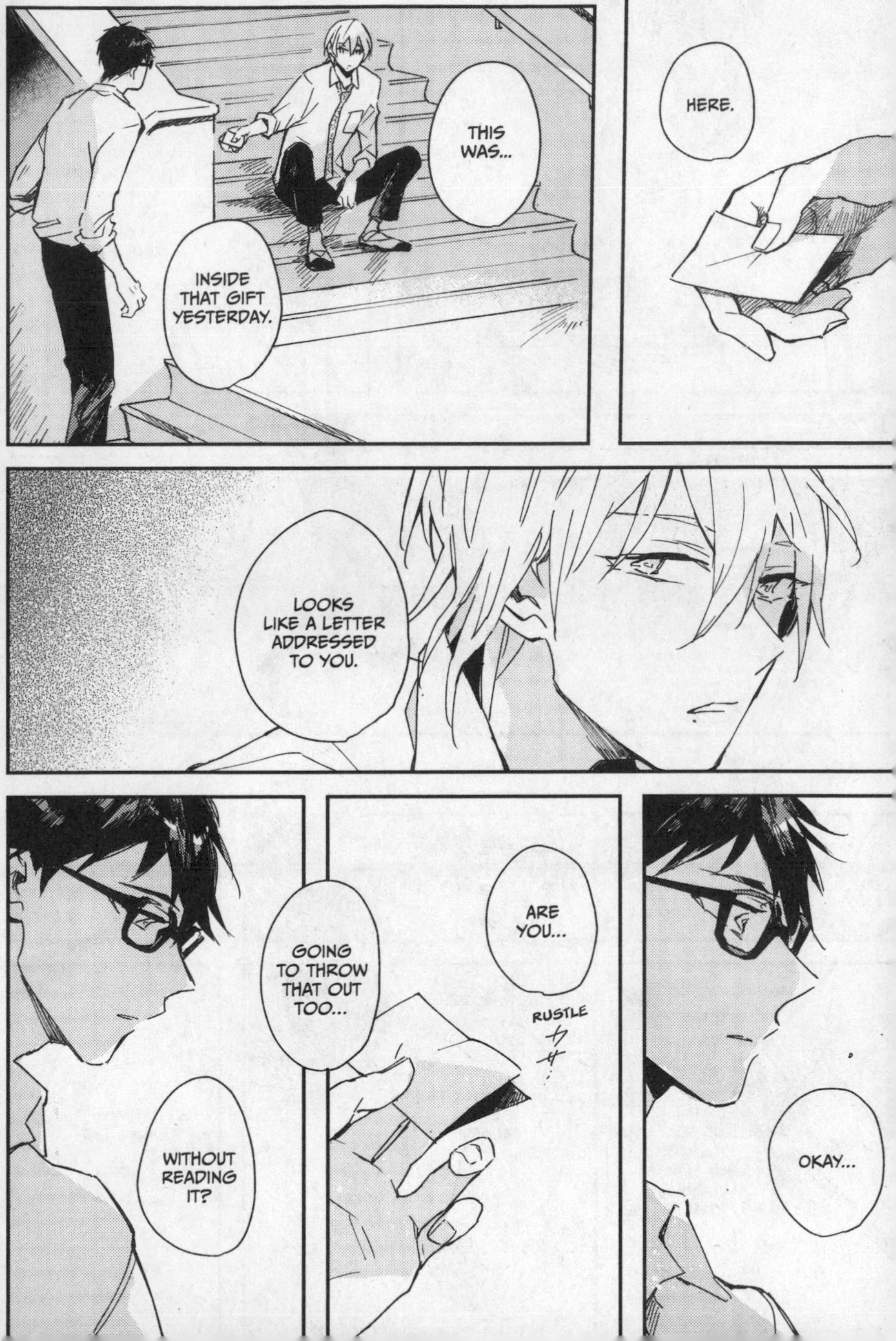
HERE.
THIS WAS...
INSIDE THAT GIFT YESTERDAY.
LOOKS LIKE A LETTER ADDRESSED TO YOU.
OKAY...
ARE YOU...
RUSTLE
GOING TO THROW THAT OUT TOO...
WITHOUT READING IT?

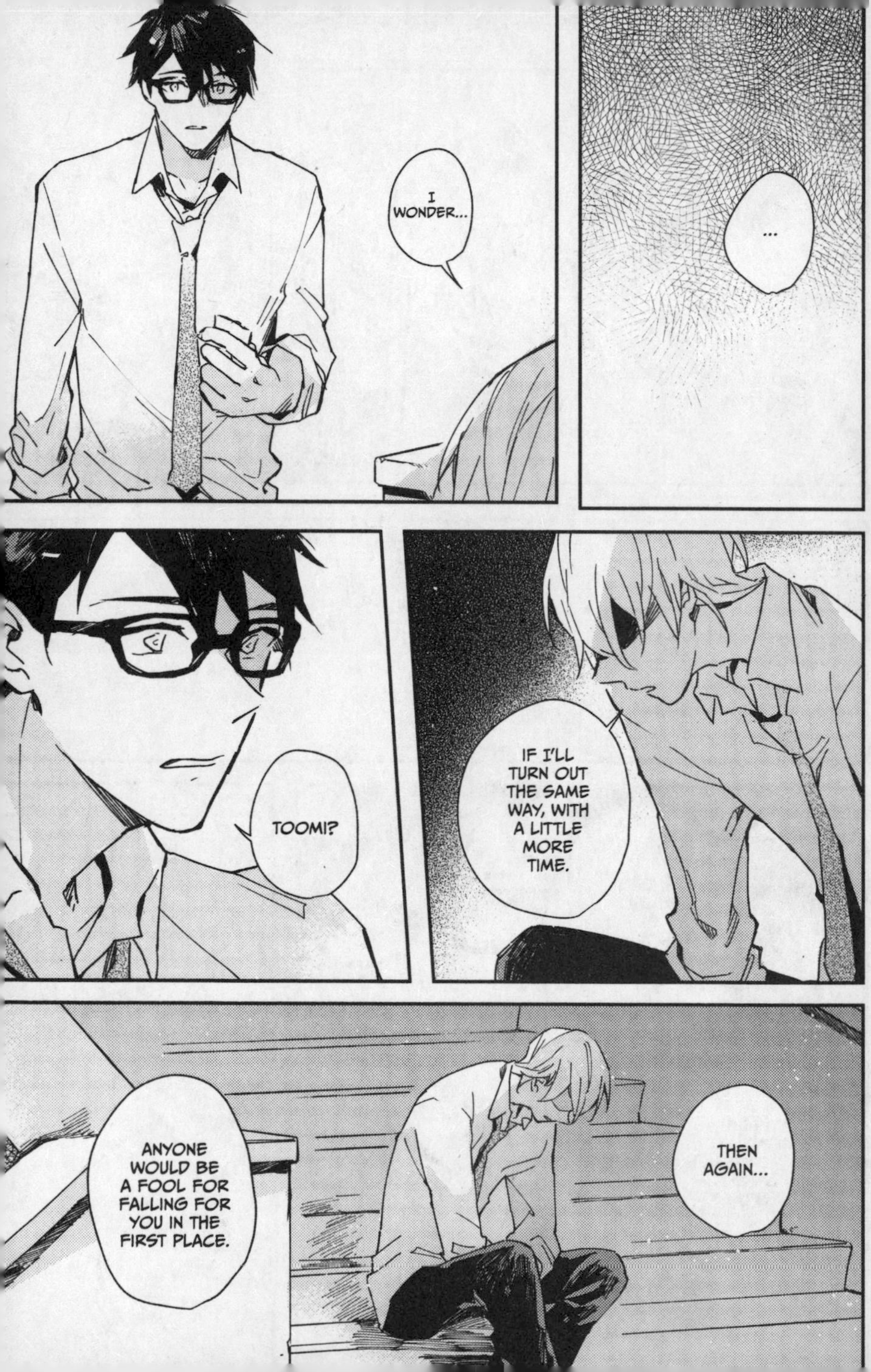
...
I WONDER...
IF I'LL TURN OUT THE SAME WAY, WITH A LITTLE MORE TIME.
TOOMI?
THEN AGAIN...
ANYONE WOULD BE A FOOL FOR FALLING FOR YOU IN THE FIRST PLACE.

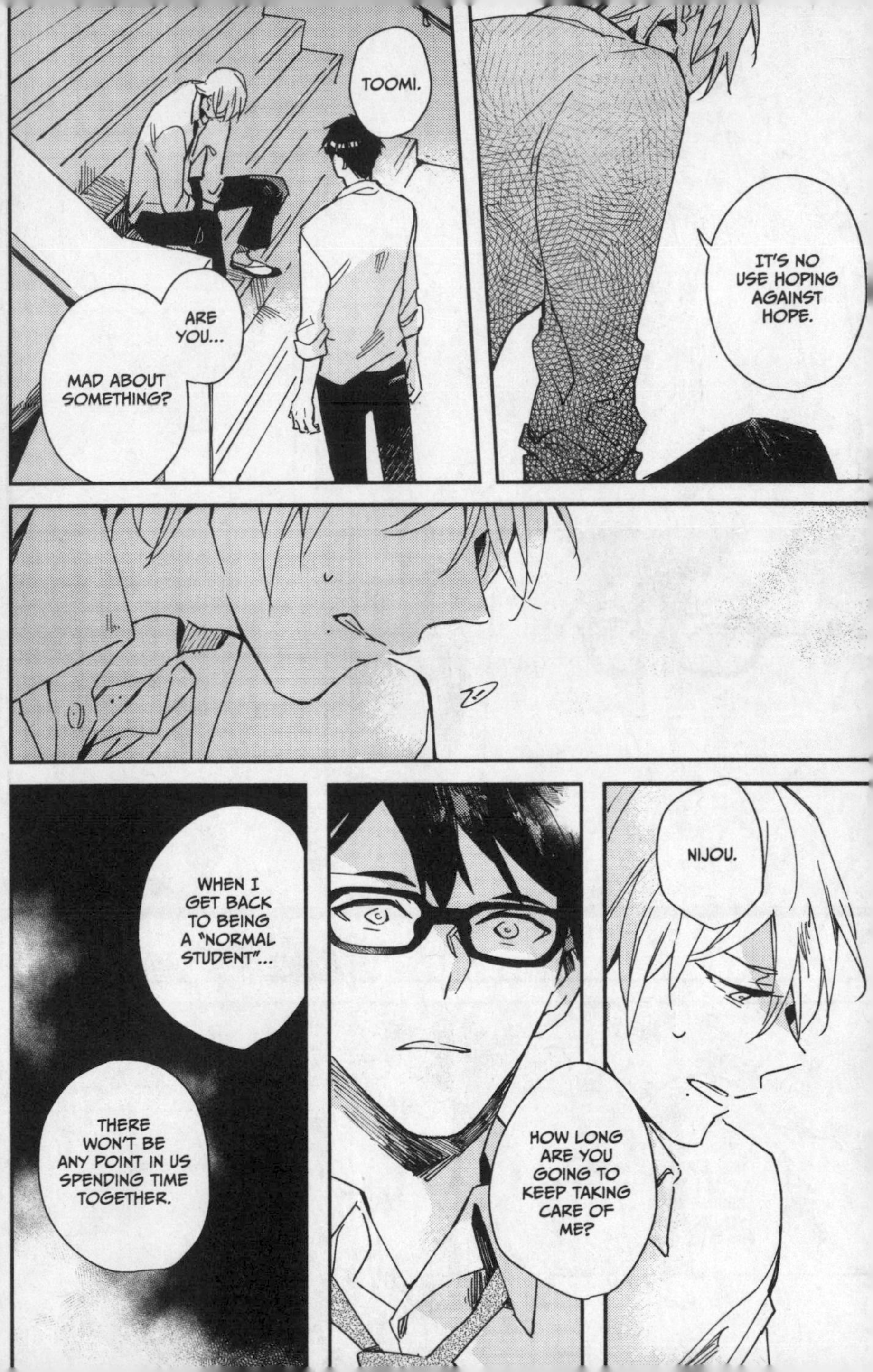
IT'S NO USE HOPING AGAINST HOPE.
TOOMI.
ARE YOU...
MAD ABOUT SOMETHING?
!?
NIJOU.
HOW LONG ARE YOU GOING TO KEEP TAKING CARE OF ME?
WHEN I GET BACK TO BEING A "NORMAL STUDENT"...
THERE WON'T BE ANY POINT IN US SPENDING TIME TOGETHER.

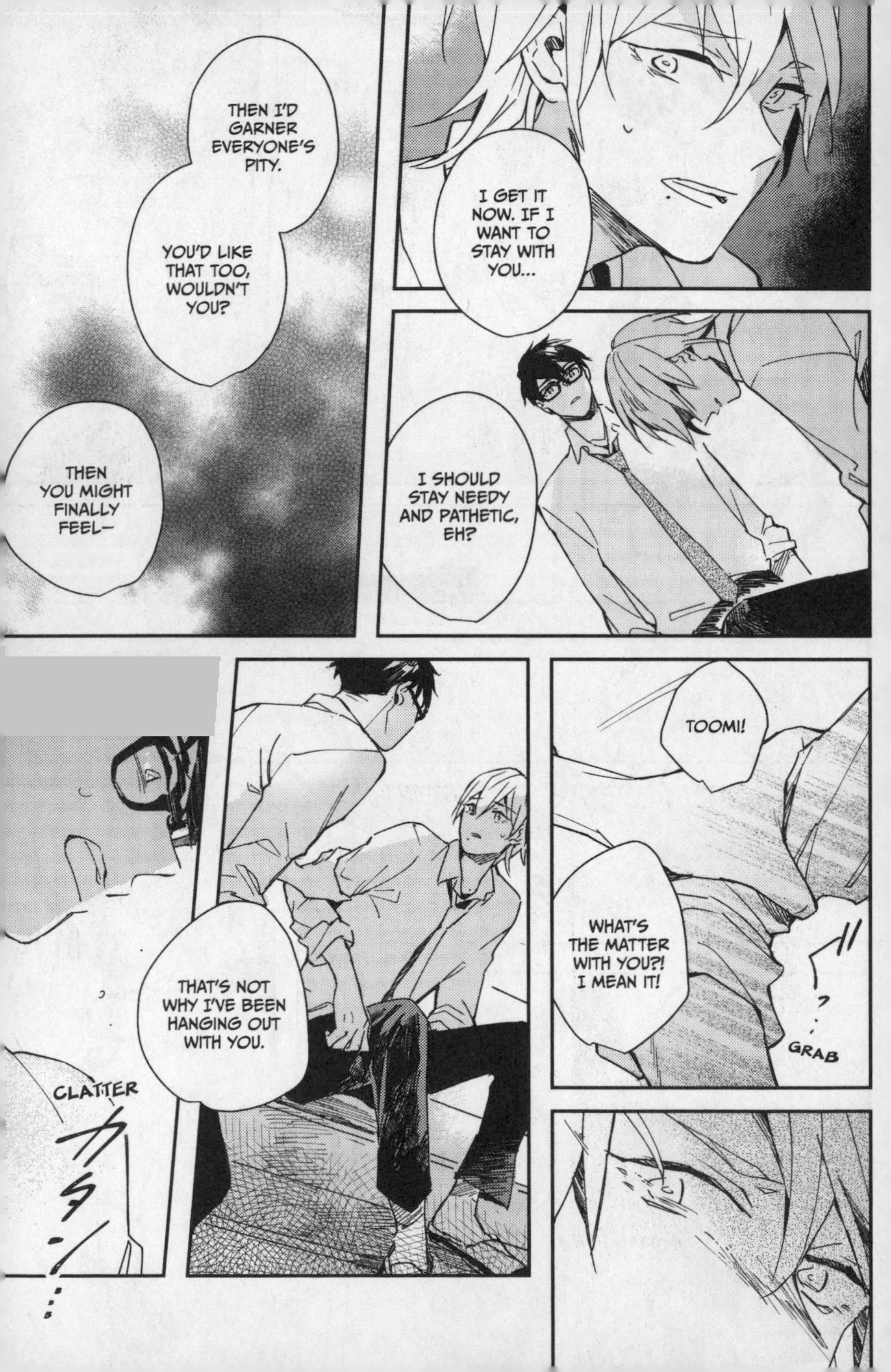
I GET IT NOW. IF I WANT TO STAY WITH YOU...
I SHOULD STAY NEEDY AND PATHETIC, EH?
THEN I'D GARNER EVERYONE'S PITY.
YOU'D LIKE THAT TOO, WOULDN'T YOU?
THEN YOU MIGHT FINALLY FEEL—
TOOMI!
WHAT'S THE MATTER WITH YOU?! I MEAN IT!
GRAB
THAT'S NOT WHY I'VE BEEN HANGING OUT WITH YOU.
CLATTER

SNATCH

I'M SORRY.

ARE YOU IN THE MIDDLE OF SOMETHING?

!

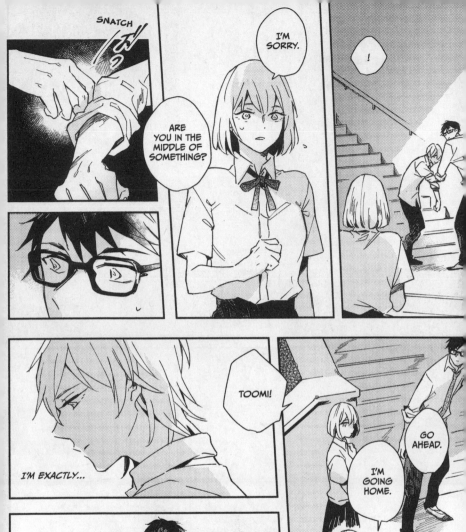

TOOMI!

I'M EXACTLY...

GO AHEAD.

I'M GOING HOME.

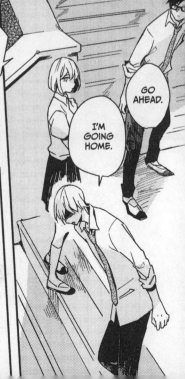

LIKE THAT "FOOL"...

I WAS TALKING ABOUT BEFORE.

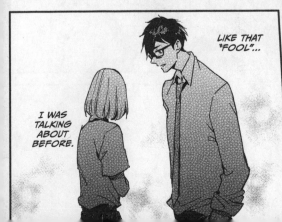

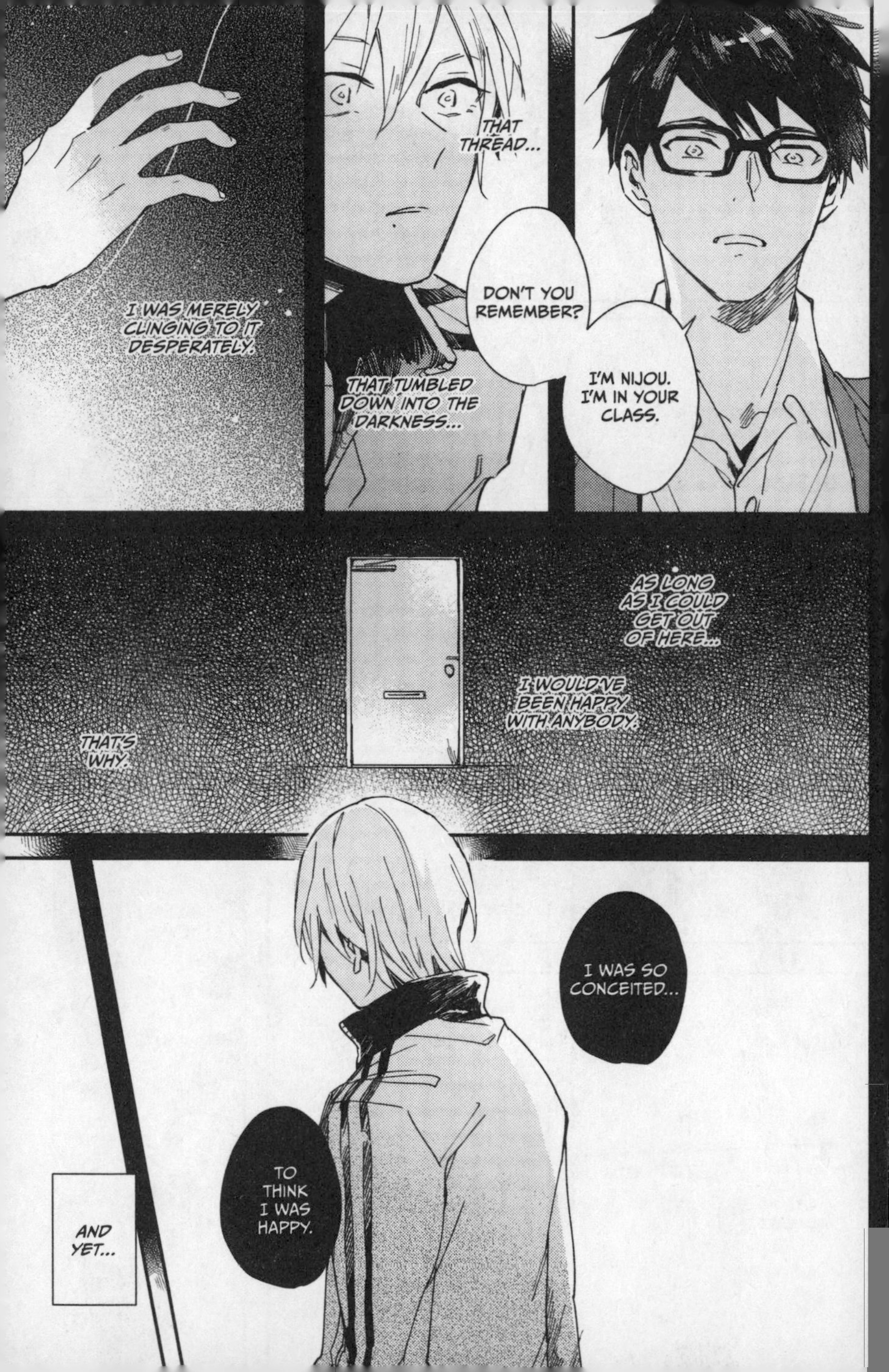
DON'T YOU REMEMBER?
I'M NIJOU. I'M IN YOUR CLASS.
THAT THREAD...
THAT TUMBLED DOWN INTO THE DARKNESS...
I WAS MERELY CLINGING TO IT DESPERATELY.
AS LONG AS I COULD GET OUT OF HERE...
I WOULD'VE BEEN HAPPY WITH ANYBODY.
THAT'S WHY.
I WAS SO CONCEITED...
TO THINK I WAS HAPPY.
AND YET...

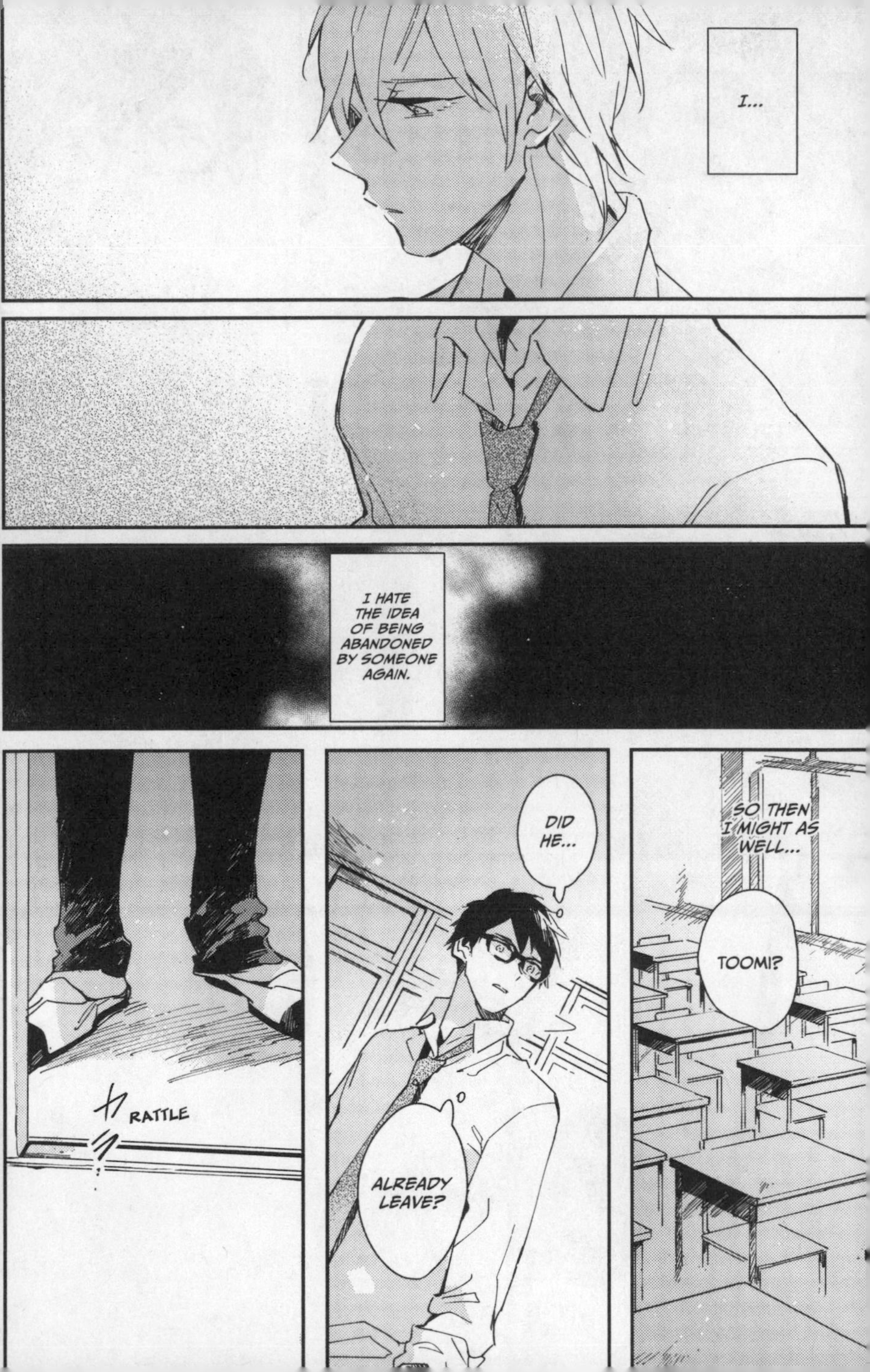
I...
I HATE THE IDEA OF BEING ABANDONED BY SOMEONE AGAIN.
SO THEN I MIGHT AS WELL...
TOOMI?
DID HE...
ALREADY LEAVE?
RATTLE

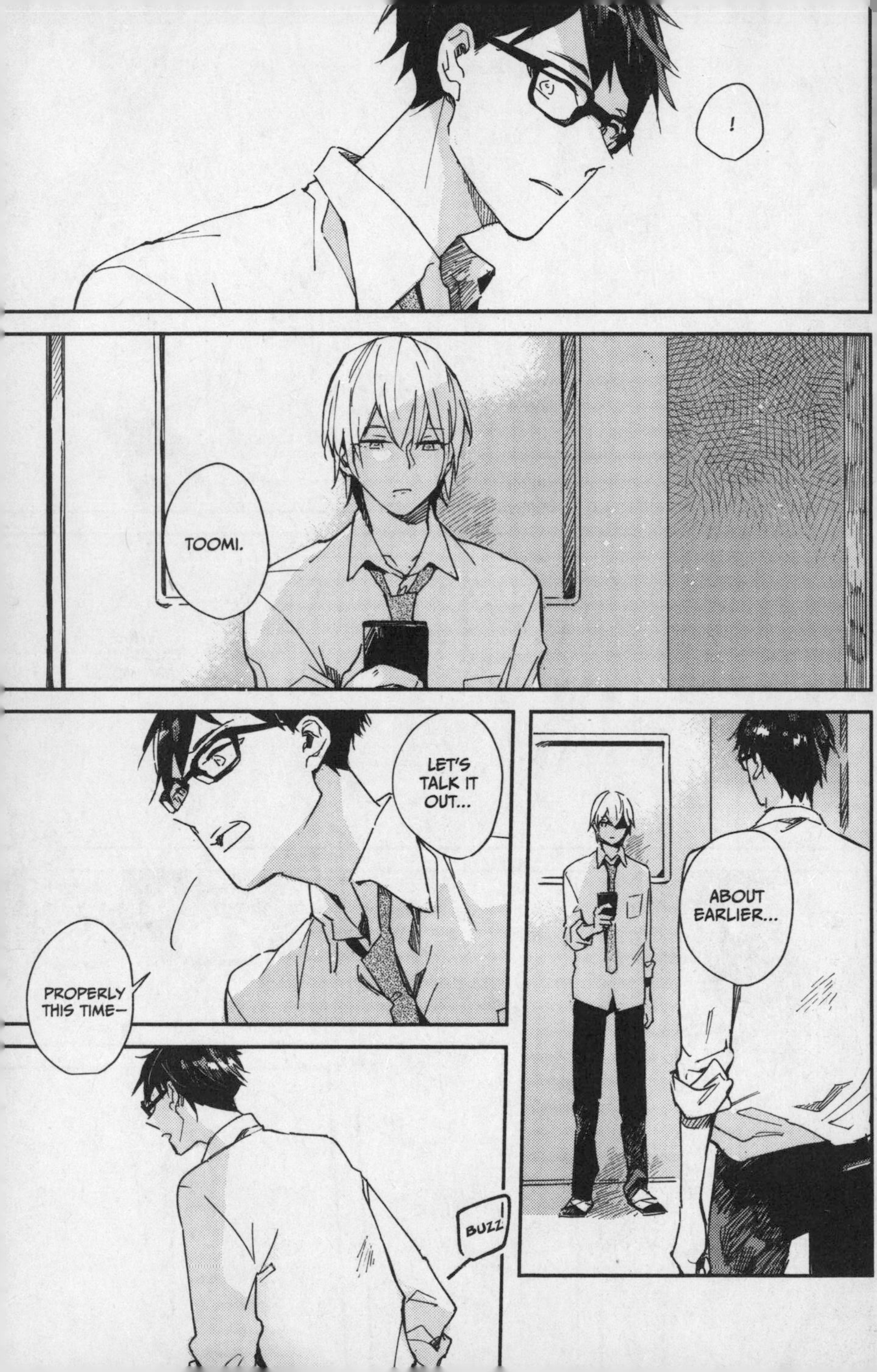
!
TOOMI.
ABOUT EARLIER...
LET'S TALK IT OUT...
PROPERLY THIS TIME—
BUZZ

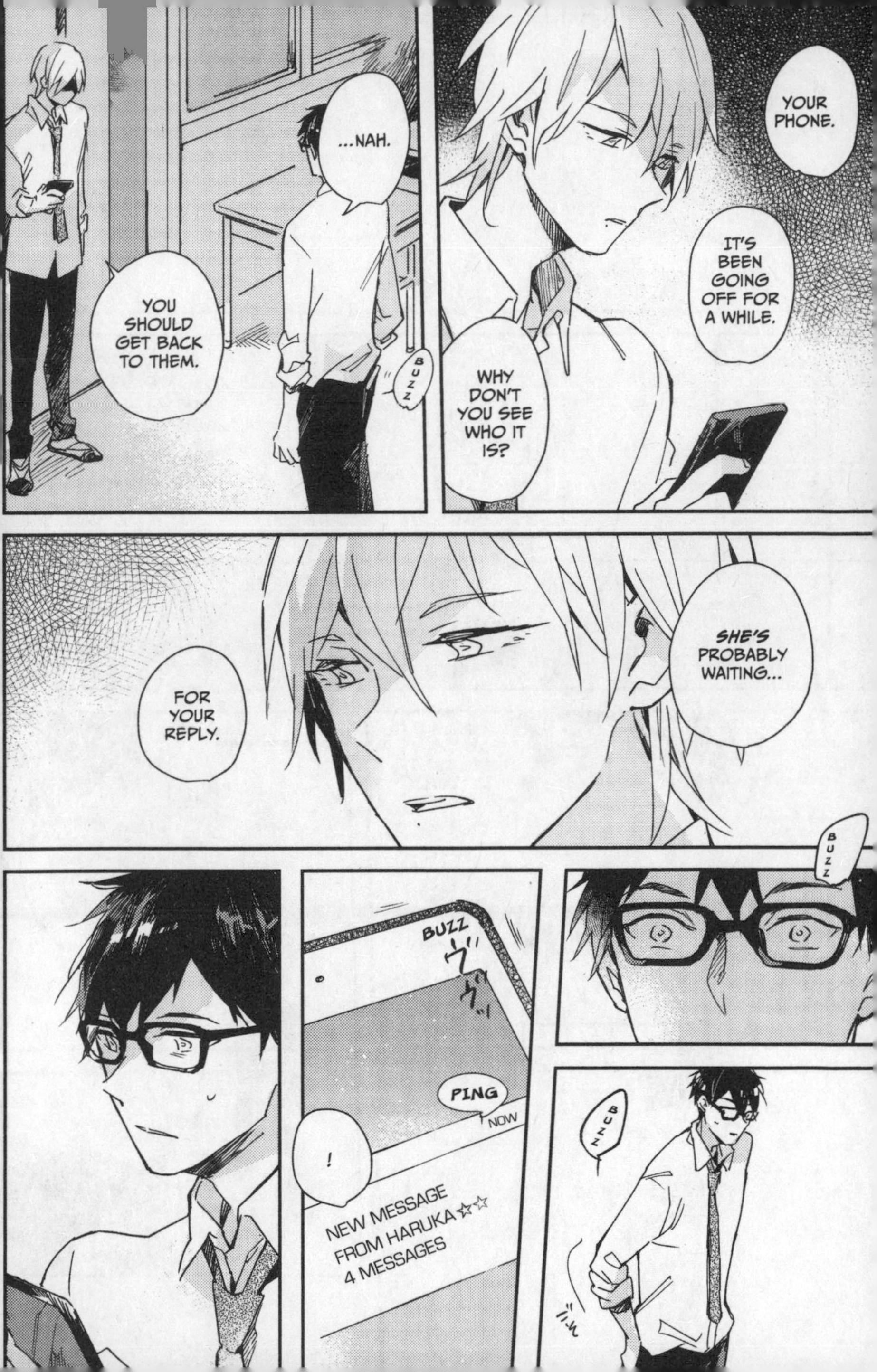
YOUR PHONE.
IT'S BEEN GOING OFF FOR A WHILE.
WHY DON'T YOU SEE WHO IT IS?
...NAH.
BUZZ
YOU SHOULD GET BACK TO THEM.
SHE'S PROBABLY WAITING...
FOR YOUR REPLY.
BUZZ
BUZZ
BUZZ
PING
NOW
!
NEW MESSAGE FROM HARUKA☆☆ 4 MESSAGES

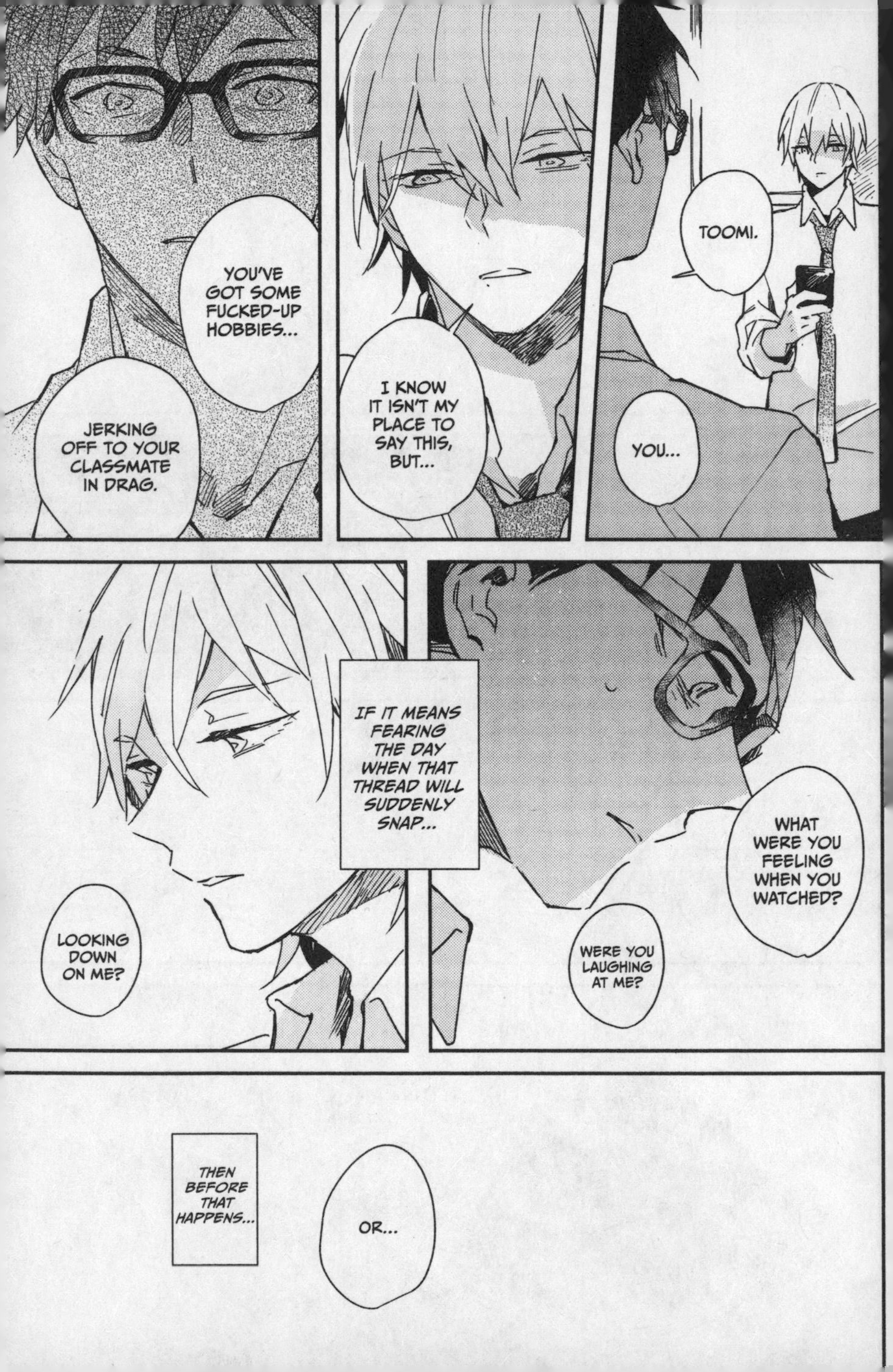
TOOMI.
YOU...
I KNOW IT ISN'T MY PLACE TO SAY THIS, BUT...
YOU'VE GOT SOME FUCKED-UP HOBBIES...
JERKING OFF TO YOUR CLASSMATE IN DRAG.
WHAT WERE YOU FEELING WHEN YOU WATCHED?
WERE YOU LAUGHING AT ME?
IF IT MEANS FEARING THE DAY WHEN THAT THREAD WILL SUDDENLY SNAP...
LOOKING DOWN ON ME?
OR...
THEN BEFORE THAT HAPPENS...

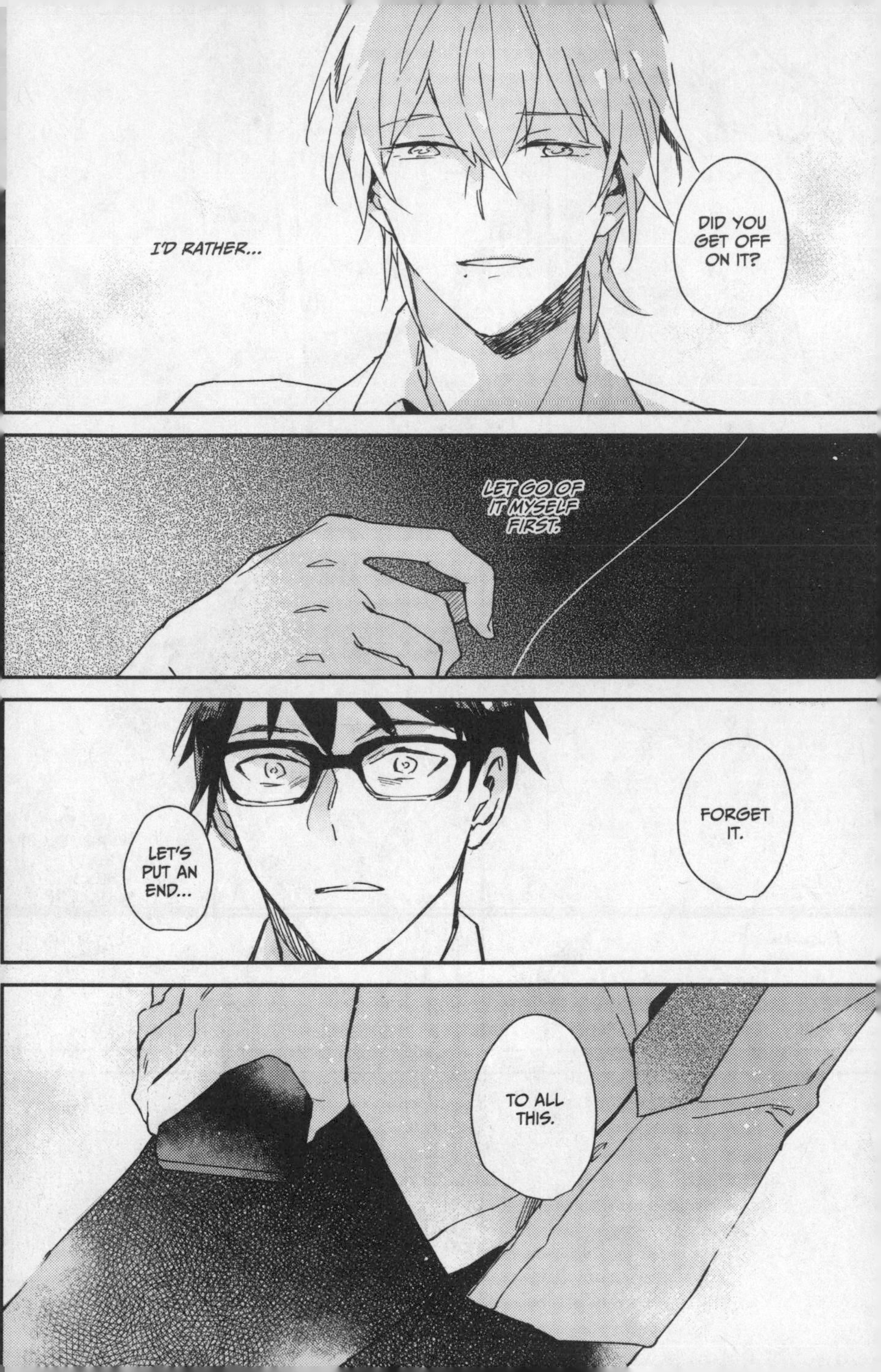
DID YOU GET OFF ON IT?
I'D RATHER...
LET GO OF IT MYSELF FIRST.
FORGET IT.
LET'S PUT AN END...
TO ALL THIS.

#4

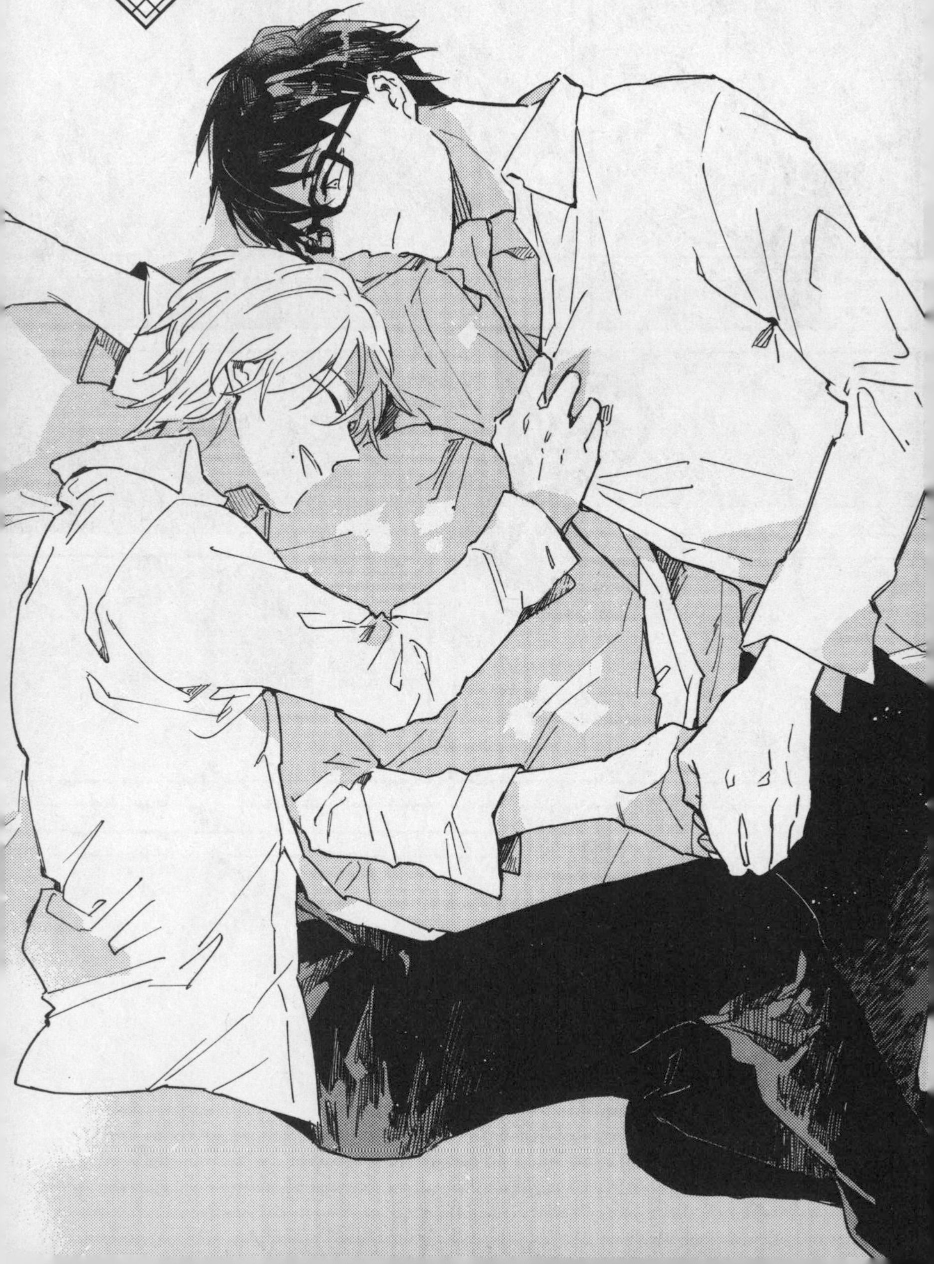

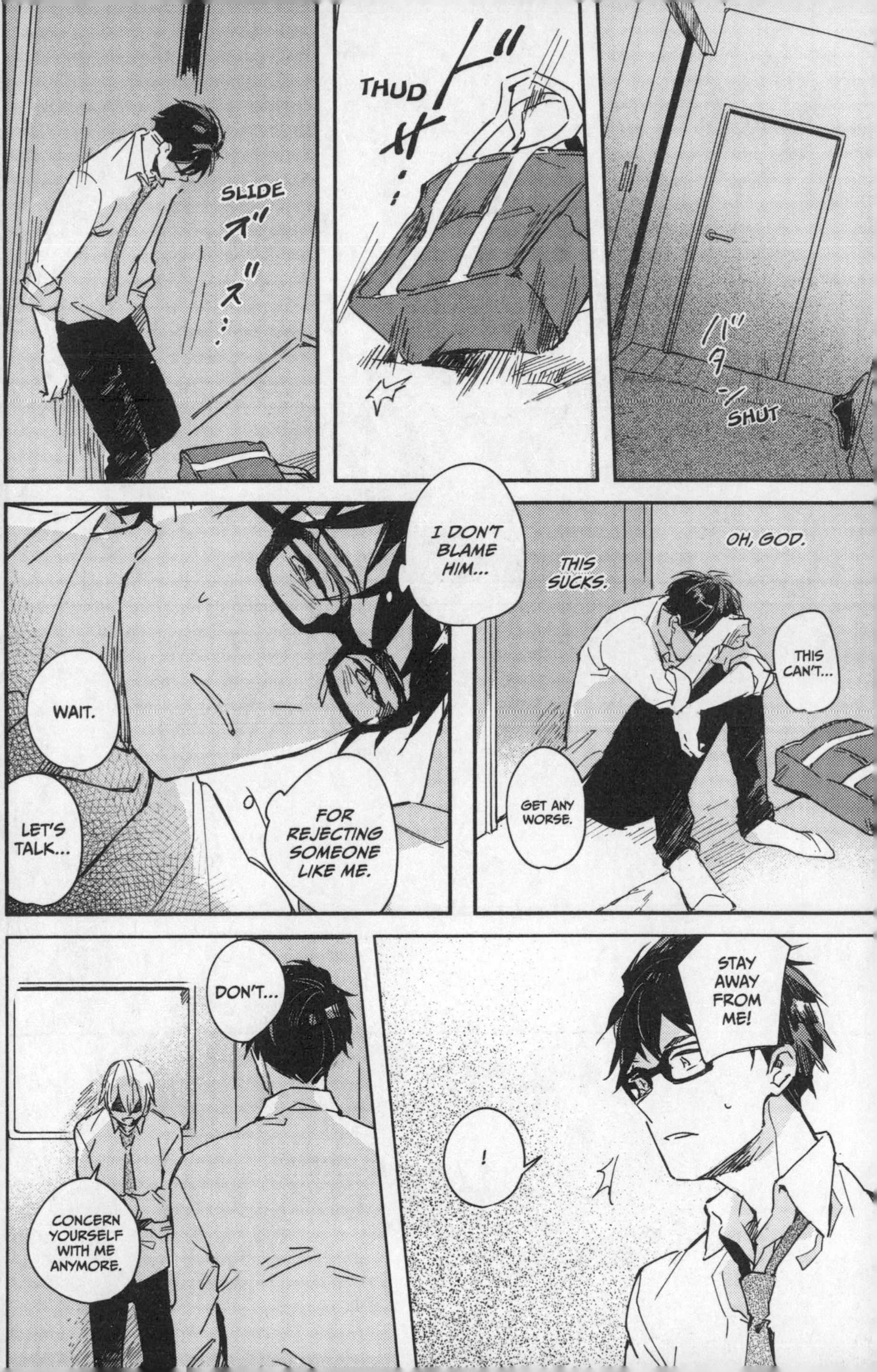
バタン
SHUT
ドサ…
THUD
ズズ…
SLIDE
OH, GOD.
THIS SUCKS.
THIS CAN'T...
GET ANY WORSE.
I DON'T BLAME HIM...
FOR REJECTING SOMEONE LIKE ME.
WAIT.
LET'S TALK...
STAY AWAY FROM ME!
!
DON'T...
CONCERN YOURSELF WITH ME ANYMORE.

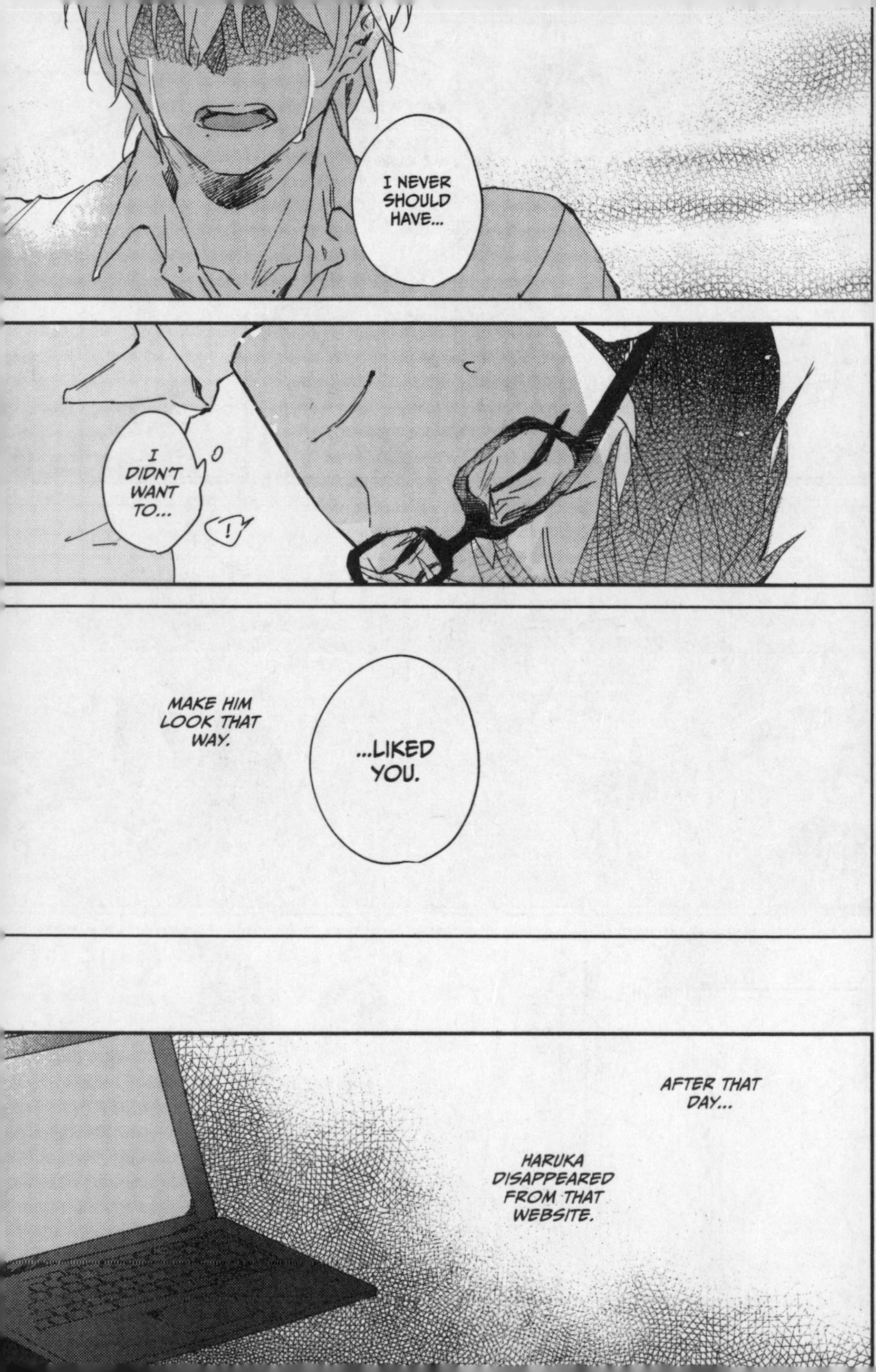
I NEVER SHOULD HAVE...
I DIDN'T WANT TO...
!
...LIKED YOU.
MAKE HIM LOOK THAT WAY.
AFTER THAT DAY...
HARUKA DISAPPEARED FROM THAT WEBSITE.

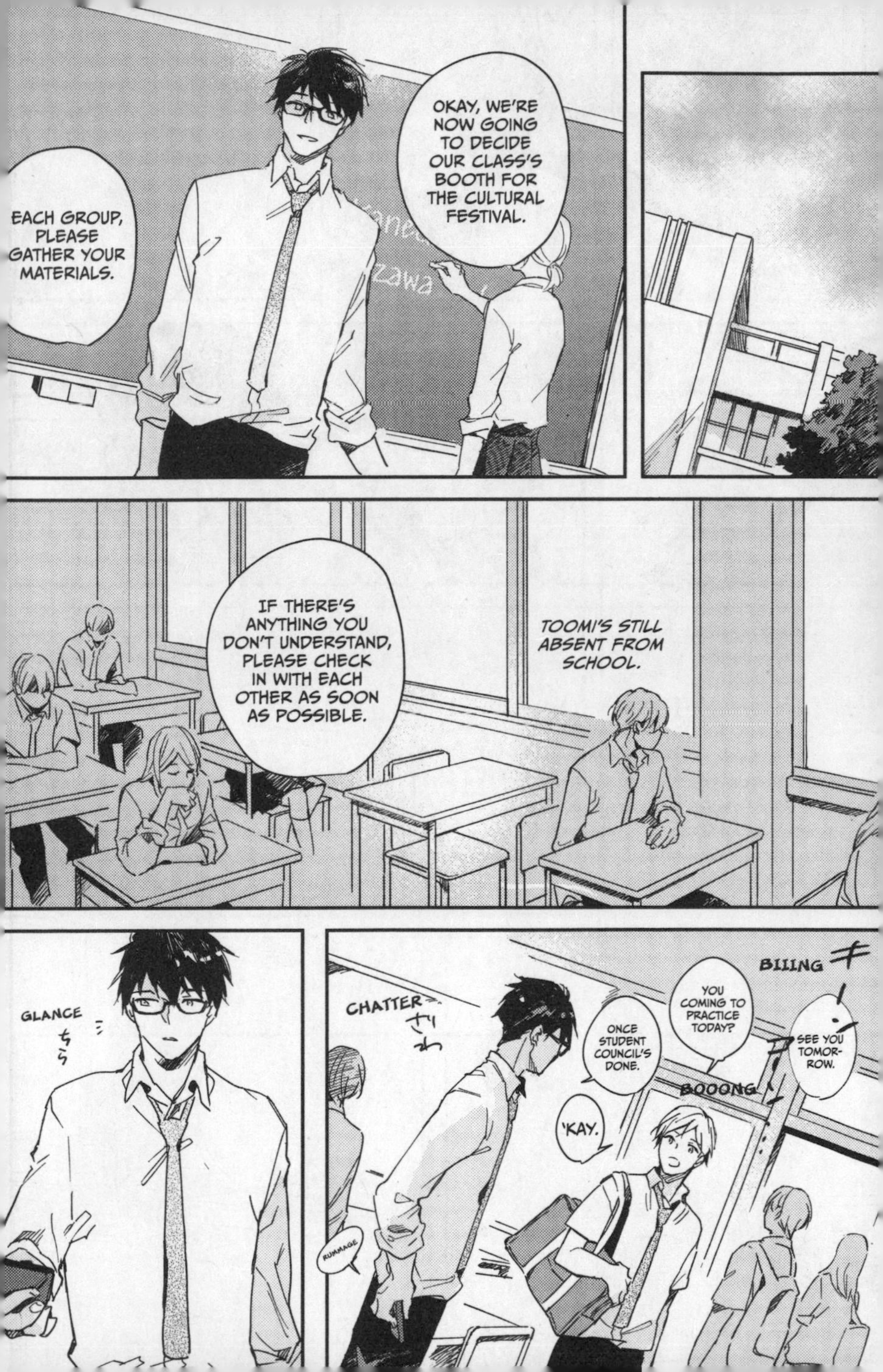
OKAY, WE'RE NOW GOING TO DECIDE OUR CLASS'S BOOTH FOR THE CULTURAL FESTIVAL.
EACH GROUP, PLEASE GATHER YOUR MATERIALS.
IF THERE'S ANYTHING YOU DON'T UNDERSTAND, PLEASE CHECK IN WITH EACH OTHER AS SOON AS POSSIBLE.
TOOMI'S STILL ABSENT FROM SCHOOL.
BIIING
SEE YOU TOMORROW.
YOU COMING TO PRACTICE TODAY?
ONCE STUDENT COUNCIL'S DONE.
BOOONG
'KAY.
CHATTER
ざわ
RUMMAGE
GLANCE
ちら

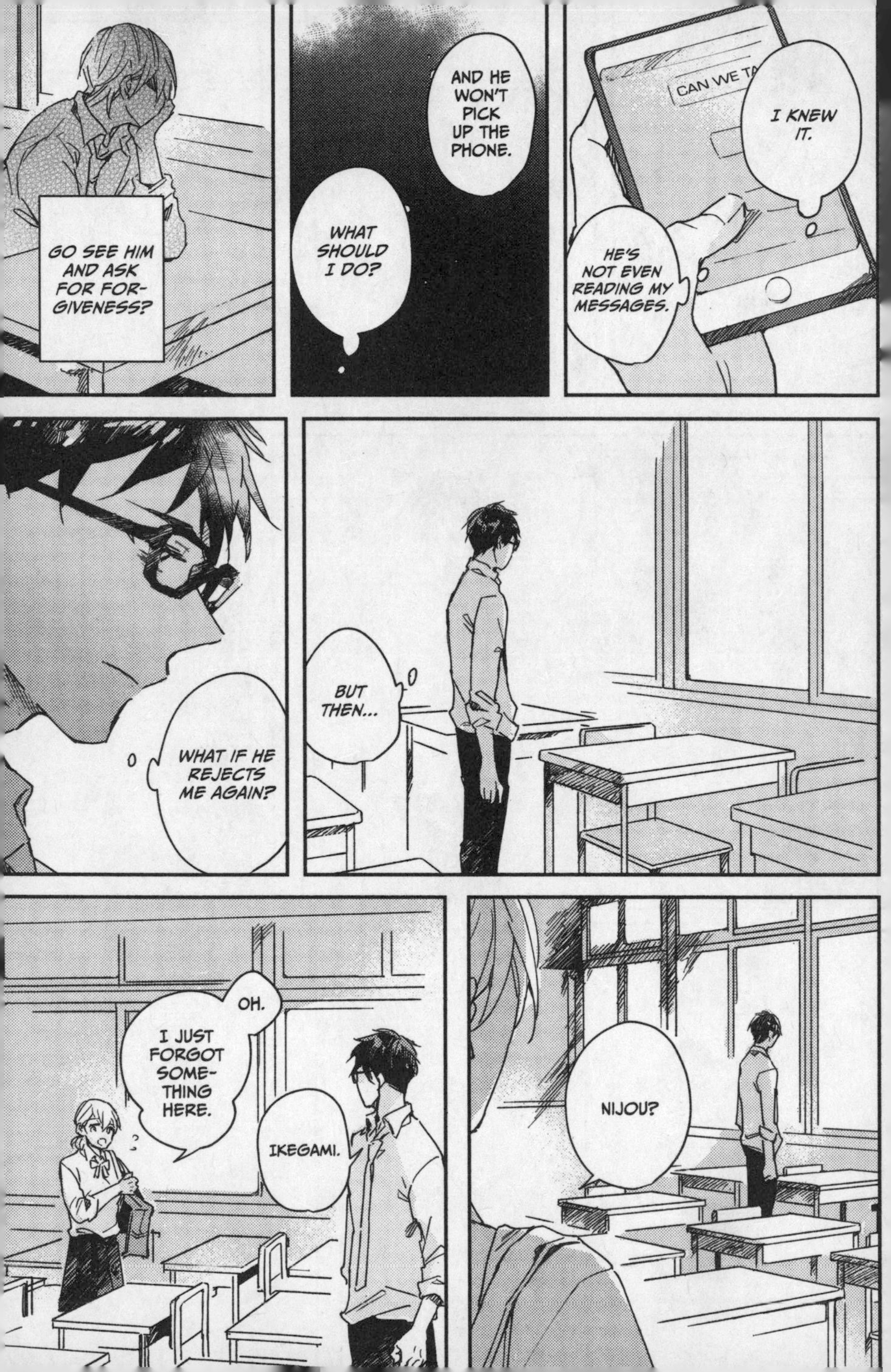
CAN WE TA
I KNEW IT.
HE'S NOT EVEN READING MY MESSAGES.
AND HE WON'T PICK UP THE PHONE.
WHAT SHOULD I DO?
GO SEE HIM AND ASK FOR FOR-GIVENESS?
BUT THEN...
WHAT IF HE REJECTS ME AGAIN?
NIJOU?
OH. I JUST FORGOT SOME-THING HERE.
IKEGAMI.

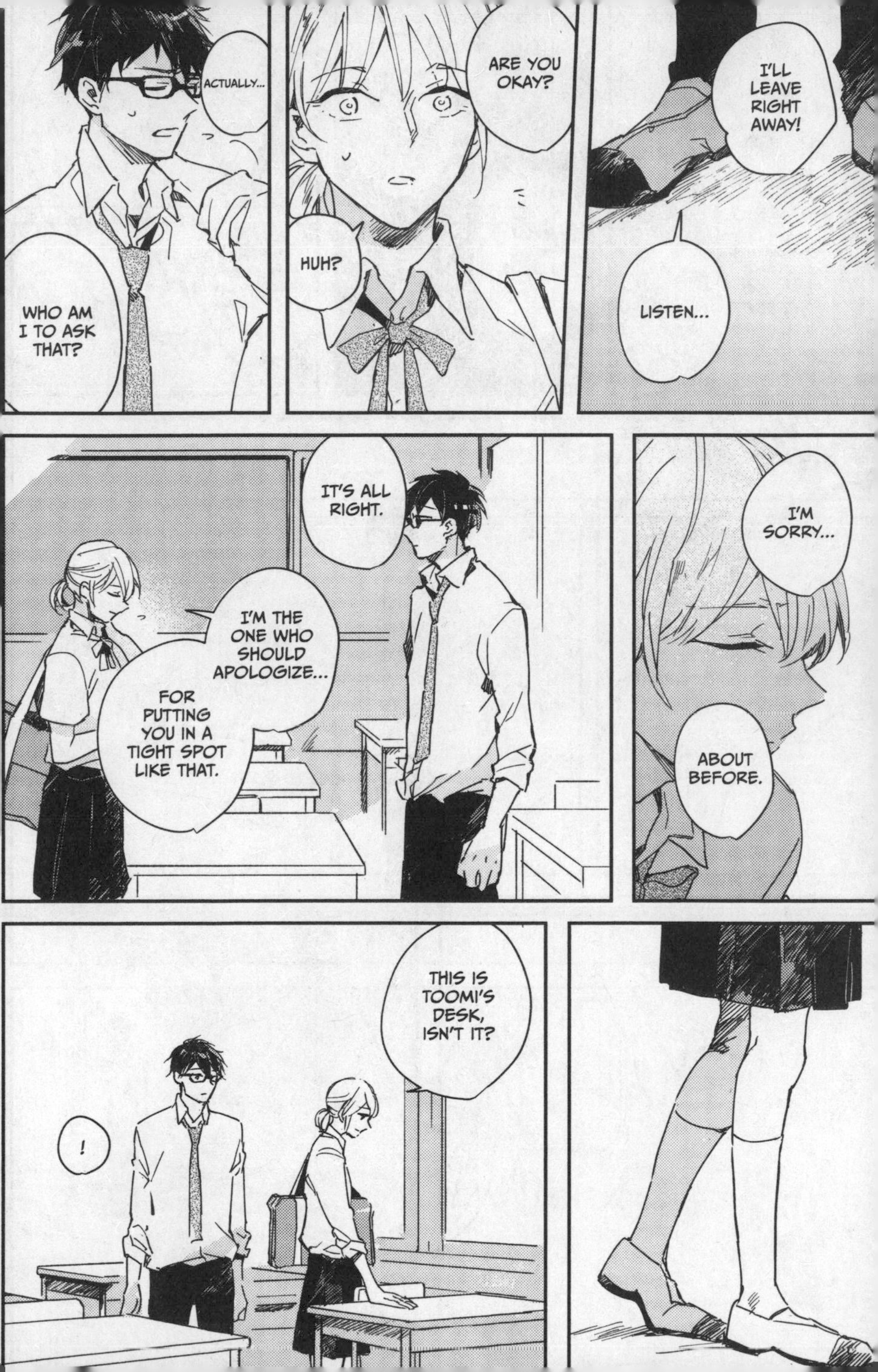
I'LL LEAVE RIGHT AWAY!
LISTEN...
ARE YOU OKAY?
HUH?
ACTUALLY...
WHO AM I TO ASK THAT?
I'M SORRY...
ABOUT BEFORE.
IT'S ALL RIGHT.
I'M THE ONE WHO SHOULD APOLOGIZE...
FOR PUTTING YOU IN A TIGHT SPOT LIKE THAT.
THIS IS TOOMI'S DESK, ISN'T IT?
!

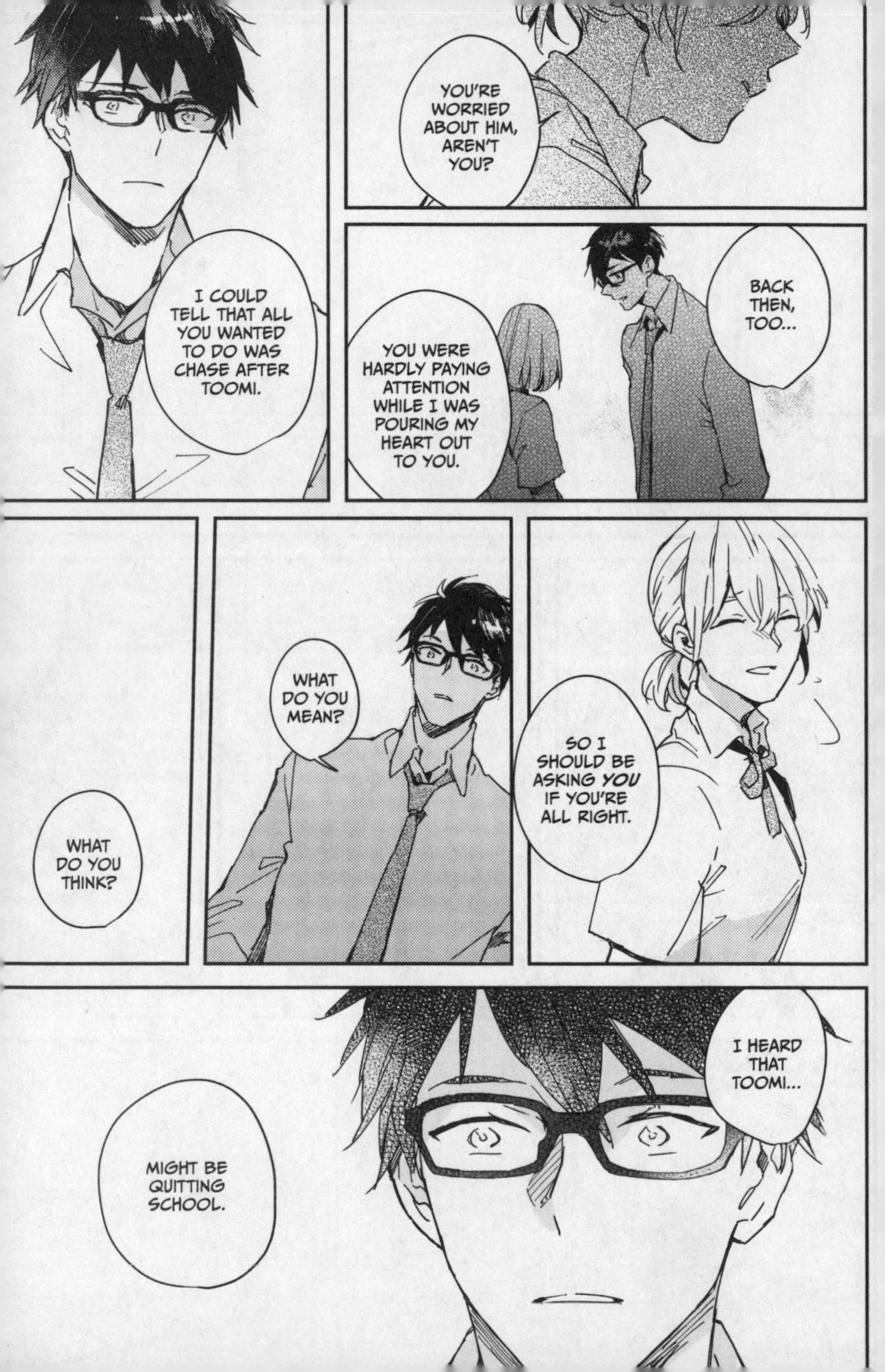
YOU'RE WORRIED ABOUT HIM, AREN'T YOU?
BACK THEN, TOO...
YOU WERE HARDLY PAYING ATTENTION WHILE I WAS POURING MY HEART OUT TO YOU.
I COULD TELL THAT ALL YOU WANTED TO DO WAS CHASE AFTER TOOMI.
SO I SHOULD BE ASKING *YOU* IF YOU'RE ALL RIGHT.
WHAT DO YOU MEAN?
WHAT DO YOU THINK?
I HEARD THAT TOOMI...
MIGHT BE QUITTING SCHOOL.

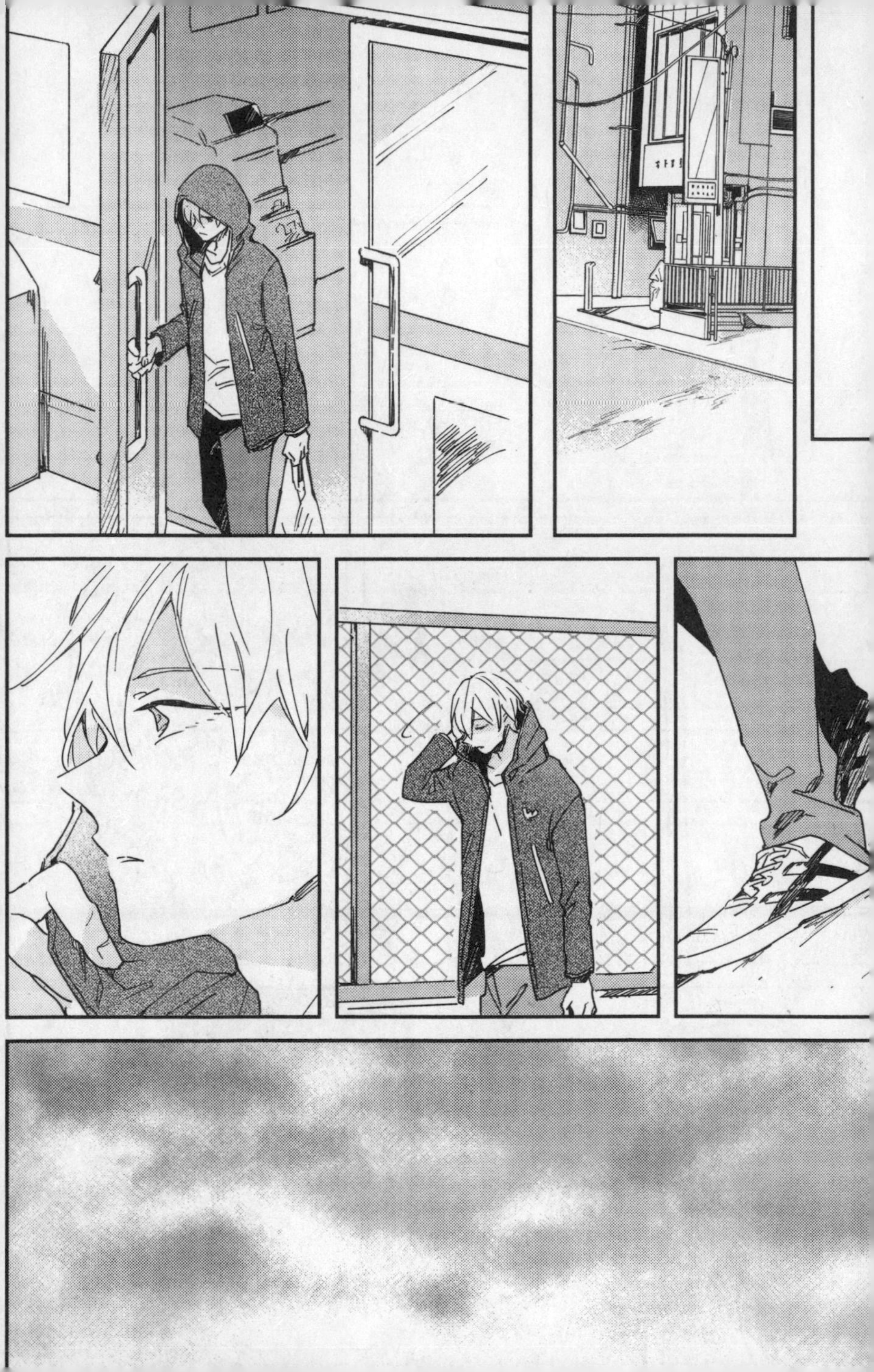

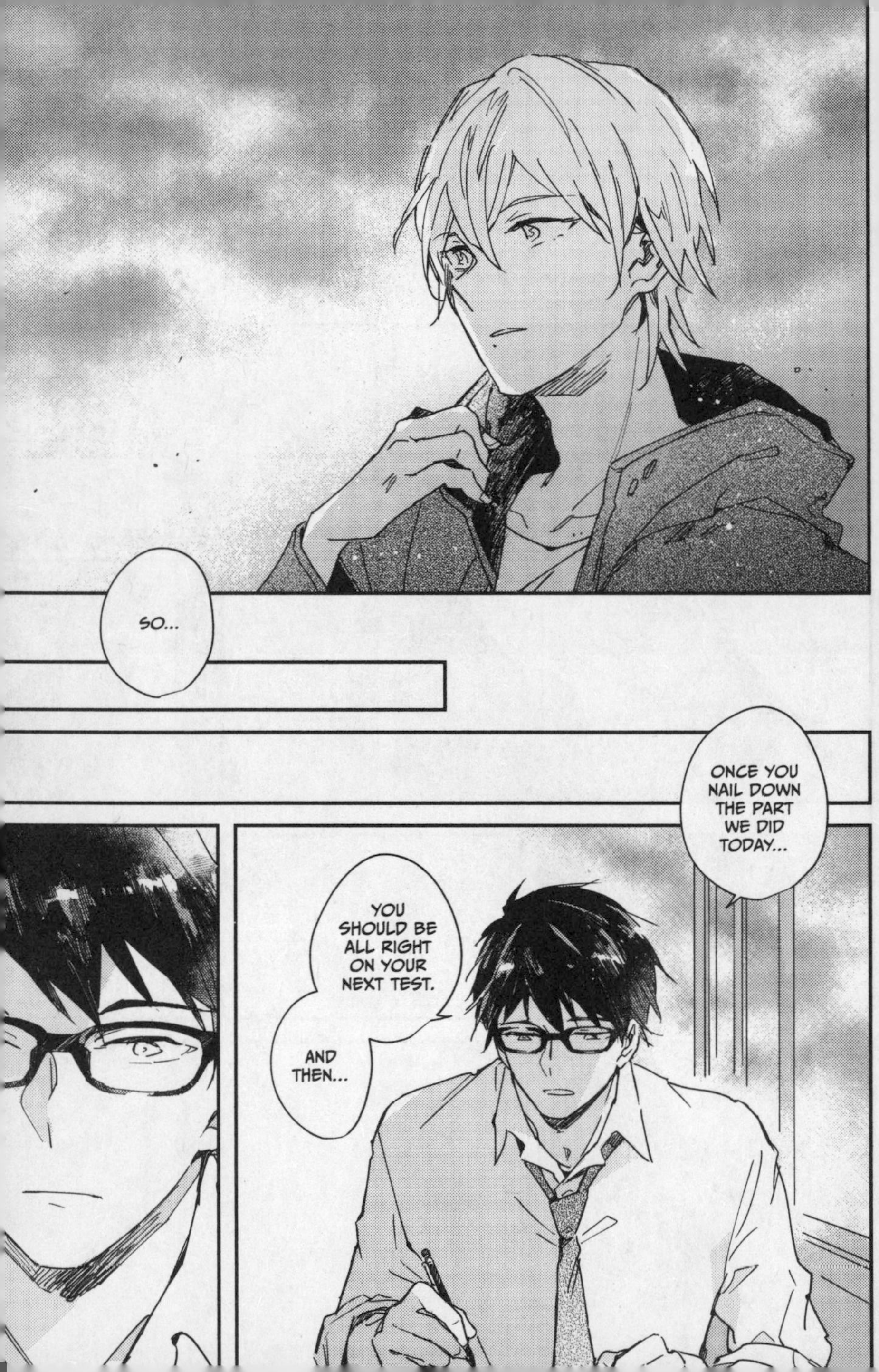
SO...
ONCE YOU NAIL DOWN THE PART WE DID TODAY...
YOU SHOULD BE ALL RIGHT ON YOUR NEXT TEST.
AND THEN...

WHAT IS IT?

TOOMI.

TCH.

WHY AM I REMEMBERING THAT?

I DON'T REGRET ANYTHING.

SCUFF

SO WHY...

AT LEAST, I SHOULDN'T.

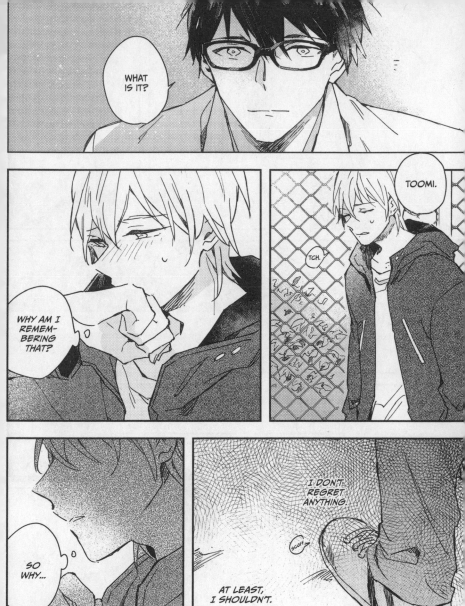
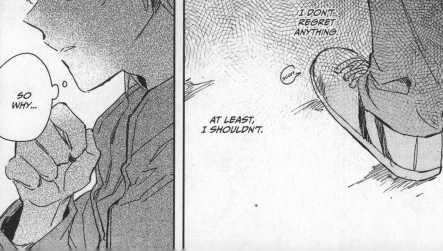

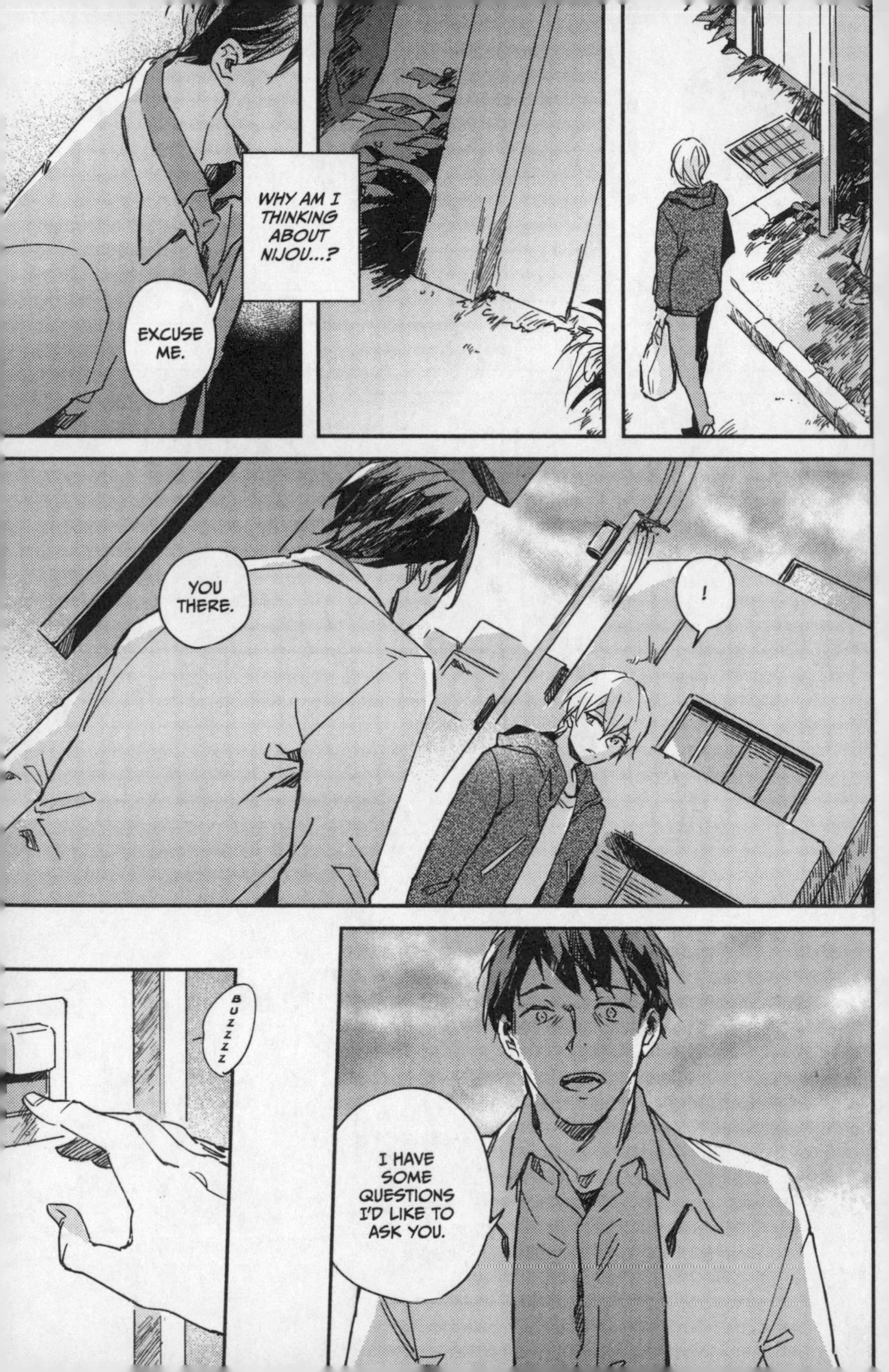
WHY AM I THINKING ABOUT NIJOU...?
EXCUSE ME.
!
YOU THERE.
I HAVE SOME QUESTIONS I'D LIKE TO ASK YOU.
BUZZZZ

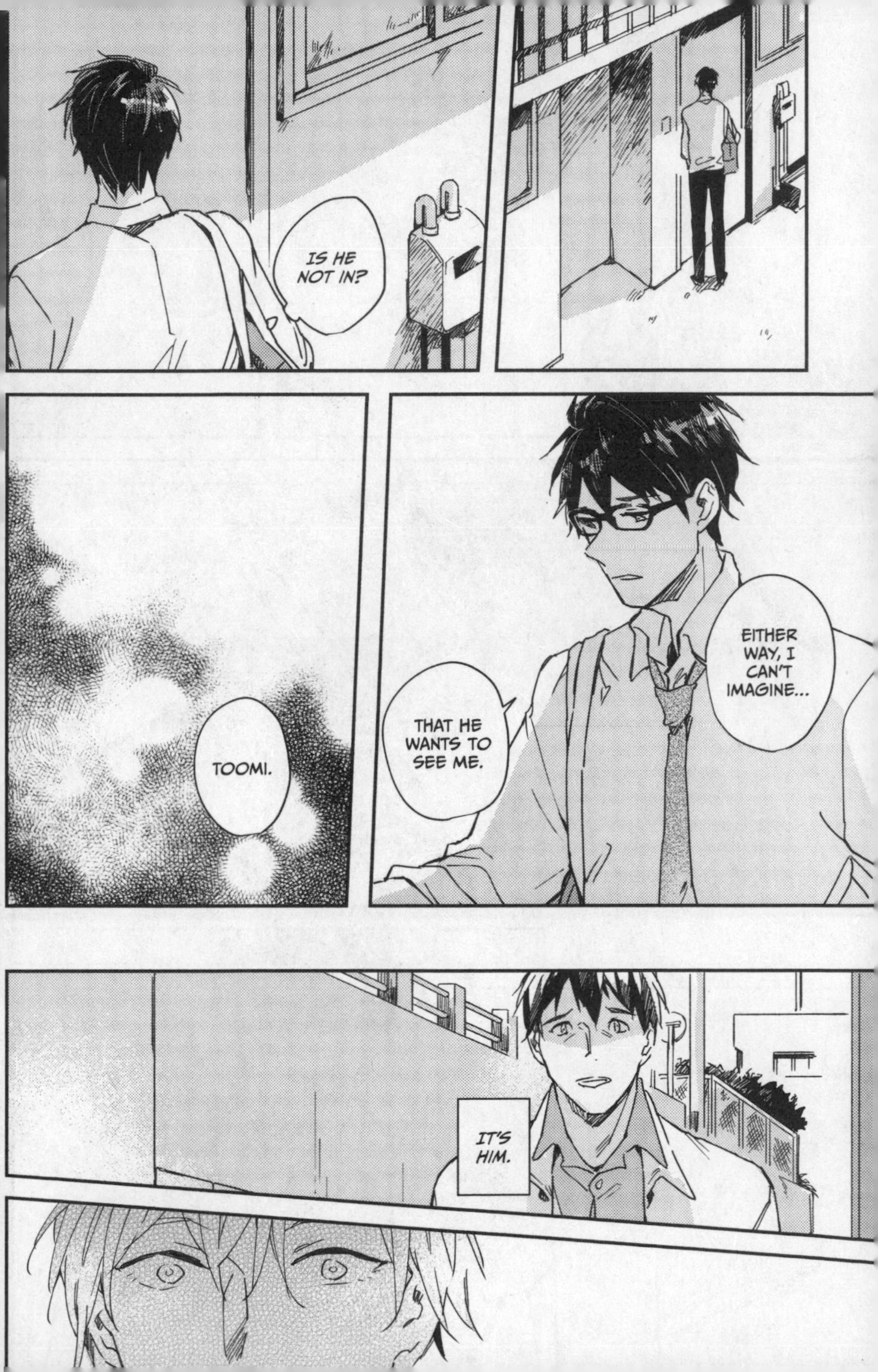
IS HE NOT IN?
EITHER WAY, I CAN'T IMAGINE...
THAT HE WANTS TO SEE ME.
TOOMI.
IT'S HIM.

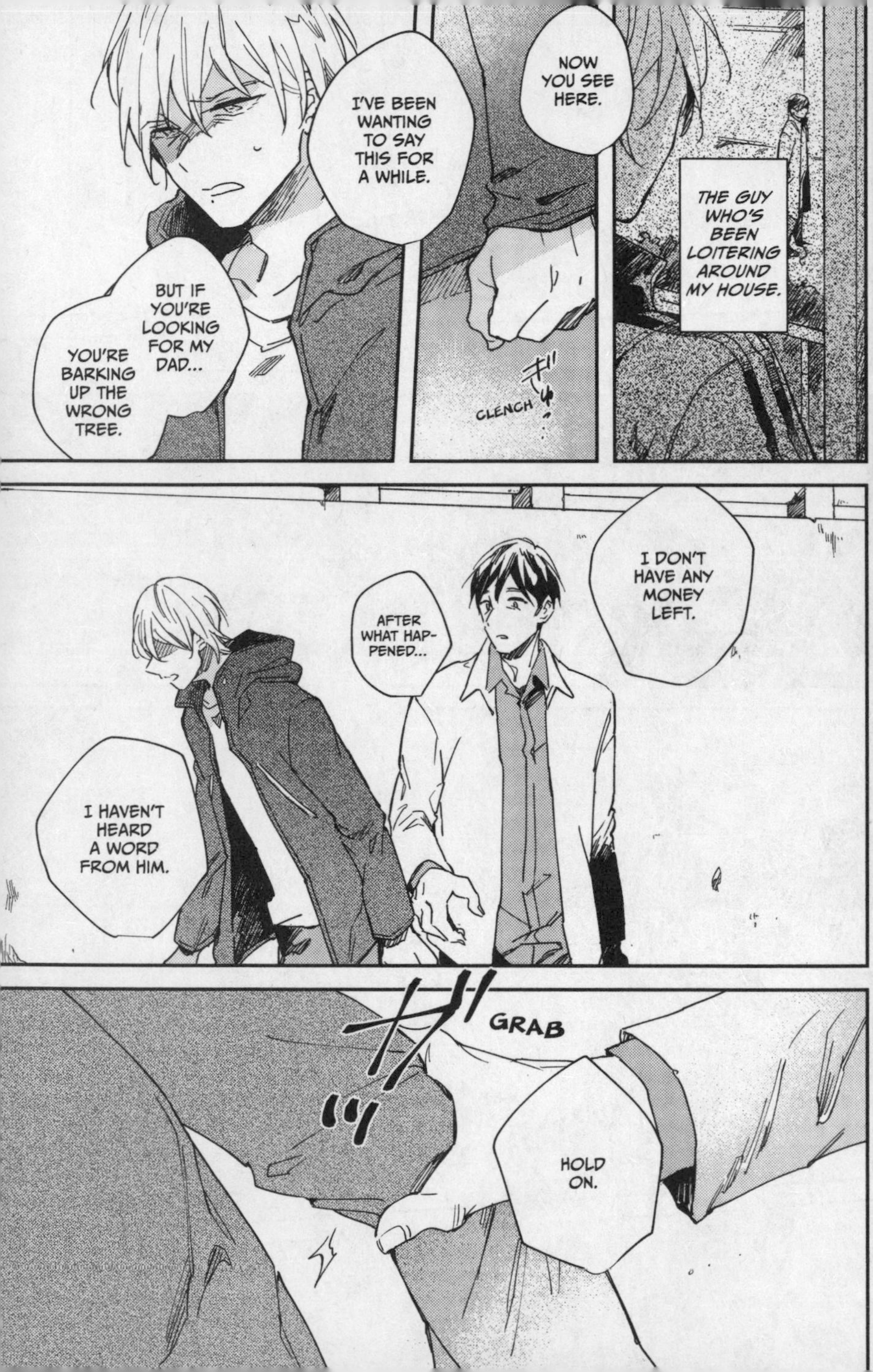
NOW YOU SEE HERE.
THE GUY WHO'S BEEN LOITERING AROUND MY HOUSE.
I'VE BEEN WANTING TO SAY THIS FOR A WHILE.
CLENCH
BUT IF YOU'RE LOOKING FOR MY DAD...
YOU'RE BARKING UP THE WRONG TREE.
I DON'T HAVE ANY MONEY LEFT.
AFTER WHAT HAP-PENED...
I HAVEN'T HEARD A WORD FROM HIM.
GRAB
HOLD ON.

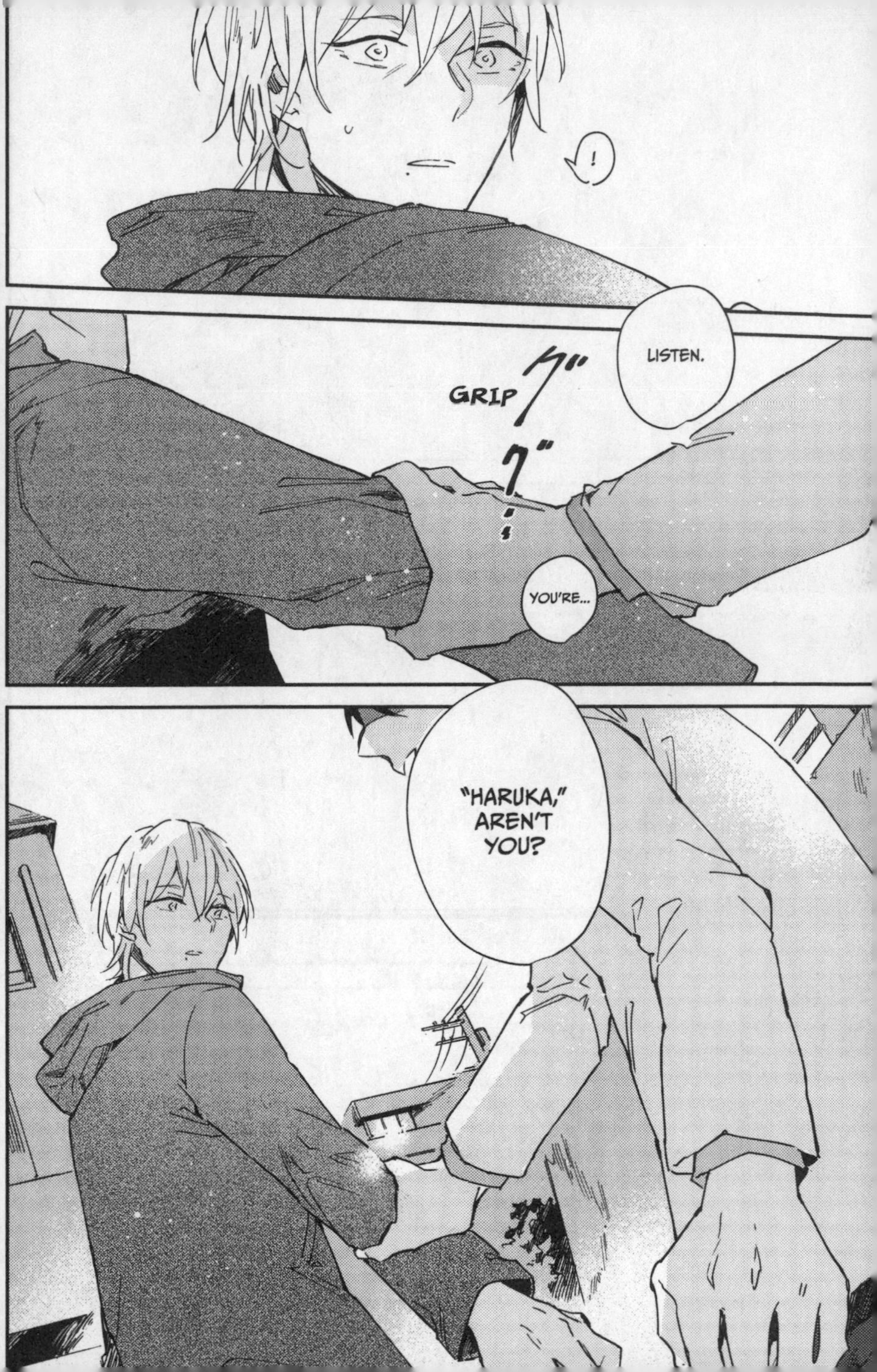
!
LISTEN.
GRIP
YOU'RE...
"HARUKA," AREN'T YOU?

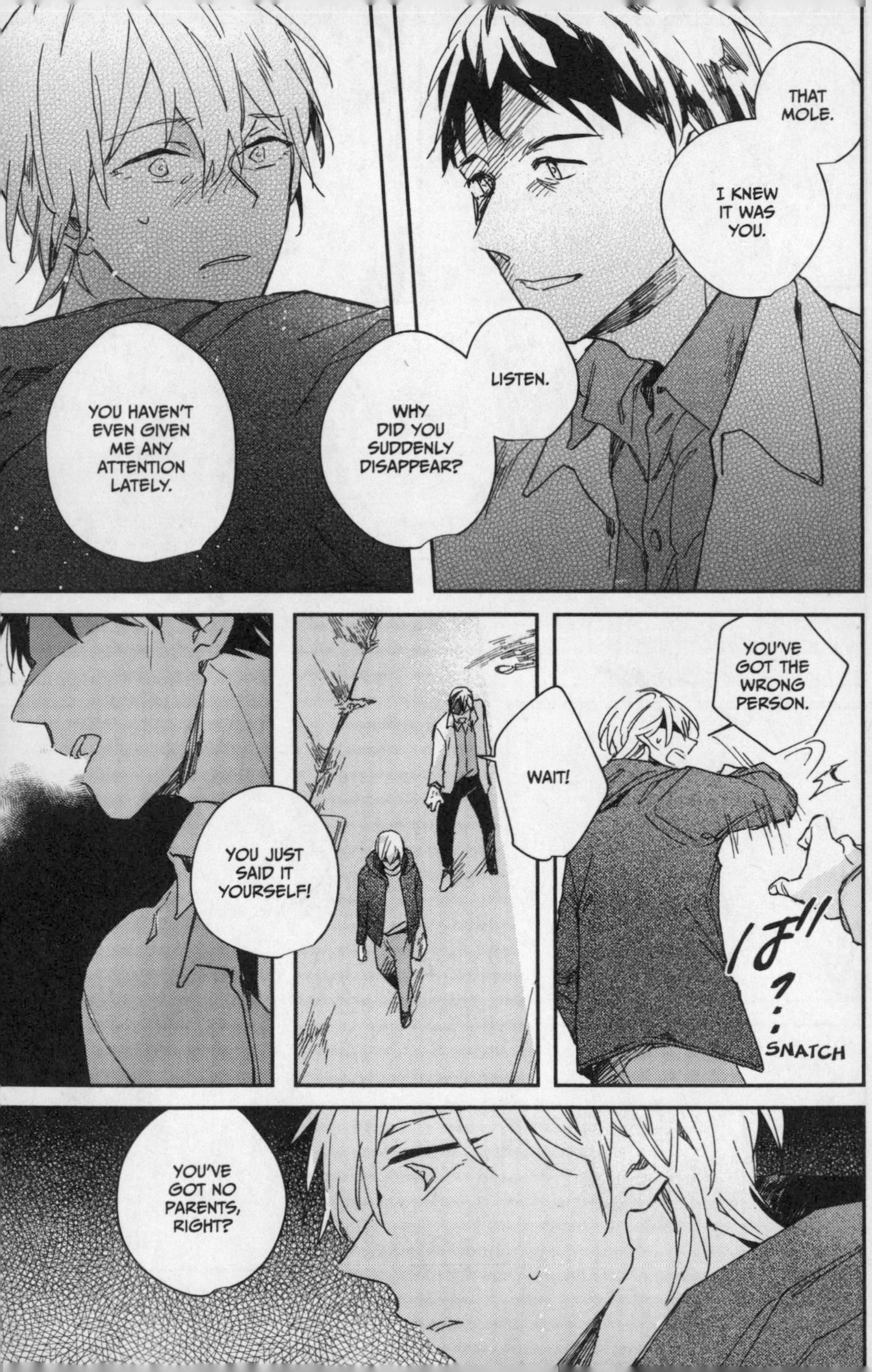
THAT MOLE.
I KNEW IT WAS YOU.
LISTEN.
WHY DID YOU SUDDENLY DISAPPEAR?
YOU HAVEN'T EVEN GIVEN ME ANY ATTENTION LATELY.
YOU'VE GOT THE WRONG PERSON.
SNATCH
WAIT!
YOU JUST SAID IT YOURSELF!
YOU'VE GOT NO PARENTS, RIGHT?

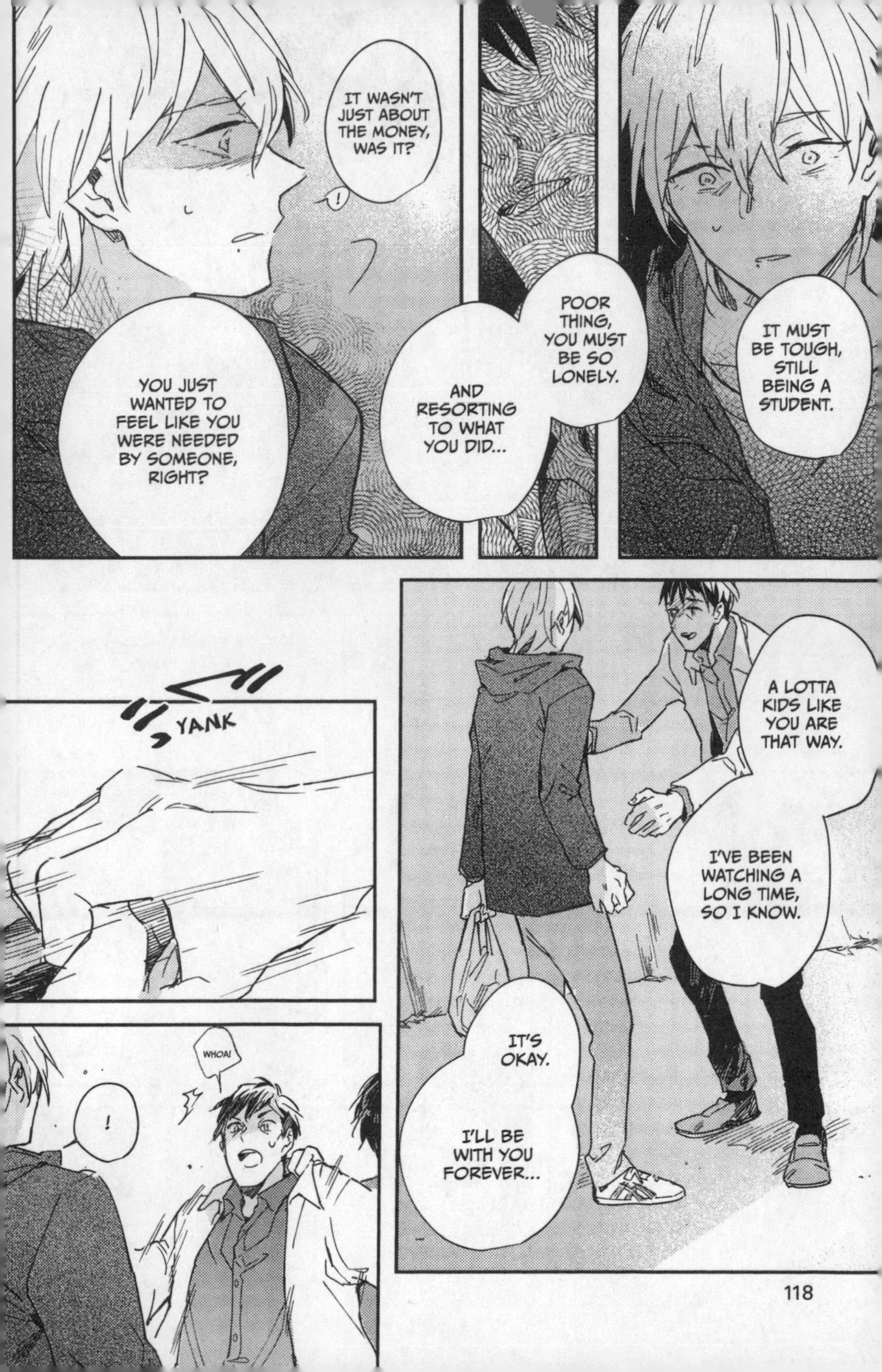
IT MUST BE TOUGH, STILL BEING A STUDENT.
POOR THING, YOU MUST BE SO LONELY.
AND RESORTING TO WHAT YOU DID...
IT WASN'T JUST ABOUT THE MONEY, WAS IT?
!
YOU JUST WANTED TO FEEL LIKE YOU WERE NEEDED BY SOMEONE, RIGHT?
A LOTTA KIDS LIKE YOU ARE THAT WAY.
I'VE BEEN WATCHING A LONG TIME, SO I KNOW.
IT'S OKAY.
I'LL BE WITH YOU FOREVER...
YANK
!
WHOA!

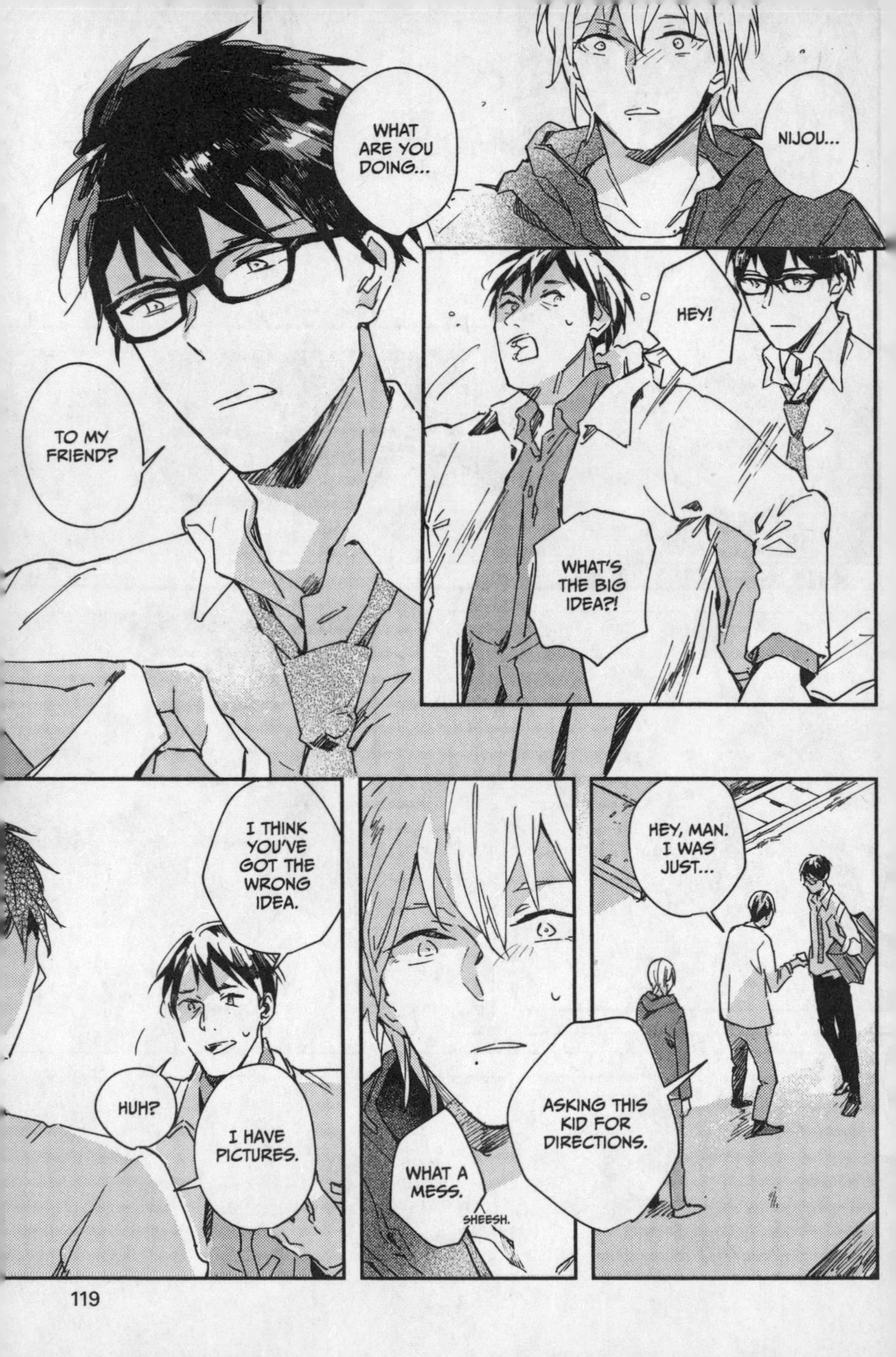
NIJOU...
WHAT ARE YOU DOING...
TO MY FRIEND?
HEY!
WHAT'S THE BIG IDEA?!
HEY, MAN. I WAS JUST...
ASKING THIS KID FOR DIRECTIONS.
WHAT A MESS.
SHEESH.
I THINK YOU'VE GOT THE WRONG IDEA.
HUH?
I HAVE PICTURES.

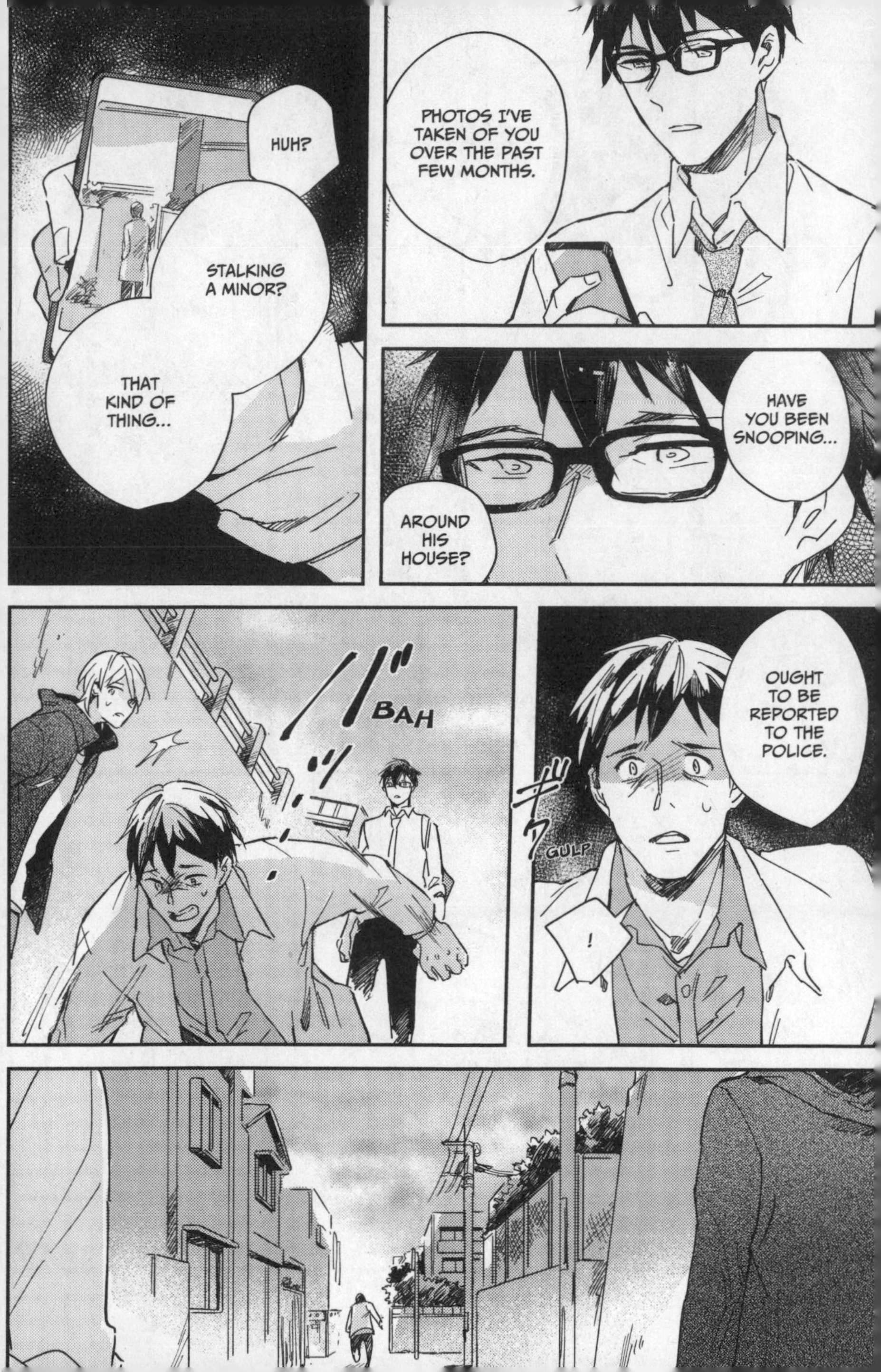
PHOTOS I'VE TAKEN OF YOU OVER THE PAST FEW MONTHS.
HAVE YOU BEEN SNOOPING...
AROUND HIS HOUSE?
HUH?
STALKING A MINOR?
THAT KIND OF THING...
OUGHT TO BE REPORTED TO THE POLICE.
GULP
!
BAH

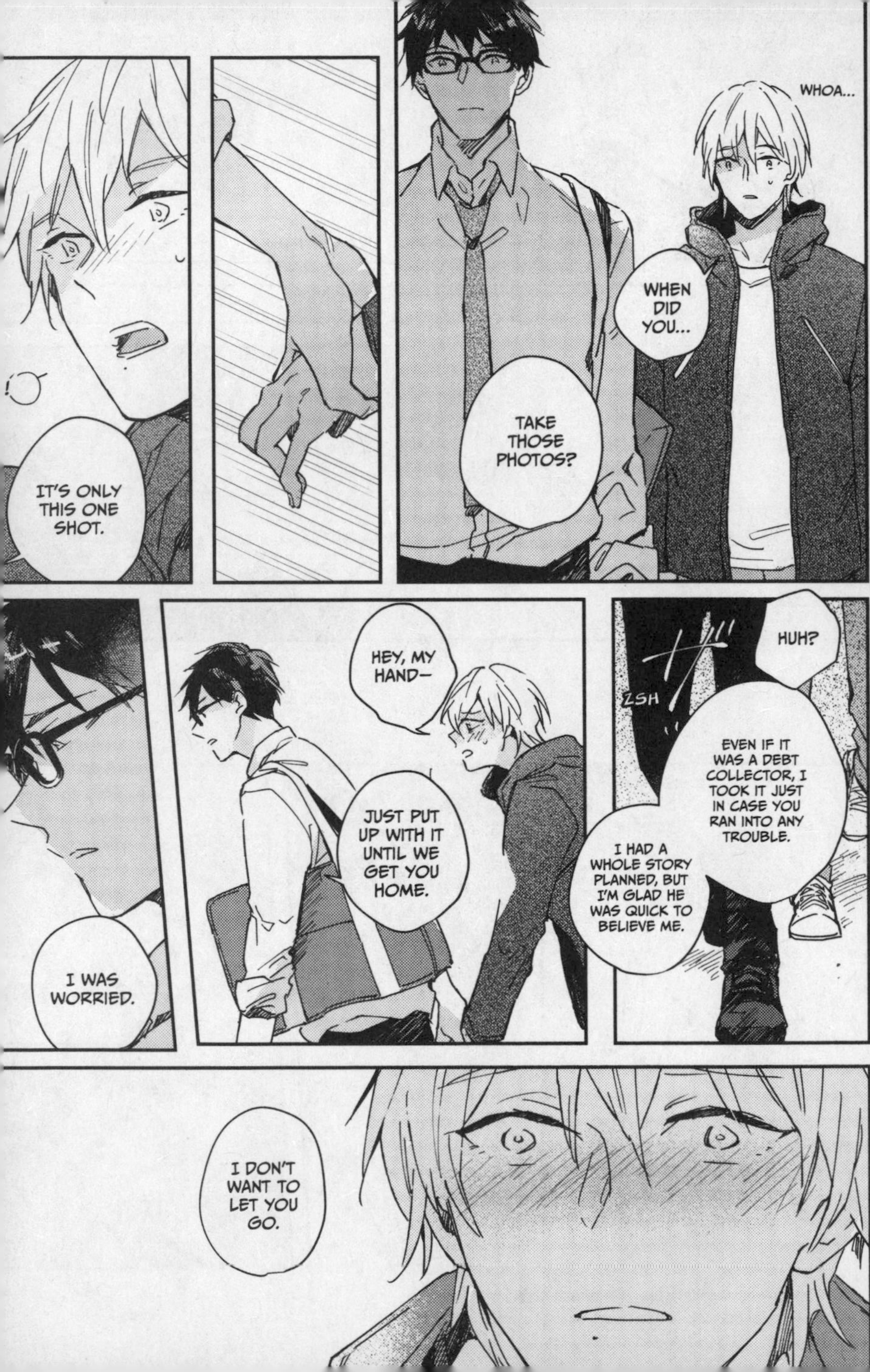
WHOA...
WHEN DID YOU...
TAKE THOSE PHOTOS?
!
IT'S ONLY THIS ONE SHOT.
ZSH
HUH?
EVEN IF IT WAS A DEBT COLLECTOR, I TOOK IT JUST IN CASE YOU RAN INTO ANY TROUBLE.
I HAD A WHOLE STORY PLANNED, BUT I'M GLAD HE WAS QUICK TO BELIEVE ME.
HEY, MY HAND—
JUST PUT UP WITH IT UNTIL WE GET YOU HOME.
I WAS WORRIED.
I DON'T WANT TO LET YOU GO.

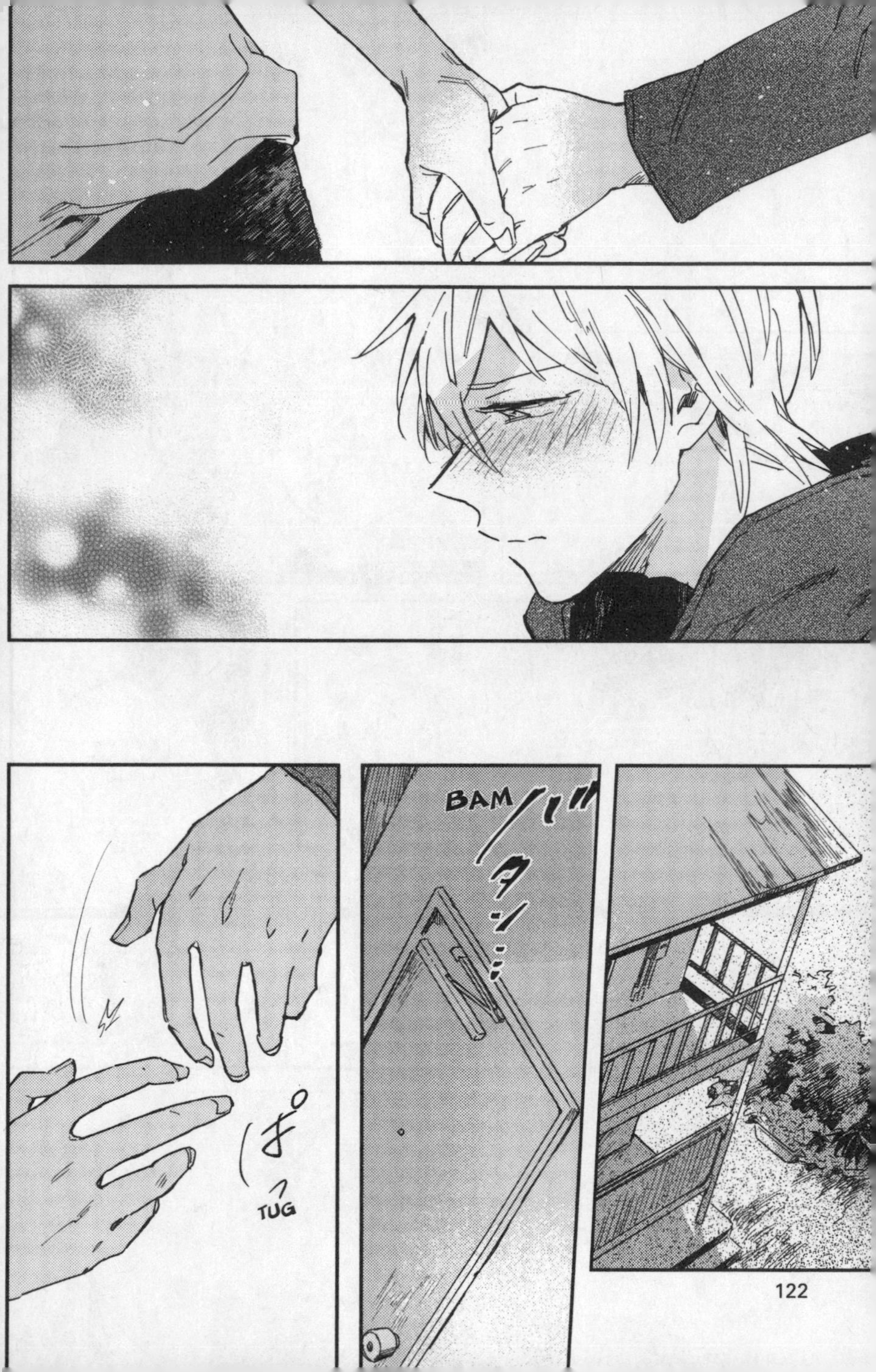
BAM
ぱっ
TUG

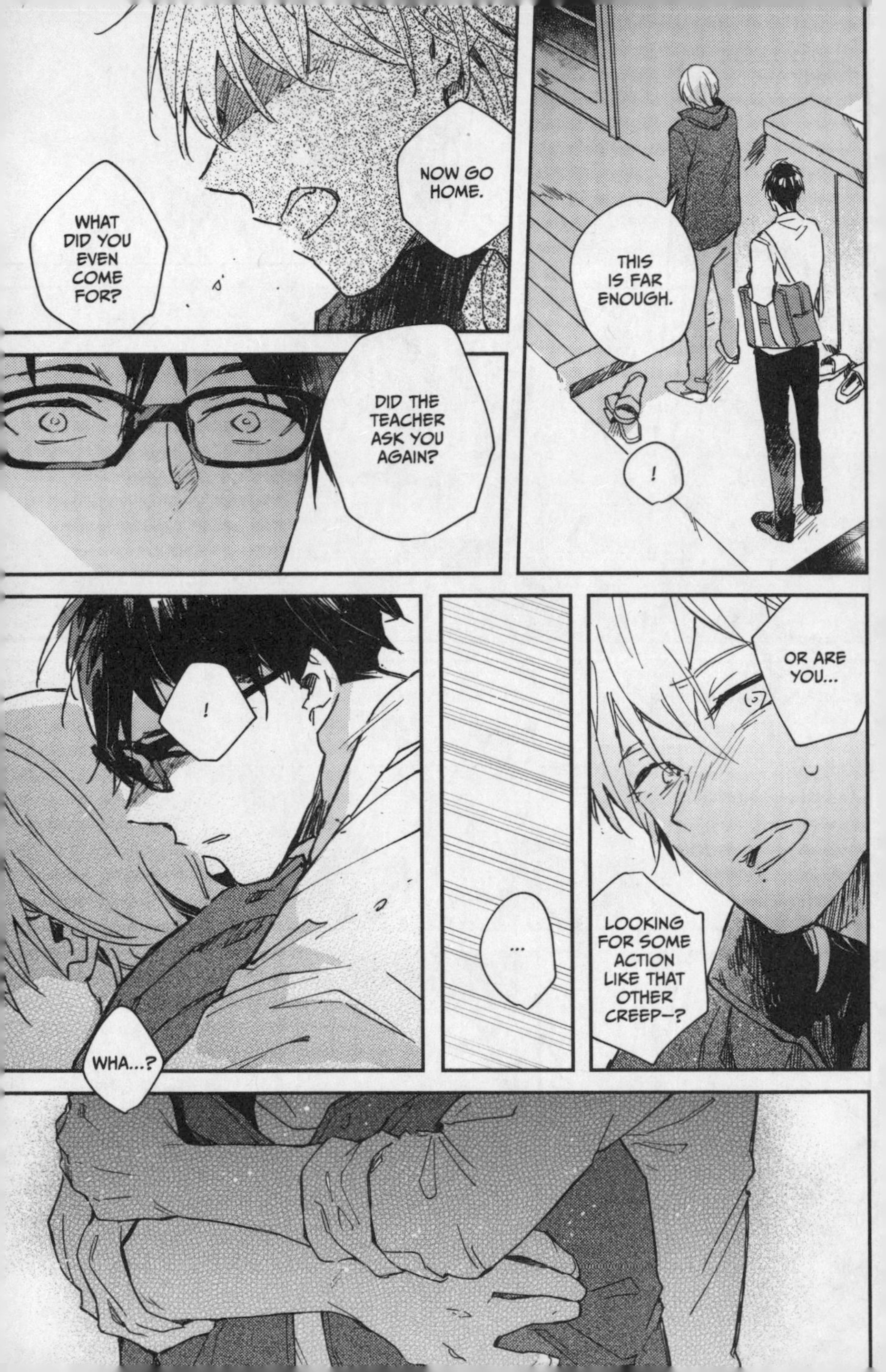
THIS IS FAR ENOUGH.
!
NOW GO HOME.
WHAT DID YOU EVEN COME FOR?
DID THE TEACHER ASK YOU AGAIN?
OR ARE YOU...
LOOKING FOR SOME ACTION LIKE THAT OTHER CREEP–?
...
!
WHA...?

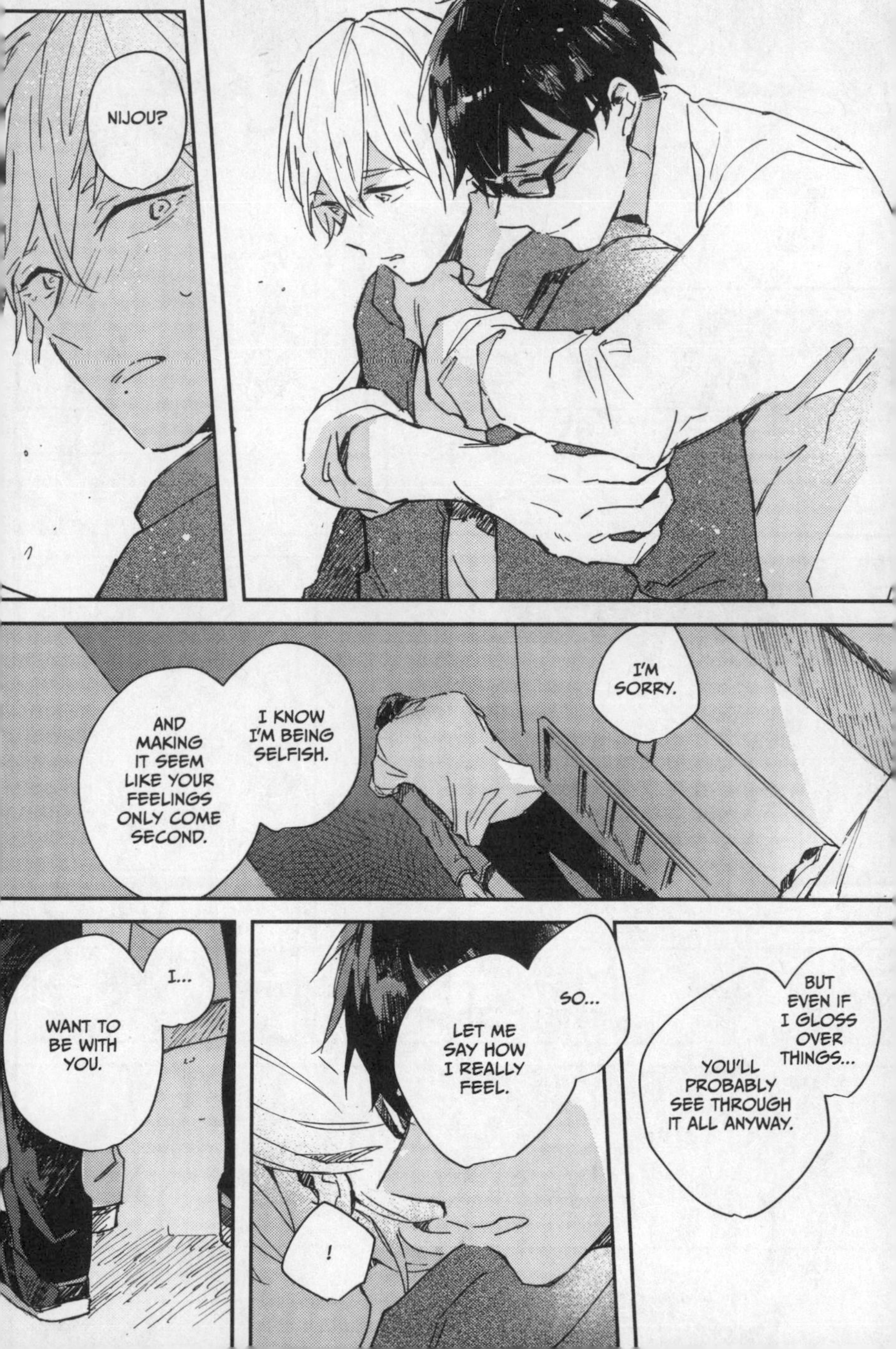
NIJOU?
I'M SORRY.
I KNOW I'M BEING SELFISH.
AND MAKING IT SEEM LIKE YOUR FEELINGS ONLY COME SECOND.
BUT EVEN IF I GLOSS OVER THINGS...
YOU'LL PROBABLY SEE THROUGH IT ALL ANYWAY.
SO...
LET ME SAY HOW I REALLY FEEL.
!
I...
WANT TO BE WITH YOU.

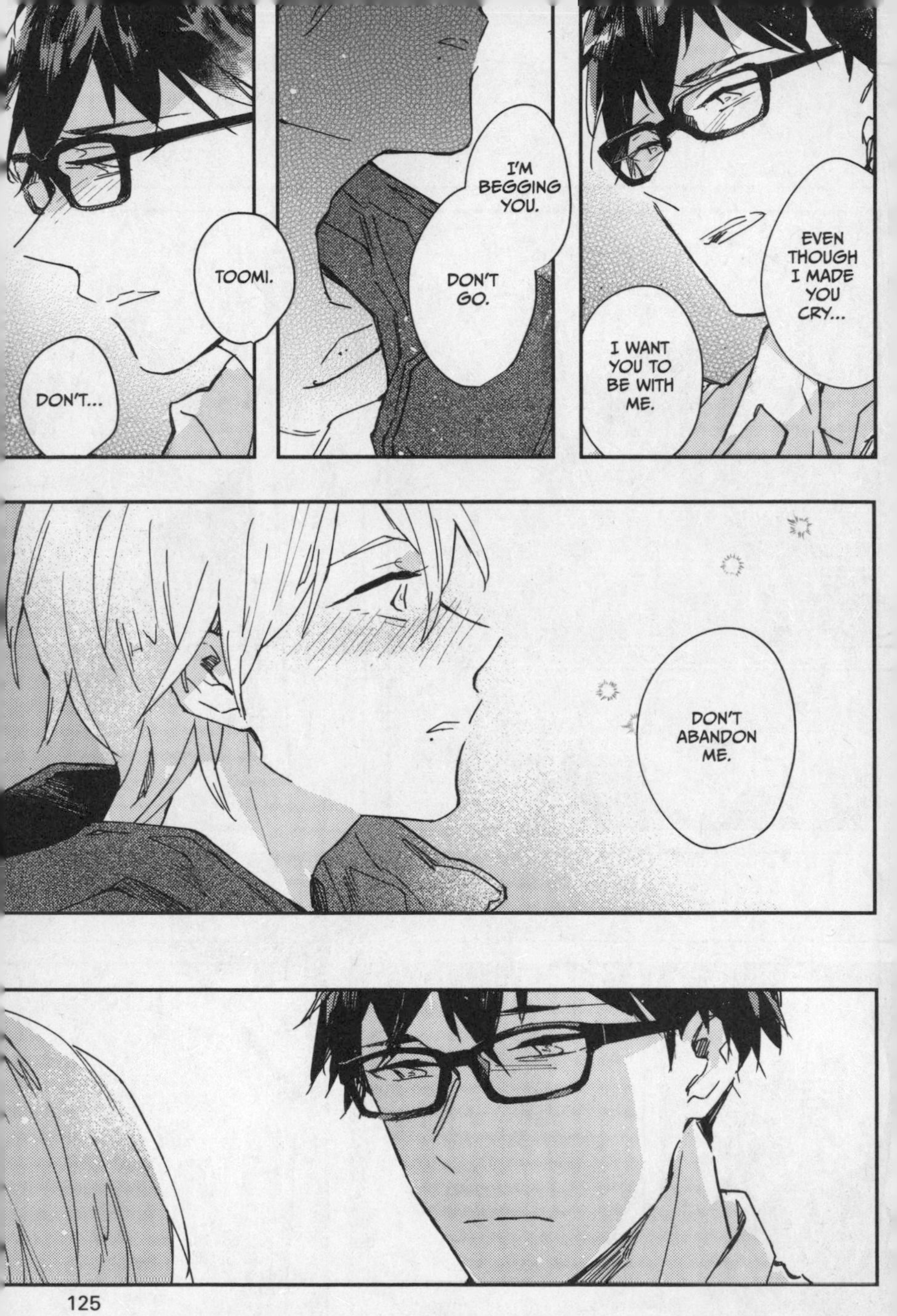
EVEN THOUGH I MADE YOU CRY...
I WANT YOU TO BE WITH ME.
I'M BEGGING YOU.
DON'T GO.
TOOMI.
DON'T...
DON'T ABANDON ME.

WHAT THE HELL?

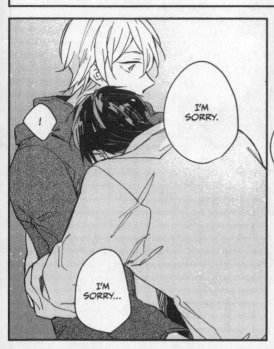

I'M SORRY.

I'M SORRY...

TOOMI.

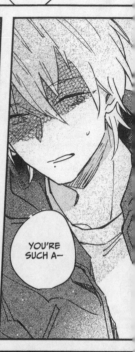

YOU'RE SUCH A—

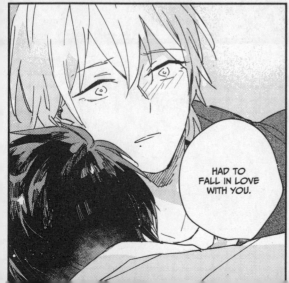

HAD TO FALL IN LOVE WITH YOU.

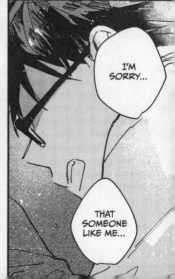

I'M SORRY...

THAT SOMEONE LIKE ME...

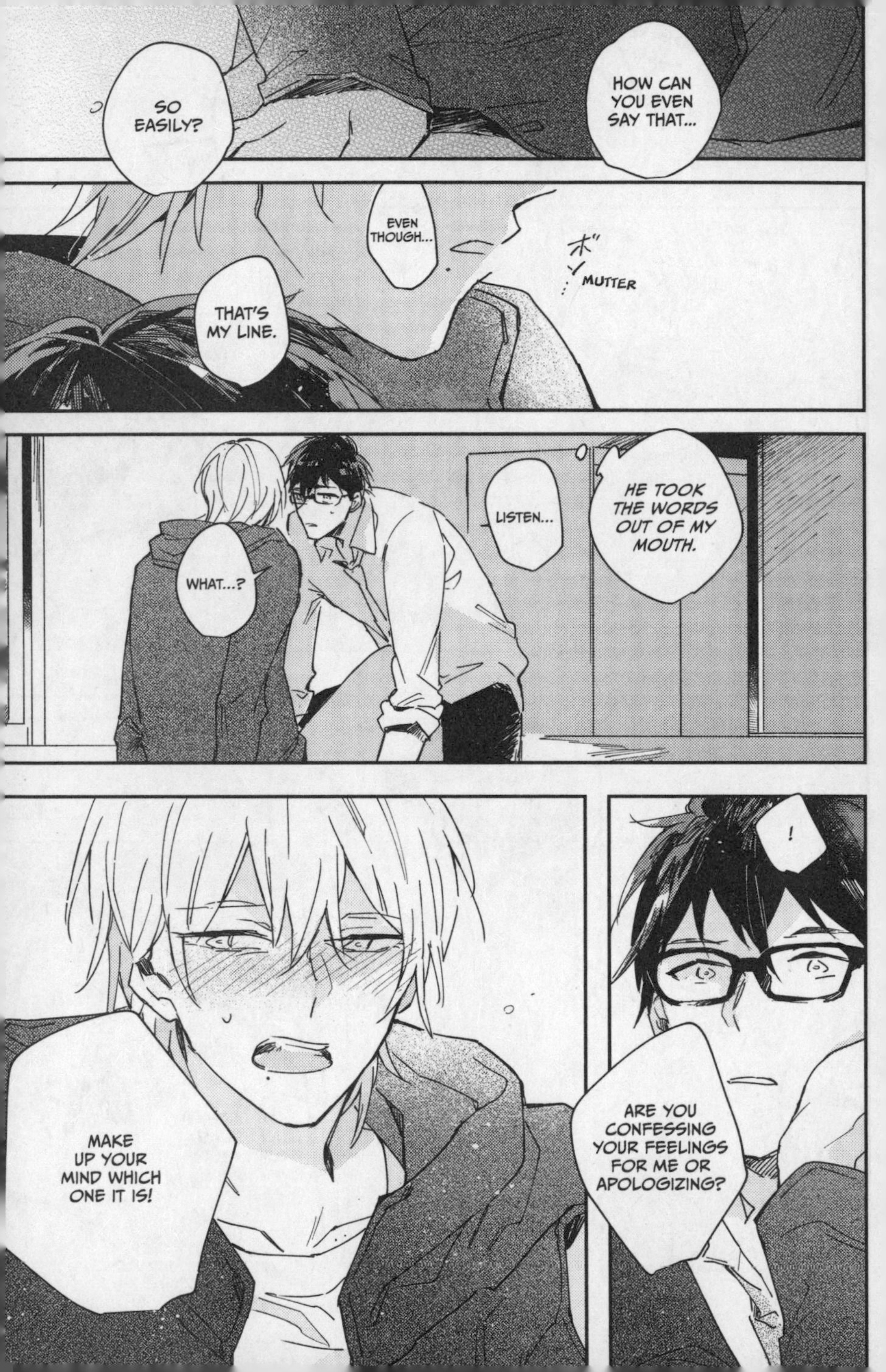
HOW CAN YOU EVEN SAY THAT...
SO EASILY?
MUTTER
EVEN THOUGH...
THAT'S MY LINE.
HE TOOK THE WORDS OUT OF MY MOUTH.
LISTEN...
WHAT...?
!
ARE YOU CONFESSING YOUR FEELINGS FOR ME OR APOLOGIZING?
MAKE UP YOUR MIND WHICH ONE IT IS!

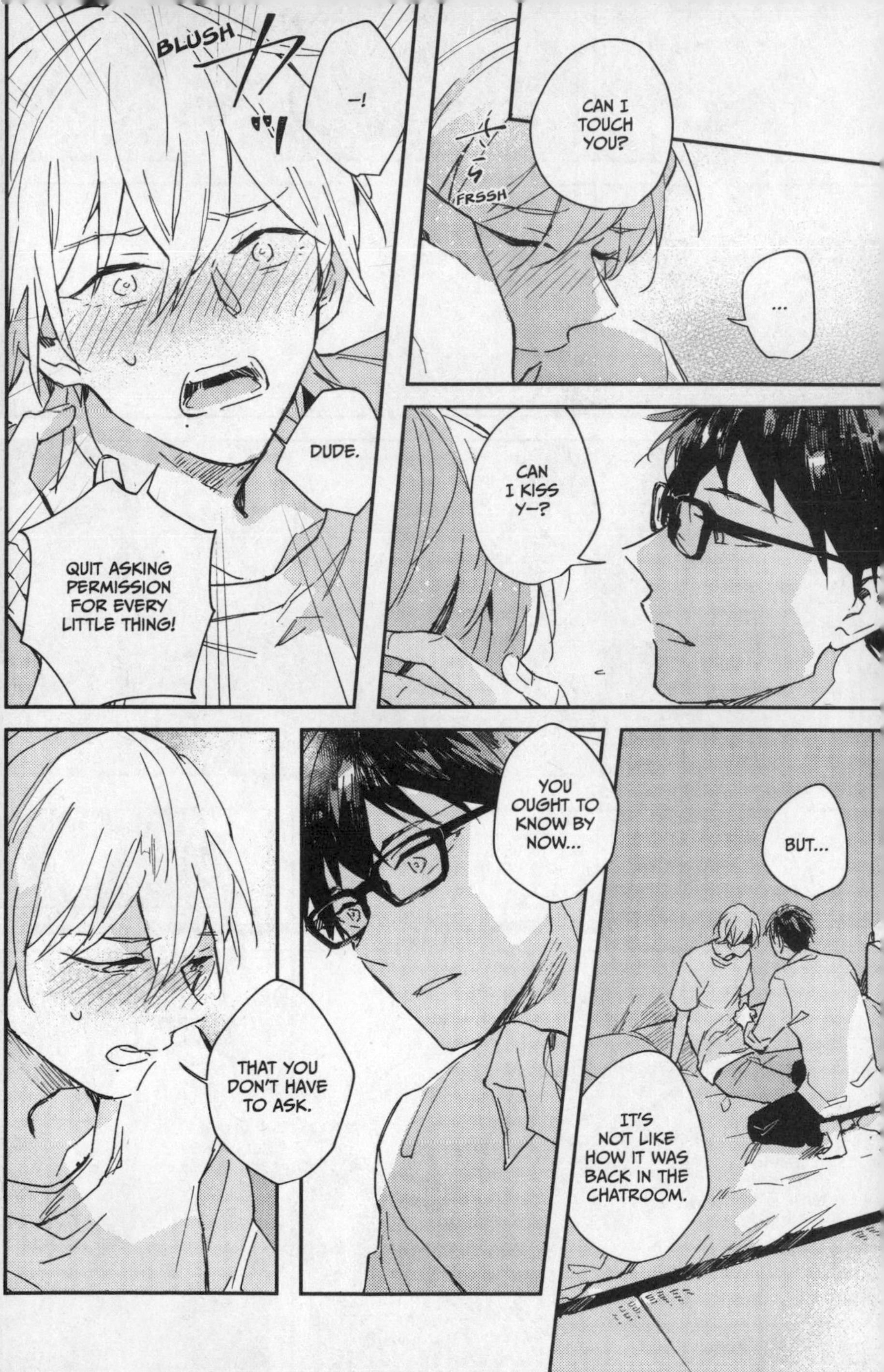
CAN I TOUCH YOU?
FRSSH
...
CAN I KISS Y—?
BLUSH
—!
DUDE.
QUIT ASKING PERMISSION FOR EVERY LITTLE THING!
BUT...
IT'S NOT LIKE HOW IT WAS BACK IN THE CHATROOM.
YOU OUGHT TO KNOW BY NOW...
THAT YOU DON'T HAVE TO ASK.

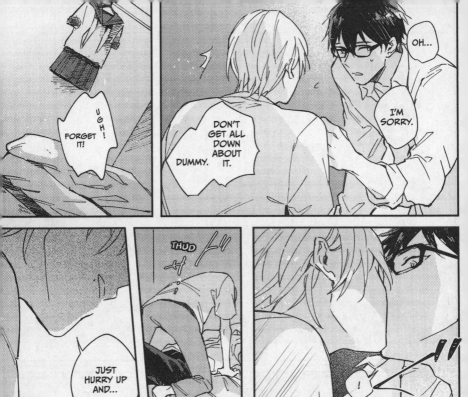

UGH!

FORGET IT!

DON'T GET ALL DOWN ABOUT IT. DUMMY.

OH...

I'M SORRY.

JUST HURRY UP AND...

THUD

YANK

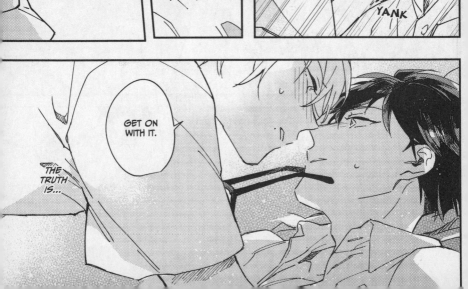

GET ON WITH IT.

THE TRUTH IS...

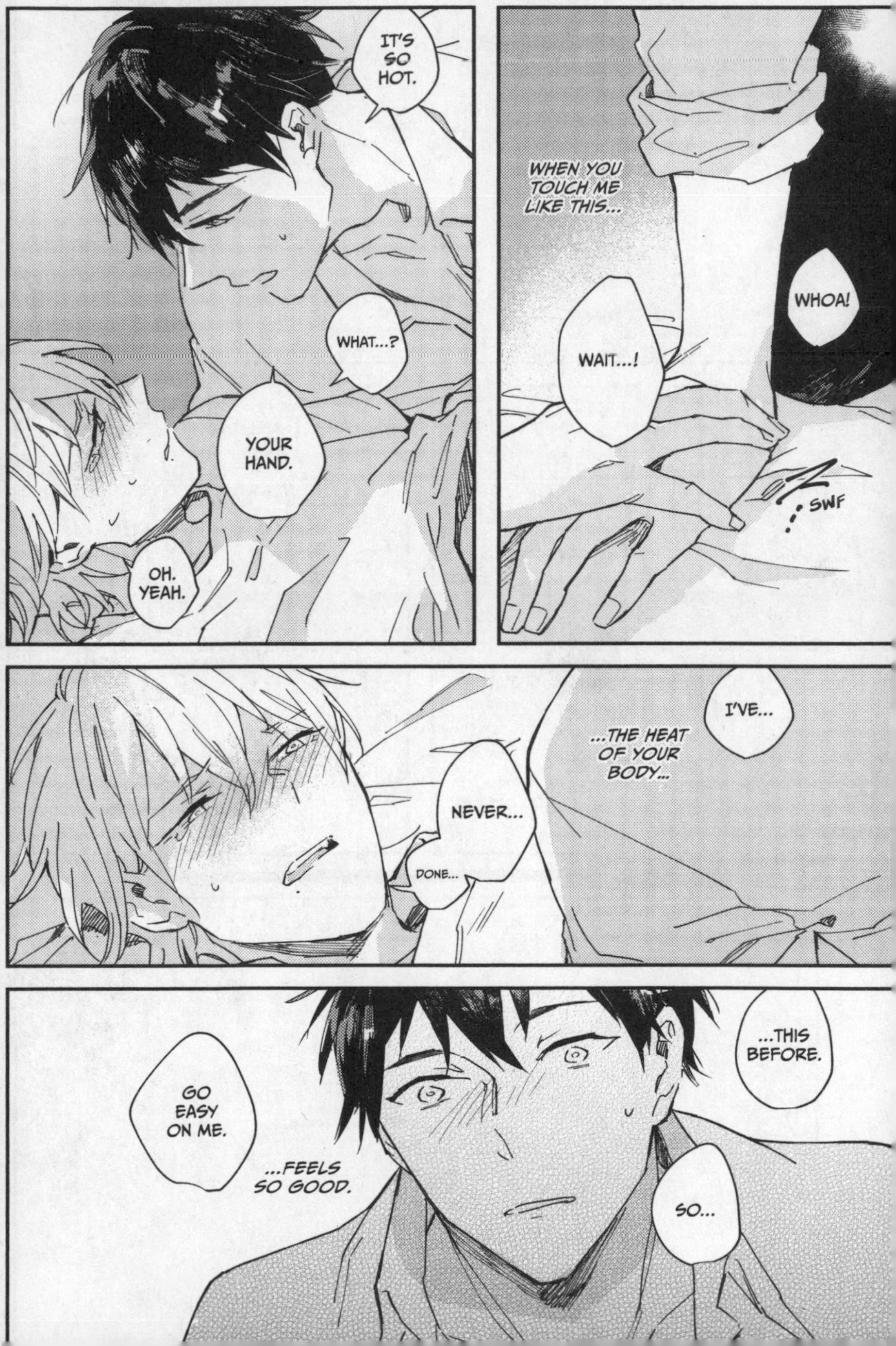
WHEN YOU TOUCH ME LIKE THIS...
WHOA!
WAIT...!
SWF
IT'S SO HOT.
WHAT...?
YOUR HAND.
OH. YEAH.
I'VE...
...THE HEAT OF YOUR BODY...
NEVER...
DONE...
...THIS BEFORE.
SO...
GO EASY ON ME.
...FEELS SO GOOD.

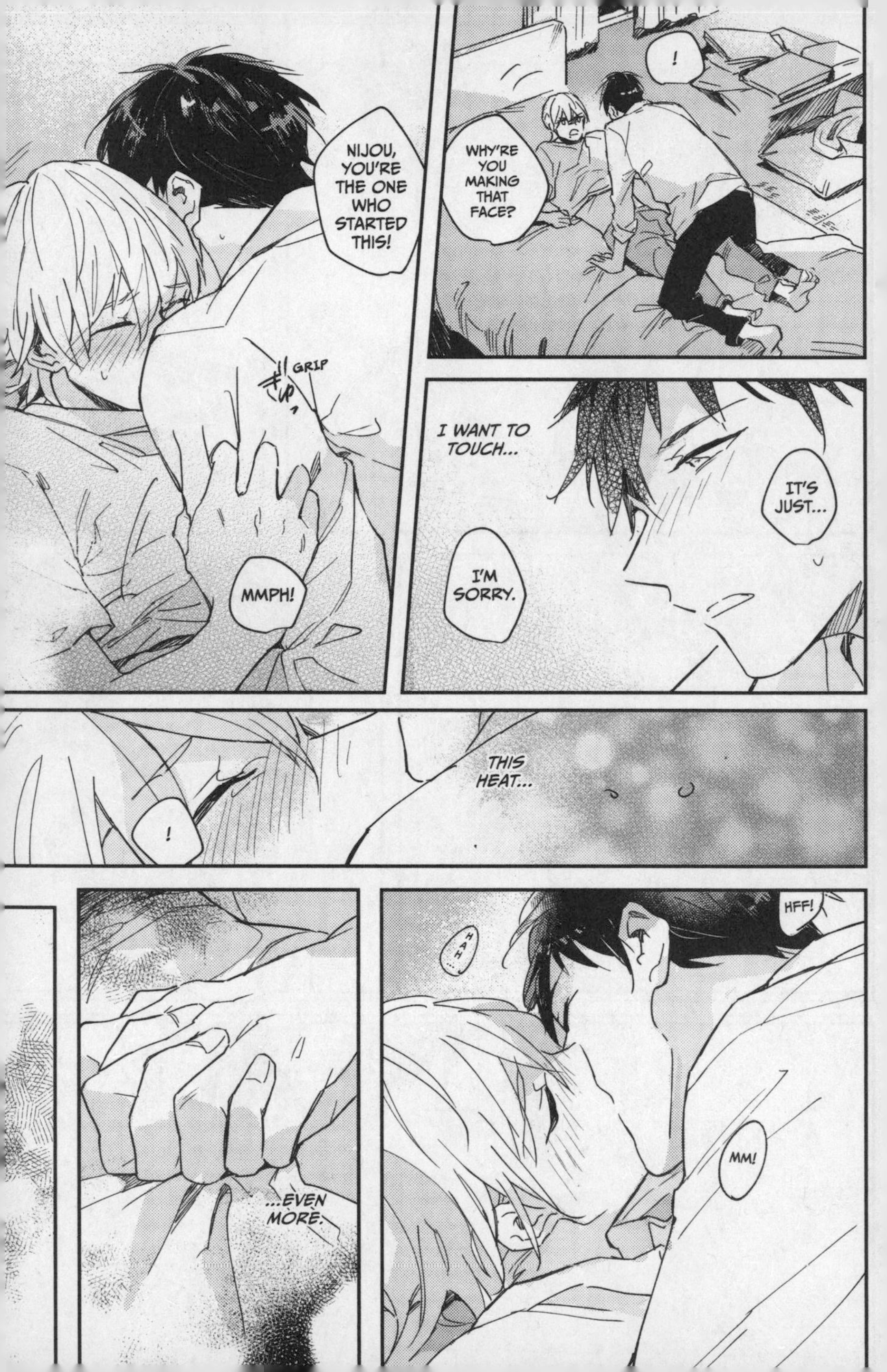
!
WHY'RE YOU MAKING THAT FACE?
IT'S JUST...
I'M SORRY.
I WANT TO TOUCH...
NIJOU, YOU'RE THE ONE WHO STARTED THIS!
ぎゅ
GRIP
MMPH!
THIS HEAT...
!
HFF!
HAH...
MM!
...EVEN MORE.

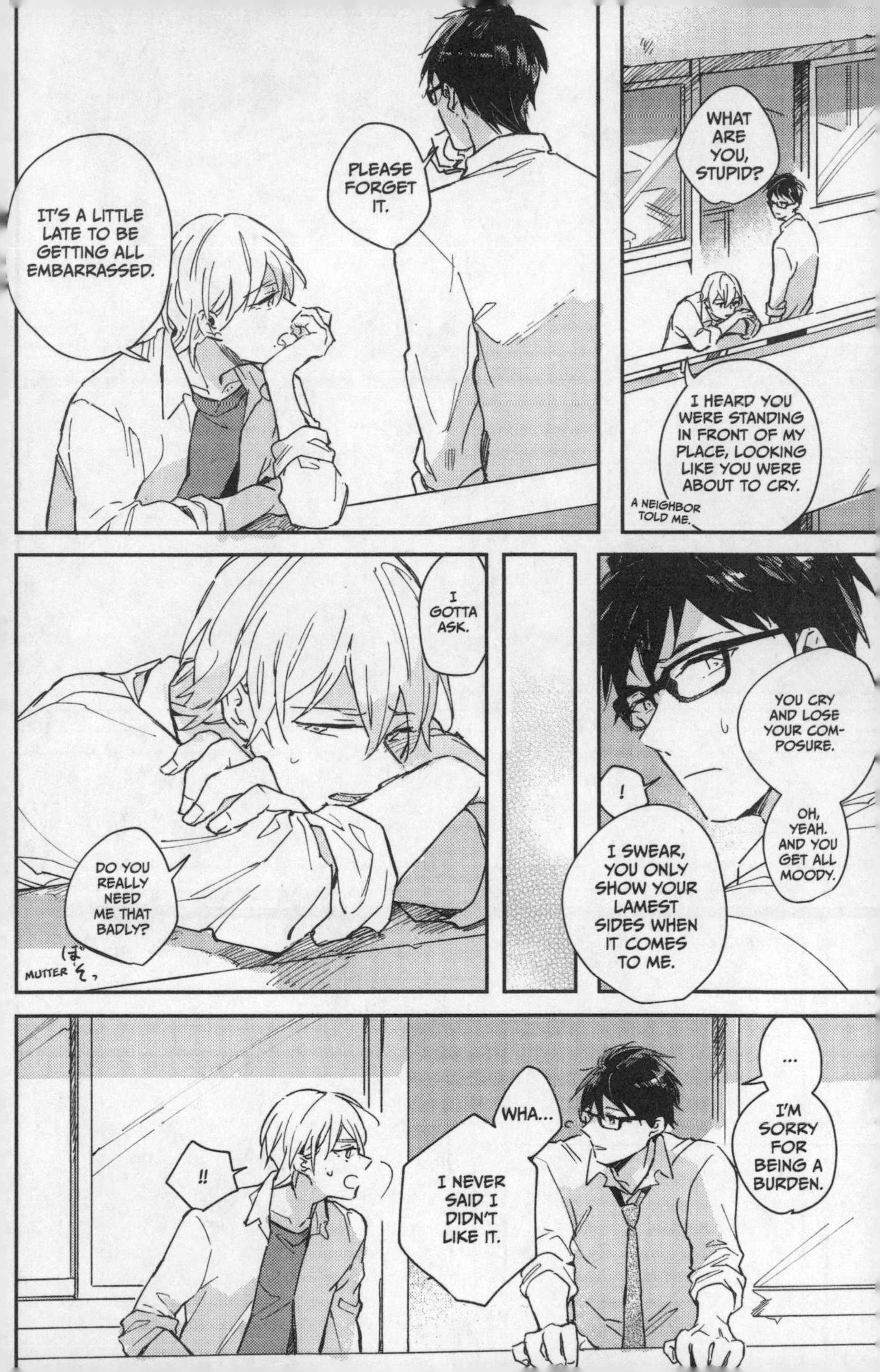
WHAT ARE YOU, STUPID?
I HEARD YOU WERE STANDING IN FRONT OF MY PLACE, LOOKING LIKE YOU WERE ABOUT TO CRY.
A NEIGHBOR TOLD ME.
PLEASE FORGET IT.
IT'S A LITTLE LATE TO BE GETTING ALL EMBARRASSED.
YOU CRY AND LOSE YOUR COMPOSURE.
OH, YEAH. AND YOU GET ALL MOODY.
!
I SWEAR, YOU ONLY SHOW YOUR LAMEST SIDES WHEN IT COMES TO ME.
I GOTTA ASK.
DO YOU REALLY NEED ME THAT BADLY?
MUTTER
...
I'M SORRY FOR BEING A BURDEN.
WHA...
I NEVER SAID I DIDN'T LIKE IT.
!!

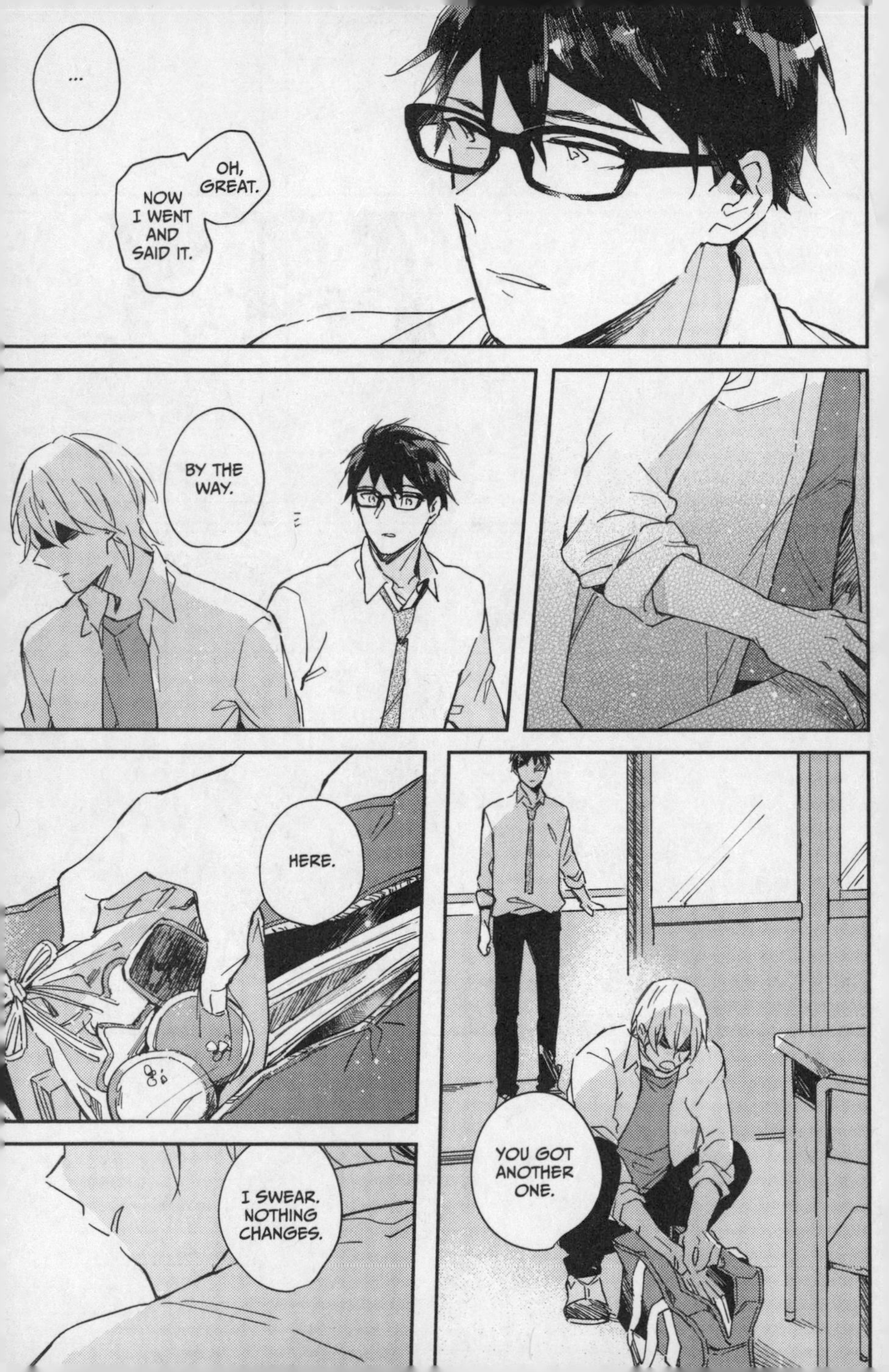
...
OH, GREAT. NOW I WENT AND SAID IT.
BY THE WAY.
YOU GOT ANOTHER ONE.
HERE.
I SWEAR. NOTHING CHANGES.

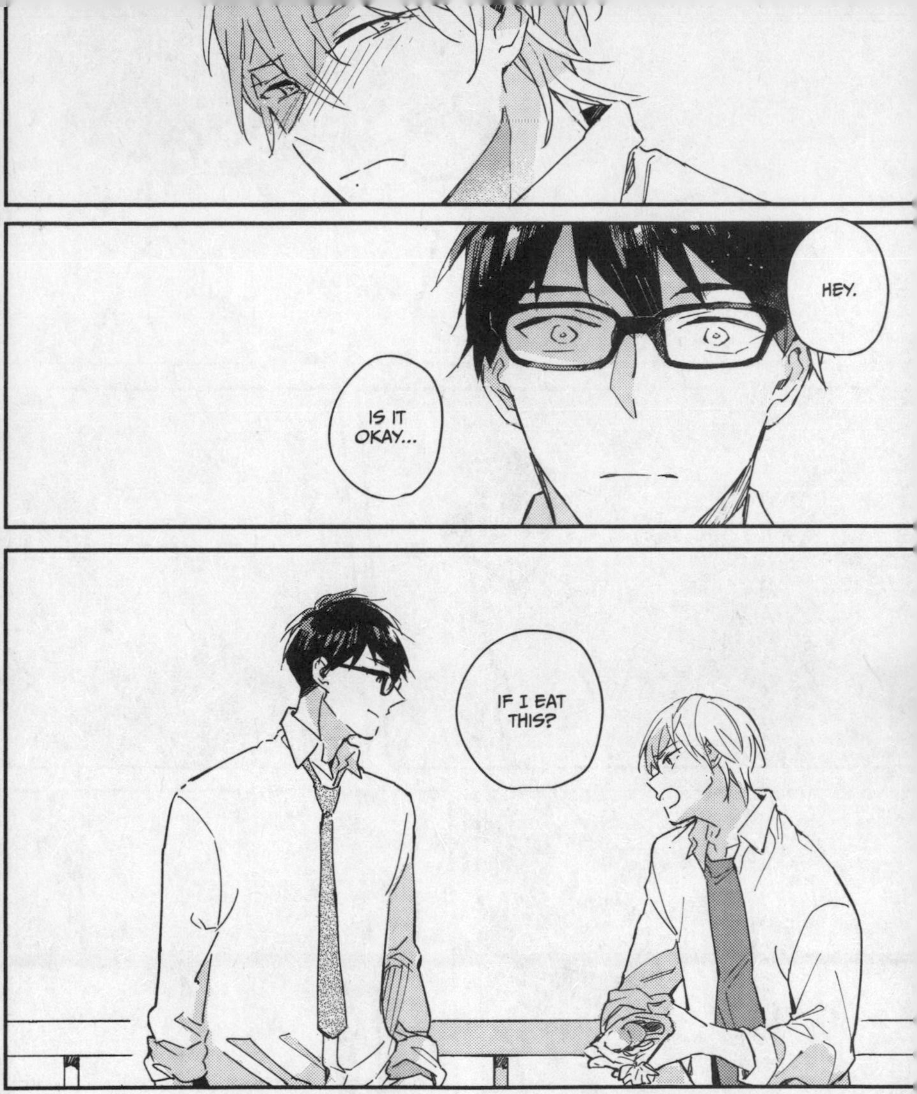
HEY.
IS IT OKAY...
IF I EAT THIS?

end

glass syndrome

glass syndrome

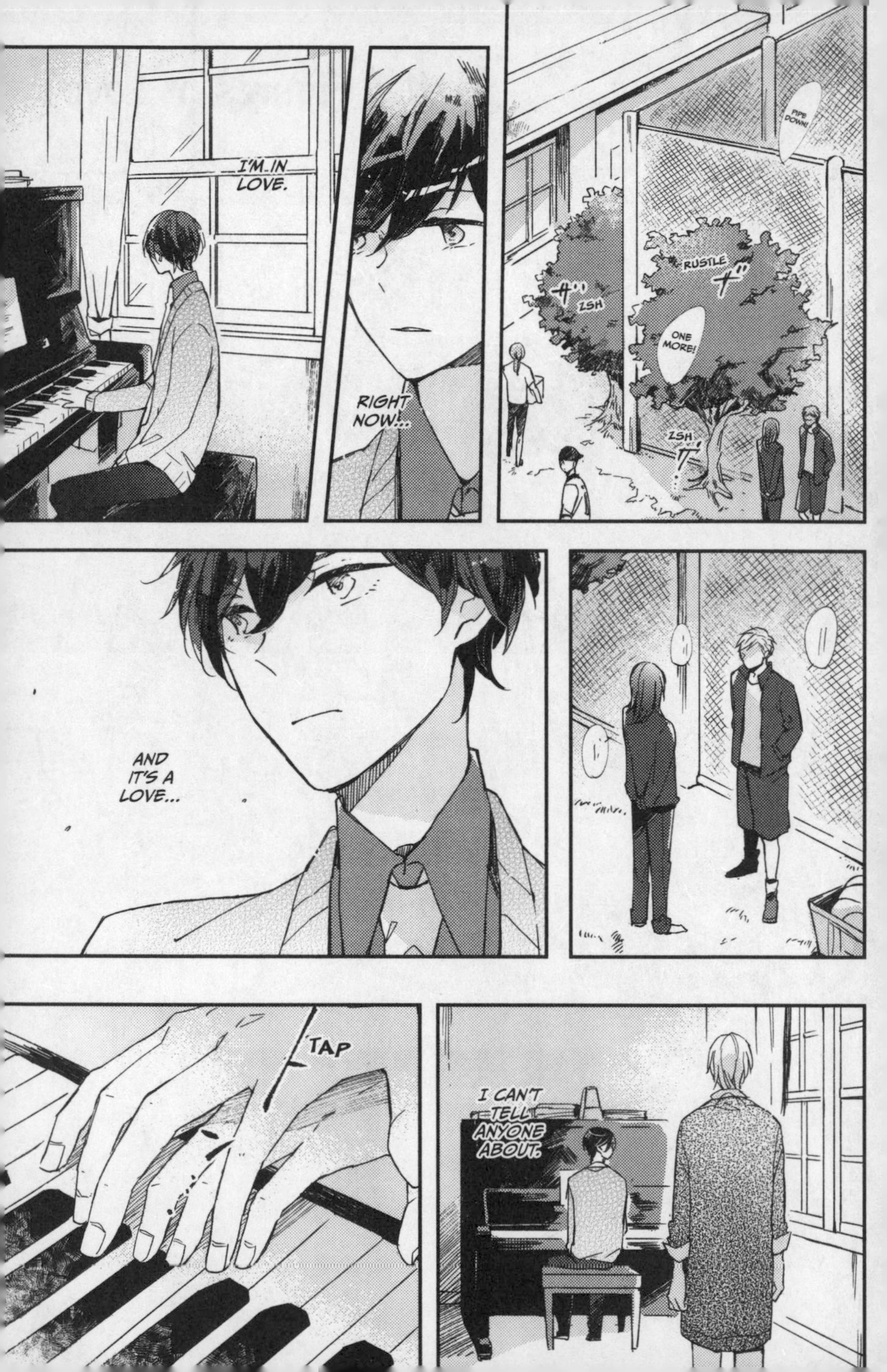
PIPE DOWN!
RUSTLE
ZSH
ONE MORE!
ZSH
RIGHT NOW...
I'M IN LOVE.
!!
!
!
AND IT'S A LOVE...
I CAN'T TELL ANYONE ABOUT.
TAP

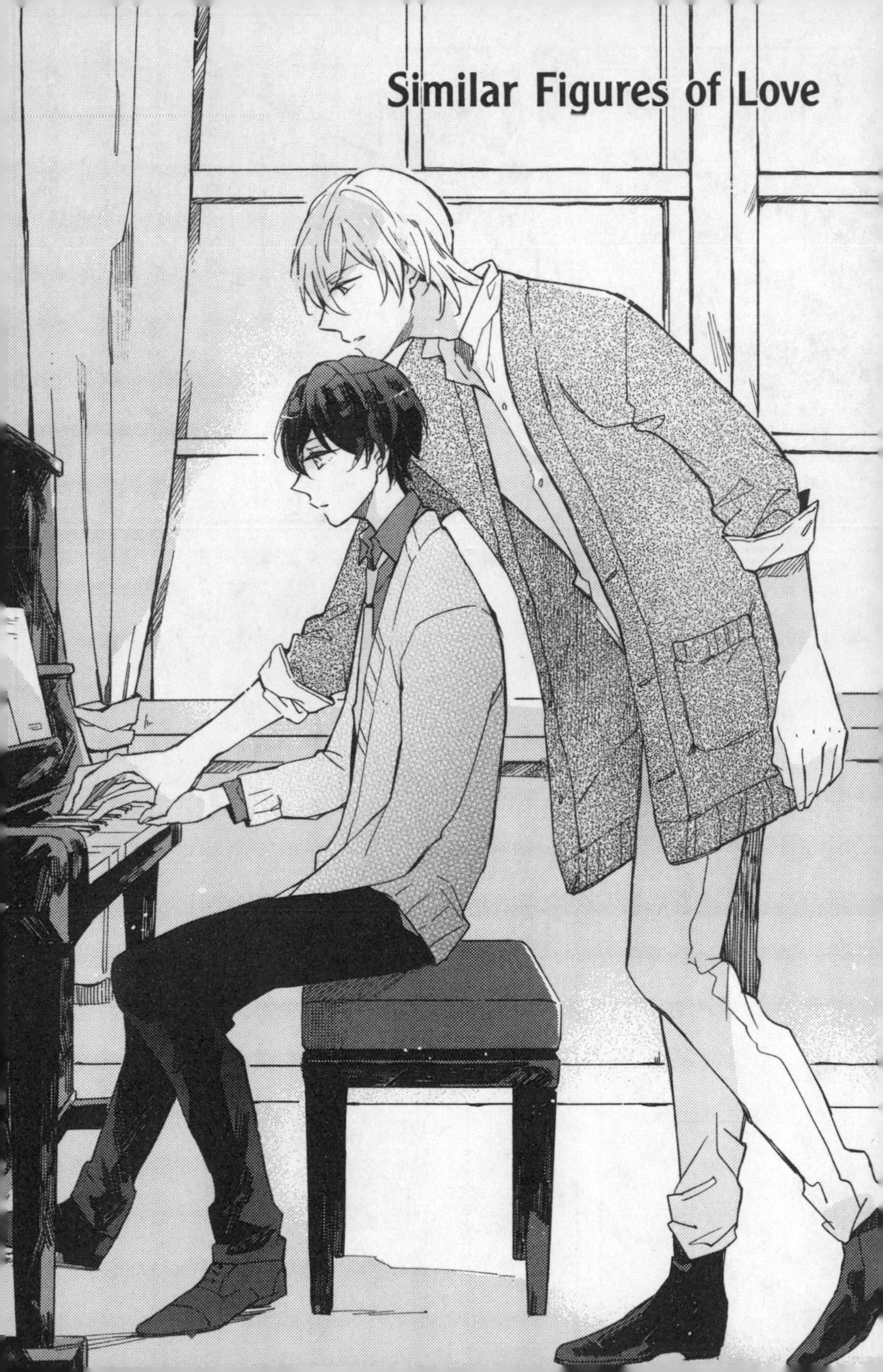
Similar Figures of Love

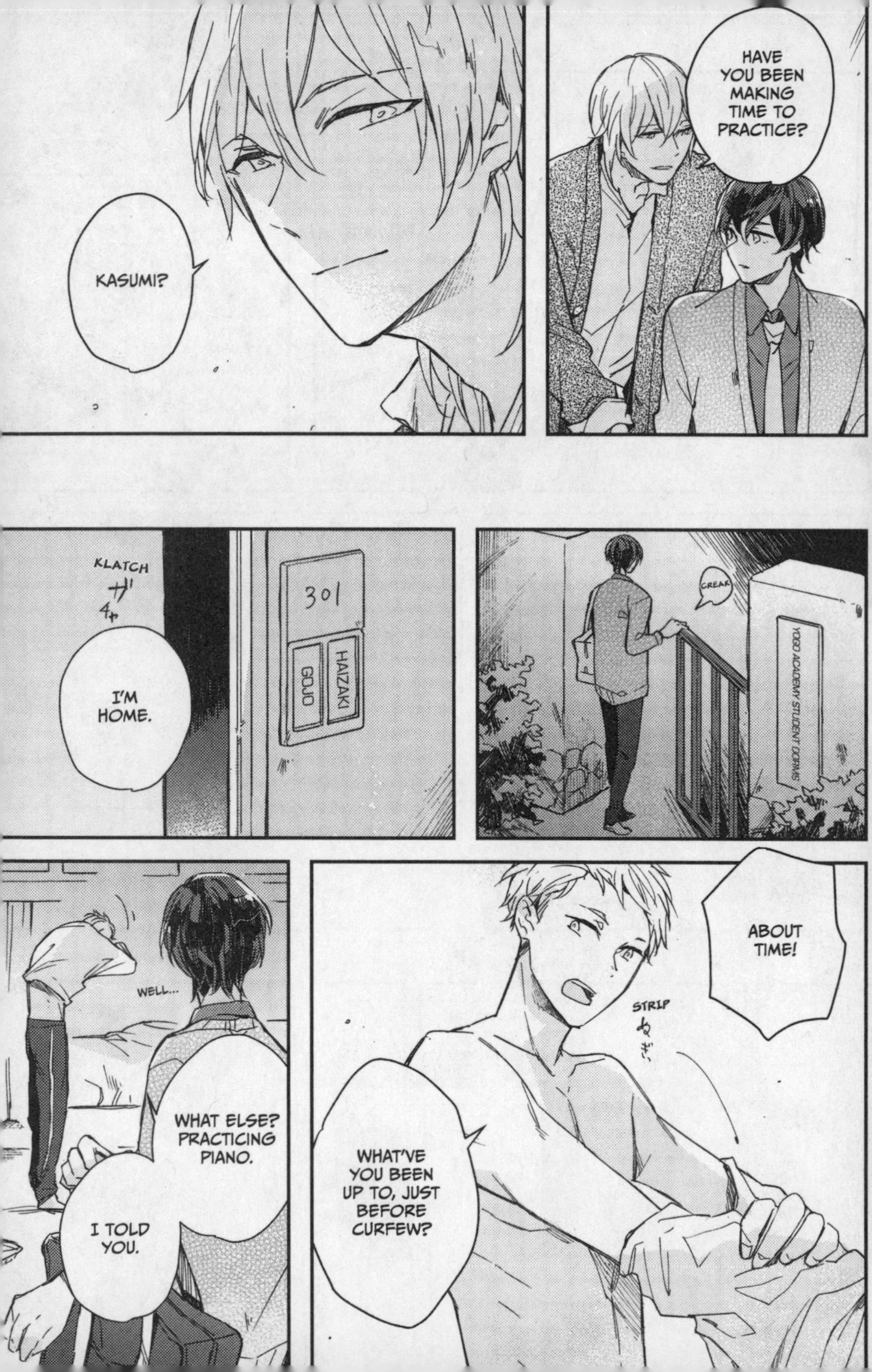
HAVE YOU BEEN MAKING TIME TO PRACTICE?
KASUMI?
CREAK
YOGO ACADEMY STUDENT DORMS
KLATCH
I'M HOME.
301
HAIZAKI
GOJO
ABOUT TIME!
STRIP
WHAT'VE YOU BEEN UP TO, JUST BEFORE CURFEW?
WELL...
WHAT ELSE? PRACTICING PIANO.
I TOLD YOU.

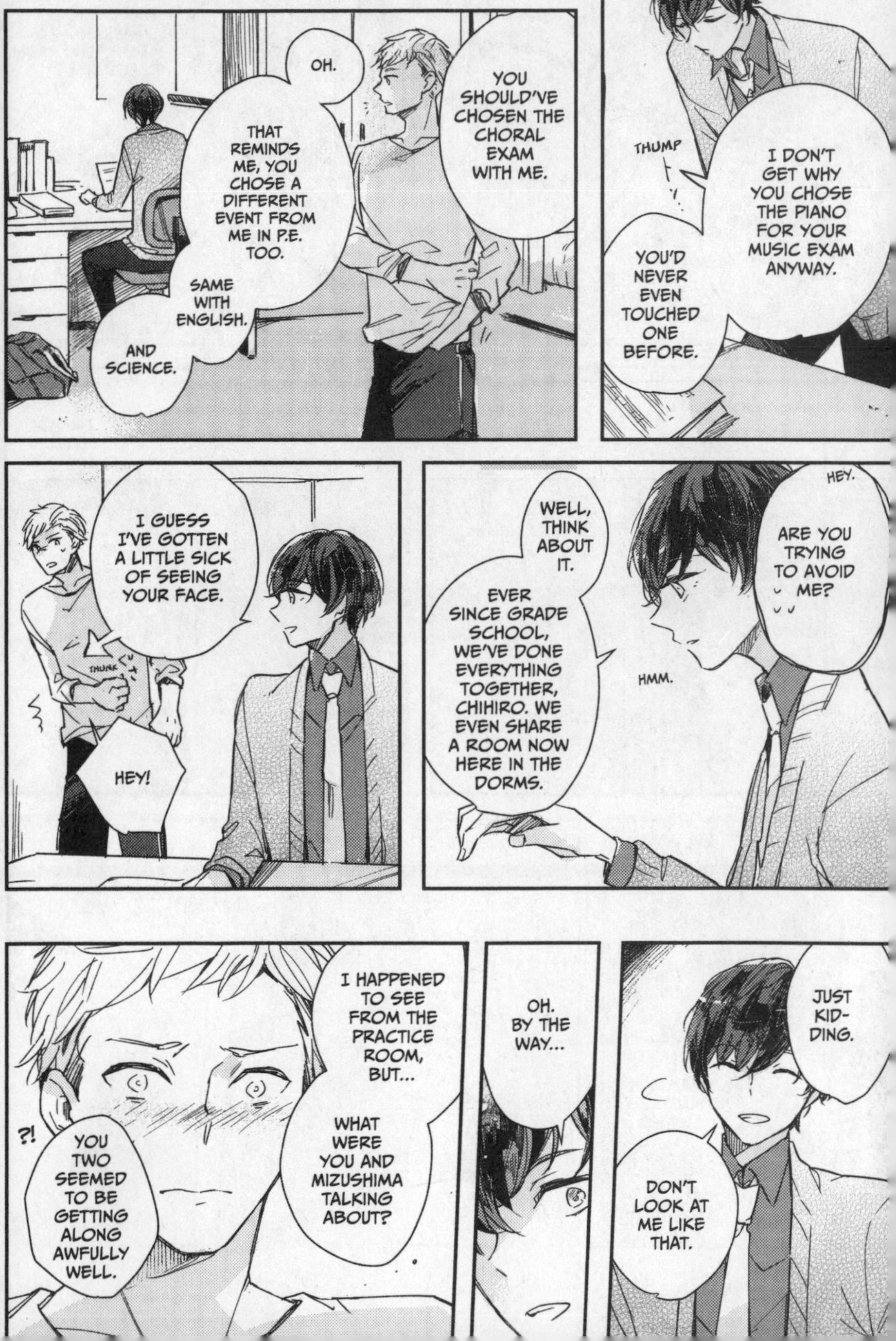
THUMP
I DON'T GET WHY YOU CHOSE THE PIANO FOR YOUR MUSIC EXAM ANYWAY.
YOU'D NEVER EVEN TOUCHED ONE BEFORE.
YOU SHOULD'VE CHOSEN THE CHORAL EXAM WITH ME.
OH.
THAT REMINDS ME, YOU CHOSE A DIFFERENT EVENT FROM ME IN P.E. TOO.
SAME WITH ENGLISH.
AND SCIENCE.
HEY.
ARE YOU TRYING TO AVOID ME?
HMM.
WELL, THINK ABOUT IT.
EVER SINCE GRADE SCHOOL, WE'VE DONE EVERYTHING TOGETHER, CHIHIRO. WE EVEN SHARE A ROOM NOW HERE IN THE DORMS.
I GUESS I'VE GOTTEN A LITTLE SICK OF SEEING YOUR FACE.
THUNK
HEY!
JUST KID-DING.
DON'T LOOK AT ME LIKE THAT.
OH. BY THE WAY...
I HAPPENED TO SEE FROM THE PRACTICE ROOM, BUT...
WHAT WERE YOU AND MIZUSHIMA TALKING ABOUT?
?!
YOU TWO SEEMED TO BE GETTING ALONG AWFULLY WELL.

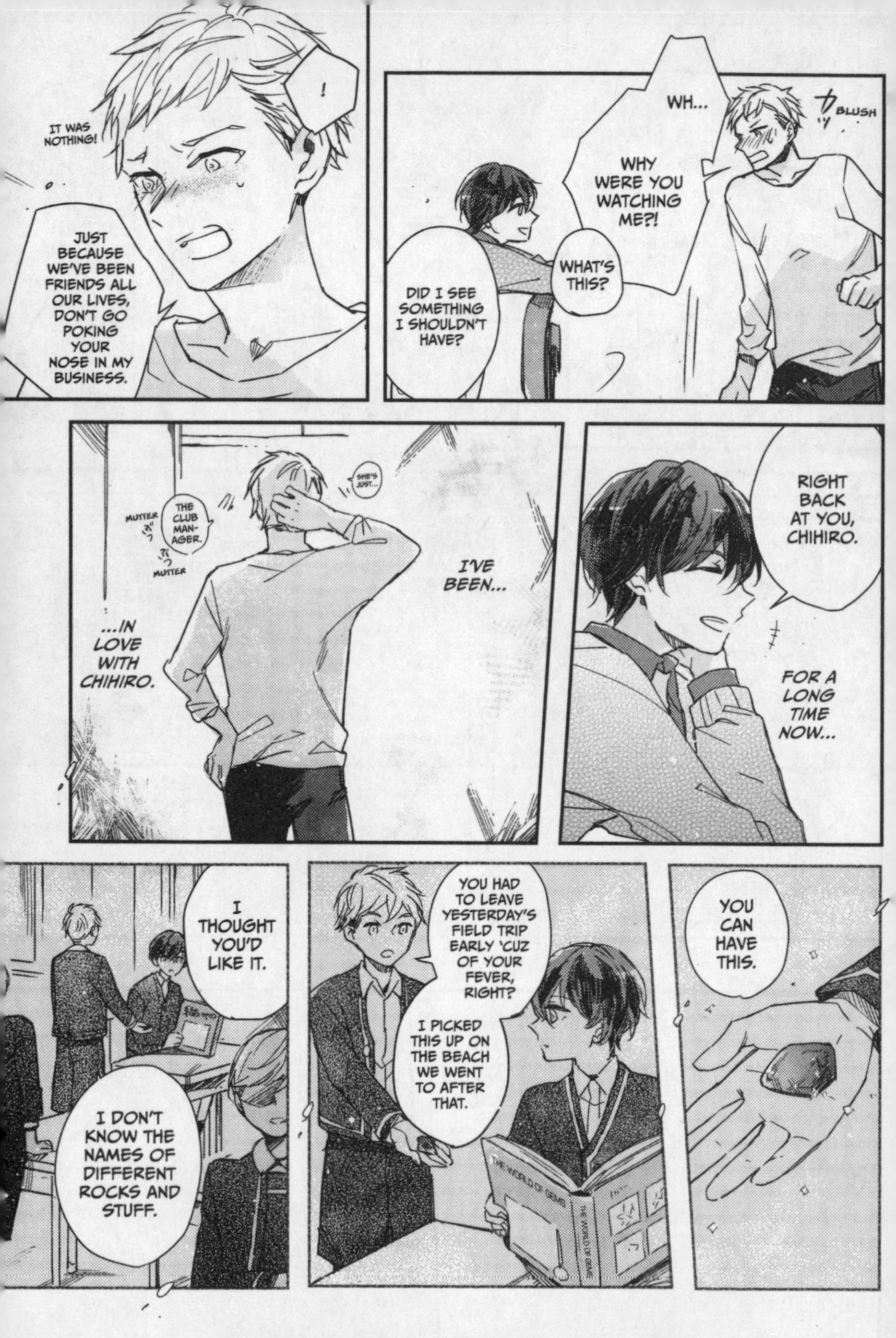
WH...
WHY WERE YOU WATCHING ME?!
BLUSH
WHAT'S THIS?
DID I SEE SOMETHING I SHOULDN'T HAVE?
!
IT WAS NOTHING!
JUST BECAUSE WE'VE BEEN FRIENDS ALL OUR LIVES, DON'T GO POKING YOUR NOSE IN MY BUSINESS.
RIGHT BACK AT YOU, CHIHIRO.
FOR A LONG TIME NOW...
I'VE BEEN...
SHE'S JUST...
THE CLUB MANAGER.
MUTTER
MUTTER
...IN LOVE WITH CHIHIRO.
YOU CAN HAVE THIS.
YOU HAD TO LEAVE YESTERDAY'S FIELD TRIP EARLY 'CUZ OF YOUR FEVER, RIGHT?
I PICKED THIS UP ON THE BEACH WE WENT TO AFTER THAT.
THE WORLD OF GEMS
I THOUGHT YOU'D LIKE IT.
I DON'T KNOW THE NAMES OF DIFFERENT ROCKS AND STUFF.

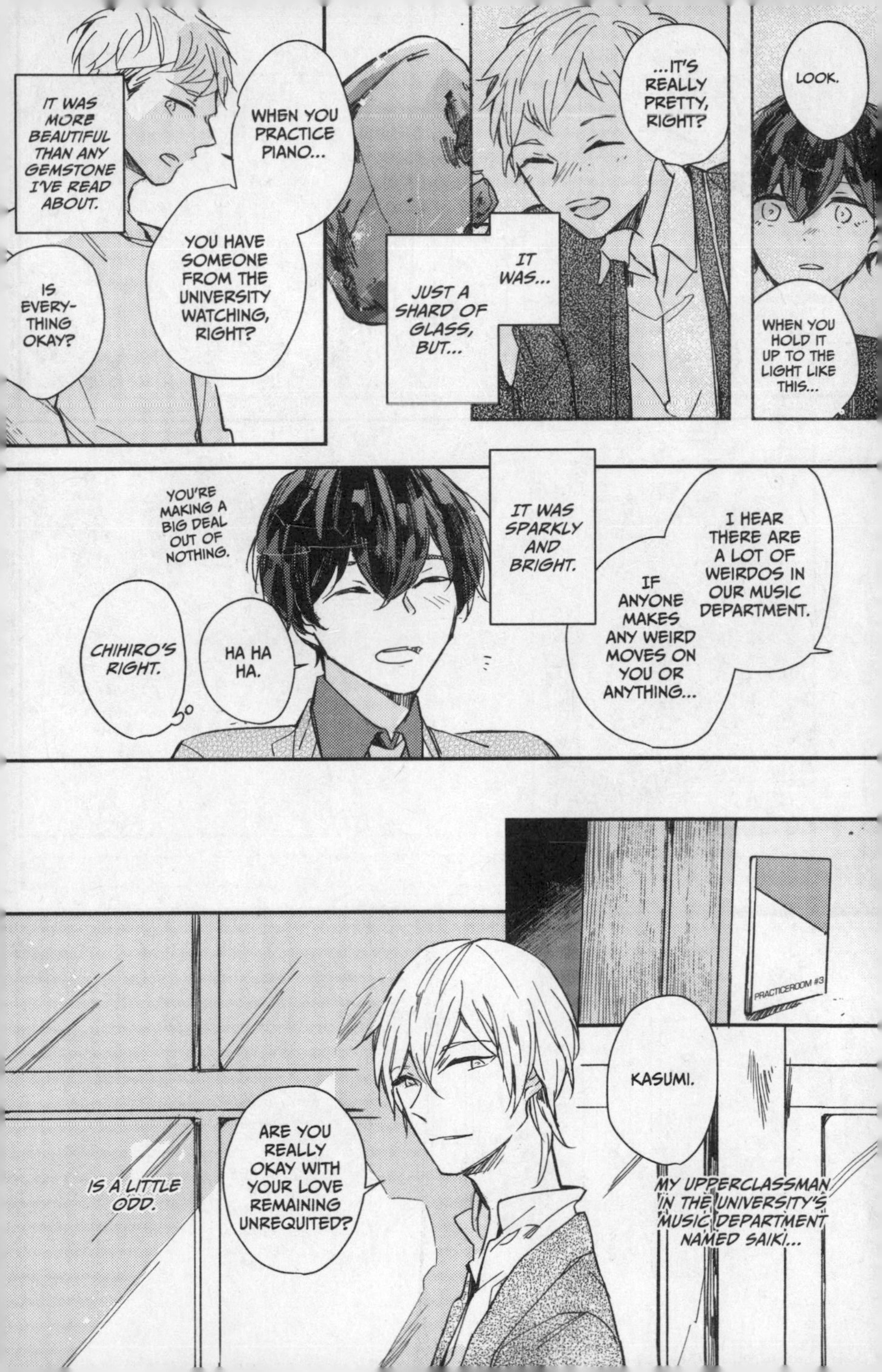
LOOK.
WHEN YOU HOLD IT UP TO THE LIGHT LIKE THIS...
...IT'S REALLY PRETTY, RIGHT?
IT WAS... JUST A SHARD OF GLASS, BUT...
IT WAS MORE BEAUTIFUL THAN ANY GEMSTONE I'VE READ ABOUT.
WHEN YOU PRACTICE PIANO...
YOU HAVE SOMEONE FROM THE UNIVERSITY WATCHING, RIGHT?
IS EVERYTHING OKAY?
IT WAS SPARKLY AND BRIGHT.
I HEAR THERE ARE A LOT OF WEIRDOS IN OUR MUSIC DEPARTMENT.
IF ANYONE MAKES ANY WEIRD MOVES ON YOU OR ANYTHING...
YOU'RE MAKING A BIG DEAL OUT OF NOTHING.
HA HA HA.
CHIHIRO'S RIGHT.
PRACTICEROOM #3
KASUMI.
MY UPPERCLASSMAN IN THE UNIVERSITY'S MUSIC DEPARTMENT NAMED SAIKI...
ARE YOU REALLY OKAY WITH YOUR LOVE REMAINING UNREQUITED?
IS A LITTLE ODD.

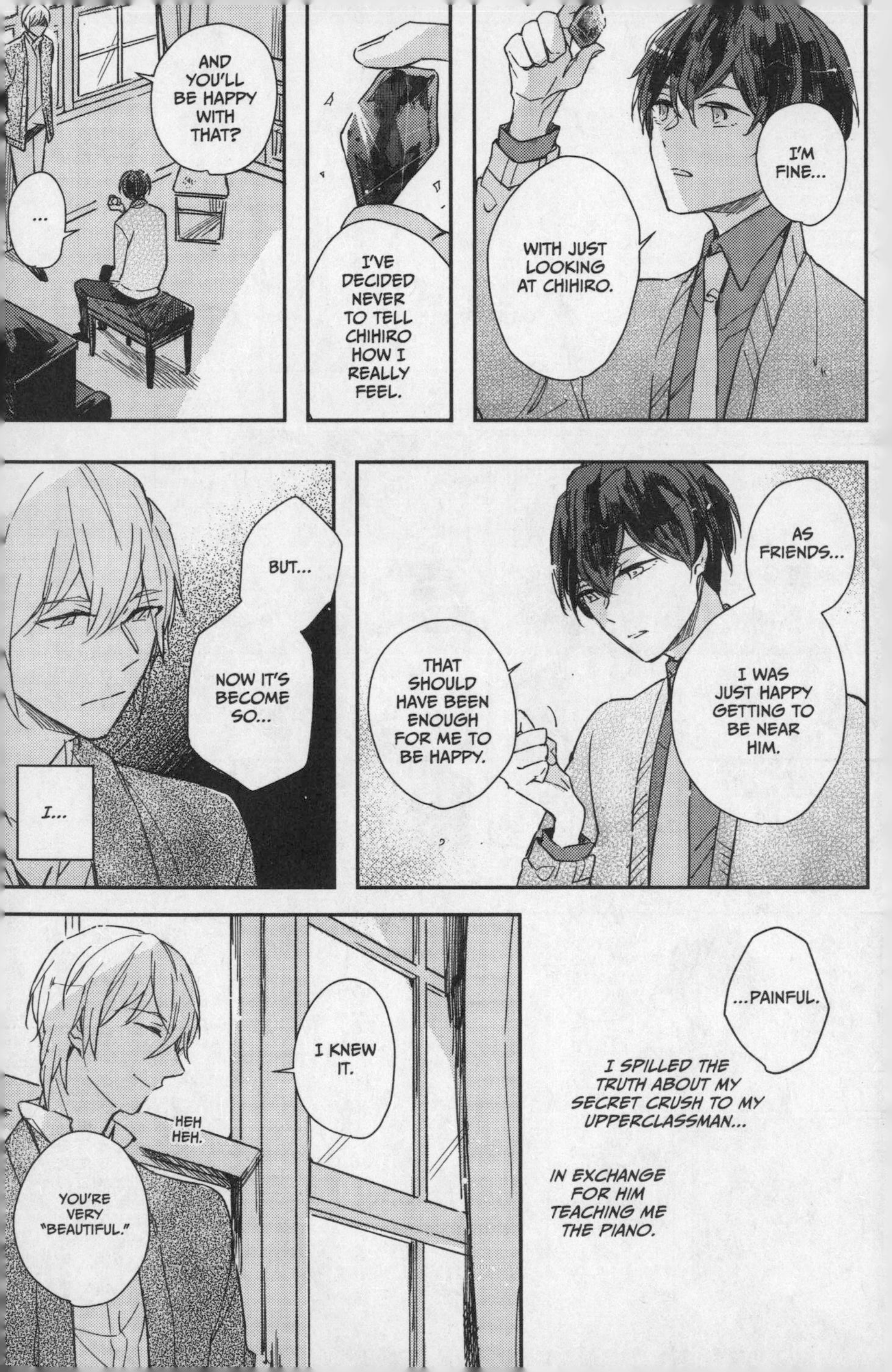
I'M FINE...
WITH JUST LOOKING AT CHIHIRO.
I'VE DECIDED NEVER TO TELL CHIHIRO HOW I REALLY FEEL.
AND YOU'LL BE HAPPY WITH THAT?
...
AS FRIENDS...
I WAS JUST HAPPY GETTING TO BE NEAR HIM.
THAT SHOULD HAVE BEEN ENOUGH FOR ME TO BE HAPPY.
BUT...
NOW IT'S BECOME SO...
I...
...PAINFUL.
I SPILLED THE TRUTH ABOUT MY SECRET CRUSH TO MY UPPERCLASSMAN...
IN EXCHANGE FOR HIM TEACHING ME THE PIANO.
I KNEW IT.
HEH HEH.
YOU'RE VERY "BEAUTIFUL."

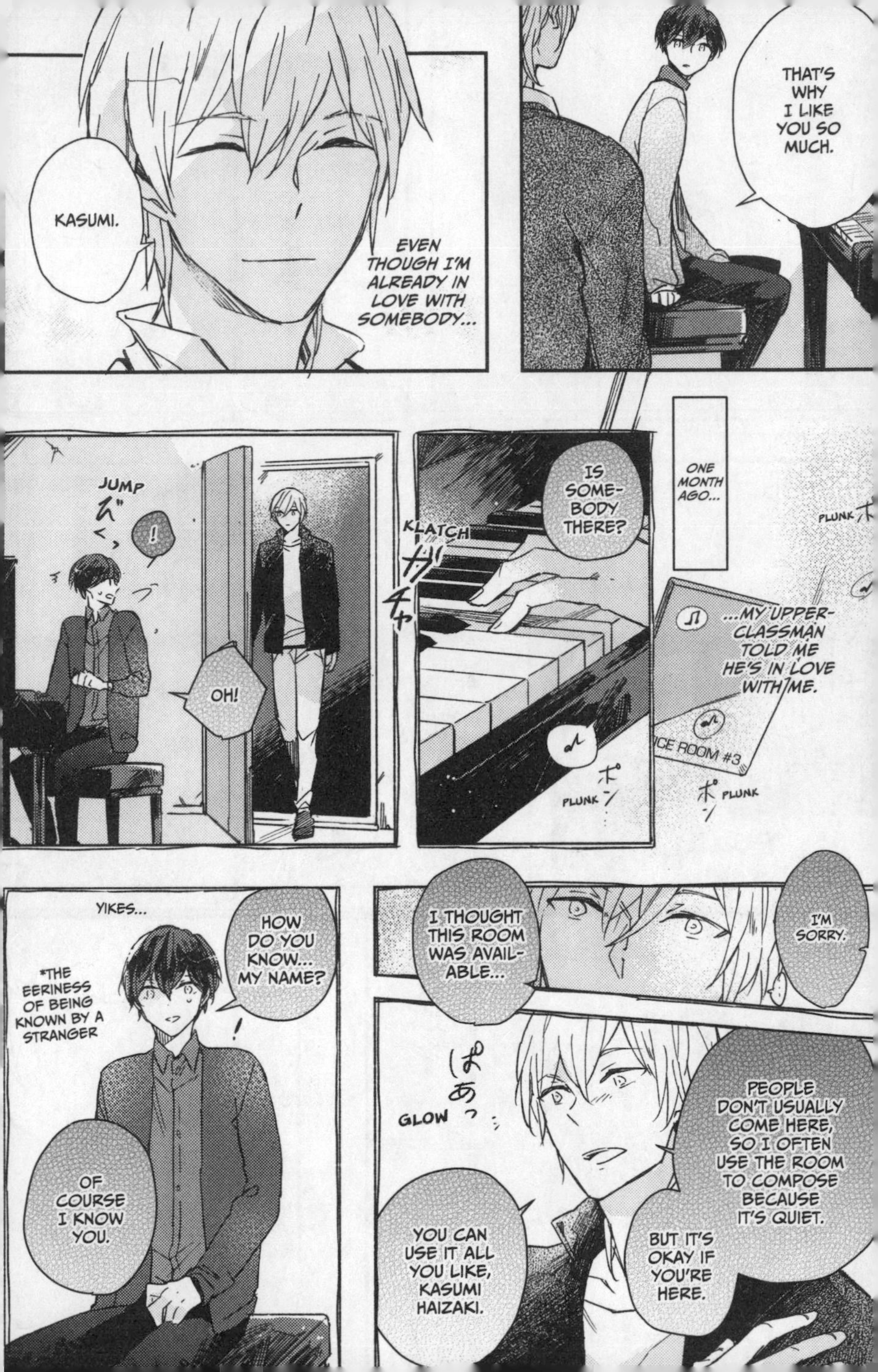
THAT'S WHY I LIKE YOU SO MUCH.
KASUMI.
EVEN THOUGH I'M ALREADY IN LOVE WITH SOMEBODY...
ONE MONTH AGO...
PLUNK
...MY UPPER-CLASSMAN TOLD ME HE'S IN LOVE WITH ME.
ICE ROOM #3
PLUNK
IS SOME-BODY THERE?
KLATCH
PLUNK
JUMP
!
OH!
I'M SORRY.
I THOUGHT THIS ROOM WAS AVAIL-ABLE...
PEOPLE DON'T USUALLY COME HERE, SO I OFTEN USE THE ROOM TO COMPOSE BECAUSE IT'S QUIET.
GLOW
BUT IT'S OKAY IF YOU'RE HERE.
YOU CAN USE IT ALL YOU LIKE, KASUMI HAIZAKI.
HOW DO YOU KNOW... MY NAME?
YIKES...
*THE EERINESS OF BEING KNOWN BY A STRANGER
!
OF COURSE I KNOW YOU.

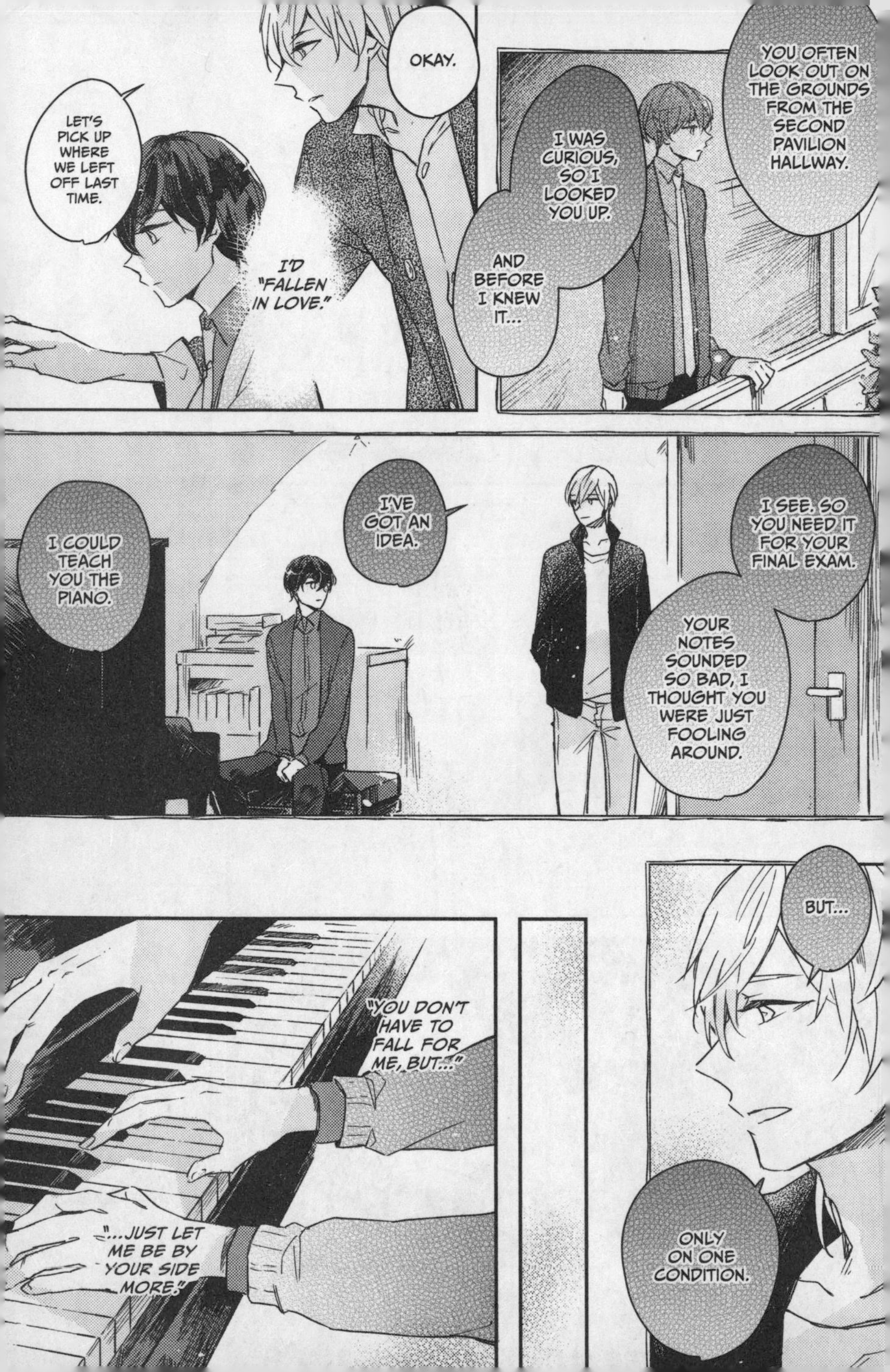
YOU OFTEN LOOK OUT ON THE GROUNDS FROM THE SECOND PAVILION HALLWAY.
I WAS CURIOUS, SO I LOOKED YOU UP.
AND BEFORE I KNEW IT...
OKAY.
LET'S PICK UP WHERE WE LEFT OFF LAST TIME.
I'D "FALLEN IN LOVE."
I SEE. SO YOU NEED IT FOR YOUR FINAL EXAM.
YOUR NOTES SOUNDED SO BAD, I THOUGHT YOU WERE JUST FOOLING AROUND.
I'VE GOT AN IDEA.
I COULD TEACH YOU THE PIANO.
BUT...
ONLY ON ONE CONDITION.
"YOU DON'T HAVE TO FALL FOR ME, BUT..."
"...JUST LET ME BE BY YOUR SIDE MORE."

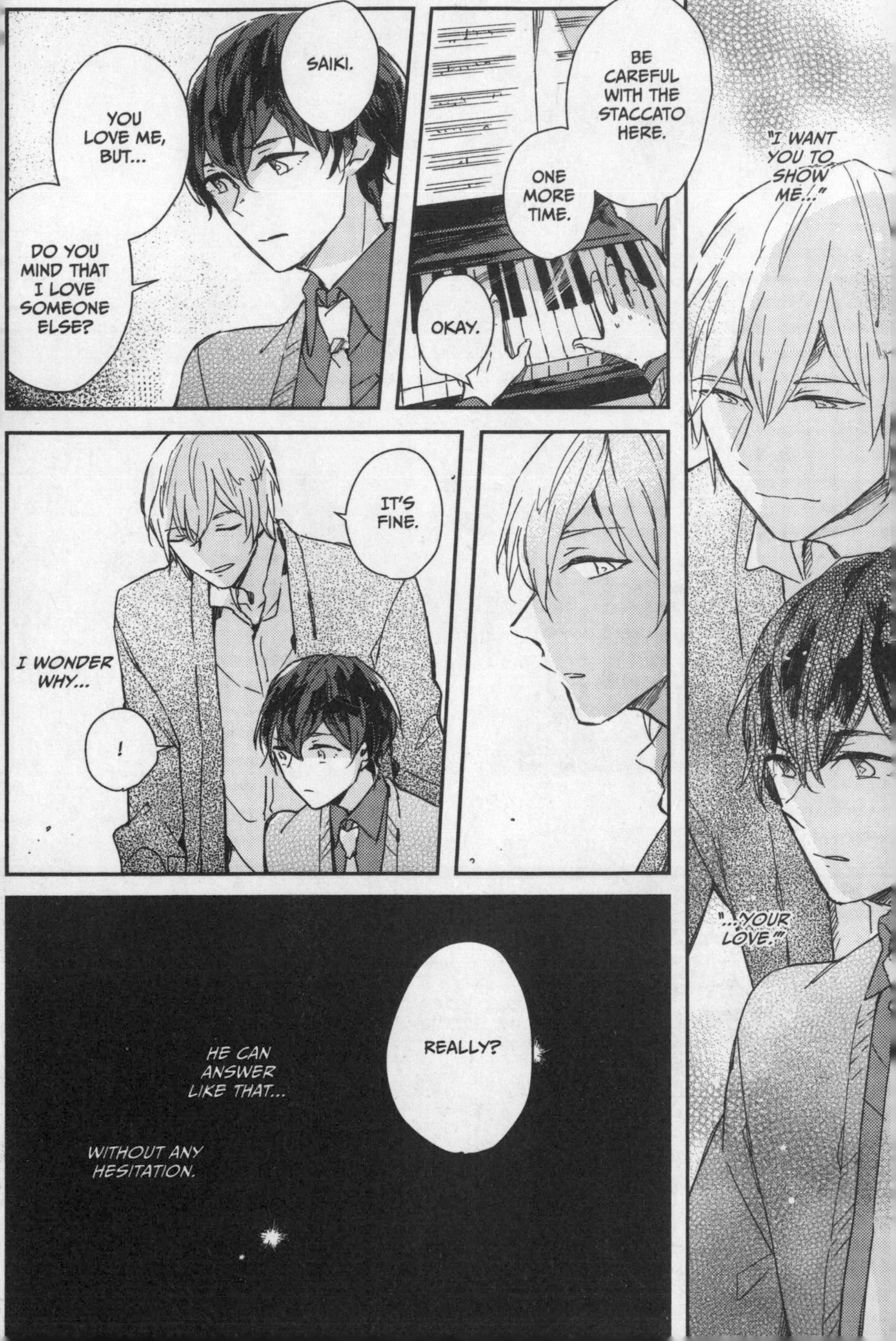
"I WANT YOU TO SHOW ME..."
"...YOUR LOVE."
BE CAREFUL WITH THE STACCATO HERE.
ONE MORE TIME.
OKAY.
SAIKI.
YOU LOVE ME, BUT...
DO YOU MIND THAT I LOVE SOMEONE ELSE?
IT'S FINE.
I WONDER WHY...
!
REALLY?
HE CAN ANSWER LIKE THAT...
WITHOUT ANY HESITATION.

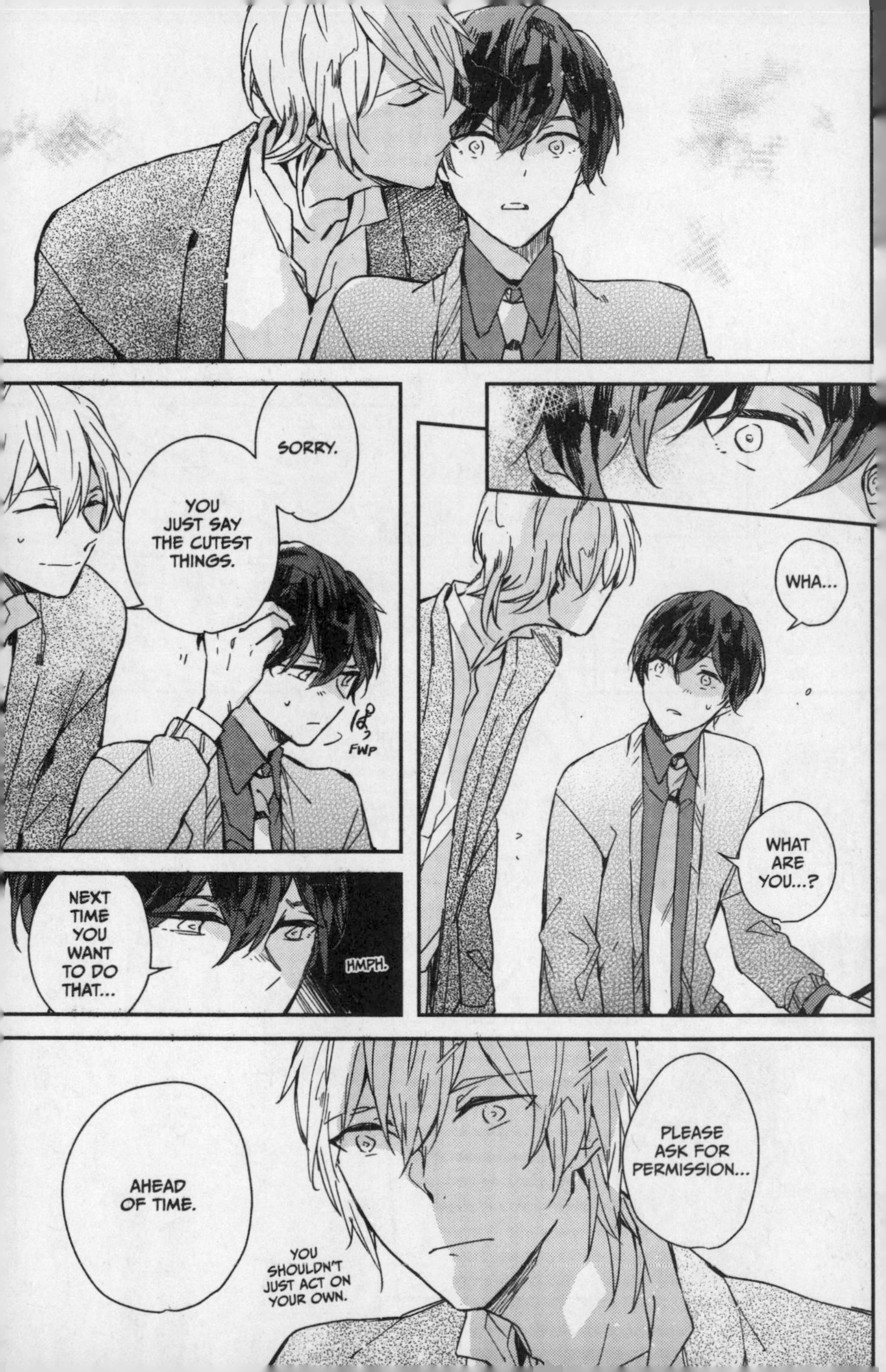
WHA...
WHAT ARE YOU...?
SORRY.
YOU JUST SAY THE CUTEST THINGS.
FWP
NEXT TIME YOU WANT TO DO THAT...
HMPH.
PLEASE ASK FOR PERMISSION...
AHEAD OF TIME.
YOU SHOULDN'T JUST ACT ON YOUR OWN.

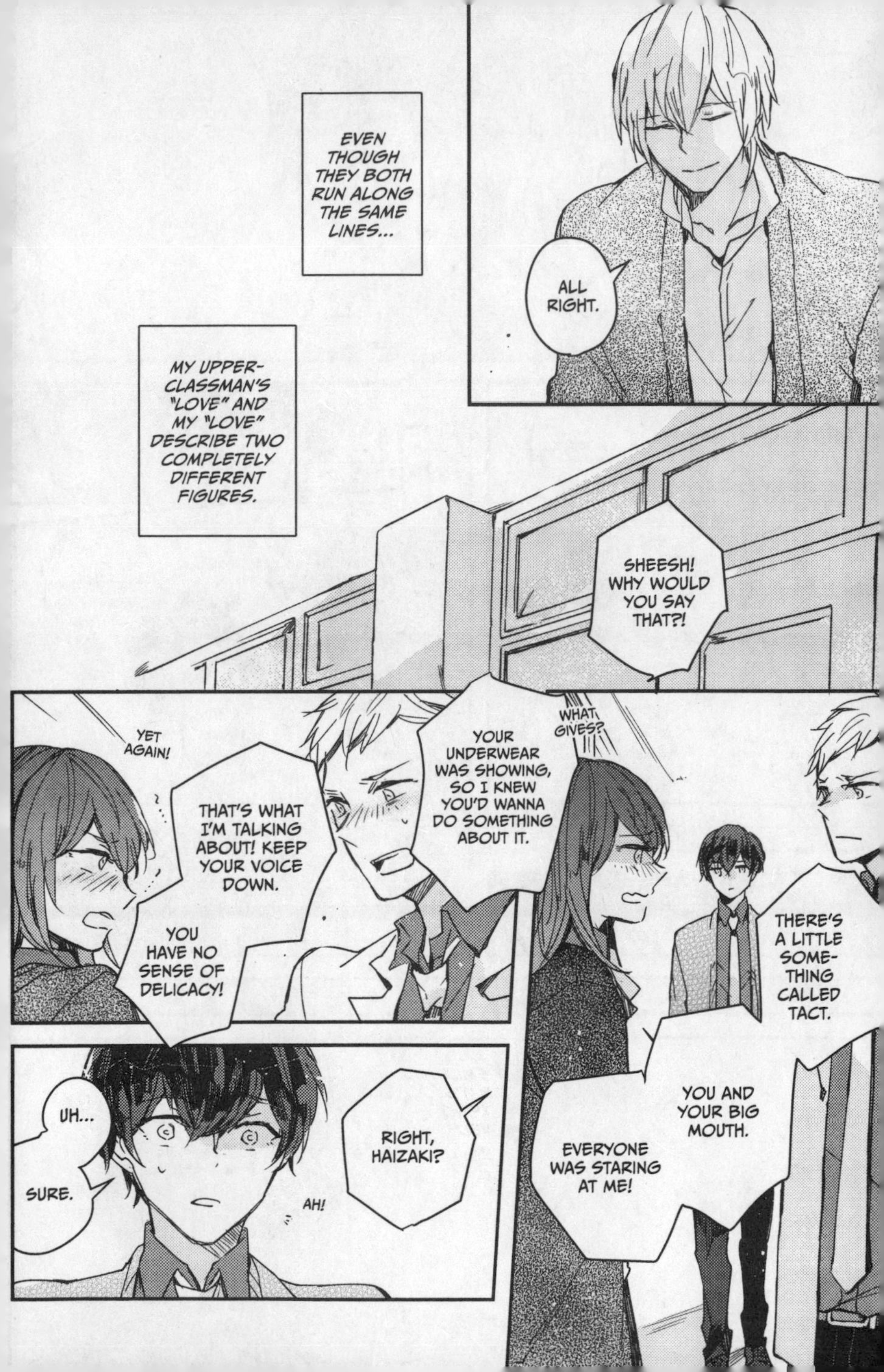
ALL RIGHT.
EVEN THOUGH THEY BOTH RUN ALONG THE SAME LINES...
MY UPPER-CLASSMAN'S "LOVE" AND MY "LOVE" DESCRIBE TWO COMPLETELY DIFFERENT FIGURES.
SHEESH! WHY WOULD YOU SAY THAT?!
WHAT GIVES?
YOUR UNDERWEAR WAS SHOWING, SO I KNEW YOU'D WANNA DO SOMETHING ABOUT IT.
THERE'S A LITTLE SOME-THING CALLED TACT.
YOU AND YOUR BIG MOUTH.
EVERYONE WAS STARING AT ME!
YET AGAIN!
THAT'S WHAT I'M TALKING ABOUT! KEEP YOUR VOICE DOWN.
YOU HAVE NO SENSE OF DELICACY!
RIGHT, HAIZAKI?
AH!
UH...
SURE.

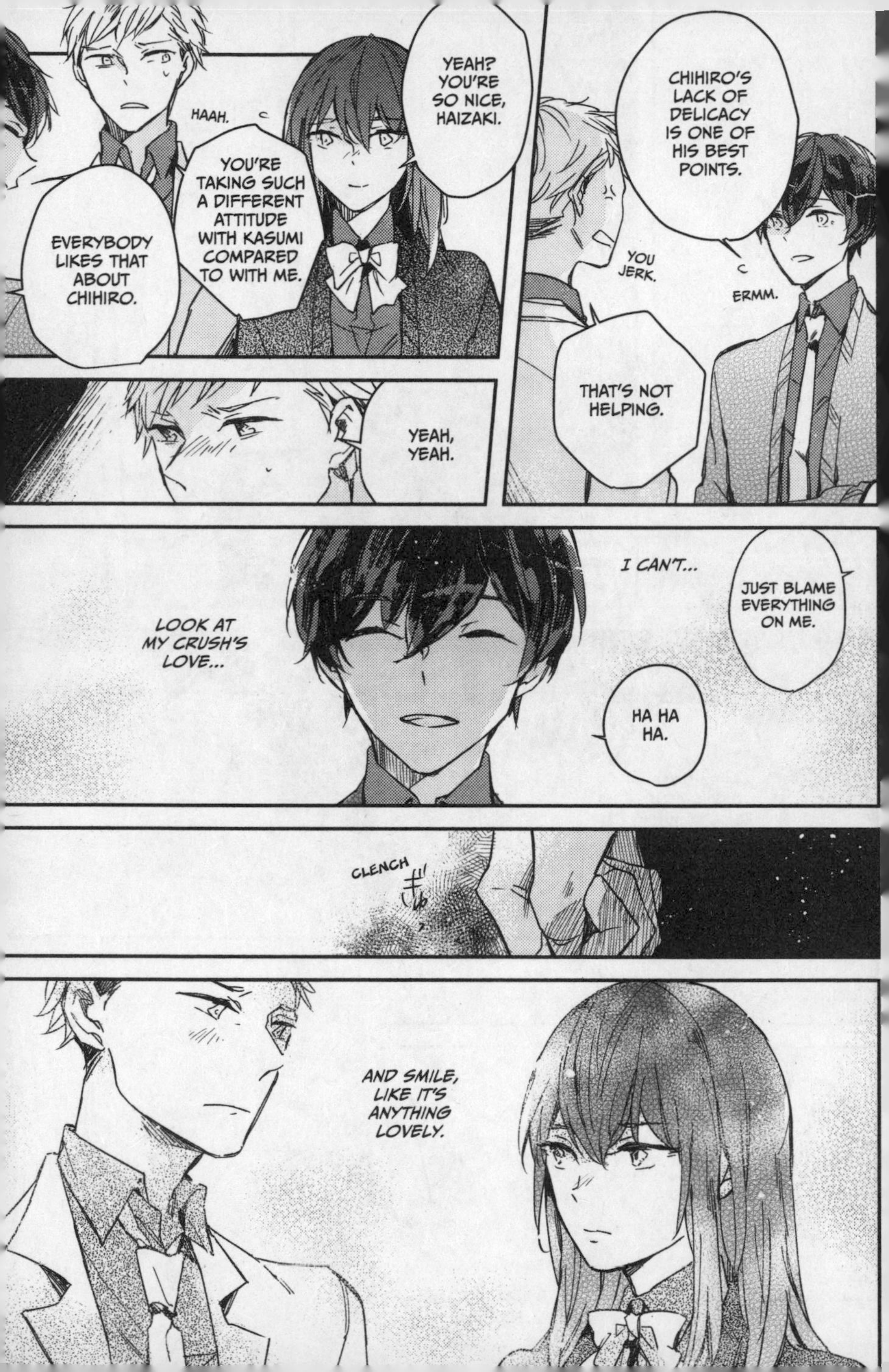

CHIHIRO'S LACK OF DELICACY IS ONE OF HIS BEST POINTS.
YOU JERK.
ERMM.
THAT'S NOT HELPING.
YEAH? YOU'RE SO NICE, HAIZAKI.
YOU'RE TAKING SUCH A DIFFERENT ATTITUDE WITH KASUMI COMPARED TO WITH ME.
HAAH.
EVERYBODY LIKES THAT ABOUT CHIHIRO.
YEAH, YEAH.
JUST BLAME EVERYTHING ON ME.
I CAN'T...
HA HA HA.
LOOK AT MY CRUSH'S LOVE...
CLENCH
AND SMILE, LIKE IT'S ANYTHING LOVELY.

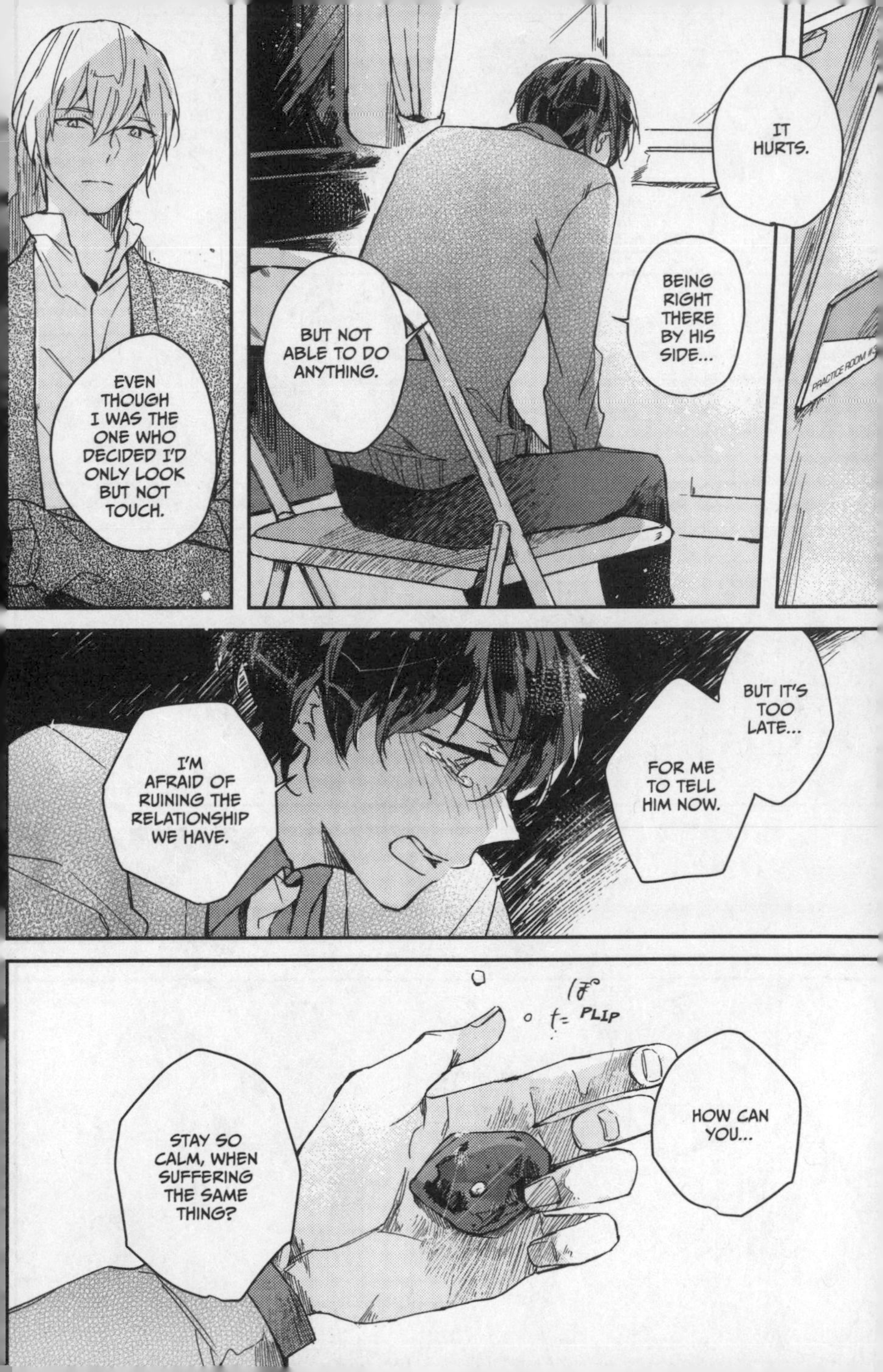
PRACTICE ROOM
IT HURTS.
BEING RIGHT THERE BY HIS SIDE...
BUT NOT ABLE TO DO ANYTHING.
EVEN THOUGH I WAS THE ONE WHO DECIDED I'D ONLY LOOK BUT NOT TOUCH.
BUT IT'S TOO LATE...
FOR ME TO TELL HIM NOW.
I'M AFRAID OF RUINING THE RELATIONSHIP WE HAVE.
PLIP
HOW CAN YOU...
STAY SO CALM, WHEN SUFFERING THE SAME THING?

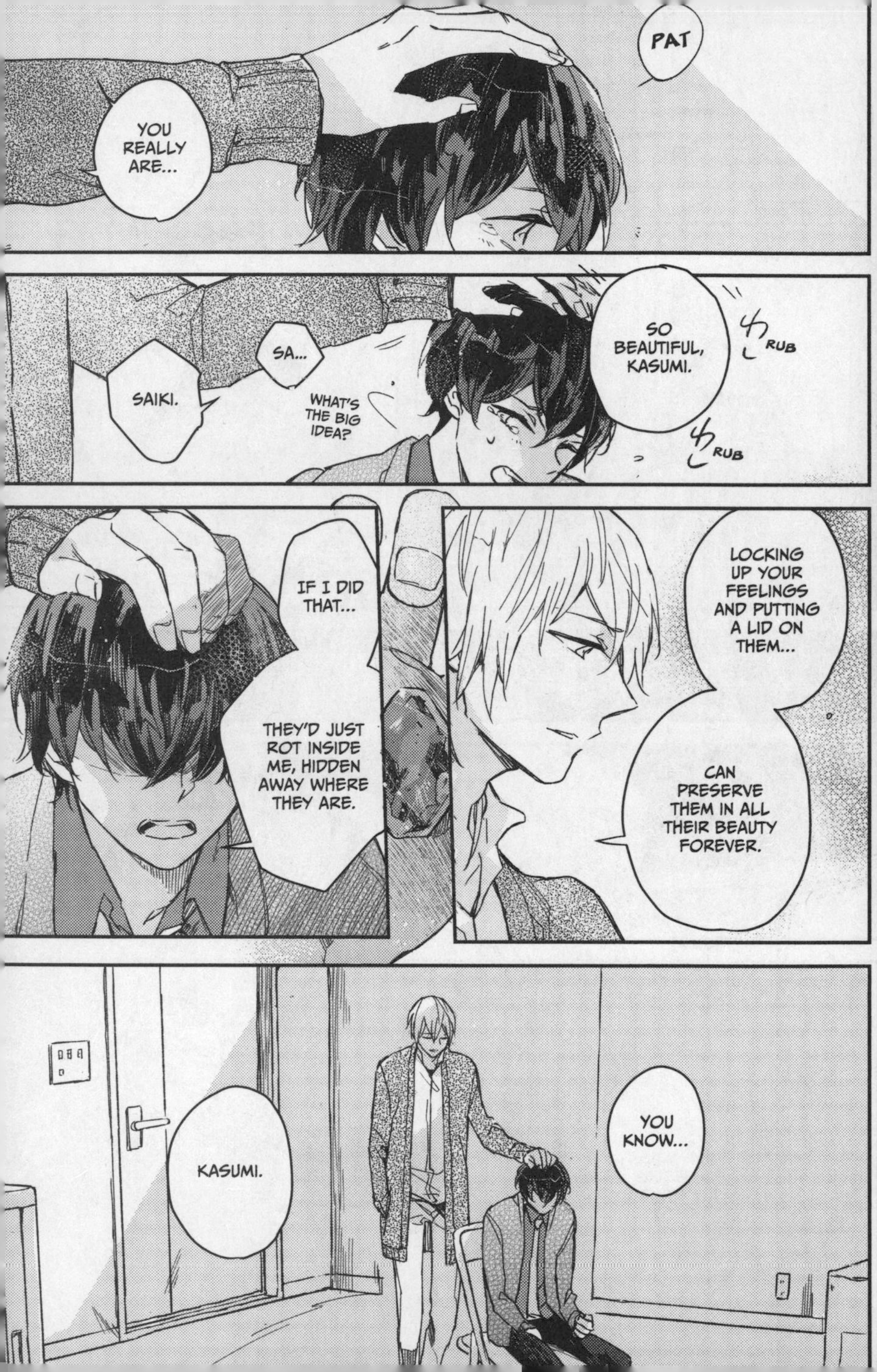
PAT
YOU REALLY ARE...
SO BEAUTIFUL, KASUMI.
RUB
RUB
SA...
WHAT'S THE BIG IDEA?
SAIKI.
LOCKING UP YOUR FEELINGS AND PUTTING A LID ON THEM...
CAN PRESERVE THEM IN ALL THEIR BEAUTY FOREVER.
IF I DID THAT...
THEY'D JUST ROT INSIDE ME, HIDDEN AWAY WHERE THEY ARE.
YOU KNOW...
KASUMI.

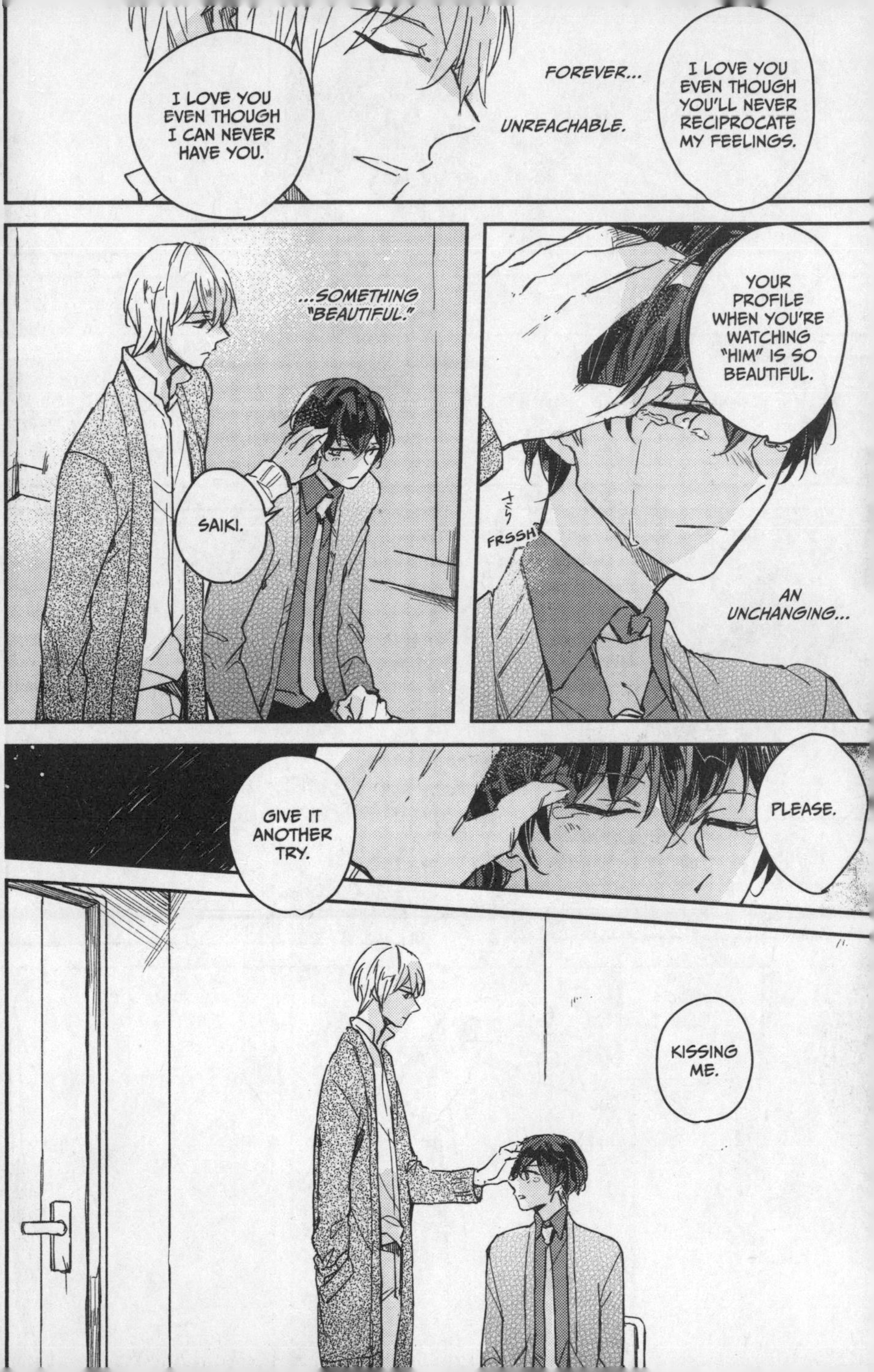
I LOVE YOU EVEN THOUGH YOU'LL NEVER RECIPROCATE MY FEELINGS.
FOREVER...
UNREACHABLE.
I LOVE YOU EVEN THOUGH I CAN NEVER HAVE YOU.
YOUR PROFILE WHEN YOU'RE WATCHING "HIM" IS SO BEAUTIFUL.
FRSSH
AN UNCHANGING...
...SOMETHING "BEAUTIFUL."
SAIKI.
PLEASE.
GIVE IT ANOTHER TRY.
KISSING ME.

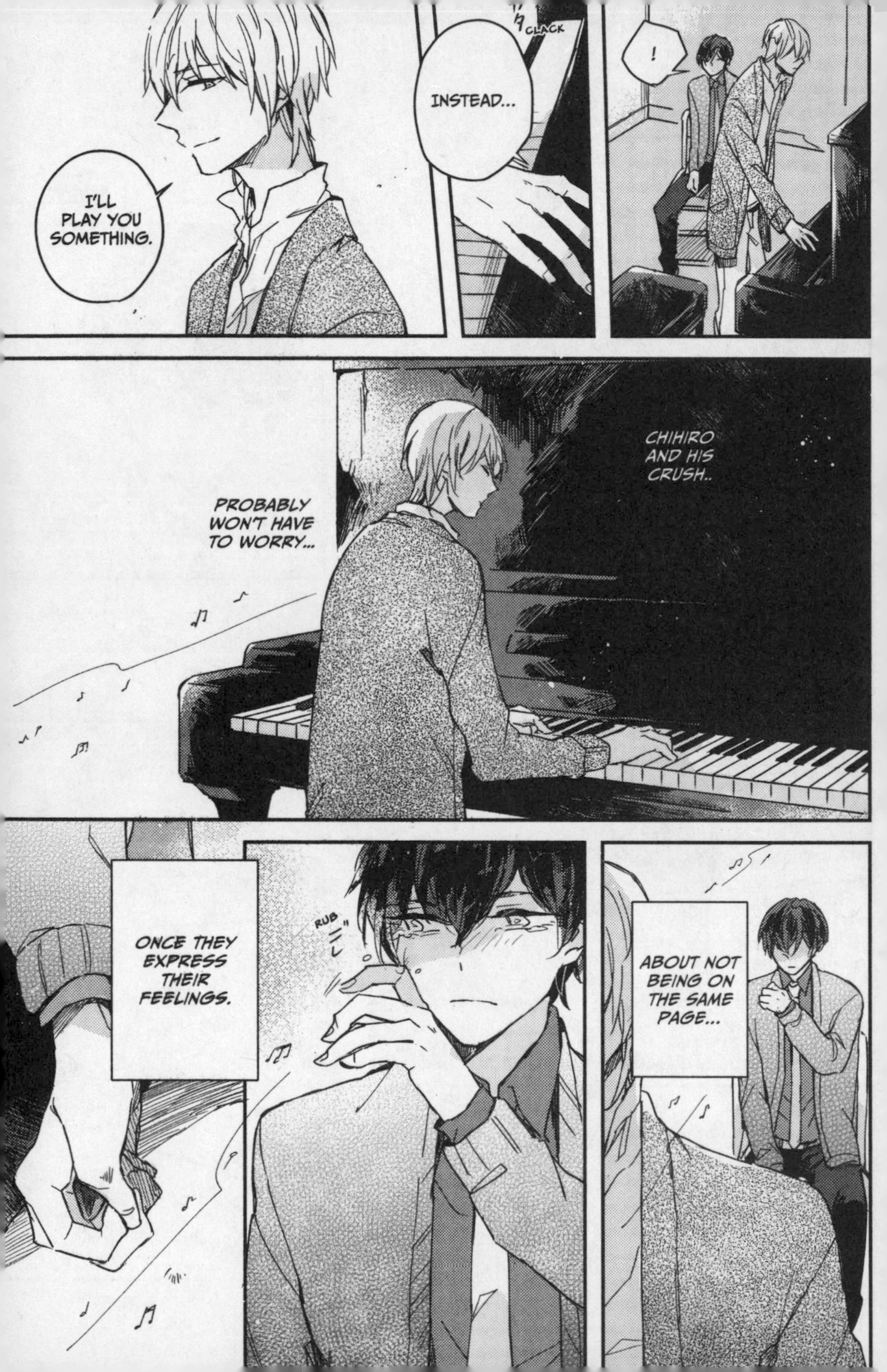
!
CLACK
INSTEAD...
I'LL PLAY YOU SOMETHING.
CHIHIRO AND HIS CRUSH..
PROBABLY WON'T HAVE TO WORRY...
ABOUT NOT BEING ON THE SAME PAGE...
RUB
ONCE THEY EXPRESS THEIR FEELINGS.

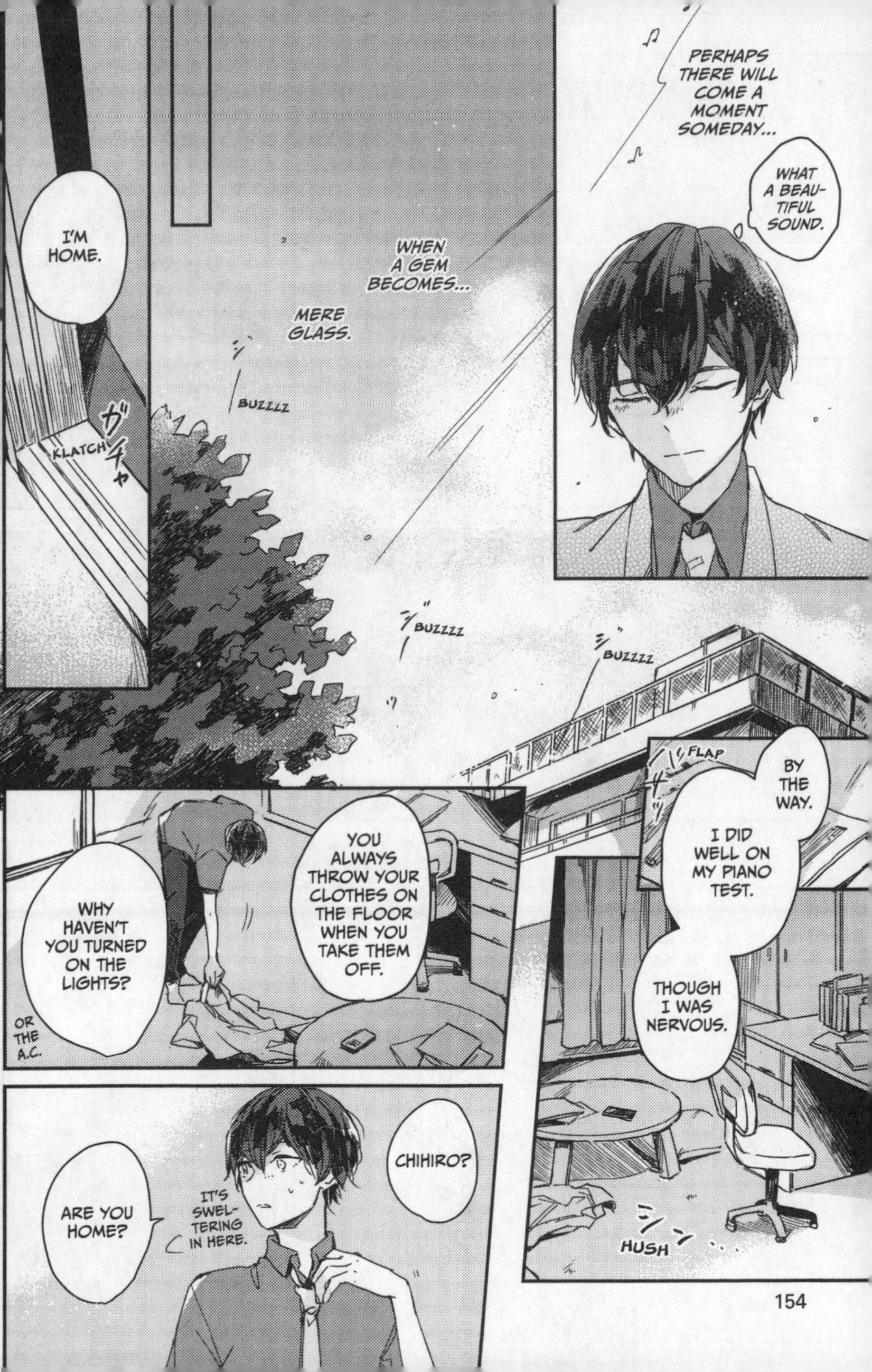

PERHAPS THERE WILL COME A MOMENT SOMEDAY...
WHAT A BEAUTIFUL SOUND.
WHEN A GEM BECOMES...
MERE GLASS.
BUZZZZ
I'M HOME.
ガチャ
KLATCH
BUZZZZ
BUZZZZ
FLAP
BY THE WAY.
I DID WELL ON MY PIANO TEST.
THOUGH I WAS NERVOUS.
HUSH
YOU ALWAYS THROW YOUR CLOTHES ON THE FLOOR WHEN YOU TAKE THEM OFF.
WHY HAVEN'T YOU TURNED ON THE LIGHTS?
OR THE A.C.
CHIHIRO?
ARE YOU HOME?
IT'S SWELTERING IN HERE.

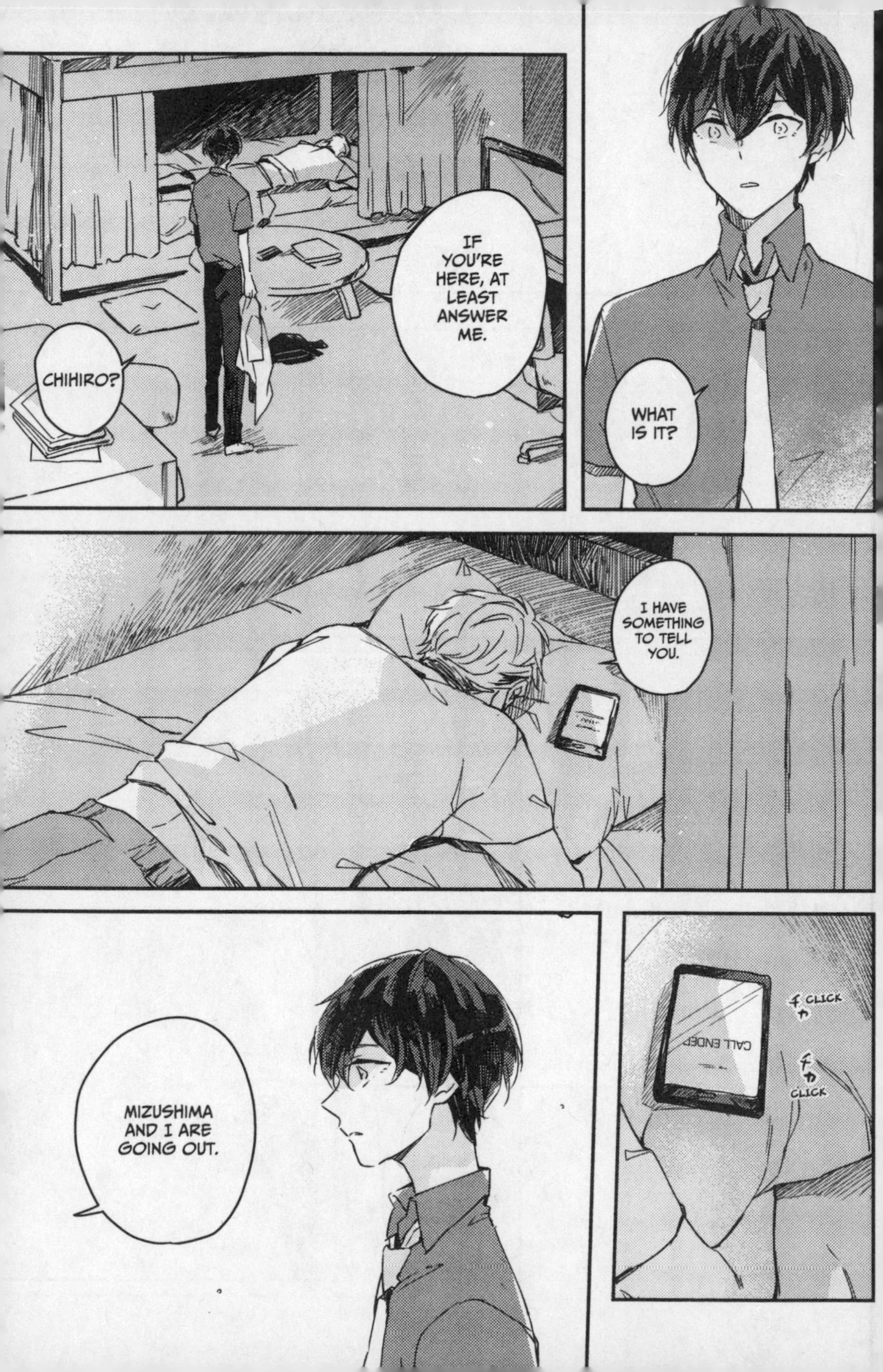
WHAT IS IT?
IF YOU'RE HERE, AT LEAST ANSWER ME.
CHIHIRO?
I HAVE SOMETHING TO TELL YOU.
CALL ENDED
チカ CLICK
チカ CLICK
MIZUSHIMA AND I ARE GOING OUT.

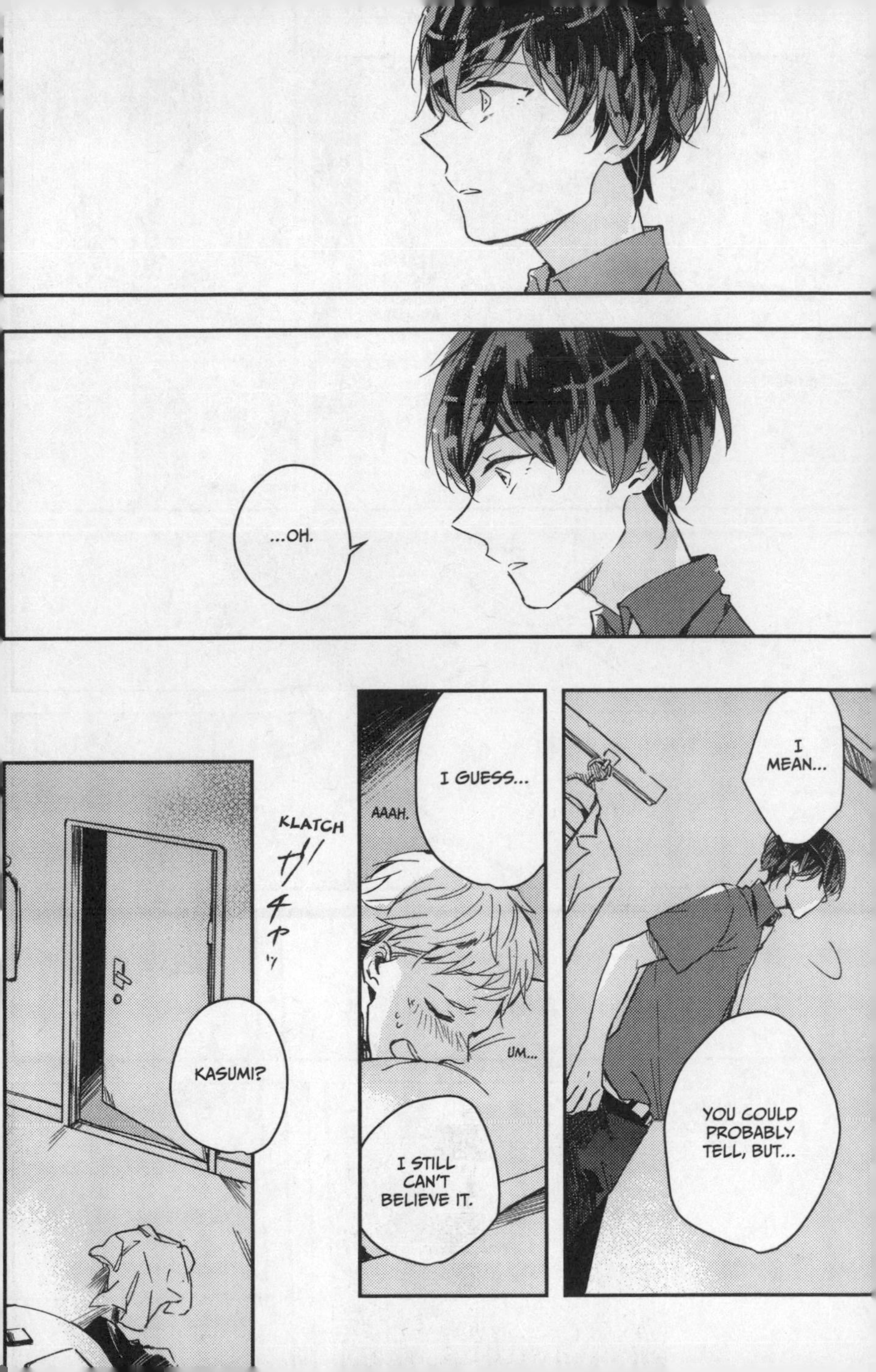
...OH.
I MEAN...
YOU COULD PROBABLY TELL, BUT...
I GUESS...
AAAH.
UM...
I STILL CAN'T BELIEVE IT.
KLATCH
ガチャッ
KASUMI?

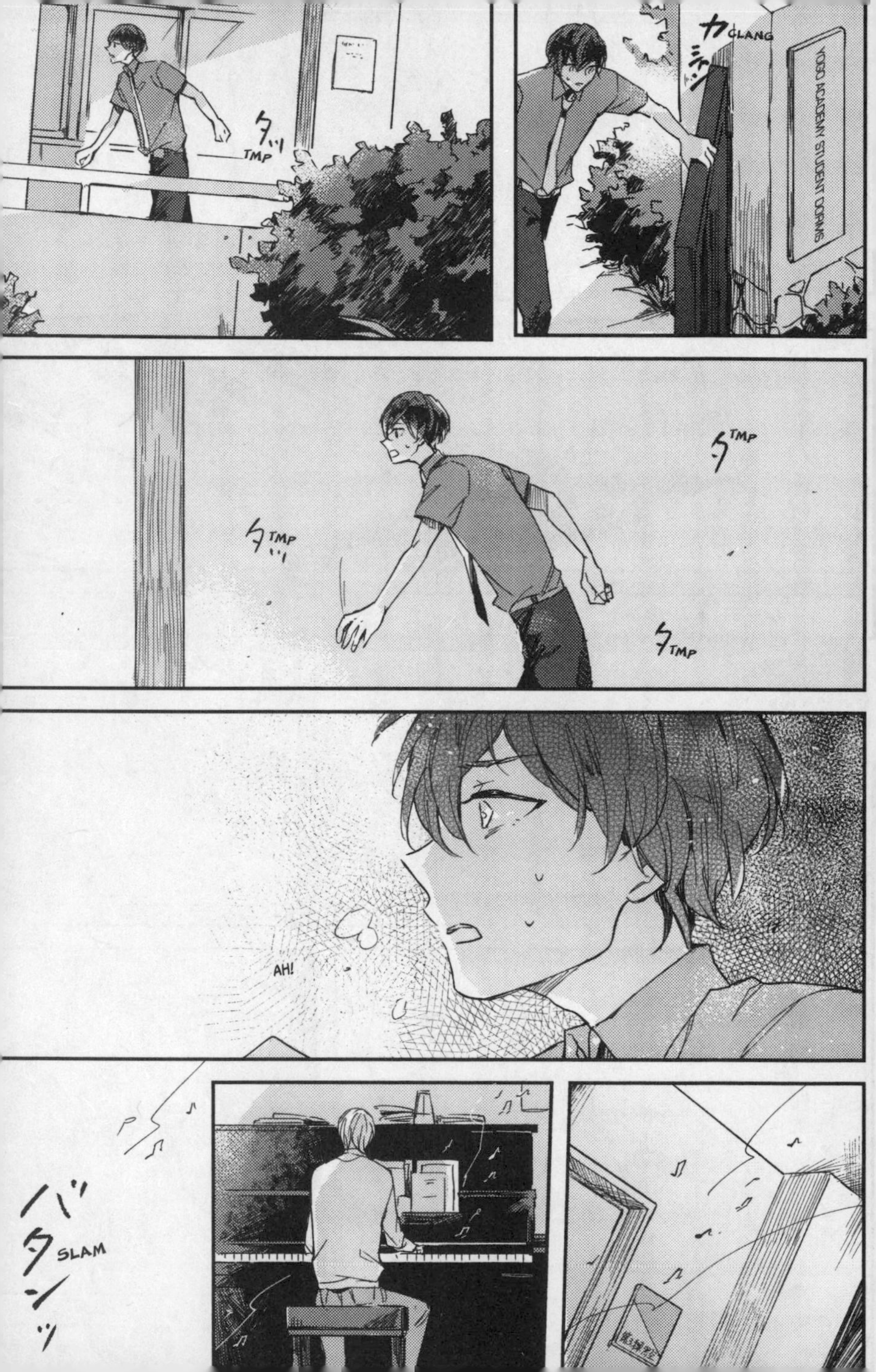
カシャン CLANG
YOGO ACADEMY STUDENT DORMS
タッ TMP
TMP
TMP
TMP
AH!
バタンッ SLAM

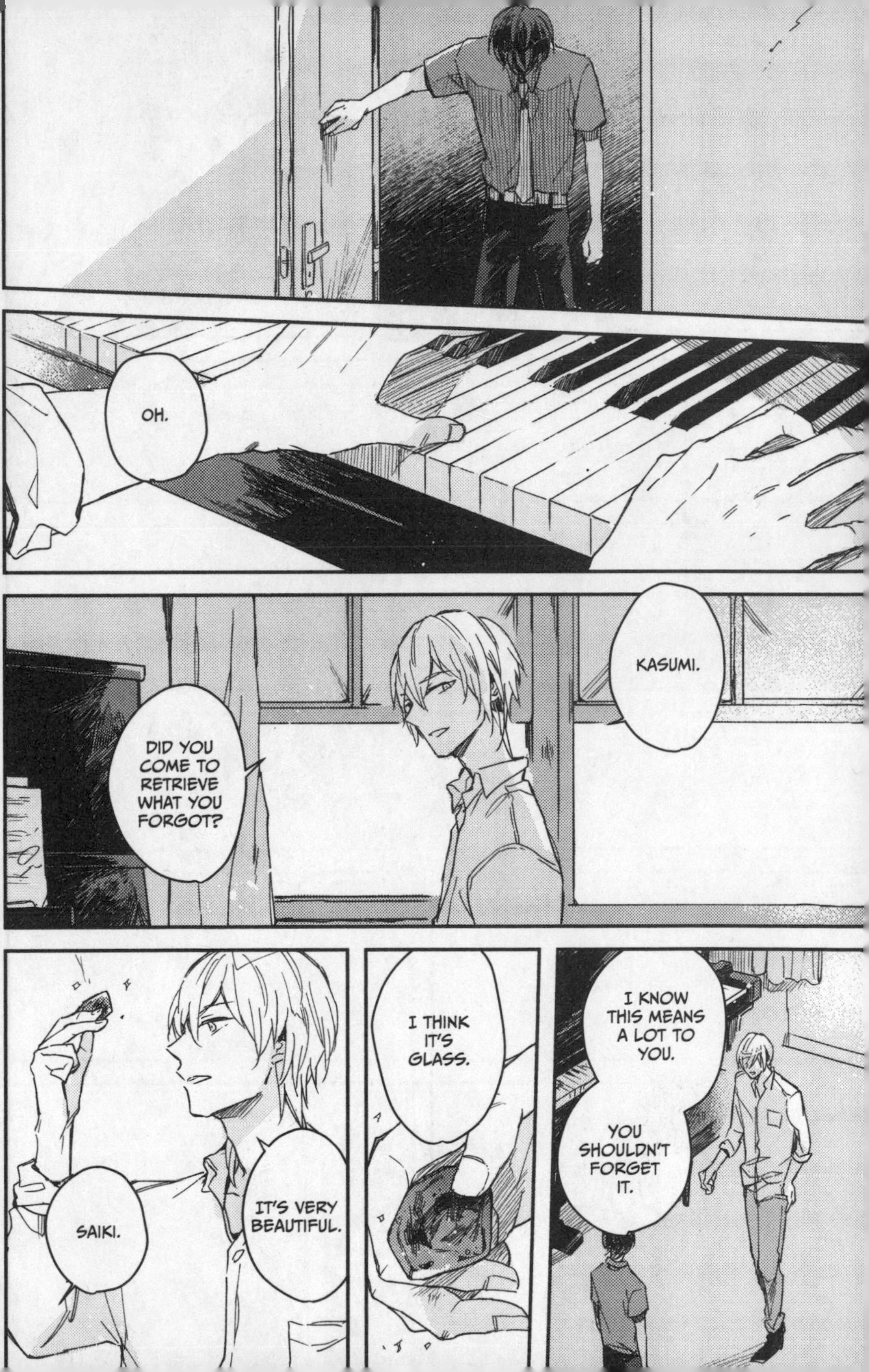
OH.
KASUMI.
DID YOU COME TO RETRIEVE WHAT YOU FORGOT?
I KNOW THIS MEANS A LOT TO YOU.
YOU SHOULDN'T FORGET IT.
I THINK IT'S GLASS.
IT'S VERY BEAUTIFUL.
SAIKI.

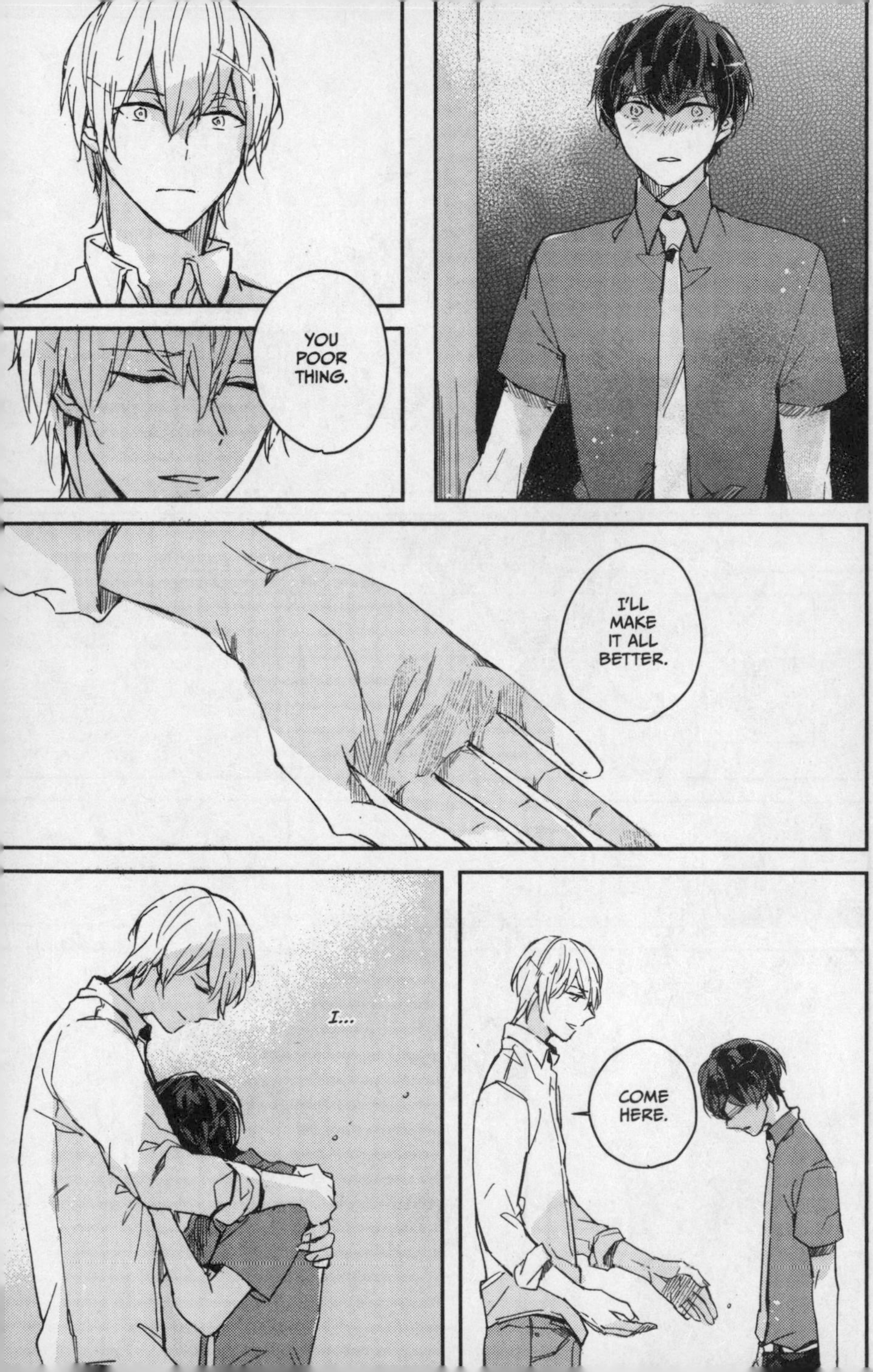
YOU POOR THING.
I'LL MAKE IT ALL BETTER.
COME HERE.
I...

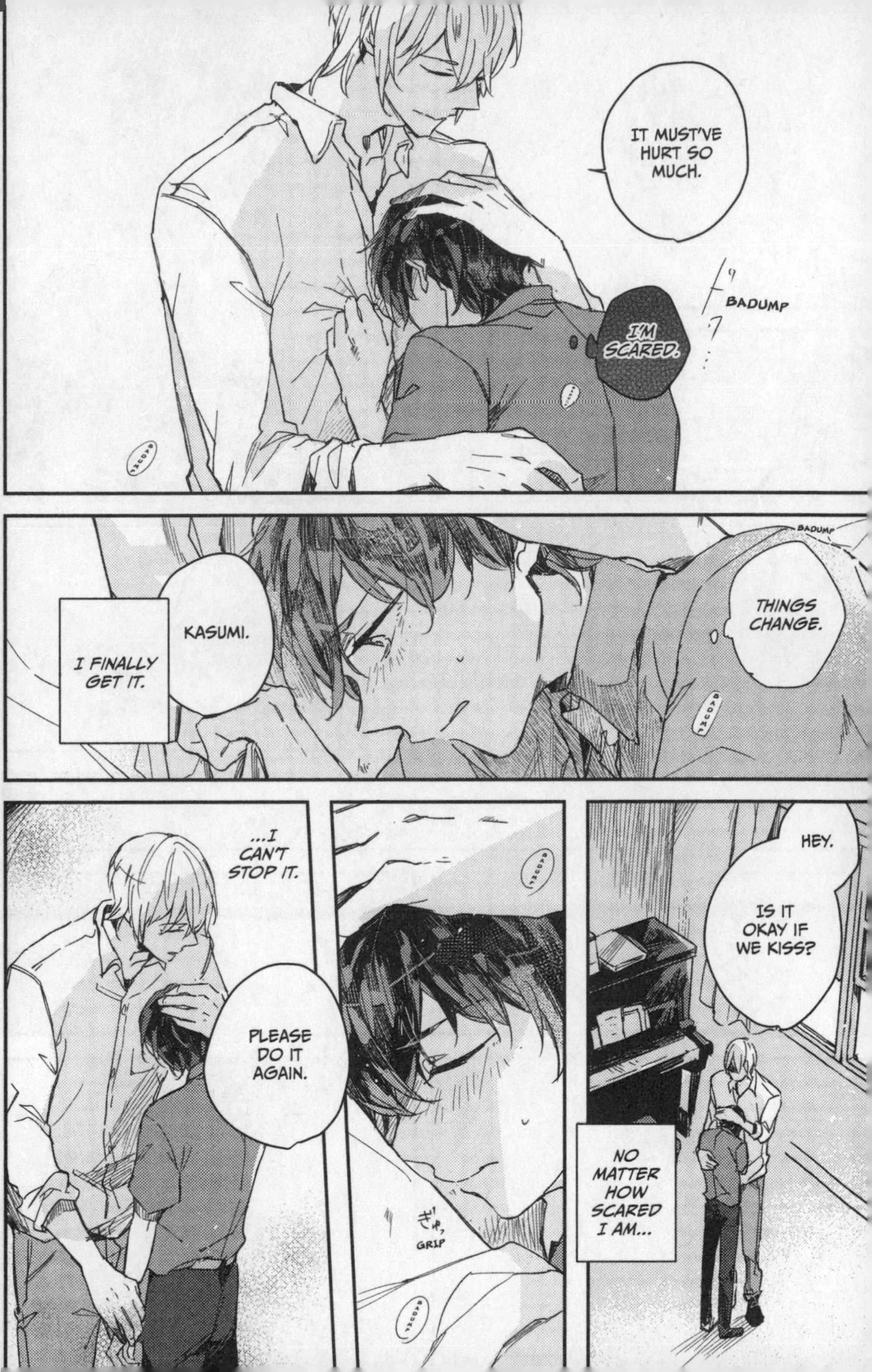
IT MUST'VE HURT SO MUCH.
BADUMP
I'M SCARED.
BADUMP
THINGS CHANGE.
BADUMP
KASUMI.
I FINALLY GET IT.
HEY.
IS IT OKAY IF WE KISS?
NO MATTER HOW SCARED I AM...
BADUMP
ぎゅ
GRIP
BADUMP
...I CAN'T STOP IT.
PLEASE DO IT AGAIN.

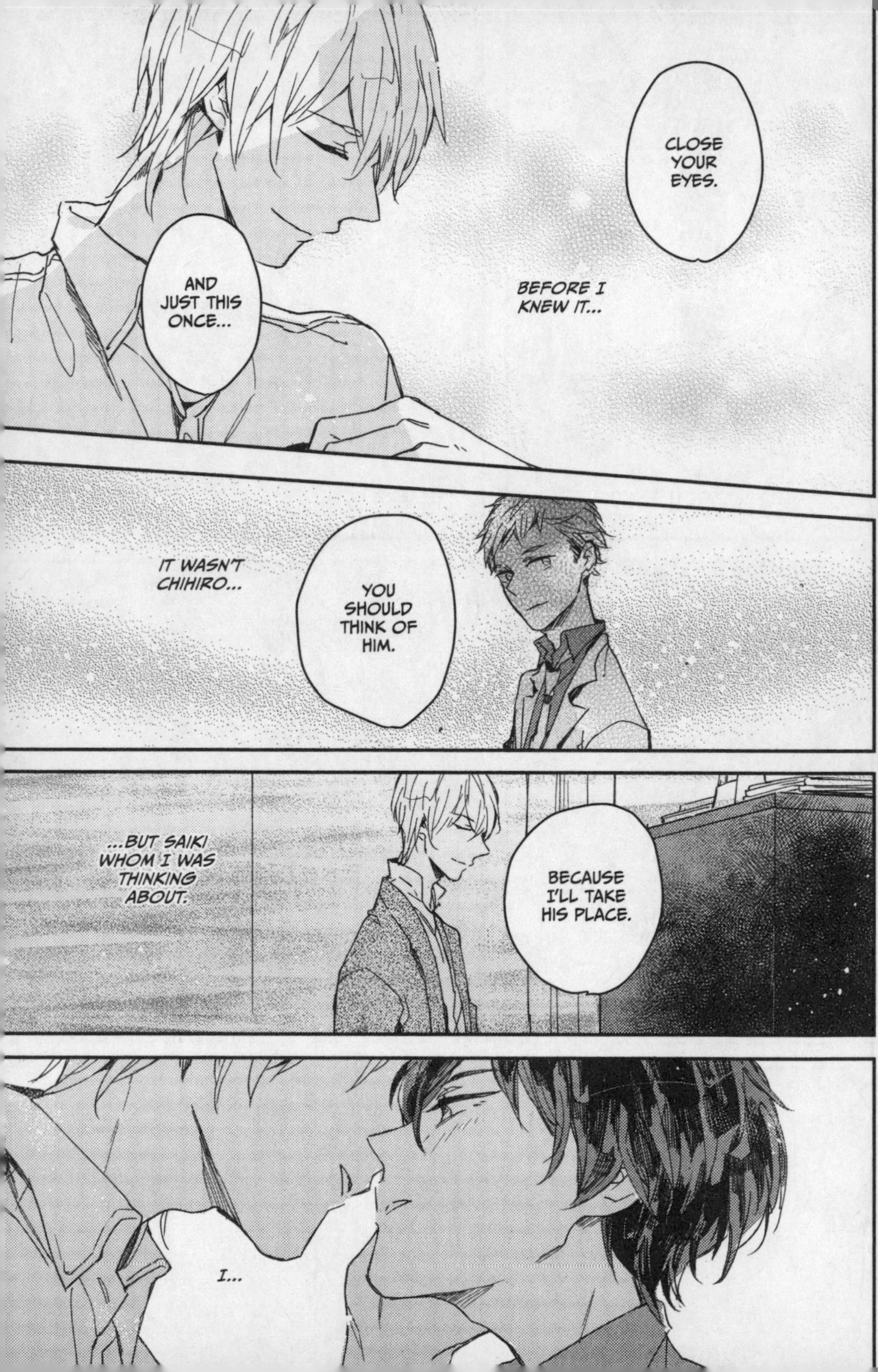
CLOSE YOUR EYES.
BEFORE I KNEW IT...
AND JUST THIS ONCE...
YOU SHOULD THINK OF HIM.
IT WASN'T CHIHIRO...
BECAUSE I'LL TAKE HIS PLACE.
...BUT SAIKI WHOM I WAS THINKING ABOUT.
I...

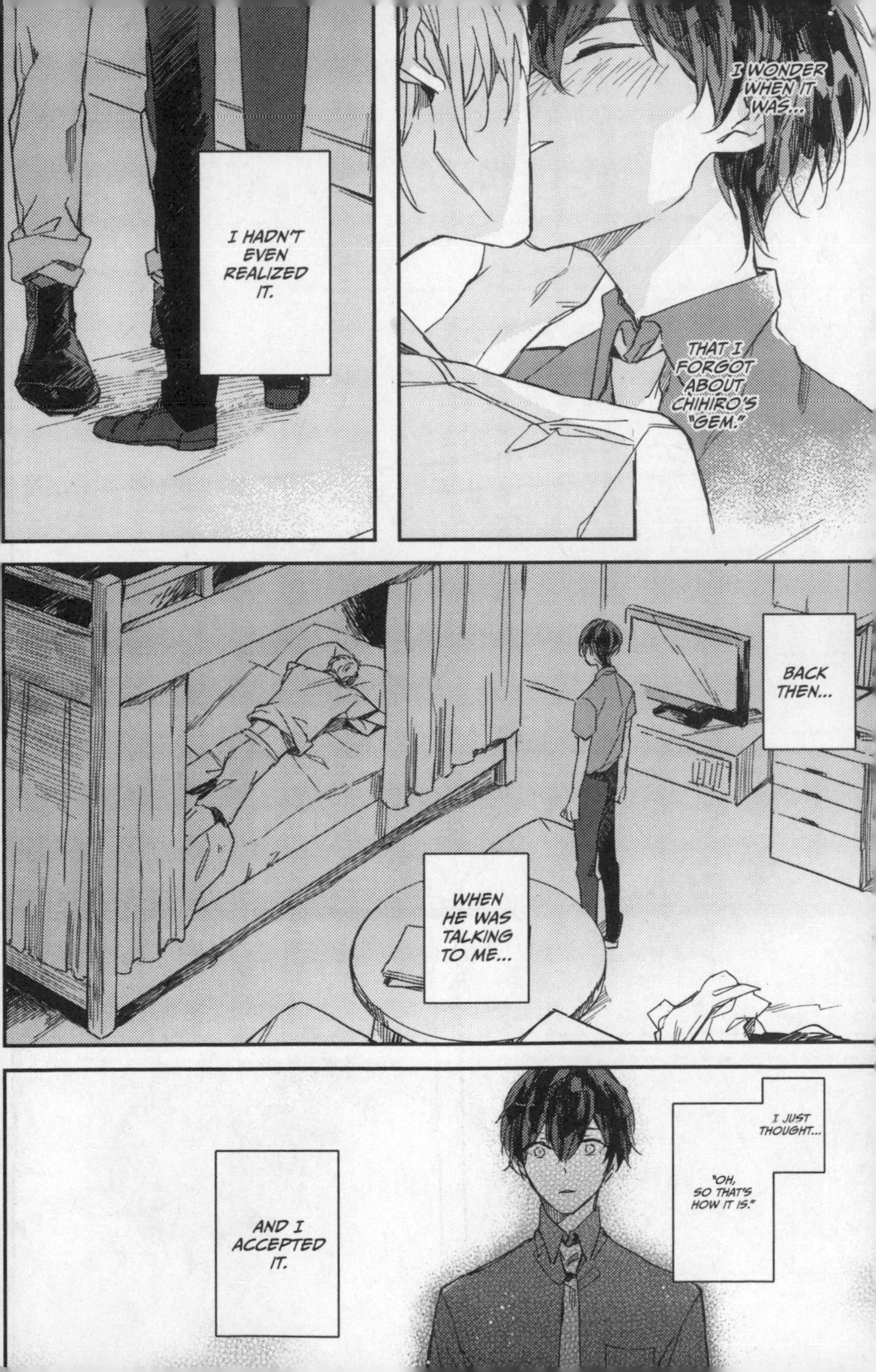
I WONDER WHEN IT WAS...
THAT I FORGOT ABOUT CHIHIRO'S "GEM."
I HADN'T EVEN REALIZED IT.
BACK THEN...
WHEN HE WAS TALKING TO ME...
I JUST THOUGHT...
"OH, SO THAT'S HOW IT IS."
AND I ACCEPTED IT.

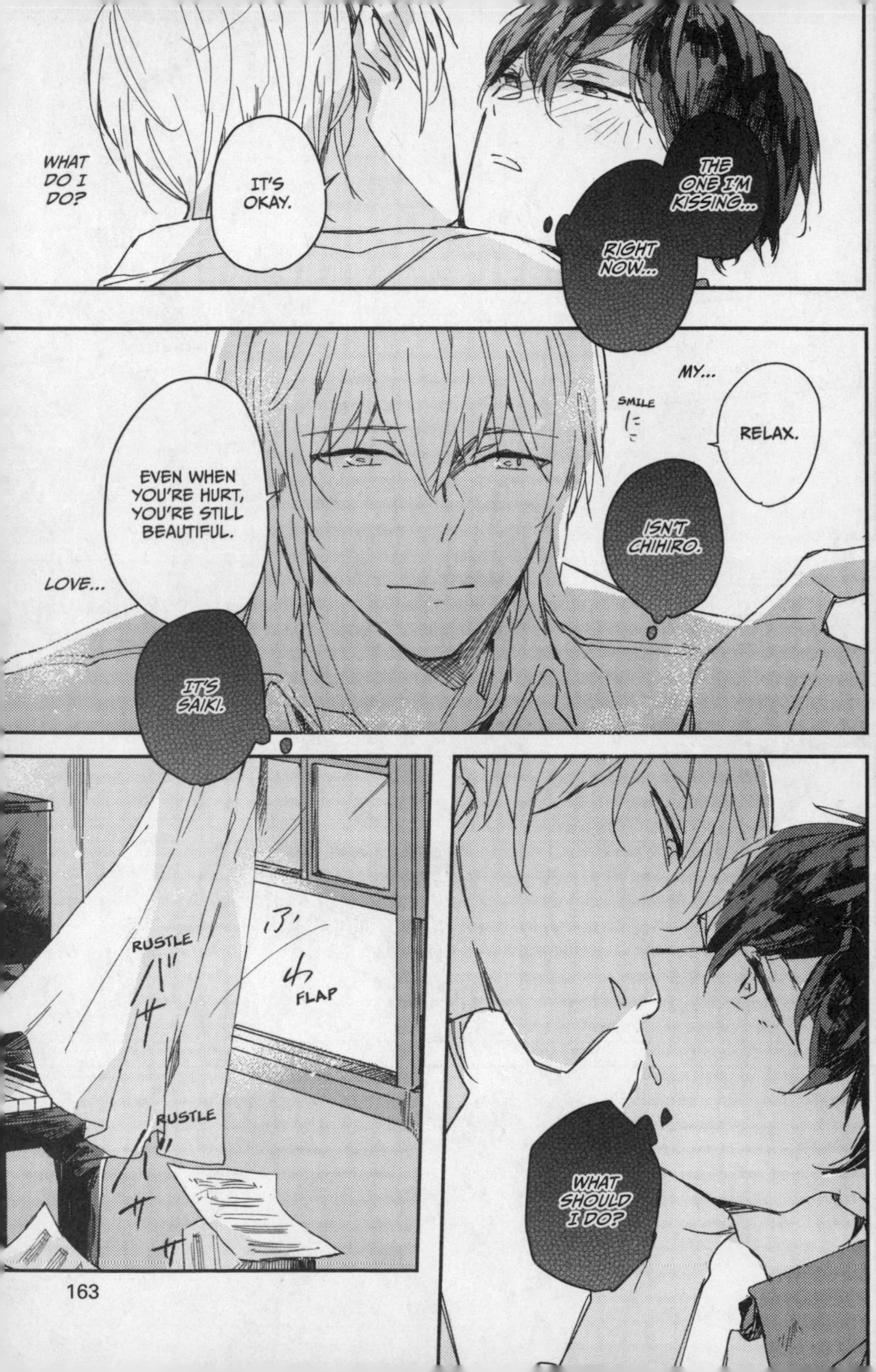
THE ONE I'M KISSING...
RIGHT NOW...
IT'S OKAY.
WHAT DO I DO?
MY...
SMILE
RELAX.
ISN'T CHIHIRO.
EVEN WHEN YOU'RE HURT, YOU'RE STILL BEAUTIFUL.
LOVE...
IT'S SAIKI.
WHAT SHOULD I DO?
RUSTLE
FLAP
RUSTLE

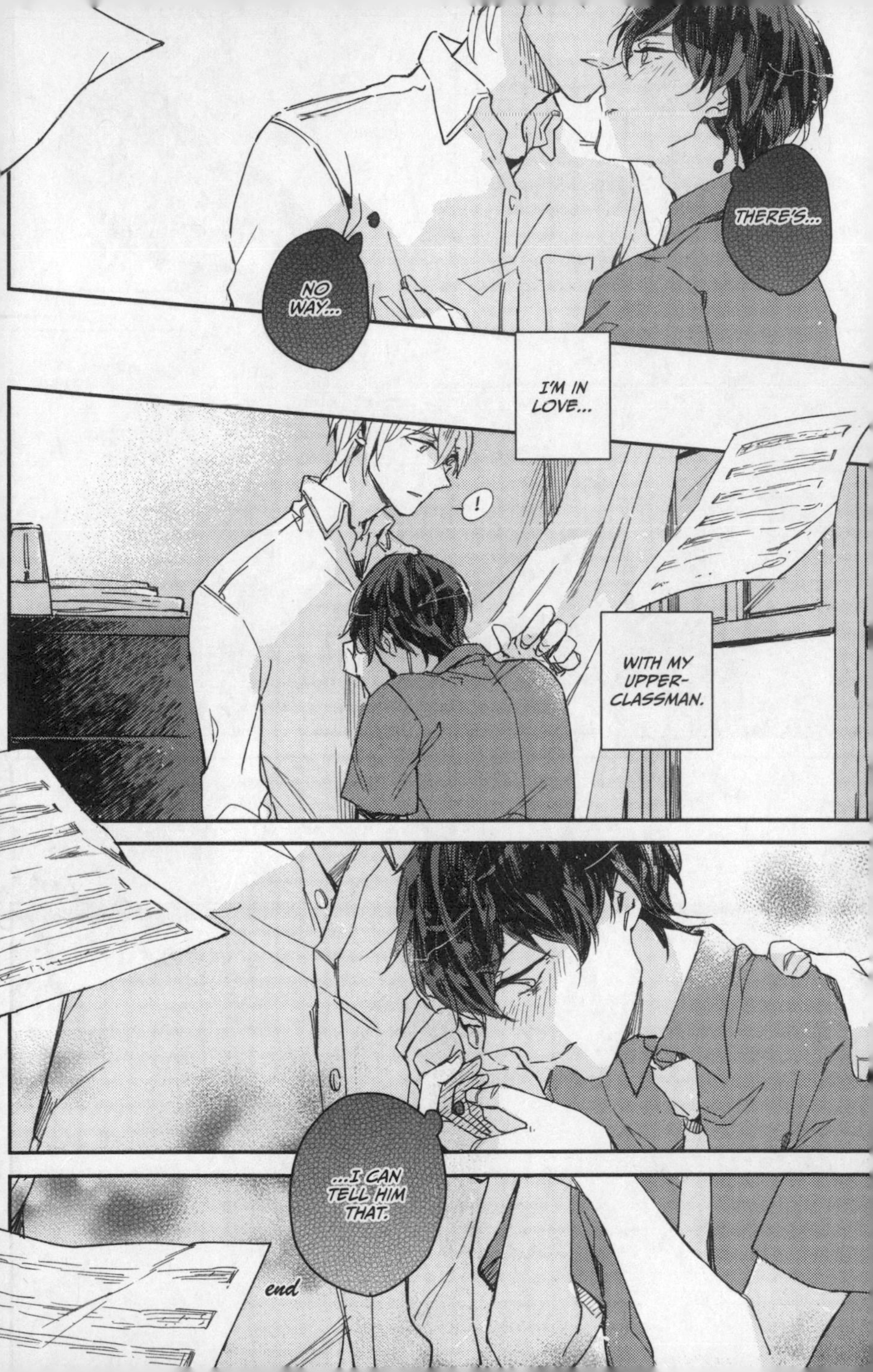
THERE'S...
NO WAY...
I'M IN LOVE...
!
WITH MY UPPER-CLASSMAN.
...I CAN TELL HIM THAT.
end

Glass Syndrome

Sequel

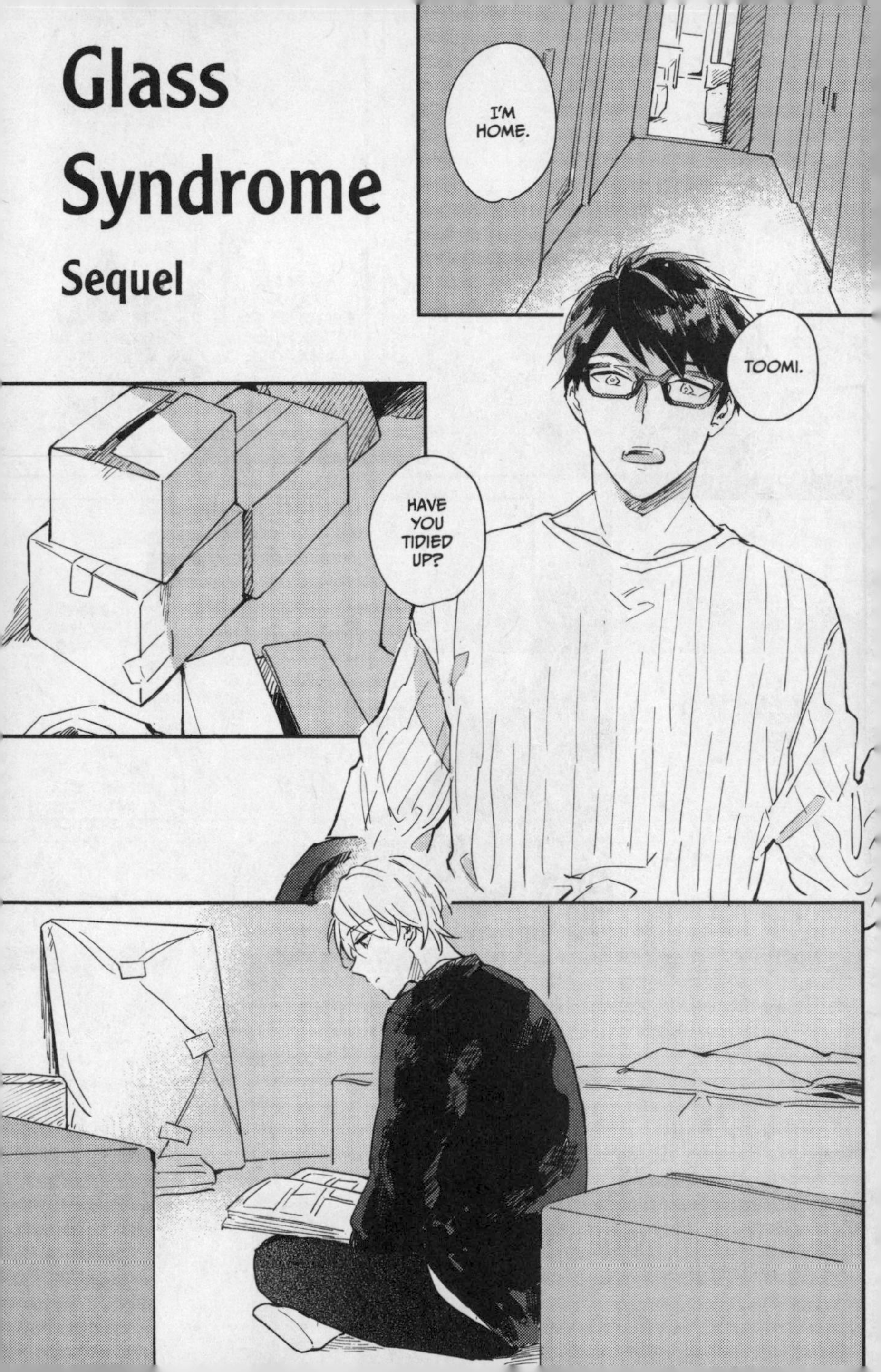
I'M HOME.
TOOMI.
HAVE YOU TIDIED UP?

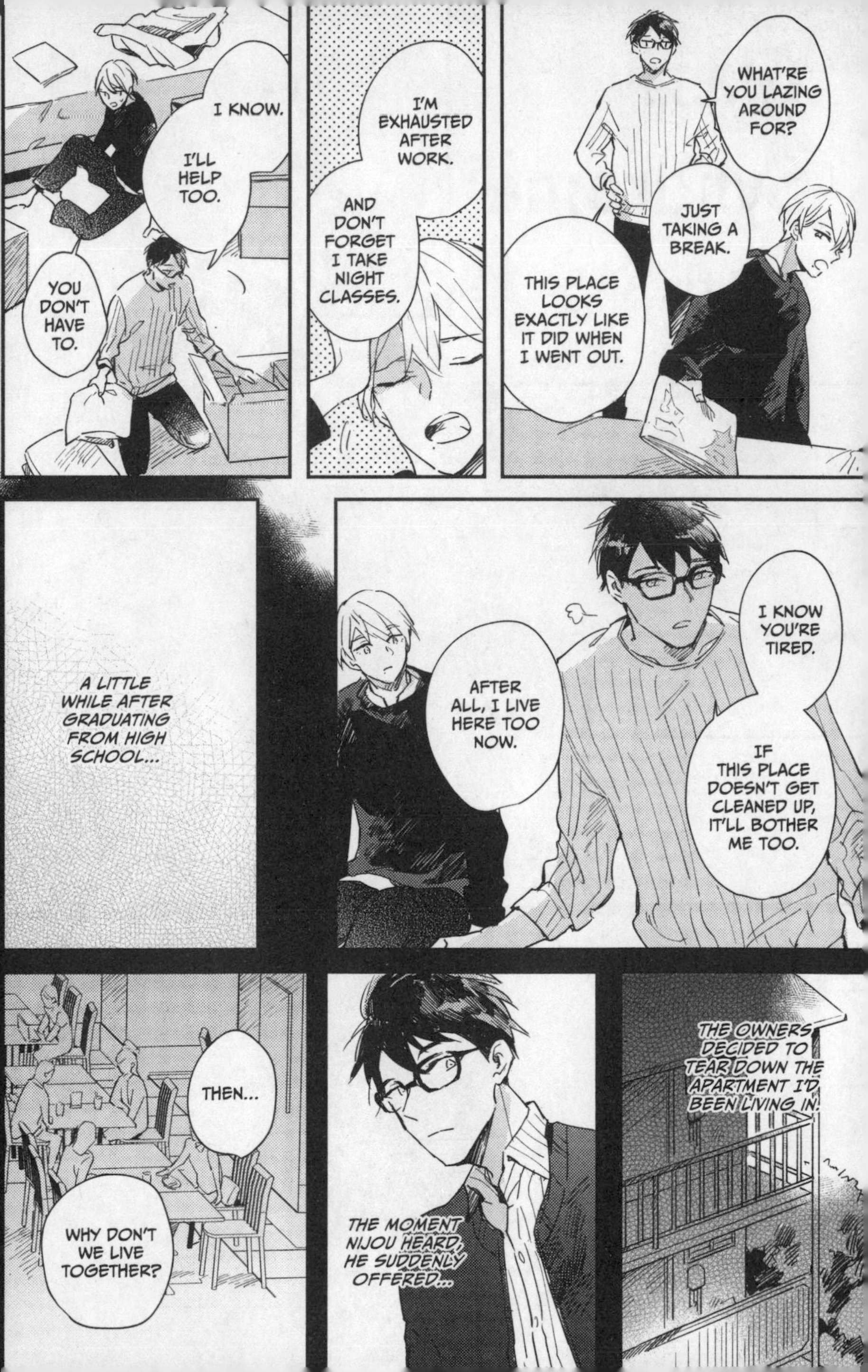
WHAT'RE YOU LAZING AROUND FOR?
JUST TAKING A BREAK.
THIS PLACE LOOKS EXACTLY LIKE IT DID WHEN I WENT OUT.
I'M EXHAUSTED AFTER WORK.
AND DON'T FORGET I TAKE NIGHT CLASSES.
I KNOW.
I'LL HELP TOO.
YOU DON'T HAVE TO.
I KNOW YOU'RE TIRED.
IF THIS PLACE DOESN'T GET CLEANED UP, IT'LL BOTHER ME TOO.
AFTER ALL, I LIVE HERE TOO NOW.
A LITTLE WHILE AFTER GRADUATING FROM HIGH SCHOOL...
THE OWNERS DECIDED TO TEAR DOWN THE APARTMENT I'D BEEN LIVING IN.
THE MOMENT NIJOU HEARD, HE SUDDENLY OFFERED...
THEN...
WHY DON'T WE LIVE TOGETHER?

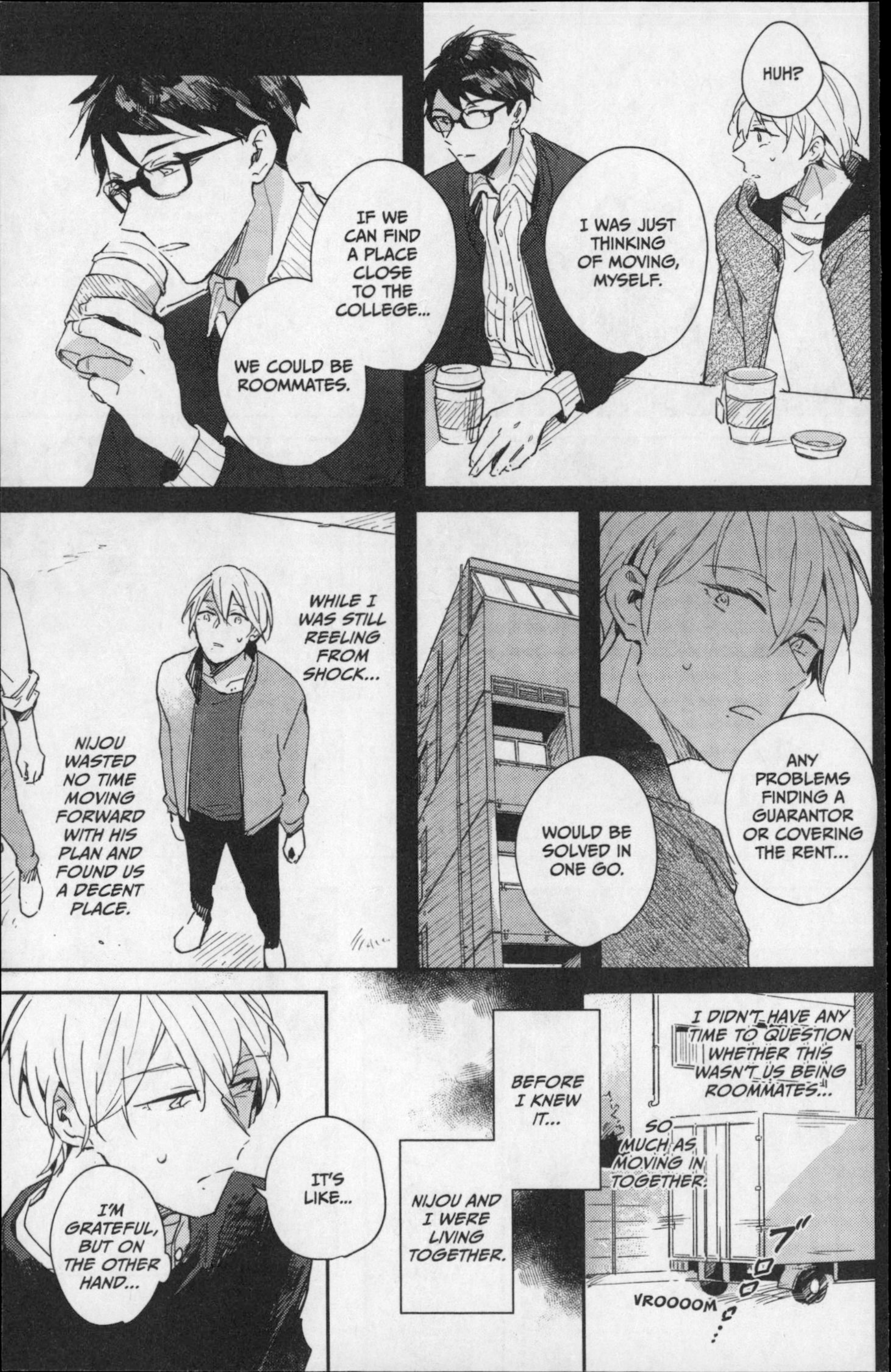
HUH?
I WAS JUST THINKING OF MOVING, MYSELF.
IF WE CAN FIND A PLACE CLOSE TO THE COLLEGE...
WE COULD BE ROOMMATES.
ANY PROBLEMS FINDING A GUARANTOR OR COVERING THE RENT...
WOULD BE SOLVED IN ONE GO.
WHILE I WAS STILL REELING FROM SHOCK...
NIJOU WASTED NO TIME MOVING FORWARD WITH HIS PLAN AND FOUND US A DECENT PLACE.
I DIDN'T HAVE ANY TIME TO QUESTION WHETHER THIS WASN'T US BEING ROOMMATES...
SO MUCH AS MOVING IN TOGETHER.
VROOOOM
BEFORE I KNEW IT...
NIJOU AND I WERE LIVING TOGETHER.
IT'S LIKE...
I'M GRATEFUL, BUT ON THE OTHER HAND...

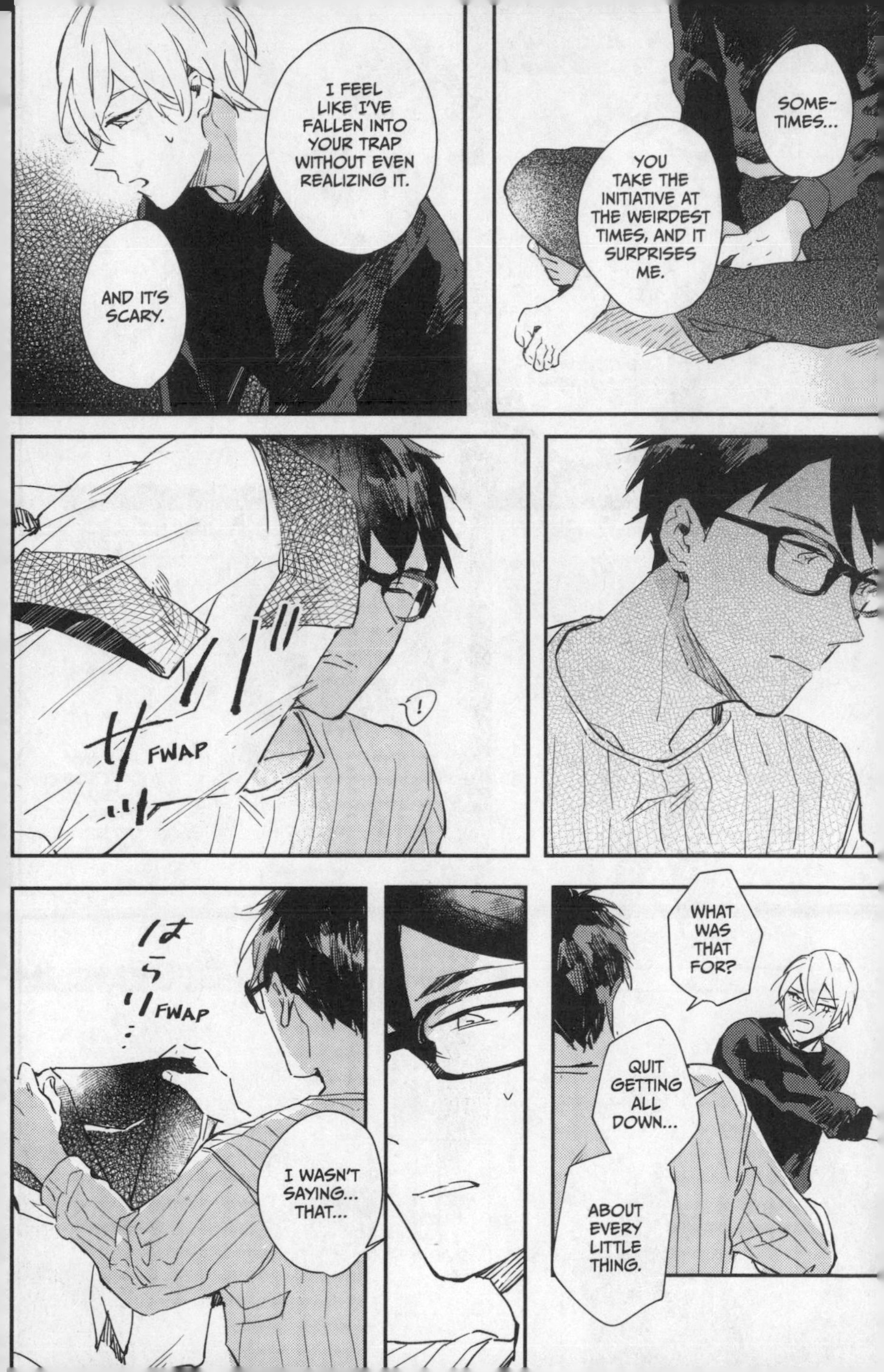
SOME-TIMES...
YOU TAKE THE INITIATIVE AT THE WEIRDEST TIMES, AND IT SURPRISES ME.
I FEEL LIKE I'VE FALLEN INTO YOUR TRAP WITHOUT EVEN REALIZING IT.
AND IT'S SCARY.
!
FWAP
WHAT WAS THAT FOR?
QUIT GETTING ALL DOWN...
ABOUT EVERY LITTLE THING.
I WASN'T SAYING... THAT...
FWAP

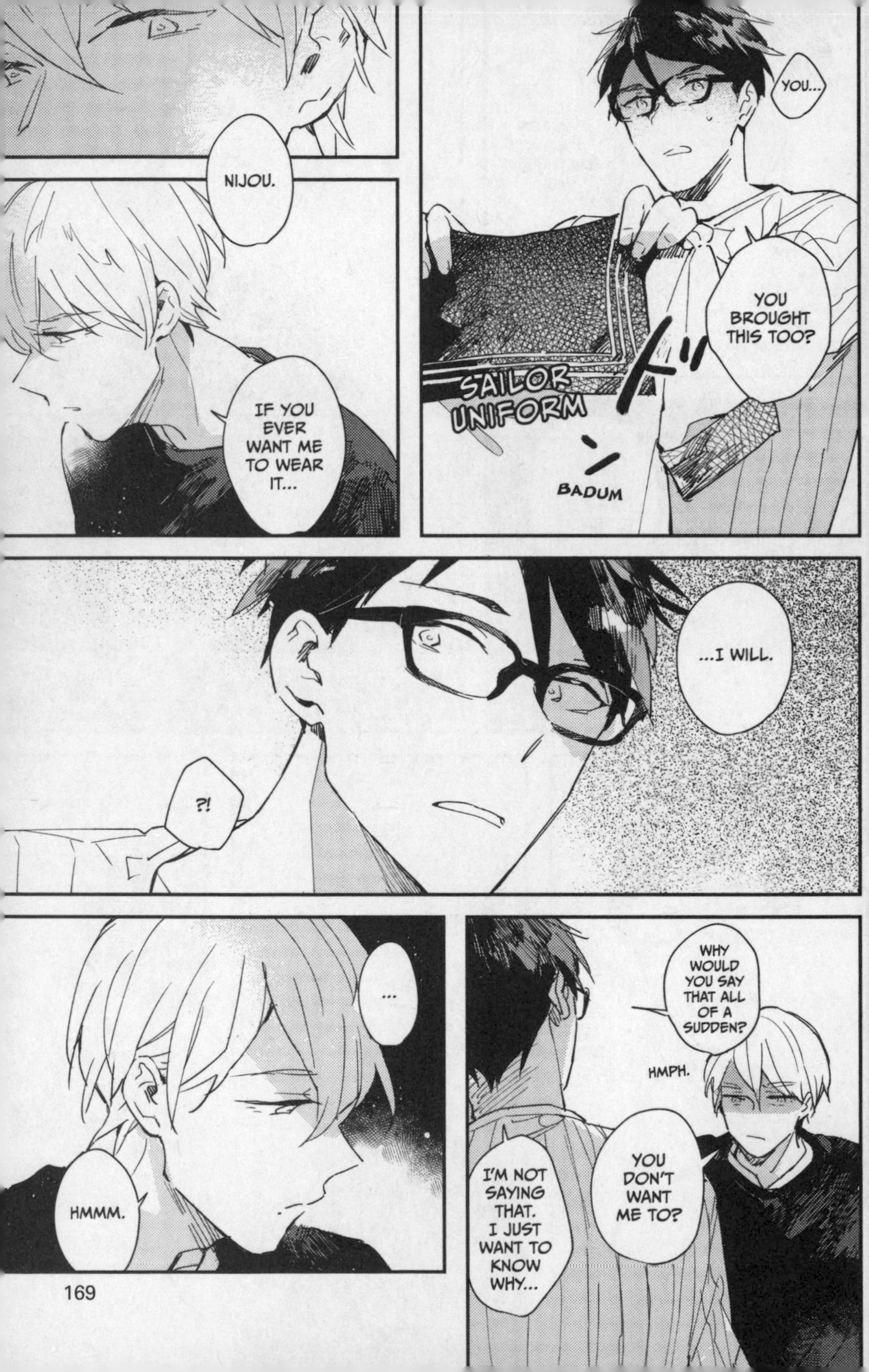
YOU...
YOU BROUGHT THIS TOO?
SAILOR UNIFORM
BADUM
NIJOU.
IF YOU EVER WANT ME TO WEAR IT...
...I WILL.
?!
WHY WOULD YOU SAY THAT ALL OF A SUDDEN?
HMPH.
YOU DON'T WANT ME TO?
I'M NOT SAYING THAT. I JUST WANT TO KNOW WHY...
...
HMMM.

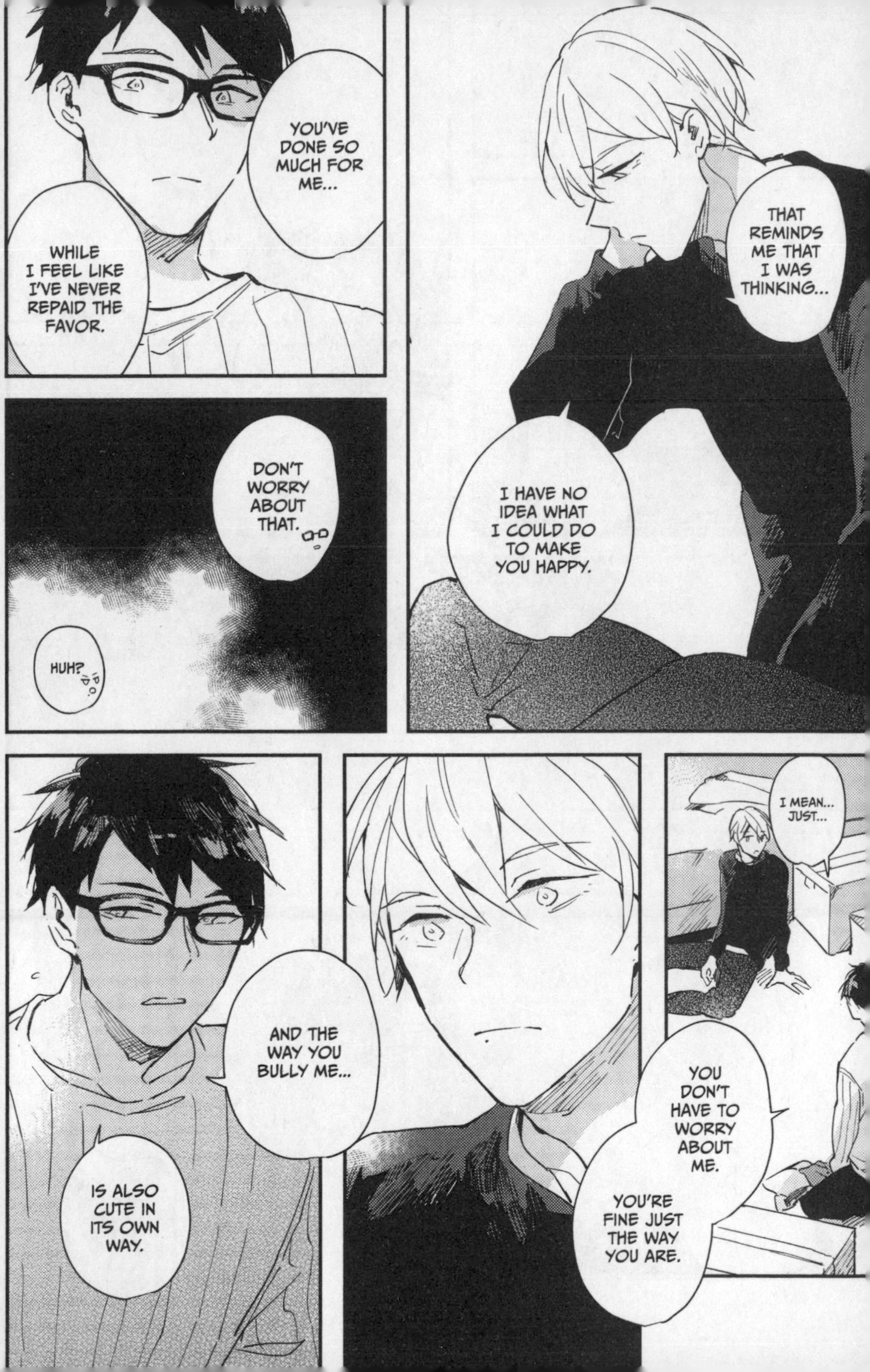
THAT REMINDS ME THAT I WAS THINKING...
I HAVE NO IDEA WHAT I COULD DO TO MAKE YOU HAPPY.
YOU'VE DONE SO MUCH FOR ME...
WHILE I FEEL LIKE I'VE NEVER REPAID THE FAVOR.
DON'T WORRY ABOUT THAT.
HUH?
I MEAN... JUST...
YOU DON'T HAVE TO WORRY ABOUT ME.
YOU'RE FINE JUST THE WAY YOU ARE.
AND THE WAY YOU BULLY ME...
IS ALSO CUTE IN ITS OWN WAY.

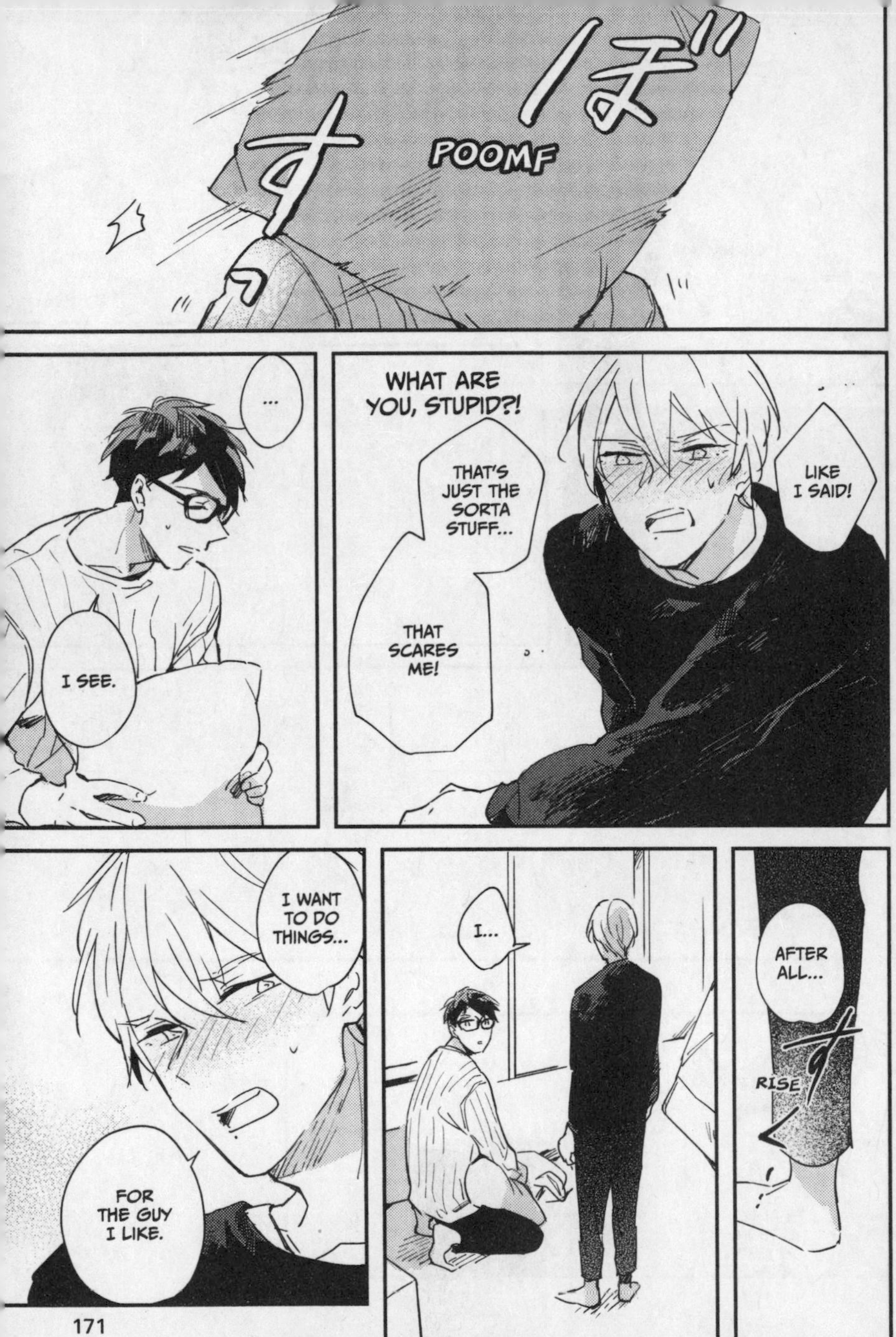

ぼ
す
POOMF
LIKE I SAID!
WHAT ARE YOU, STUPID?!
THAT'S JUST THE SORTA STUFF...
THAT SCARES ME!
...
I SEE.
AFTER ALL...
RISE
I...
I WANT TO DO THINGS...
FOR THE GUY I LIKE.

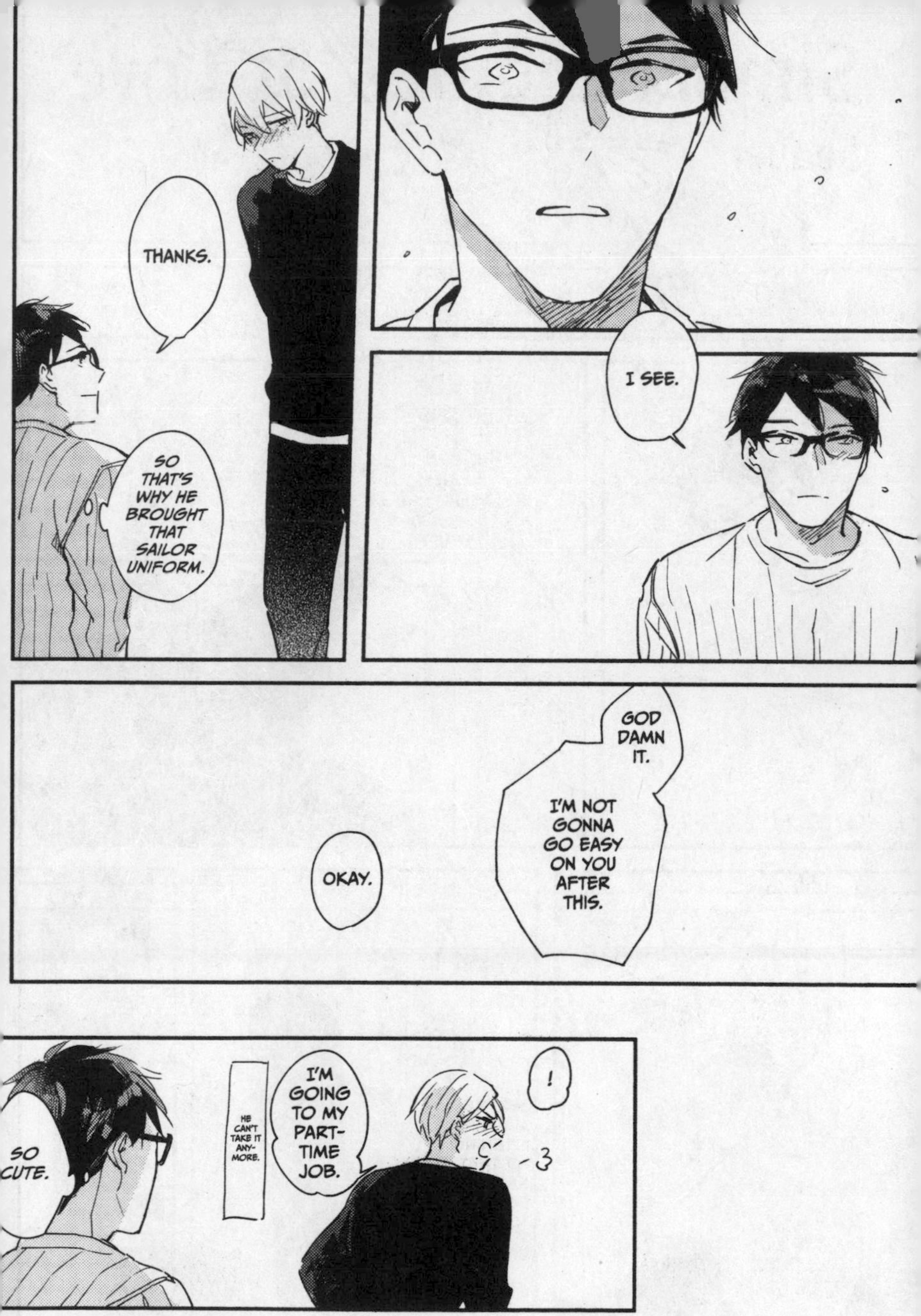
I SEE.
THANKS.
SO THAT'S WHY HE BROUGHT THAT SAILOR UNIFORM.
GOD DAMN IT.
I'M NOT GONNA GO EASY ON YOU AFTER THIS.
OKAY.
!
I'M GOING TO MY PART-TIME JOB.
HE CAN'T TAKE IT ANY-MORE.
SO CUTE.

end

Similar Figures of Love

Sequel

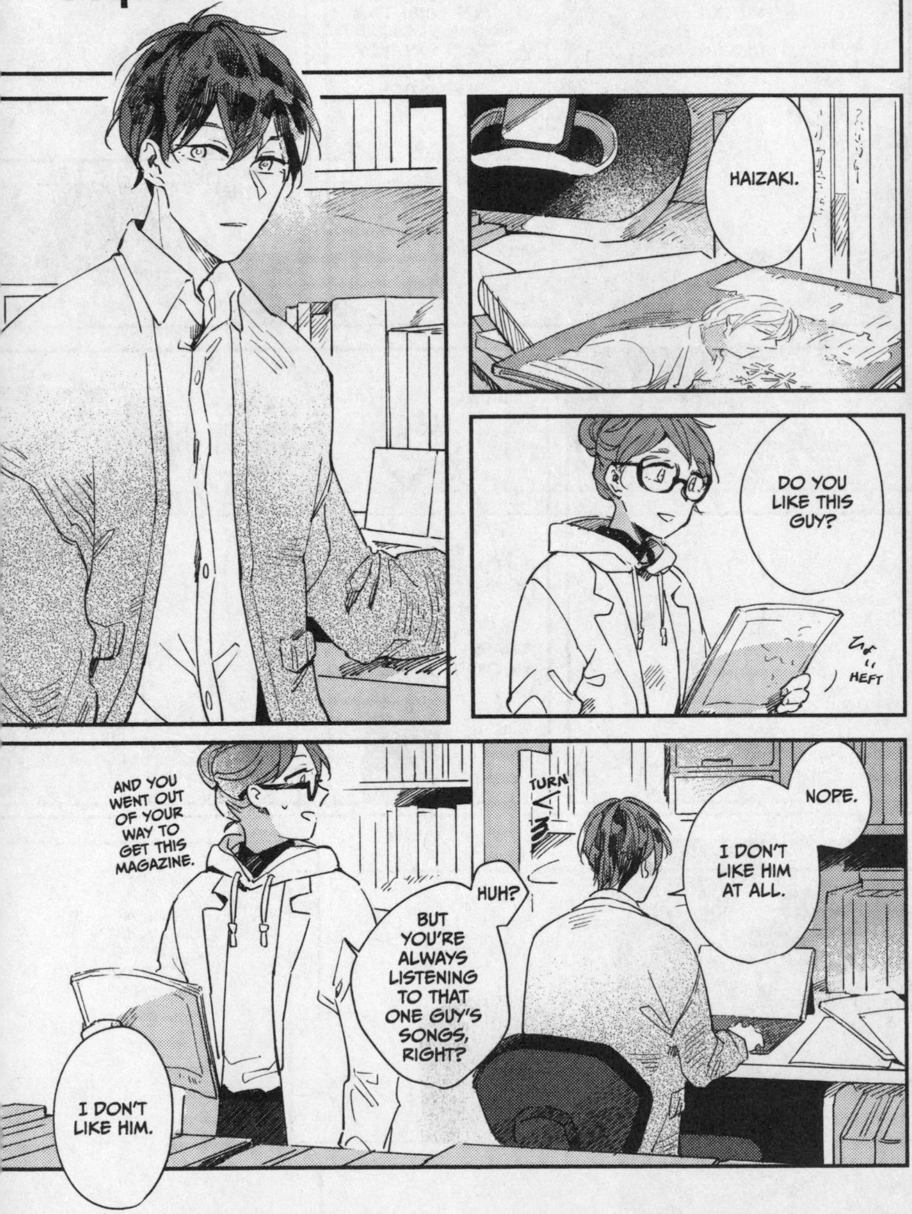
HAIZAKI.
DO YOU LIKE THIS GUY?
HEFT
NOPE.
I DON'T LIKE HIM AT ALL.
TURN
HUH?
BUT YOU'RE ALWAYS LISTENING TO THAT ONE GUY'S SONGS, RIGHT?
AND YOU WENT OUT OF YOUR WAY TO GET THIS MAGAZINE.
I DON'T LIKE HIM.

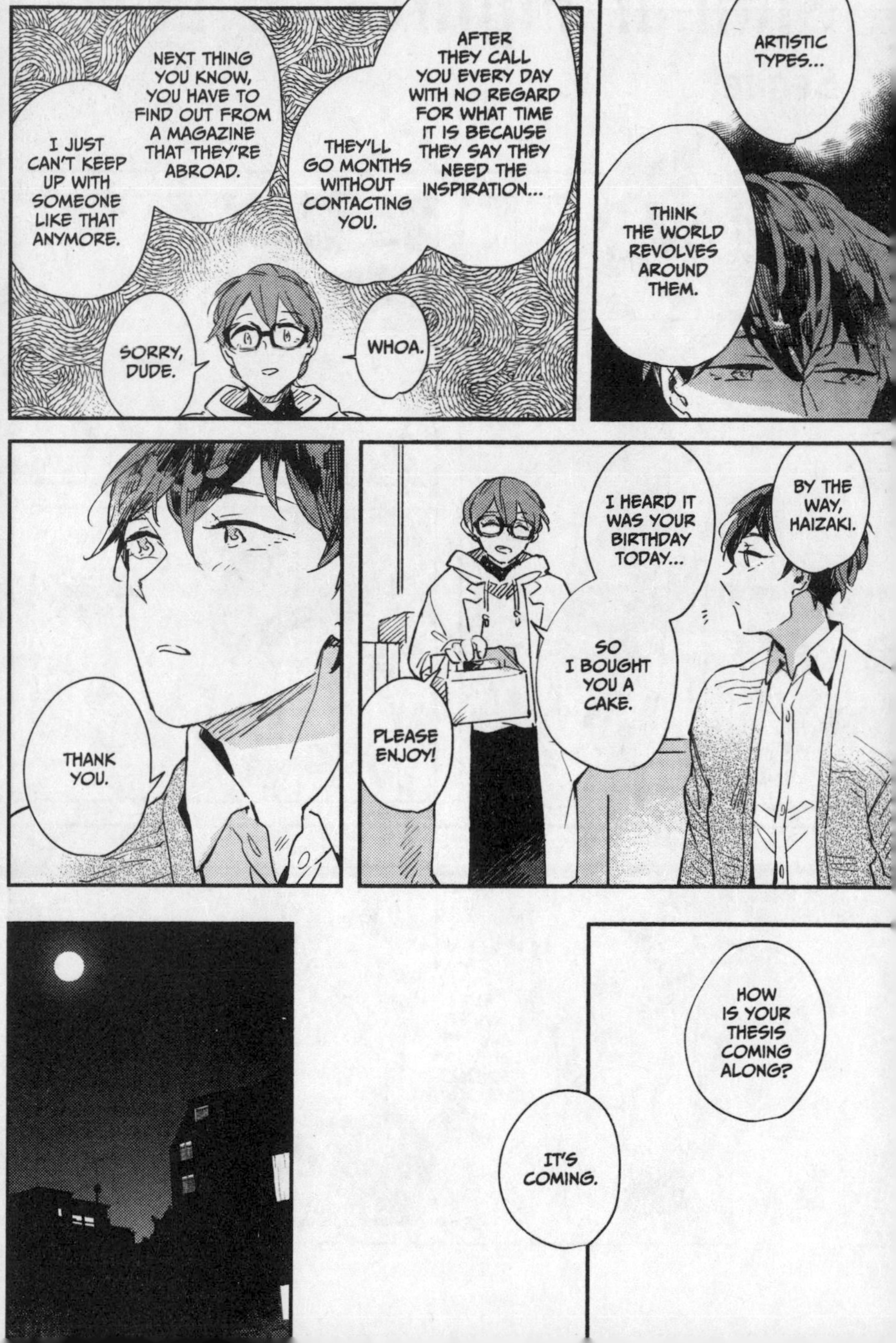
ARTISTIC TYPES...
THINK THE WORLD REVOLVES AROUND THEM.
AFTER THEY CALL YOU EVERY DAY WITH NO REGARD FOR WHAT TIME IT IS BECAUSE THEY SAY THEY NEED THE INSPIRATION...
THEY'LL GO MONTHS WITHOUT CONTACTING YOU.
NEXT THING YOU KNOW, YOU HAVE TO FIND OUT FROM A MAGAZINE THAT THEY'RE ABROAD.
I JUST CAN'T KEEP UP WITH SOMEONE LIKE THAT ANYMORE.
WHOA.
SORRY, DUDE.
BY THE WAY, HAIZAKI.
I HEARD IT WAS YOUR BIRTHDAY TODAY...
SO I BOUGHT YOU A CAKE.
PLEASE ENJOY!
THANK YOU.
HOW IS YOUR THESIS COMING ALONG?
IT'S COMING.

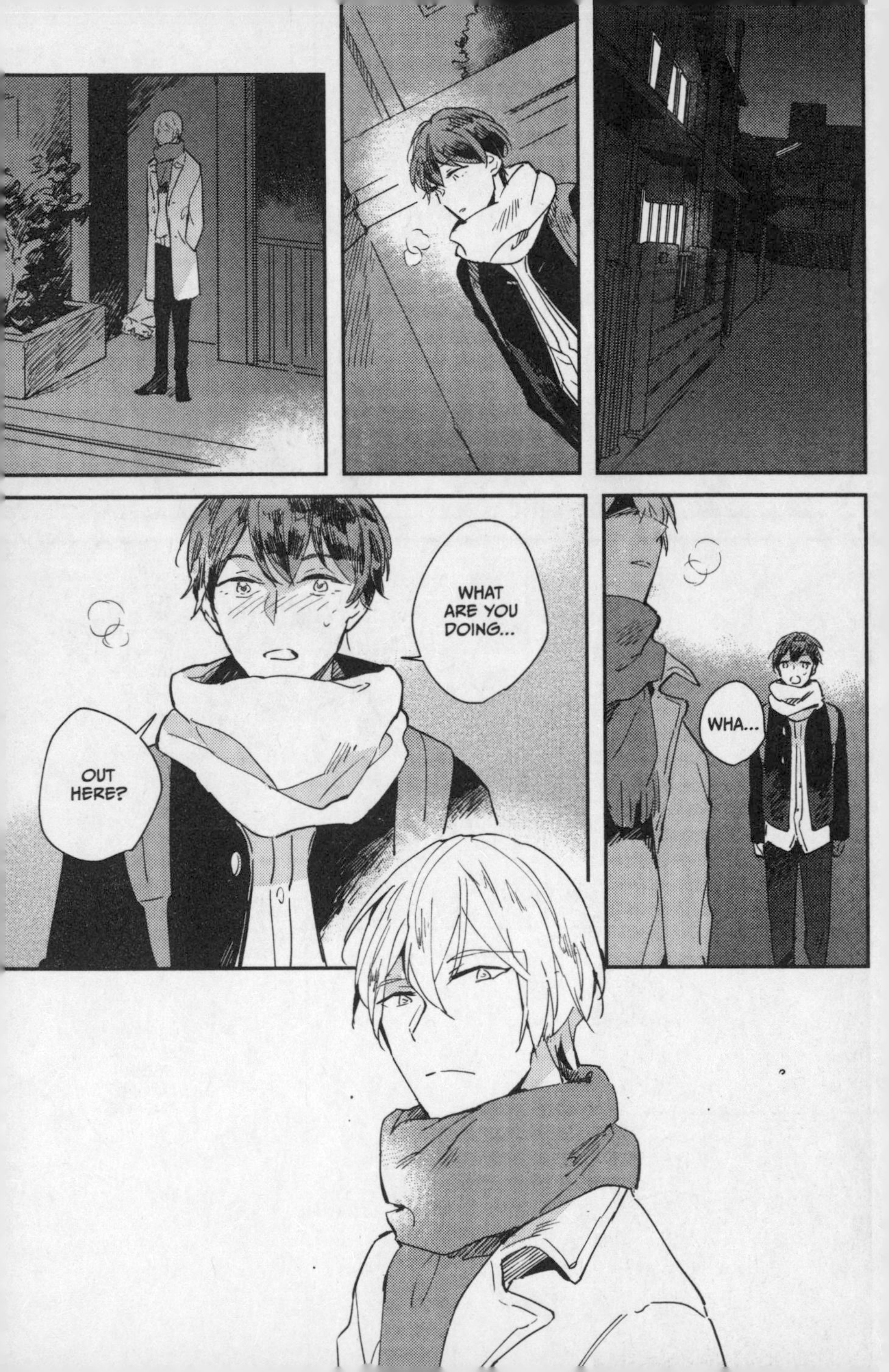
WHA...
WHAT ARE YOU DOING...
OUT HERE?

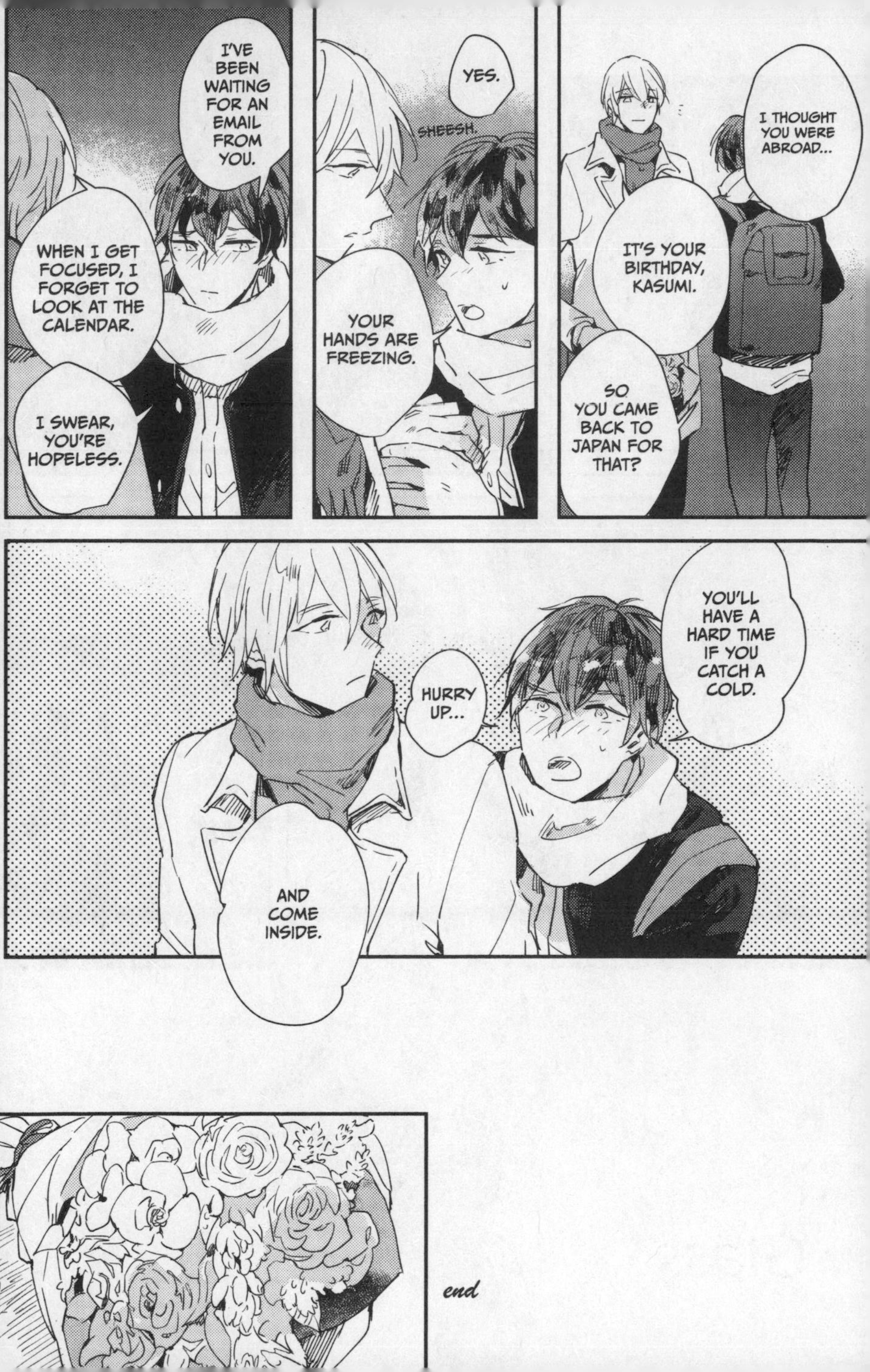
I THOUGHT YOU WERE ABROAD...
IT'S YOUR BIRTHDAY, KASUMI.
SO YOU CAME BACK TO JAPAN FOR THAT?
YES.
SHEESH.
YOUR HANDS ARE FREEZING.
I'VE BEEN WAITING FOR AN EMAIL FROM YOU.
WHEN I GET FOCUSED, I FORGET TO LOOK AT THE CALENDAR.
I SWEAR, YOU'RE HOPELESS.
YOU'LL HAVE A HARD TIME IF YOU CATCH A COLD.
HURRY UP...
AND COME INSIDE.
end

Glass *Syndrome*

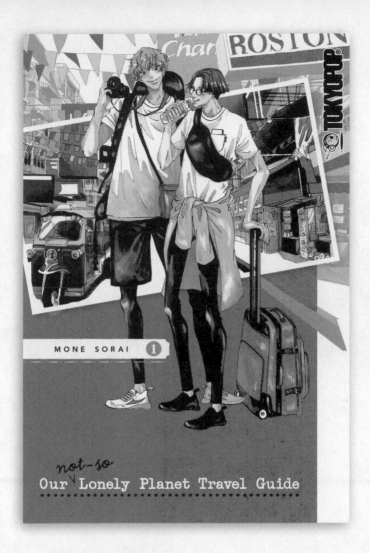

MONE SORAI ①

not-so
Our ˅Lonely Planet Travel Guide

◊LOVE-x-LOVE◊

Super serious Asahi Suzumura and laidback, easygoing Mitsuki Sayama might seem like an odd couple, but they made a deal; they'll vacation around the world and when they get back to Japan, they'll get married. As they travel from country to country, the different people, cultures and cuisine they encounter begin to bring them closer together. After all they're not just learning about the world, but about themselves too.

© Mone Sorai 2020 / MAG Garden

KATAKOI LAMP

Kyohei Azumi

Katakoi Lamp
TOKYOPOP
KYOHEI AZUMI

LOVE x LOVE

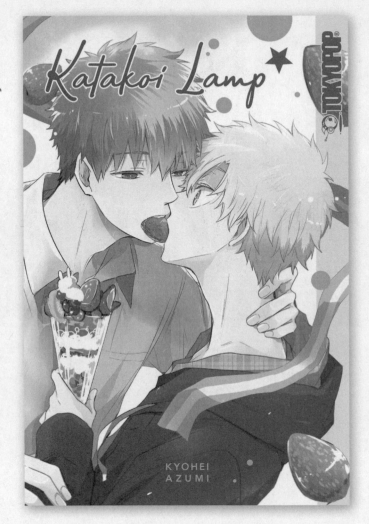

Kazuto Muronoi runs a cute little coffee shop, where many people enjoy doing some work or writing papers for school. Among his coffee shop's regulars is a college student named Jun, who often studies there. It was love at first sight for Kazuto! Will Kazuto be able to find the courage to confess his crush before Jun graduates college and stops frequenting the shop? And to make matters even more complicated... it seems Jun has his sights set on another worker at the café!

TOKYOPOP

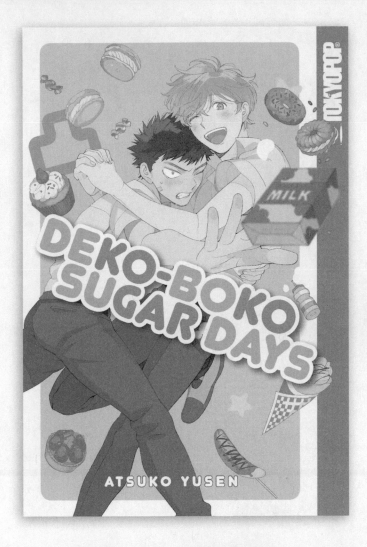

DEKO-BOKO SUGAR DAYS

ATSUKO YUSEN

💍LOVE-x-LOVE💍   MATURE 18+

Yuujirou Matsukaze has been close friends with Rui Hanamine since the two of them were children. Back then, Yuujirou was the one who stood up for and took care of his adorable, soft-hearted friend. But as it turns out, Yuujirou's childhood dreams end up growing a little too big to handle — or, rather, too tall! At over six feet in height, the cute and easygoing Rui towers over his would-be protector... and still has no idea Yuujirou's had a crush on him since they were kids!

THIS WONDERFUL SEASON WITH YOU
Atsuko Yusen

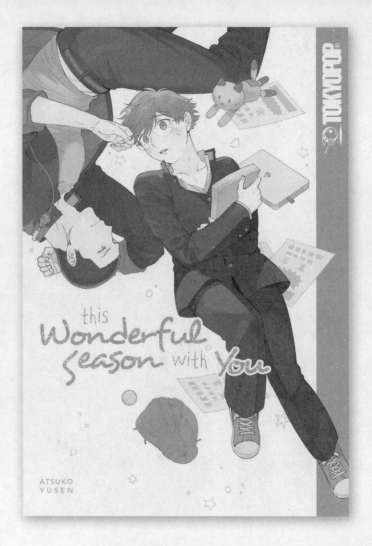

this
Wonderful
season with You

ATSUKO
YUSEN

TOKYOPOP®

MATURE 18+   δLOVE-x-LOVEδ

TOKYOPOP®

Enoki is practically the poster-boy for what a typical nerd looks like: short and slight, complete with big round glasses and social awkwardness. His main hobby is making video games, and he's used to not having many friends at school. Then, he meets Shirataki, a former member of the baseball club and his exact opposite; tall, muscular and sporty. Despite their many differences, the spark of friendship between the two boys begins to grow into something more...

© YUSEN ATSUKO / GENTOSHA COMICS INC.

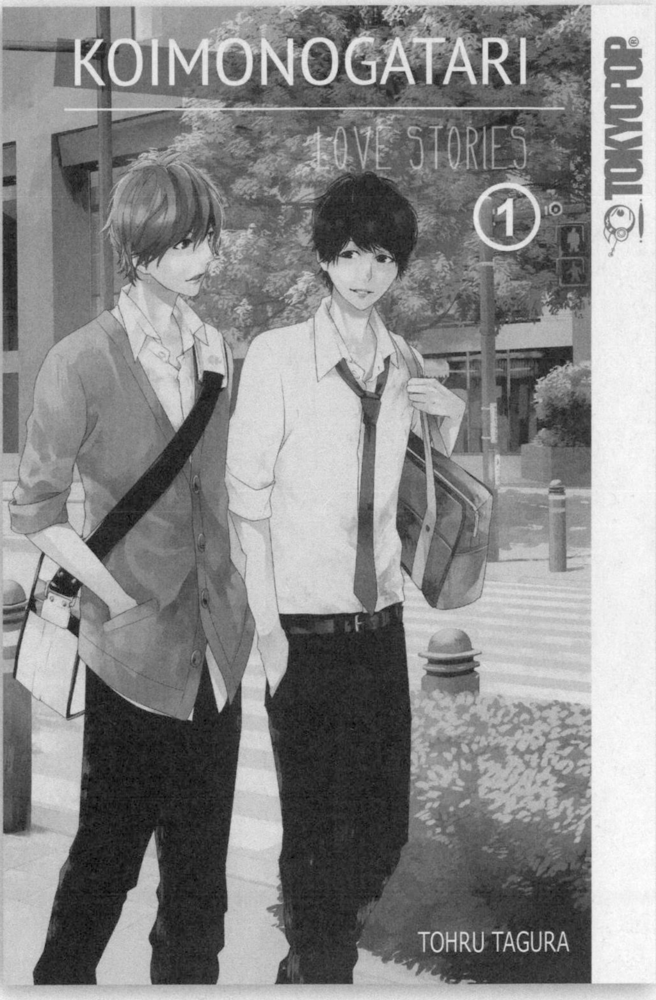
KOIMONOGATARI
LOVE STORIES
1
TOKYOPOP
TOHRU TAGURA

KOIMONOGATARI: LOVE STORIES, VOLUME 1

Tohru Tagura

LOVE-x-LOVE

When Yuiji accidentally overhears his classmate Yamato confessing to another friend that he's gay, his perspective shifts. Seeing Yamato in a new light, Yuiji does his best not to let prejudice color his view, but he still finds himself overthinking his classmates' interactions now. He especially notices the way Yamato looks at one particular boy: Yuiji's own best friend. Even though he tells himself he shouldn't get involved, Yuiji finds he just can't help it; watching Yamato's one-sided love draws him in a way he never expected. At first, it's empathy, knowing that the boy Yamato has his sights on is definitely straight and has no idea. But as his own friendship with Yamato develops and the two of them grow closer through a mutual study group, Yuiji comes to truly care about Yamato as a person, regardless of his sexuality. He only wants Yamato to be happy, and to be able to express his true self.

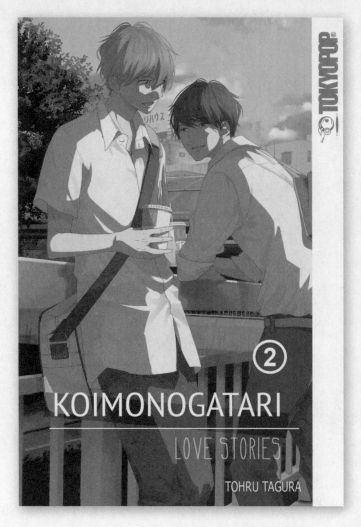

KOIMONOGATARI: LOVE STORIES, VOLUME 2

Tohru Tagura

TOKYOPOP
2
KOIMONOGATARI
LOVE STORIES
TOHRU TAGURA

LOVE-x-LOVE

When Yuiji accidentally finds out his classmate Yamato is gay and has a crush on his best friend, he doesn't know how to react at first. But after spending more time together, the two of them become close friends. While Yamato struggles with his sexuality, Yuiji supports him and keeps his secret, hoping that Yamato can find a way to accept himself and be happy. Meanwhile, Yuiji is having trouble feeling connected to his long-time girlfriend, realizing that although he still cares about her, the spark in their relationship has faded. Love is a complicated, messy thing — especially in high school, where hurtful rumors and intolerant classmates can make life unbearable. Yamato and Yuiji face their own individual struggles, but together, they learn one very important lesson: it's hard to search for romance if you don't love yourself first.

TOKYOPOP

REPLAY

Saki Tsukahara

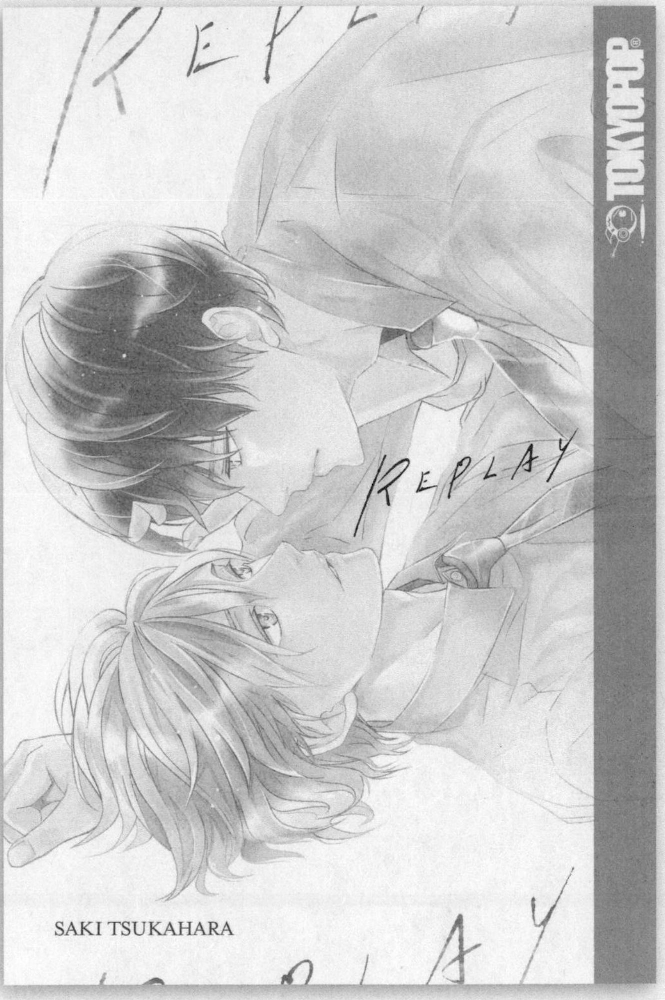
TOKYOPOP
REPLAY
SAKI TSUKAHARA

LOVE-x-LOVE MATURE 18+

Yuta and Ritsu have been playing baseball together since they were children, but after being defeated in a local tournament over the summer, they must retire from the high school team to study for university entrance exams. Still, Yuta finds himself unable to give up his lingering attachment to baseball. The one person who can truly understand him is Ritsu, who has been acting worryingly distant since they quit the team. But there's something Yuta himself doesn't understand... Does he think of Ritsu as his partner in the way that a teammate would, or is the affection between them something stronger?

TOKYOPOP

THERE ARE THINGS I CAN'T TELL YOU
Edako Mofumofu

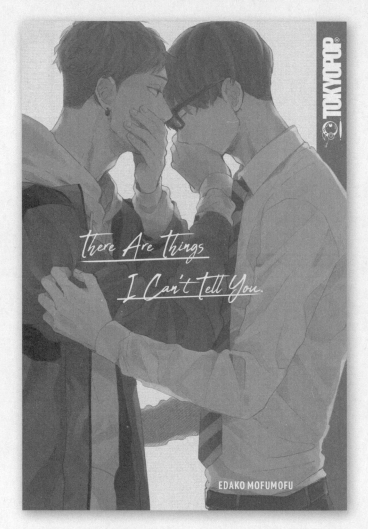

there Are things
I Can't tell You.

EDAKO MOFUMOFU

TOKYOPOP®

MATURE 18+   ♂LOVE-x-LOVE♂

Kasumi and Kyousuke are polar opposites when it comes to personality. Kasumi is reserved, soft-spoken and shy; Kyousuke is energetic and has always been popular among their peers. As the saying goes though, opposites have a tendency to attract, and these two have been fast friends since elementary school. To Kasumi, Kyousuke has always been a hero to look up to, someone who supports him and saves him from the bullies. But now, school is over; their relationship suddenly becomes a lot less simple to describe. Facing the world — and one another — as adults, both men find there are things they struggle to say out loud, even to each other.

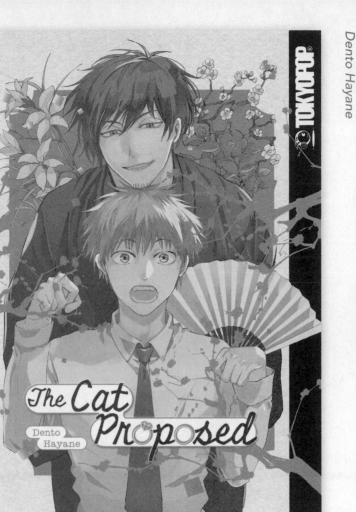

Dento Hayane

THE CAT PROPOSED

δLOVE-x-LOVEδ

Matoi Souta is an overworked office worker tired of his life. Then, on his way home from a long day of work one day, he decides to watch a traditional Japanese play. But something strange happens. He could have sworn he saw one of the actors has cat ears. It turns out that the man is actually a bakeneko — a shapeshifting cat from Japanese folklore. And then, the cat speaks: "From now on, you will be my mate."

© 2020 Dento Hayane/ FRANCE SHOIN

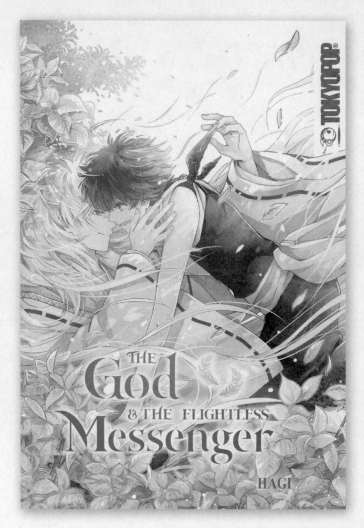

THE GOD AND THE FLIGHTLESS MESSENGER

Hagi

TOKYOPOP
THE God
& THE FLIGHTLESS
Messenger
HAGI

LOVE x LOVE

"My lord, were you the one who stayed by my side?"

Shin is a messenger to the gods, but he's always been alone because of his tiny wings. And when he's finally assigned a god to serve, it turns out to be... a huge ball of fluff?! Stranger still, he feels an odd, nostalgic connection with the funny-looking god.

This is not the story of how a shape-shifting god and an earnest messenger with a short temper meet, but of how they find each other again.

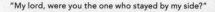

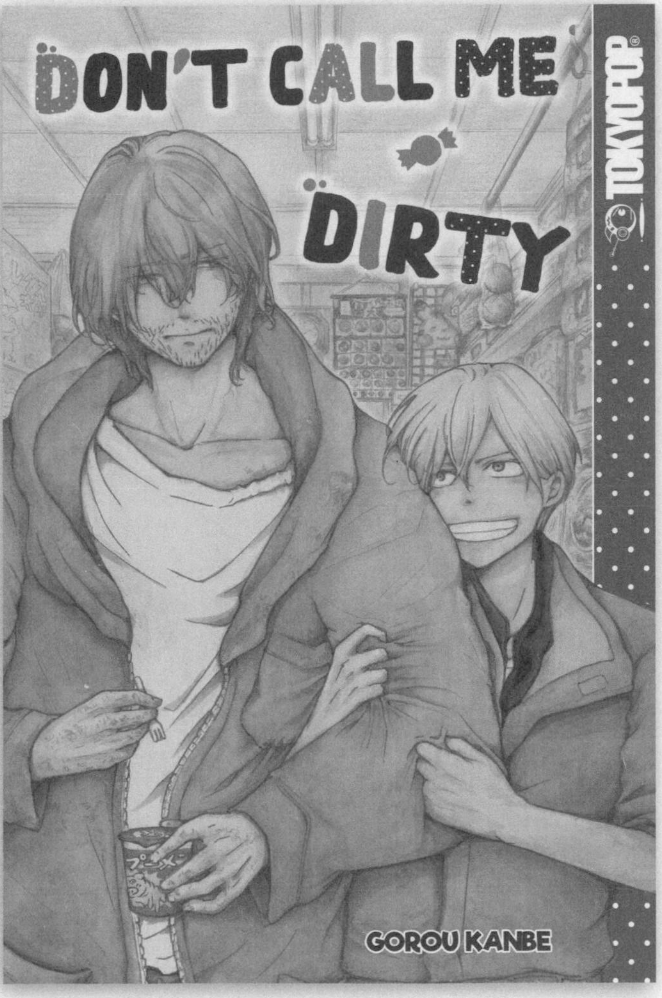

DON'T CALL ME DIRTY

GOROU KANBE

♂LOVE-x-LOVE♂

After some time attempting a long-distance relationship, Shouji is crestfallen when he finds out his crush isn't gay. Having struggled with his sexuality for years, he tries to distract himself from the rejection, in part by helping out at the neighboring sweets shop — but when a young homeless man called Hama shows up at the store, Shouji finds himself curious to learn more about him. Attempting to make their way in a society that labels each of them as 'outcasts' and 'dirty,' the two men grow closer. Together, they begin to find they have more in common than either of them could have anticipated.

DON'T CALL ME DADDY
Gorou Kanbe

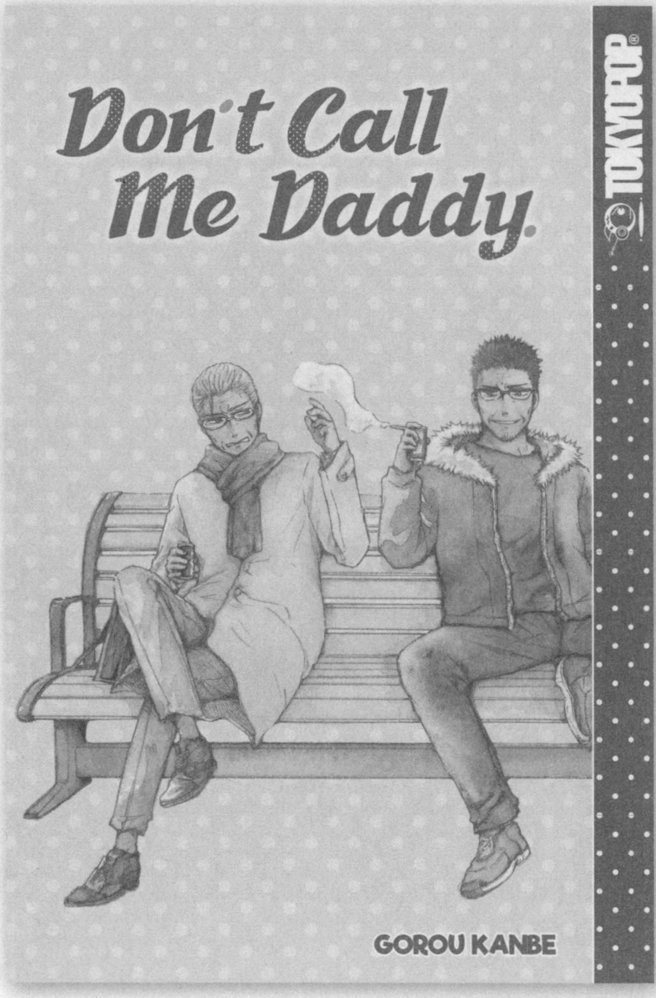

Don't Call Me Daddy.

TOKYOPOP®

GOROU KANBE

◊LOVE-x-LOVE◊

TOKYOPOP®

Long before the events of Don't Call Me Dirty, Hanao Kaji and Ryuuji Mita were close friends... When Ryuuji is left to raise his son Shouji as a single father, Hanao steps up to help him out. At first, their family life is happy and content, but Hanao's true feelings for Ryuuji become more and more difficult for him to ignore. The pressure of staying closeted eventually becomes too much to bear; Hanao leaves, choosing to run from his feelings and his fears of somehow "messing up" Shouji's life when he starts getting teased at school for having two dads. Years later, when he comes home to care for his aging father and ends up advising Shouji on his blossoming relationship with Hama, Hanao realizes it's time to face his own past... and his future.

© 2019 Gorou Kanbe / MAG Garden

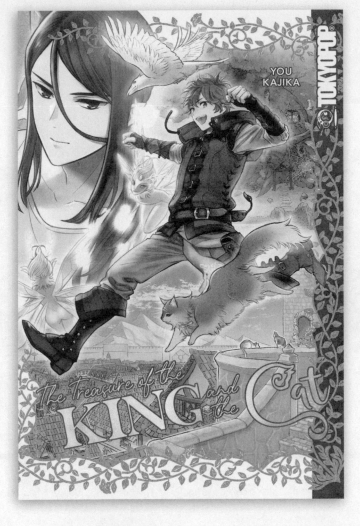

YOU KAJIKA

The Treasure of the KING and the Cat

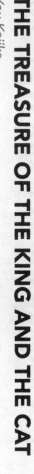

You Kajika

THE TREASURE OF THE KING AND THE CAT

♂LOVE-x-LOVE♂

One day, a large number of people suddenly disappeared in the royal capital. When young King Castio goes out to investigate this occurrence, he comes across the culprit... but the criminal puts a spell on him! To help him out, the king calls the wizard O'Feuille to his castle, along with Prince Volks and his loyal retainer Nios. Together, they're determined to solve this strange, fluffy mystery full of cats, swords and magic!

TOKYOPOP

© KAJIKA YOU / GENTOSHA COMICS INC.

BL FANS LOVE MY BROTHER?!

Mimu Oyamada

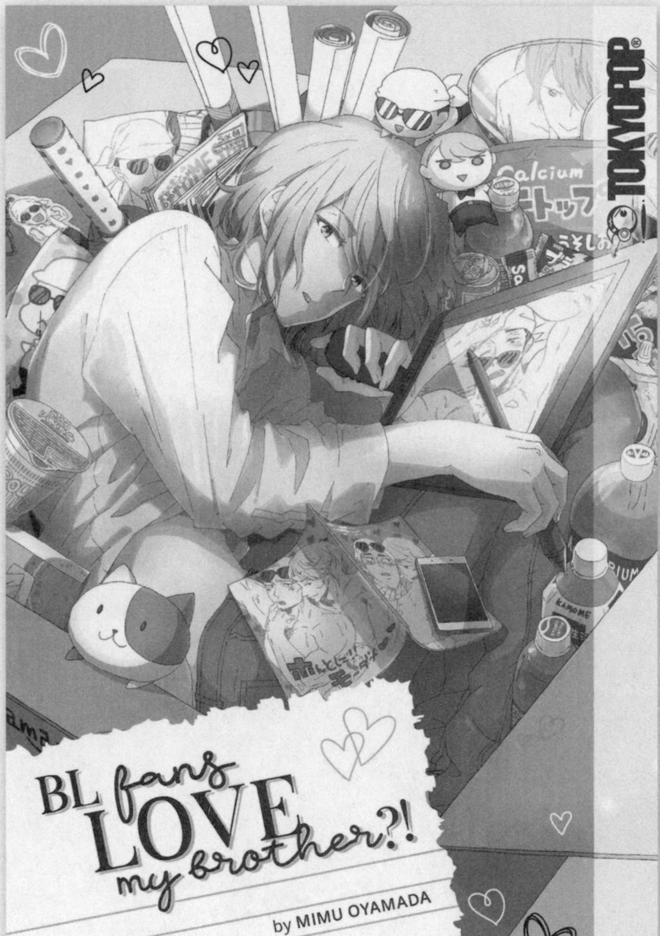
TOKYOPOP
Calcium
KAMOME
BL fans LOVE my brother?!
by MIMU OYAMADA

COMEDY

Four years ago, Kirika Amano's older brother became a shut-in. Since then, he's barely even left his own room, constantly working on something at his desk. When Kirika finally finds out what he's been doing all that time, she's shocked — her brother creates boys love comics! Not only that, but it turns out that he's actually quite good at it, and he's got a dedicated fanbase.

Even though Kirika doesn't understand her brother's hobbies or the fandom that surrounds him, he's still family. Maybe if she helps him sell his comics, she can convince him to step outside into the world again and greet his fans in person.

TOKYOPOP

Glass Syndrome

Manga by Eiko Ariki

Editor	- Lena Atanassova
Translator	- Christine Dashiell
Copy Editor	- Tina Tseng
Editorial Associate	- Janae Young
Marketing Associate	- Kae Winters
Graphic Designer	- Sol DeLeo
Retouching and Lettering	- Vibrraant Publishing Studio
Editor-in-Chief & Publisher	- Stu Levy

A TOKYOPOP® Manga

TOKYOPOP inc.
5200 W Century Blvd
Suite 705
Los Angeles, CA 90045 USA

E-mail: info@TOKYOPOP.com
Come visit us online at www.TOKYOPOP.com

www.facebook.com/TOKYOPOP
www.twitter.com/TOKYOPOP
www.pinterest.com/TOKYOPOP
www.instagram.com/TOKYOPOP

First published in Japan in 2019 by Kaiohsha Publishing Co., Ltd.
English translation rights arranged with Kaiohsha Publishing Co., Ltd.

ISBN: 978-1-4278-6821-3

First TOKYOPOP Printing: June 2021

Printed in CANADA

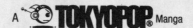

STOP

THIS IS THE BAC

How do you read man

Let's practice -- just s

panel and follow th

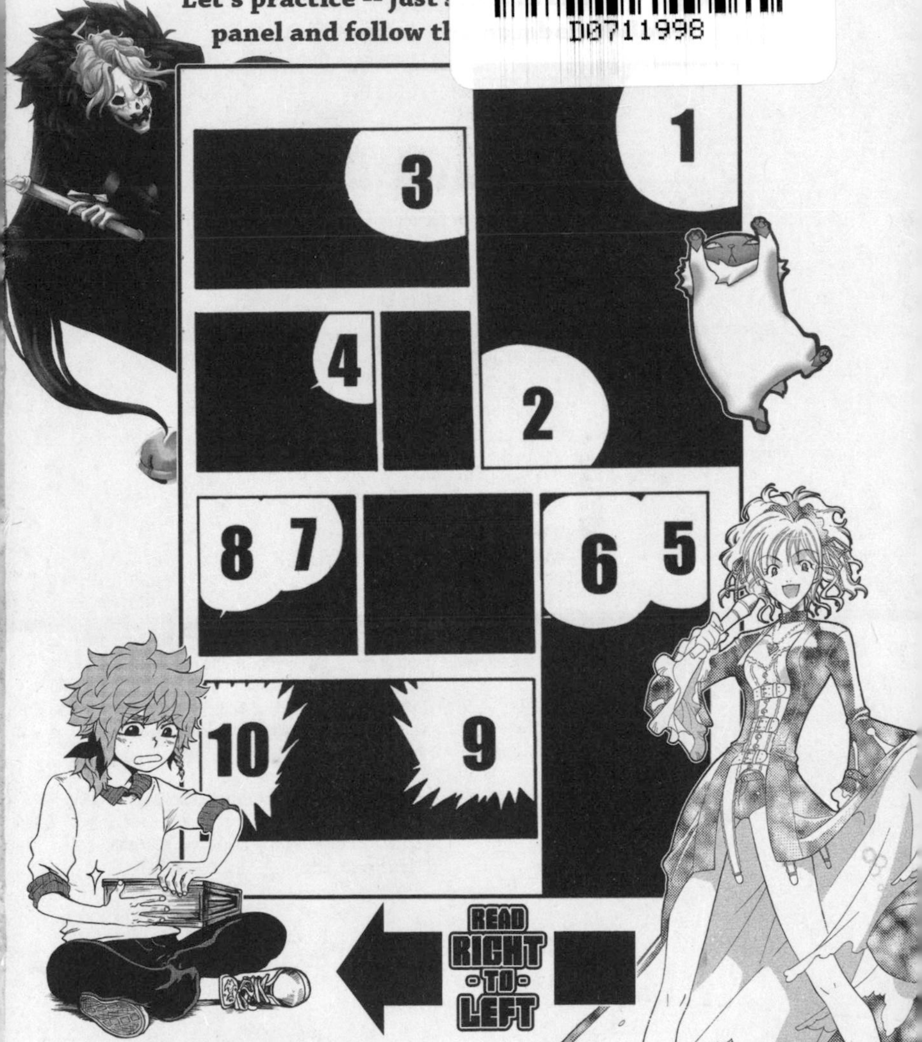
1
2
3
4
5
6
7
8
9
10
READ RIGHT -TO- LEFT

Crimson from ***Kamo*** / Fairy Cat from ***Grimms Manga Tales***
Morrey from ***Goldfisch*** / Princess Ai from ***Princess Ai***